国家双语教学示范课程配套教材

农业生态学
Agroecology

王松良〔加〕C. D. 考德威尔
〔加〕S. 基利尼克〔加〕J. 西克利　编著

科学出版社
北京

内 容 简 介

本书是国家双语教学示范课程的配套教材，也是“（中国）福建农林大学-（加拿大）新斯科舍农学院‘2+2’本科教学合作项目”的成果之一。本书紧紧围绕“农业是把太阳光转变成人们健康、幸福生活的科学、艺术、政治学和社会学”这一对“农业”的新理解，把“农业生态学”定义为农学与生态学联姻的学科和实现农业生态系统可持续管理的应用科学。主要介绍农业生态学的学科内涵、农业生态系统的基本过程及其人为问题、可持续农业生态系统的构建与管理等内容，并包括该课程系列实践教学指导书。

本书视角独特，图文并茂，适合于高等农林院校同名课程的双语教学用书，也可作为农业院校和科研院所研究生考试的参考书。

图书在版编目（CIP）数据

农业生态学/王松良等编著. —北京：科学出版社，2012.1
国家双语教学示范课程配套教材
ISBN 978-7-03-032999-8

Ⅰ.①农… Ⅱ.①王… Ⅲ.①农业生态学-双语教学-高等学校-教材-汉、英 Ⅳ.①S181

中国版本图书馆 CIP 数据核字（2011）第 256976 号

责任编辑：丛 楠/责任校对：李 影
责任印制：徐晓晨/封面设计：谜底书装

科学出版社出版
北京东黄城根北街 16 号
邮政编码：100717
http://www.sciencep.com

北京凌奇印刷有限责任公司印刷
科学出版社发行 各地新华书店经销
*
2012 年 1 月第 一 版 开本：787×1092 1/16
2020 年 1 月第十三次印刷 印张：17 1/4
字数：400 000

定价：58.00 元

（如有印装质量问题，我社负责调换）

Preface

—Agroecology: A Discipline for Our Time

One may say that agriculture moulded our culture before the onset of the Industrial Revolution in the 18th century. We are a culture dependent upon food, fibres and other by-products to sustain life. Today however, we as a people have learned how to transform and mould agriculture to suit our culture (including ideology, needs and sciences). Agriculture is so far removed from its agrarian origins that it is now more an expression of human power and intelligence and less of a way of simply feeding oneself.

How can human culture control agriculture? Through reductionism thinking and the power of science and modern technology, people have learned to dissemble nature and agriculture in order to provide enough food for our growing population. Many modern perspectives of agriculture regard nature as raw materials for human use rather than as a naturally occurring, balanced ecosystem for an abundance of life forms. For example, the modern, classical world viewpoint considers nature as reductive materials and mechanical aggregates; likewise, "conventional" industrial agriculture follows the Newtonian mechanical model of nature while "modern" industrial agriculture perceives soil as potential monocultures, assembled from fossil fuels, synthetic fertilizers and chemical pesticides (Callicott, 1988). As a result, we have limited our ability to maximise food availability, security and safety by destroying the very foundation of agriculture, leaving us in a conflict with nature, rather than working within its natural constraints.

Undoubtedly, agricultural restoration will require a new ideological and disciplinary revolution (reverse reductionism thinking) returning a balance to the people-nature interface. The Newtonian mechanical model and Darwinian agriculture need to adopt holistic, systematic, ecological thinking and approaches; a marriage of agriculture and other disciplines (particularly ecology) is extremely necessary and urgent. In this textbook, the nascent discipline of agroecology expresses and reflects the new paradigm emerging from agriculture and ecology. Agroecology translates this abstract new vision into concrete agricultural vocabulary. In agroecology, the farmstead is regarded as a managed ecosystem with an abundance of diversified plant and animal constituents, interacting in complex, symbiotic ways with each other and their natural surrounding ecosystems (Callicott, 1988).

Sustainable land use has gone from the unique minority to the common paradigm for the future of agriculture. Sustainable Agriculture derives substance and function from applied ecology, governed by naturally occurring biological and physical processes. Internal competition in natural ecosystems is designed to divert greater amounts of energy, nutrients, and water into crops, a necessary component of agriculture; however, where natural ecosystems favour biodiversity, modern agriculture has curtailed diversity in favour of vulnerable monocultures (Thomas, 1993). Modern agriculture has established crop systems that inherently lack the ability to resist perturbations. Sustainable agriculture, therefore, uses natural ecological succession as a model for single crop rotations, preparing the land for continual crop production. Crop rotations resembling ecological succession retain nutrients for future crop growth, reduce pest accumulation and increase soil organic processes (i. e. decomposition and material cycling) (Thomas, 1993). In the r-K continuum of reproductive maturity (growth vs stability; see McArthur and Wilson, 1967) modern agriculture is nearing the r-extreme as a result of clearing forests, rotational burning and cereal monocultures (Thomas, 1993). Mimicking natural landscapes (e. g. hedgerows) may enhance agricultural production through naturally beneficial ecological processes.

Principles of Agroecology are:

(1) Sustainable agroecosystems designed and managed through applied ecology.

(2) Holistic approach to agriculture and agricultural development, combining traditional, alternative and local small-scale practices.

(3) Links ecology, socioeconomics and culture for sustainable agricultural production in rural communities and environmental health.

In order to apply these principles of Agroecology, it is important to understand several basic questions:

(1) What is agroecology?

(2) What are agroecosystems?

(3) What is sustainability?

(4) What are their intrinsic connections?

(5) What are the agroecological principles that guide development of sustainable agroecosystems?

(6) How do we measure sustainability in agroecosystems?

(7) What are the best agroecological indicators of sustainability?

The unique purpose of this book is to answer the questions stated above and introduce you to the theoretical framework of agroecology, bridging your knowledge between agriculture and ecology. This book is organized in five units (twenty-four chapters), with three field practices, three lab experiments and one class training activity. These chapters use the core concepts of agroecosystems to define the discipline of Agroecology and to explain management practices in agricultural industry within agroecosystems. For students, the purpose of this textbook is to define agroecology as a comprehensive learning paradigm that can be applied to both local and global agriculture in order to decrease loss of ecological capital while still attaining productive agriculture.

The first Unit, The Context of Agroecology, introduces the history, key terms and characteristics of agroecology; Unit 2, Basic Analysis of Agroecosystems, describes matter, energy, information and monetary flows within agroecosystems, based on natural ecosystems without human interference, and highlights soil ecosystems and agrobiodiversity reconstruction; Unit 3, Agroecosystematic Processes and their Anthropocentric Problems, emphasizes the problems and solutions associated with resource use and the consequences of soil misuse; Unit 4, Sustainable Production Systems, uses agroecological principles in agricultural production systems to pursue the goal of sustainability; Unit 5, Agroecosystem Management: Issues, Problems and Solutions, examines several key practices in agriculture from the macro and micro viewpoints of sustainable agroecosystem management; The Epilogue at the end of this textbook reviews content taught throughout the six units, in addition to an exercise revisiting the concept of agroecology as a discipline of food science of 21st century.

This Agro-ecology textbook is one of the outcomes of NSAC-FAFU 2 + 2 program, an international cooperative education program, initiated in 2003 between Fujian Agriculture and Forestry University (FAFU) in China and Nova Scotia Agricultural College (NSAC) in Canada. Under this framework, Dr. Claude Caldwell of NSAC introduced the course to FAFU in collaboration with Dr. Wang Songliang. The course is currently available for the undergraduate students majoring in Horticulture and Agricultural Resources & Environment at FAFU. After four years of cooperative effort since the program's implementation in 2004, the course has been certified with the name of "Provincial Elite Course" in 2007, and subsequently has become a model for bilingual education in China in 2009. This course provides an excellent opportunity for the students to become familiar with western style lecturing and practice teaching in the same manner while using English textbooks and referencing system. In that regard, the authors thought it was important to compose a textbook for three reasons: ① to summarize the outcomes of the cooperative teaching program; ② to provide a textbook geared toward the specific structure and scope of the program, and ③ to offer a model of bilingual teaching materials and methodologies for Chinese agroecology groups.

The authors are grateful to the Canadian and Chinese governments for their sponsorship of the 2 + 2 educational program and agroecology course cooperative teaching. Thanks go to the scientists from NSAC who provided the teaching materials for this book, they are: Dr. Tarjei Tennessen, Dr. Crag Miller, Dr. Ralph C. Martin, Dr. Rajasekaran Lada, Ms. Maggie Hope-Simpson, Mr. L. Mapplebeck, Mr. Tracey MacKenzie, Dr. Gordon R. Brewster, Mr. Jim Duston and Prof. Nigel Firth. Additional thanks go to our colleagues at FAFU and NSAC and particularly to Ms Wenfeng Zhu, who offerred much help in editing this textbook, and finally many thanks go to Ms. Cong Nan as the higher editor of this book for her elaborate efforts.

References:

Callicott B. J. (1988) Agroecology in Context. *Journal of Agricultural Ethics*, 1: 3-9.

MacArthur R. and Wilson E. O. (1967) The Theory of Island Biogeography. Princeton: Princeton University Press.

Thomas V. G. and Kevan P. G. (1993) Basic Principles of Agroecology and Sustainable Agriculture. *Journal of Agriculture and Environmental Ethics*, 6 (1): 1-19.

Songliang Wang & Claude Caldwell
July, 2011 in FAFU

前言：时代需要农业生态学

纵观我国的农耕史，我们有理由认为，在18世纪工业革命之前，农业塑造了人类的文化和文明。今天则相反，人类的文化（包括意识形态、需要和科学）已经牢牢地控制了“农业”，使后者完全失去作为“自然”一部分的属性，而成为人类“生存权力”的牺牲品：庞大的人口产生对食物的巨大需求；现代科学和技术及其归纳思维的压倒性力量形成巨大的拆解（dissemble）自然与农业的内在联系，丧失对总体农业生态系统的思考能力。和现代世界观把“自然”视为外部关联的、原子的、还原的、物质的、机械的“配件”一样，产业化的农业更是把土壤作为单一化种植、化石农业的附属。结果是，当我们面临食物安全（包括粮食安全和食品安全，food security and safety）的农业可持续性（agricultural sustainability）的问题时，发现我们已经完全摧毁了其赖以存在的基础，而使其成为我们真正的敌人。

无疑，还农业与自然之间的平衡，我们需要意识和学科的变革以扭转归纳论思维，把牛顿机械论和达尔文进化论的功利农业变回到整体的和系统思维的本源农业，一种跨学科的农业生态学方法——生态学与农学的联姻——是极为必要和迫切的。在这个背景下，初生的农业生态学表达、反映产生于生态学和量子物理学的各类范式，后两者则以在各自的方式代表了一种把自然当作相互联系的、系统的、整合的、有机的整体。农业生态学能转译这个精要成一个具体的农业词汇。在这里，农场及其建筑物被认为是一个人工的生态系统，包含多样的、相互作用的植物和动物组分，并和周围自然生态系统形成一个复杂而相互支撑的方式。

发展可持续农业已经成为全球共识，也是唯一的未来农业发展范式。可持续农业必须从应用生态学中，特别是从物种多度和分布（即所谓的生物多样性）的调节，以及物种的时空配置中获得实质内容和功能。自然生态系统的中间竞争同样为设计新型的农业服务，即通过人工设计把大量养分和水分输入到作物身上。鉴于自然生态系统是从群落中多样的物种，当前的农业通过喜好易受攻击的单一种植最大程度减少了物种多样性。这样的系统注定是稳定性低的，且不易从扰动中恢复。作物轮作与生演替有些类似，因为一种作物是为了获得连续的产量而种植的。这种有些轮作将提高土壤的有机过程，如养分的分解和循环等，为下一季作物产量的维持提供养分，且减少害虫积累的程度。自然群落的物种通过离散的点分布最终形成r-K类别的统一繁殖体。清除林地作为农业用地，流动的燃烧活动，以及以单一的农作物替代多年生的草地，都是农业生物群落向极端的r-生物演变。植物育种者选育那些尽早形成高产、高生物量的品种也使r-生物的形成更为有效。类似于灌木篱笆的自然景观可以扮演农业生产形成的物理和生物的助手，它们作为农地最有效使用的网络而存在。土壤在农业生态系统中最为重要，其活力和从农业波动恢复的能力是土壤可持续性形成的至关重要的基础。

农业生态学的主线索是监管未来的可持续农业，它包括三个方面：

（1）应用生态科学设计和管理可持续的农业生态系统。

（2）寻找一种基于传统的、替代的和地方小型农业的农业和农业发展系统方法。

（3）整合生态学、社会经济学和文化于维持农业生产、农场群落和环境健康。

为此，我们必须清晰如下几个基本概念：

（1）什么是农业生态学？

（2）什么是农业生态系统？

(3) 什么是可持续性?

(4) 什么是以上概念的内在联系?

(5) 指导可持续农业生态系统管理的农业生态学原理有哪些?

(6) 如何衡量农业生态系统的可持续性?

(7) 关于可持续性的农业生态学的最佳指标有哪些?

回答以上问题正是本书的唯一目标。为此，本书分成 2 个部分。第一部分是农业生态学的理论框架，它包含 5 个单元（共分 24 章），内容对接农学与生态学的 2 个学科内涵，以及基于农业生态系统核心概念下，把农业生态学定义为一个联合的学科和农业生态系统内部管理农业产业的学科。对学生而言，本教材的目的是把农业生态学培养其演绎论思维（从区域和全球农业系统的角度）的综合学习范式定义，以在实现农业的功能目标时尽可能地减少生态资本的丧失。第一单元“农业生态学的内涵”介绍农业生态学历史演变、基本术语和学科特征；第二单元“农业生态系统的基本分析”描述了农业生态系统内部有别于无人为干扰的自然生态系统的物质、能量、信息和价值（经济）流，强调了土壤生态系统和农业生物多样性的重建；第三单元“农业生态系统过程及其人为问题”则重点在于资源利用过程的问题和解决途径，特别是土壤的不合理利用及其后果；第四单元是“可持续生产体系的建立”，立足于农业生态学学科的原理，分析各类农业生产体系以实现其可持续性；第五单元为“农业生态系统管理：话题、问题和途径”，它将提供基于可持续的农业生态系统管理视野下（包括微观和宏观的）的若干关键农业生态过程。本书第二部分提供了实践教学过程所含的 3 个田间实习、3 个实验和 1 个课程学习方法培训活动的指导。最后以“农业生态学：全球食品系统的科学”作为本书的结尾，回顾学生从本课程的所学和所思。

这本农业生态学教材是“（中国）福建农林大学-（加拿大）新斯科舍农学院‘2+2’项目”的成果之一。该国际教育合作项目创始于 2003 年，在项目框架下，农业生态学由新斯科舍农学院的 Claude Caldwell 博士引进对框架内的园艺和农业资源与环境专业开设。经过 4 年（2004～2007）课程教学的执行，该课程于 2007 年被评为“福建省精品课程”，而在双方教师的努力下，由于其有别于我国高校的双语课程，相继于 2009 年被确认为“国家级双语教学示范课程”。对于项目框架学生而言，该课程提供给他们熟悉西方教学风格、英语教材和参考书。也因此，本书作者确信给框架内学生编写本教材的意义，一方面是对过去 7 年中外教师共同教学成果的总结；另一方面，也是给国内其他大学的农业生态学教学组提供本课程双语教学的模式和方法。

作者非常感激发起和资助国际教育合作的中加双方政府。同时，感谢双方合作学院参与组织和教学的教师们。感谢那些为本书提供教学资料的 NSAC 的先生和女士，他们是：Tarjei Tennessen 博士、Crag Miller 博士、Ralph C. Martin 博士、Gordon R. Brewster 博士、Rajasekavan Lada 博士、Maggie Hope-Simpson 女士、Lloyd Mapplebeck 先生、Tracey MacKenzie 先生、Jim Duston 先生与 Nigel Firth 教授。特别感谢 Jamie Sziklay、祝文烽女士为全书的文字校正作出的贡献，最后感谢科学出版社的丛楠女士作为本书编辑的精心付出。

王松良 and Claude Caldwell
2011 月 7 月 24 日于福建农林大学

Contents

Part Ⅱ Practical Teaching

Epilogue

Part Ⅰ Theoretical Framework

Unit 1 Context of Agroecology

Chapter 1 Agriculture and its anthropocentric sciences

Learning objectives

1. Define the terms agriculture, ecology, ecosystems and agroecology.
2. Discuss how the science of agroecology fits in the realm of natural and social sciences.
3. Explain why corn is a good symbol for the study of agroecology.
4. Compare and contrast the characteristics of natural and managed ecosystems.
5. Explain how the concept of "Making money and respecting the environment" is central to agroecology.

1.1 What are agriculture, ecology and agroecology?

"Agriculture is the science, art, politics and sociology of changing sunlight into healthy, happy people"

——C. D. Caldwell, 1996

When we first learn the principles of ecology, we stand apart from the system; we are observers of nature—measuring, modelling and predicting behaviour and outcomes in various systems from puddle to biosphere. We see ourselves as unbiased, highly interested observers of the interactions within and between our biotic and abiotic environments. Thus, ecology has become defined as the scientific study, through observation and analysis, of the relationships between living organisms with each other and their environment.

By comparison, agriculture seems to be a misunderstood science, tainted with the ideas that our endeavours are solely self-serving. In fact, the *Oxford Concise Dictionary* dismisses agriculture as anything more than, the "science or practice of cultivating the soil and rearing animals." This cursory definition only explores one facet of the complex scientific study and practice of agriculture.

1.1.1 Definitions of agriculture

Let's refer to the definition of agriculture as the science and industry of managing the growth of plants and animals for human use (Skanavis, 2004). Traditionally, agriculture includes cultivation of the soil, growing and harvesting crops, breeding and raising livestock, dairying and forestry (Skanavis, 2004). Agriculture sectors usually consist of crop farming, animal husbandry, dairy farming, forestry, poultry farming and soil management.

Over time, human use and interpretation of agriculture has evolved. Agriculture played a key role in population settlement and the rise of modern civilization. The husbandry of domesticated plants and animals allowed for these societal changes, creating food surpluses that enabled more densely populated and stratified communities.

A general agronomic textbook defines agriculture as "the infrastructure of national economy, and main source of living, as well as industrial material for human beings" (Zhai, 1999). This definition regards agriculture as a source of food, clothing and financial income, focusing on agriculture as "money-based" and economy driven. Agricultural practices under these defining ideologies have deteriorated natural resources and the environment (soil, water and atmosphere). This has become apparent by the depletion of ecological diversity and productivity from increased agricultural production, in an effort to meet an ever-increasing demand for food by an overpopulated society. The destroyed ecological diversity and productivity can no longer support infrastructure and provide a base for all agro-economic productivity. The Industrial Revolution replaced many organic materials with synthetic materials in agricultural ecosystems (agroecosystems), which led to the formation of "Modern Fossil Fuel Agriculture." This increased dependence on synthetic materials and fossil fuels in agriculture has only exacerbated the deterioration of agroecosystems. However, Agriculture is multi-faceted and extremely important; it is not limited to food production and economic output, but rather, it is a critical interface between humans and nature.

Ancient Chinese books, poems and paintings depicted an ideal farming-oriented society among a charming agroecological environment. The ecological functions of sound agriculture and forestry, as depicted in ancient Chinese art, are summarized as follows (Wang, 2005):

- Water and soil conservation
- Climate and rainfall regulation
- Protection of land from wind and desertification
- Landscape beautification and pollution prevention
- Living energy supply and source of fertility

Fortunately, researchers and government agencies in the world are gradually recognizing the multi-functionality of agriculture. Caldwell (1996) redefined agriculture as **"The science, art, politics and sociology of changing sunlight into healthy, happy people** (农业是把太阳光转变成人们健康、幸福生活的科学、艺术、政治学和社会学)" (Wang, 2005).

This expanded definition better recognizes the function of agriculture; it means that agriculture is a natural ecological process, whereby solar radiation converts energy and matter from natural resources (including land, atmosphere and water) for food and human environment. This definition incorporates people as an essential component, emphasizing the equilibrium point for human benefits and natural conservation, or "the basic interface between people and their environment" (Valentine, 2005). One can group the major agricultural products in the following categories: foods, fibers, fuels, raw materials, pharmaceuticals and stimulants, and an assortment of ornamental or exotic products. Ecological designs of agronomic and horticultural systems have become part of the functionality of agriculture.

The point to note here is that agriculture is homocentric. A literal interpretation of homocentric would put people at the centre; a functional interpretation puts people as a beneficiary but not central.

In addition to supporting industry and the economy, agriculture also promotes land renovation, biodiversity, nature conservation and design.

(1) Agriculture is a driver of the global economy.

- Supports the livelihoods and subsistence of people worldwide

(2) The agricultural sector must simultaneously.

- Secure enough high-quality agricultural production to meet demand
- Conserve biodiversity and manage natural resources
- Improve human health and well being, especially for the rural poor in developing countries

Agricultural management must continually increase the productivity of existing farmland to meet population demand through the adaptation of good and efficient management practices. Additionally, management should embrace the three pillars of sustainability, representing natural (environmental), social and economic factors (Fig. 1. 1).

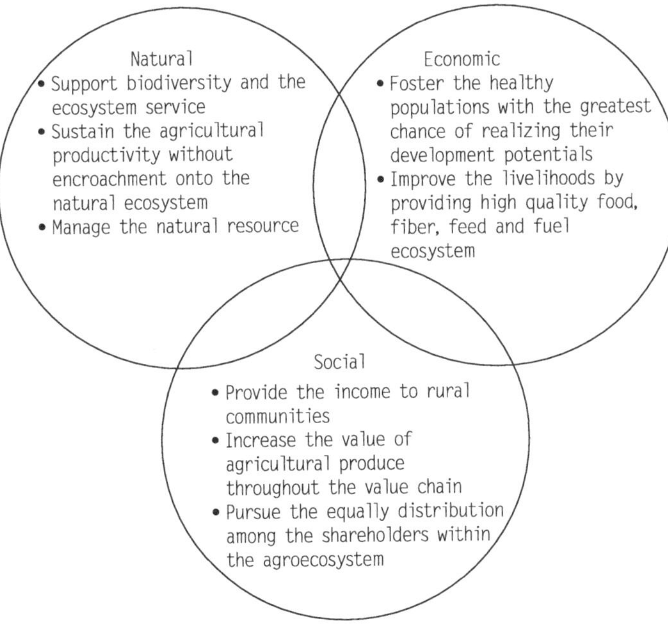

Fig. 1. 1 The three pillars of agricultural sustainability.

1. 1. 2 The science and discipline of agriculture

Science and technology are the building blocks of modern agriculture. One must understand the biological and physical sciences underlying agricultural engineering and technology. Successful farming requires the knowledge of tillage, irrigation, fertilization, drainage and sanitation. Some aspects of farming require further specialized knowledge, which agricultural engineers can carry out. Agriculture encompasses a wide variety of specialties and techniques. One such specialty is the ability to increase suitable land for plant production, usually performed by digging water-channels and other forms of irrigation. Cultivating crops on arable land and pastoral herding of livestock on rangeland are some of the fundamental practices of agriculture.

In the past few decades, plant breeding, agricultural chemistry (e. g. pesticides and fertilizers) and corresponding technological improvements have sharply increased yields from cultivation (Tab. 1. 1). For instance, plant breeding and genetics contribute immeasurably to farm productivity; meanwhile, genetics have turned livestock breeding into a science. However, some of this technology causes widespread ecological damage and negatively impacts human health. Hydroponics, a method of soilless gardening in which plants are grown in chemical nutrient solutions, may help meet the need for greater food production as the world's population increases. Similarly, selective breeding and modern practices in animal husbandry, such as intensive pig farming (and similar practices applied to chickens), have increased the output of meat. However, hydroponics can lead to pathogen attacks and selective breeding in crop varieties has led to the utilization of only a few plant species and monocropping, reducing biological diversity. In addition, concerns have increased about animal welfare and human health effects from antibiotics, growth hormones, and other chemicals often used in large-scale meat production.

Tab. 1. 1 Global productivity comparison during three phases of agricultural development (Wu, 1986)

Phase of agricultural development	Land productivity /(J/ cm^2)	Number of people fed per hm^2 of arable land	Rural population (%)	Purchased rate of agricultural product(%)
Historical agriculture	0.054×10^6	20	100	0
Labour intensive agriculture	1.020×10^6	280	85. 7	14. 3
Modern agriculture	4.180×10^6	1000	6. 4	93. 6

Agricultural chemistry which includes, but are not limited to: the application of fertilizer, insecticides and fungicides, soil makeup, analysis of agricultural products and nutritional needs of farm animals, must take into account many crucial farming concerns. The increasing use of inorganic fertilizers and synthetic pesticides poses many problems in soil degradation, ground water contamination, food safety, toxicity accumulation in natural wildlife and other environmental deterioration.

The packing, processing, and marketing of agricultural products have also been influenced by science. Methods of preservation, quick-freezing and dehydration have increased markets for farm products and decreased post-harvest losses. These processes do, however, mean the use of more chemicals and materials potentially leading to resource depletion, food safety concerns and increased environmental pollution.

Agricultural science has primarily focused on components of the production process, maximizing net returns on single products per unit of land or labour. All other resource use and environmental effects have been considered "externalities" (Francis et al. , 2003).

Many problems resulting from modern agriculture occur because of reductionist disciplines and utilitarian technologies. Thus, we need to modify our understanding of agriculture, integrating Caldwell's newer definition (1996) with a new science and discipline to investigate agriculture in a more inclusive way. Agroecology, therefore, should be considered a cutting edge discipline that bridges ecology (including human ecology) with agriculture.

1.1.3 The link to the discipline of ecology

The etymology of ecology stems from the Greek words "*oikos*" (house or place to live in) and "*logia*" (study of). The word ecology was proposed and defined by German biologist, Ernst Haeckel, in 1866. His definition states "Ecology is the science of the relations between organisms and environment" (Odum, 1969; 1983). This definition implies that ecology builds upon related biological sciences such as zoology and botany; such disciplines usually examine organisms themselves, whereas ecology explores the relationships between organisms with each other and their environment. While ecology can be considered a biological science, it spans a much broader study area, including earth science, chemistry, physics, mathematics, medicine, and certain aspects of the social and economical sciences. The famous ecologist, Eugene Odum, stated that Ecology is "a science bridging biology and social science" (Odum, 1971). This explains ecology in terms of an interdisciplinary science, mixing natural science with social science, where one can also infer a particular emphasis on economics and politics. A holistic or integrated approach to the investigation of ecosystems requires considerable knowledge, effort and scientific resources. The results of ecological studies are often contrary to what one may expect at a first glance.

Although the study of ecology traces back to ancient Greek and Roman times, modern ecology was born from and accelerated by the social and environmental problems of the 18th century Industrial Revolution. Modern ecology originated as a response to the global emergence of the "Five-Ecological-Crises," i. e. Population, Food, Resource, Energy and Environment, at the beginning of the 20th century. Essentially, ecology is the economics of nature, as opposed to the money-based economics that investigates the social economy. Economics focuses on accounting for ways to regroup resources to maximize the output, regardless of any abstract innate value.

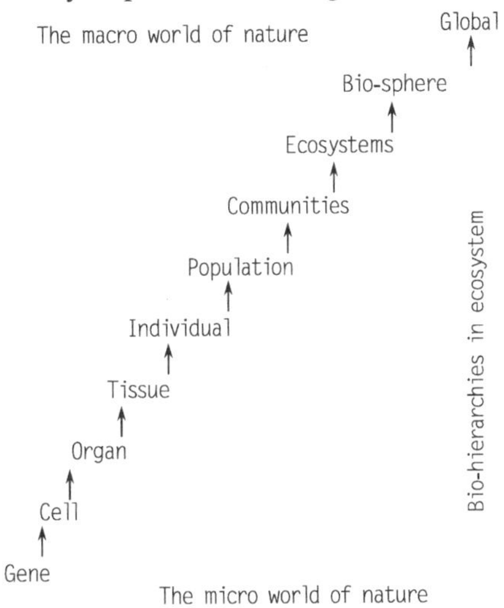

Fig. 1.2 Bio-organizational scales in ecology (Odum, 1983).

Ecology investigates the interactions among organisms and their environments at various scales, from individual organisms to a population, community, ecosystem or biosphere. Fig. 1.2 illustrates the scales of ecology, classified under subjects such as molecular ecology, autecology (species ecology), population ecology, community ecology and global ecology.

1.1.4 The link between agriculture and ecology: the inclusive discipline of agroecology

The role of ecology in agriculture is to find the pivotal balance among global food security, advantageous production, technological innovation, environmental preservation and protection of biodiversity (Ormerod, 2003). Both agriculture and ecology have common roots in the disciplines of botany, chemistry, physics and geology, with very distinct applications and management practices (Paul, 1989). Agroecology manifested from these relationships, first emerging in the 1930s; its initial phase lasted until the 1960s, after which the science expanded until it became considered a discipline in its own right and institutionalized in the 1990s (Wezzel, 2009). Prof. Luo Shiming et al (1987) defined **Agroecology as "a science of the interaction, co-evolution, regulation, control and equilibrium development between agro-organisms and their environment (both natural and social), based upon the principles of ecology and systematic theory and practice** (农业生态学是应用生态学的原理、系统论的观点和方法，把农业生物与其自然和社会系统作为整体，研究它们之间的相互联系、协调演变、调节控制和平衡发展规律的科学)". This definition is inclusive and reflects the intent of Caldwell's definition (1996) of agriculture. While agroecology is derived from the larger field of ecology, draws even more strongly on the social sciences to construct understanding and predictions about organism relationships. Ecology can be considered the "parent" theory of agroecology because the goals of the discipline are to pursue the sustainable management of particular ecosystems; i. e. agroecosystems. This is evidenced by the recent history of corn (maize, *Zea mays*) in agroecology.

1.1.5 The development of agroecology as a discipline and science

(1) Agroecology developed under the background of the global ecological crises concerning agriculture

Agroecosystems play a crucial role in our lives because they provide us with food and fibre while greatly impacting the quality of our environment (Elliott, 1989). Historically, global ecological crises concerning agriculture have been the inspiration for the development of agroecology, as well as a major source of conflict. China represents one of the Ancient Farming Societies of the world. In China, nature has been destroyed mercilessly since the first hoe was used in agriculture, transforming the "Green Grassland" into the "White Desert", and "Mother River" into the "Yellow River" . Globally, ecology has been involved in revolutions both of environmental protection and of environmental sciences. Soon after Rachel Carson revealed the far-reaching effects of chemical pesticides used broadly in agricultural practice in her famous book *Silent Spring*, many ecologists dedicated their careers to agroecosystem research.

(2) Agroecology promotes the evolution of the agricultural economy from "Industrial-based" to "Intelligence-based"

"Historical Agriculture" refers to the first 10,000 years of agricultural development. Prior to that, people lived by hunting and gathering. Historical Agriculture required extensive cultivation and productivity relied entirely on the unpredictability of nature and weather. This economic pattern could be realistically defined as a "nature-based economy." Subsequently, Labour-Intensive Agriculture was born 2000 years ago, the productivity of which depended totally on people power and land characteristics. This economic pattern could be described as a "subsistence-based economy." The agricultural pattern has changed drastically from a "nature-based economy" to an "industrial-based economy" since the Industrial Revolution. Modern agriculture can be formularized by "fossil energy + technology = commodity," showing that fossil energy and modern technology have become the dominant factors for agriculture. Consequently, agricultural productivity has increased tremendously when compared with the former two stages (Tab. 1.1). As a negative result, however, such patterns have generally destroyed the natural sustainable mechanisms of agriculture.

By the 1980s, developed countries started responding to the destructive aspects of modern agricultural patterns with several alternative agricultures such as organic, ecological, biological and natural agriculture. Since the 1990s, the concept of Sustainable Development has arisen as common sense around the world, allowing for the emergence of Sustainable Agriculture. Sustainable Agriculture is characterized by dependence on intelligence (knowledge, technology and education); it could therefore be called an "intelligence-based economy" . The primary purpose of Sustainable Agriculture is to correct the relationship between agro-organisms and the environment. As a scientific approach to sustainable agriculture, agroecology aims to study, diagnose and offer alternative low-input management strategies of agroecosystems (Altieri, 1995).

(3) Agroecology: a new research and development paradigm for world agriculture

In the last 100 years, world agriculture has been driven by intensive science and technology to achieve the tremendous increase in productivity meeting the needs of an adequate food energy supply for the increase in world population. The technologies included new cultivars, chemicals ranging from mineral fertilizers to pesticides to synthetic plant hormones and machines to supplement and replace the labour force. Many countries benefited immensely from such industrial agriculture, paying the price of monocropping, excessive tillage, short rotations and overuse of chemicals in severe soil degradation. Starting in the 1960s, a huge international effort began, the so-called "Green revolution," which extended a few high yielding crop types to many countries in order to achieve adequate world food calorie/protein production. However, this process depended on water, fertilizer and monocropping, resulting in biodiversity loss and socio-economic upheaval (Wang, 2003).

The global environmental revolution was initiated by the response to *Silent Spring* in 1962. *Rachel Carson* exposed the indiscriminate use of toxic chemicals in the "modern" agricultural industry. More and more people expressed concern about the "modern" agricultural paradigm that threatens the natural resources of land, soil, air and water. These resources are threatened through processes such as loss of soil fertility by erosion, acidification, salinization and desertification. A new model was needed, and eventually the sustainability paradigm was advocated worldwide.

As an introductory discipline of sustainable agriculture, agroecology was proposed as a new research and development paradigm for alternative, sustainable agriculture (Altieri, 1989). Agroecology advocates growing crops and raising livestock while using organic fertilizer, biological pest control, conserving soil and limiting the use of non-renewable fossil fuel energy.

Agroecology was proposed as a new scientific discipline that defined, classified and studied agricultural systems (Gliessman, 2005). Agroecology was developed to give scientific and socio-economic guidance to the management of agroecosystems (Conway, 1985; Wang and Caldwell, 2006). Therefore, going beyond the reductionist approach, agroecology provides a methodology to diagnose the "health" of agricultural systems and thus guide the design of sustainable production systems in a more fully integrated manner.

To manage an agroecosystem sustainably, agroecology uses a goal-oriented design using various methods and appropriate input technologies to achieve those goals. Input technologies improve soil fertility and conservation, maximize recycling, enhance biological pest control and diversify production. It is therefore crucial for a team of agricultural scientists and social scientists alike to be involved in the search for sustainable agricultural technologies.

1.1.6 Corn as a symbol of agroecology

Throughout the cultural, political, economic, social and gastronomic history and development of people, no species has more closely aligned with us than corn. See case study by Ruben G Mendoza (2003) entitled "The Natural History of Maize" .

Several important points discussed in Mendoza's paper link maize and people together:

(1) Maize is dependent on people for its survival as a species and, it can be argued, that people are dependent on maize for survival. While maize is a very successful crop, it is not a successful wild plant. Without the assistance of people, corn would become a very marginal plant and perhaps even disappear from the earth. Our breeding and selection efforts over millennia have produced a super-crop, but as an individual plant has poor species survivability. One needs to look no further than the seed covered cobs in one location to see the problems in independence for the plant. On the other hand, the world-wide demise of maize would decimate the human population due to wide spread famine and resultant social disorder. While people would not disappear, our numbers would drop and our lifestyle would change considerably.

(2) Agroecology deals with how people change their environment to benefit themselves. Maize is an excellent example of a crop that has co-evolved with people over the millennia. Maize has changed from a wild, relatively unproductive crop to one that can adapt and respond to many forms of human management, from low-tech to high-tech. The first maize selections made by primitive peoples set the stage for generation after generation of "improvements" to the crop, followed by targeted breeding and crop management in the development of hybrids. This means that people in various places across the globe have improved the ecotypes to respond to both climate and management so that the crop is:

- Widely adapted as a species
- Narrowly adapted as a hybrid

(3) Agroecology addresses the range of interactions of humans, plants and animals; maize is a key component of both human food and animal feed.

(4) Agroecology deals with closing the nutrient cycle and maintaining balance within systems. As a symbol of agroecology, maize is responsive to nitrogen and is particularly good at utilizing animal manures.

(5) Maize is given both praise and scorn. Maize is praised as a major source of food for people and feed for animals, while it is negatively targeted by the "Green Revolutionaries" as anything but "green." Maize was a key component in the global change in agriculture, bringing with it new seeds, inorganic fertilizers and pesticides to areas of the world that had not had them before. Theses changes produced higher yields, but also induced social and environmental disruption. Agriculture and maize have worn the mantle of scorn for that. Agroecology seeks to rehabilitate the image of agriculture.

1.2 Natural ecosystems versus people-centric ecosystems and agroecosystems

Natural ecosystem is a typical natural (unmanaged) solar energy powered ecosystem (Fig. 1.3), while An agroecosystem is an ecological and socioeconomic system, comprising domesticated plants and/or animals and the people who manage them, intended and transformed for agricultural purposes (Soemarwoto, 1992).

Fig. 1.3 A typical natural (unmanaged) solar energy powered ecosystem.

The distinctive feature of agroecosystems lies within its anthropocentricity (humans stand at the centre of system). This does not mean humans are the most important part of the system, rather, it means that humans are the species that tends to benefit most from the system's organization.

Natural ecological systems provide a model of survival and relative stability for building agroecosystems. The most distinctive characteristic of natural systems are: ① their biological diversity and ② the interaction of species and their habitats that maintain high diversity and thus stability (Tab. 1.2). Gliessman (1998) suggested, "the greater the structural and functional similarity of an agroecosystem to the natural ecosystems in its biogeographic region, the greater the likelihood that the agroecosystem will be sustainable".

Tab. 1.2 Basic structural and functional differences between natural ecosystems and agroecosystems (Odum, 1969)

Characteristics	Agroecosystem	Natural Ecosystem
Net productivity	High	Medium
Trophic chains	Simple, linear	Complex
Species diversity	Low	High
Genetic diversity	Low	High
Mineral cycles	Open	Closed
Stability (resilience)	Low	High
Entropy	High	Low
Human control	Definite	Not needed
Temporal permanence	Short	Long
Habitat heterogeneity	Simple	Complex

The transformation of an ecosystem into an agroecosystem involves a number of significant changes. The system itself becomes more clearly defined, at least in terms of its biological and physical-chemical boundaries. The system is also simplified by the elimination of much of the natural fauna and flora and by the loss of many natural physical-chemical processes. However, at the same time, the system is systematically affected through the introduction of human management and activity. This means that there are tremendous difficulties in mimicking natural ecosystems that display harmony between organisms and their environment.

What are the basic components of agroecosystems? Odum (1984) states that agroecosystems are domesticated ecosystems that are in many basic ways intermediate between natural ecosystems, such as grasslands and forests on the one hand, and fabricated ecosystems, such as cities on the other hand. Like natural ecosystems, agroecosystems are solar powered but differ from natural systems in the following ways (Tab. 1. 2):

(1) There are auxiliary energy sources used to enhance productivity; these sources are processed fuels along with animal and human labour; Species diversity is reduced in order to maximize yield of specific foodstuffs (plant or animal); Dominant plant and animal species are artificially selected rather than naturally selected; Control is external and goal-oriented rather than internal via subsystem feedback as in natural ecosystems.

(2) By definition, agroecosystems do not happen without human intervention in the landscape. Therefore, the creation and maintenance of agroecosystems are likely concerned with the balance of economic goals of productivity with the conservation of ecosystem stability. In other words, managing the ecological processes of production maintains agroecosystems. Compared with natural ecosystems, agroecosystems are extremely open with major exports of plant and animal production, in addition to an increased likelihood for nutrient loss (Spellman, 2011). To maintain an agroecosystem, humans must add energy and material subsidies. Thus, in fully industrialized agriculture, the net gain of energy from agriculture is small because so much is expended in its production (Tab. 1. 2). Also, as human labour is progressively replaced, first by animal power, and then by fuel and machinery, the energy dependency on external systems increases greatly and the energy output/energy input ratio declines significantly (Altieri, 1995).

1.3 "Making money and respecting the environment"

The early farmer selected and cultivated wild plants that had desirable characteristics such as large fruit size, sweet taste, fast growth and disease and insect resistance by natural selection. The earliest domesticated plants appear to have been cereals and legumes (such as peas, wheat and barley) after that the Egyptians (circa 3500B. C.) developed technologies for drainage, irrigation, land preparation, and food storage. The ancient Greeks listed common plants and other medicinal usage in herbals and are credited with establishing the scientific field of botany.

The agricultural pattern has changed dramatically since the Industrial Revolution. This pattern produced an undesirable change in the physical, chemical or biological characteristics of air, water, soil, or food that can adversely affect human health, survival or activities and our co-inhabitants of the ecosystems.

In an ecological view, the post-industrial agriculture has a high throughput economy (Fig. 1.4); such economy requires inputs of high quality energy and matter from nature. These resources flow through the economy and are converted to products, but also produce low quality heat energy, waste and pollutants as bi-products.

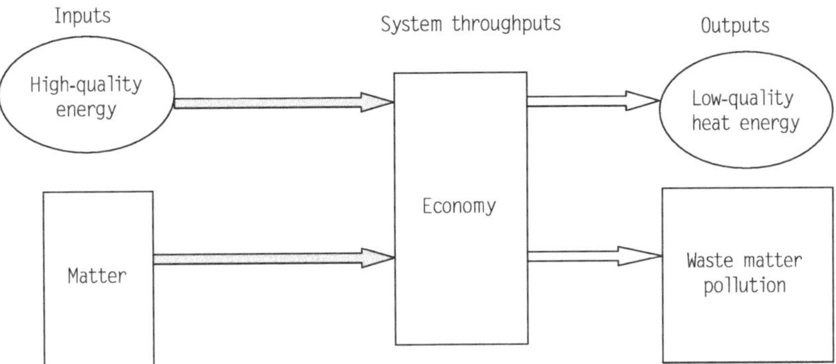

Fig. 1.4 Modern industrial agriculture is a high-throughput economy subsidized by nature and society.

1.4 What we produce is determined by what we consume: Rethinking the role of the modern supermarket

As described above, modern industrial agriculture is a commercial-based production system, within which agricultural products (particularly food) are produced, distributed and consumed at discrete stages. Supermarkets are seen to be the culmination of the system; A supermarket usually indicates or hides information on agroecosystems, including what is produced in certain agroecosystems and where and how production occurs, by means of product distribution, labelling, packaging and pricing. However, the role of the supermarket is to obscure any integration of the agricultural system. The supermarket is the great leveller: the consumer does not see the link between themselves and the complex, international industrial agriculture chain that provides the materials for their grocery basket. In particular, the consumer is isolated from the producer (farmer). This lack of communication between consumer and producer tends to breed lack of understanding of each other and eventually lack of trust (Fig. 1.5).

Many problems of modern agriculture arise from the disconnect between the consumer and the producer, in addition to the physical disconnect of the product from the agroecosystem in which it originated, by way of long distance transport. Since production is determined by consumption (supply and demand), we must pay particular attention to the information that is directly or indirectly disseminated (or not made available) to consumers in supermarkets.

Modern agriculture entails increased distances between producers and consumers, planners and beneficiaries, researchers, and practitioners. People throughout the world have differing environmental views, often based on lack of information or inaccurate information. Many people in industrial consumer societies are developing a

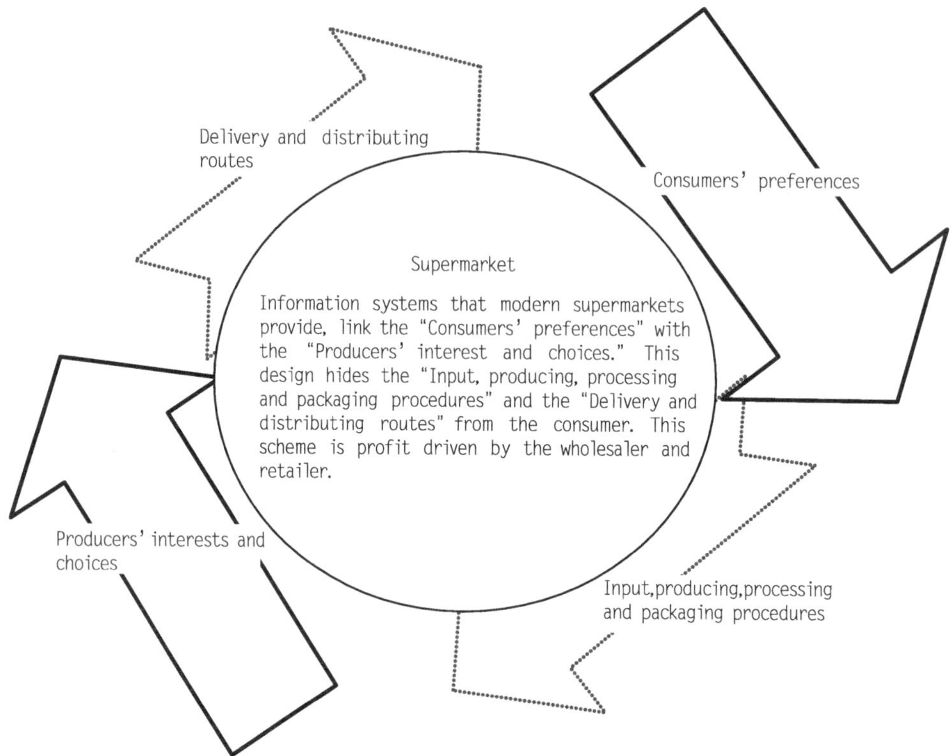

Fig. 1. 5 The central role of the modern food supermarket in disintegration of the interrelated parts of agroecosystems.

worldview of management. Advocates for environmentally sustainable economic development generally have an environmentally sustainable worldview.

A precondition to reconciliation is finding balance in views from multiple shareholders. Therefore, diverse teams should be established to deal with agroecosystems, building in knowledge and communication from both ends of the food system—in the supermarkets and from the farmers.

Literatures cited in this chapter

Altieri M. A. 1989. Agroecology: A new research and development paradigm for world agriculture. *Agriculture, Ecosystems and Environment* 27: 37-46.

Altieri M. A. 1995. *Agroecology: The Science of Sustainable Agriculture*, 2nd ed. London: Intermediate Technology Publications.

Altieri M. A. and Norgaard R. B. 1987. *Agroecology: The scientific basis of alternative agriculture*. Boulder: Westview Press.

Caldwell C. D. 1996. IN100: Agroecology course resource manual. Nora Scotia Agricultural College: 215.

Clements D. R. and Shrestha A. 2004. New dimensions in agroecology for developing a biological approach to crop production. *Journal of Crop Improvement* 11: 1-20.

Coleman D. C. 1989. Special feature: Ecology, agroecosystems, and sustainable agriculture. *Ecology* 70: 1590.

Elliott E. T. and Cole C. V. (1989) A perspective on agroecosystem science. *Ecology* 70: 1597-1602.

Francis C., Lieblein G., Gliessman S., Breland T. A., Creamer N., Harwood R., Salomonsson L., Helenius J., Rickerl D., Salvador R., Wiedenhoeft M., Simmons S., Allen P., Altieri M., Flora C., and Poincelot R. 2003. Agroecology: The ecology of food systems. *Journal of Sustainable Agriculture* 22: 99-118.

Gliessman S. R. 1990. Agroecology: *Researching the ecological basis for sustainable agriculture*. New York: Springer-Verlag.

Gliessman S. R. 2005. *Agroecology: The ecology of sustainable food system*. Boca Raton: CRC Press.

Gliessman S. R., Krieger R., and Mayne J. C. 2000. Agroecology. *American Journal of Alternative Agriculture* 15: 95-96.

Jackson W. and Piper J. 1989. The necessary marriage between ecology and agriculture. *Ecology* 70: 1591-1593.

Luo S. M., Yan F., and Chen F. 1987. Agroecology. Changsha: Hunan Science and Technology Press.

Odum E. P. 1983. *Basic Ecology*. Philadelphia: Saunders College Publications.

Odum E. P. and Barrett G. W. 1977. *Fundamentals of Ecology*. Melbourne: Cengage Publishing.

Odum, E. P. 1969. The strategy of ecosystem development. *Science* 164 (3877): 262-270.

Odum, E. P. 1984. *Properties of agroecosystems*. In: Lowranle et al. Agricultural Ecosystems: Unifying Concepts. New York: John & Wiley Press.

Ormerod S. J., Marshall E. J. P., Kerby G., and Rushton S. P. 2003. Meeting the ecological challenges of agricultural change: Editors' introduction. *Journal of Applied Ecology* 40: 939-946.

Paul E. A. and Robertson G. P. 1989. Ecology and the agricultural sciences: A false dichotomy? *Ecology* 70: 1594-1597.

Skanavis C. 2004. "Chapter 4: Environmental Education Applied to Agricultural Education." In: Filho W. L. Ecological Agriculture and Rural Development in Central and Eastern European Countries. Amsterdam, Netherlands: IOS Press.

Soemarwoto O. and Conway, G. R. 1992. The *Javanese homegarden*. *Journal for Farming Systems Research-Extension* 2 (3): 95-118.

Spellman F. R. 2011. *Spellman's Standard Handbook for Wastewater Operators, Advanced Level*. Volume III, 2nd ed. Boca Raton: CRC Press.

Valentine I. 2005. An emerging model of a systems agriculturalist. *Systems Research and Behavioral Science* 22: 109-118

Vandermeer J. 1995. The ecological basis of alternative agriculture. *Annual Review of Ecology and Systematics* 26: 201-224.

Wang S. L. 2003. Plant resource green gene and food security & safety in developing countries. *Reviews of China Agricultural Science & Technology* 5: 34-39.

Wang S. L. 2005. Information technology: toward the way to the sustainable management of agroecosystem. *Agriculture Network Information* (8): 4-12.

Welch R. M. and Graham R. D. 1990. A new paradigm for world agriculture: meeting human needs productive, sustainable, nutritious. *Field Crops Research* 60: 1-10.

Wezzel A. and Soldat V. 2009. A quantitative and qualitative historical analysis of the scientific discipline of agroecology. *International Journal of Agricultural Sustainability* 7 (1): 3-18.

Wu Z. Q. 1986. *The Basic agroecology*. Fuzhou: Fujian Science and Technology Press.

Zhai H. Q. 1999. *Introduction to agriculture*. Beijing: Higher Education Press.

Chapter 2 Agroecology: Science of synthesis of ecology and agriculture

Learning objectives

1. Describe how the discipline of agroecology bridges ecology and agronomy.
2. Draw a diagram to describe the role of agroecology in harmonizing social, environmental and economic goals in agriculture.
3. Compare the basic tenets of agroecology to those of the traditional agricultural sciences.
4. Deduce the effects of an agroecological view on food production systems on a regional and global scale.
5. List 3 food production strategies.
6. Write a summary commenting on the two cases analyses of food systems in China and Canada.

2.1 Agroecology: Bridging ecology and agronomy

There has been increasing interest in melding the basic, applied aspects of environmental and ecological sciences with agriculture since the exposure of global environmental problems in the publications *Silent Spring* (1962) and *Limits to Growth* (1972) by Rachel Carson and The Club of Rome, respectively. The impelling argument to mesh these disciplines centre around the long term needs for sustainable food and fibre production in the agricultural sector. Concerns have grown over Greenhouse Gas (GHG) emissions from agriculture, field and non-point source pollution due to the abuse of arable land and synthetic chemicals in agriculture.

To solve the problems, many have invoked the need for reviving traditional methods such as polyculture and perennial cropping systems. The intelligent use of these methods requires the joining of ecologists and agriculturists. This produces an alternative to the reductionist, bioengineered approach to agroecosystems; it requires a re-thinking, in both education and research involving interdisciplinary approaches with holistic thinking. This re-thinking appeals to both agronomists and ecologists, and has brought them together under the banner of Agroecology.

Agroecology is emerging as the bridge between ecology and agronomic sciences; simply stated, Agroecology is the study of agroecosystems and their components as they function within themselves and in the context of the landscapes that contain them. Application of this knowledge can lead to the development of more sustainable agroecosystems in harmony with their larger ecosystem and eco-region. Agroecology provides the tools and ecological concepts to carry out the study, design and management of agroecosystems in a productive, conservation-minded, culturally sensitive and economically viable way (Altieri and Nicholls, 2004).

As shown in Fig. 2. 1, traditional agronomy includes physiology, cytology, genetics, economics etc. (listed at right of diagram). While ecology deals with bio-organizational hierarchies at many levels, the problems of modern agriculture tend to occur above the community level. Agroecology brings ecological principles to bear on agriculture and can elevate the consideration of traditional agricultural disciplines to the community level (cropping system) and ecosystem level to eliminate the problem sources of modern agriculture.

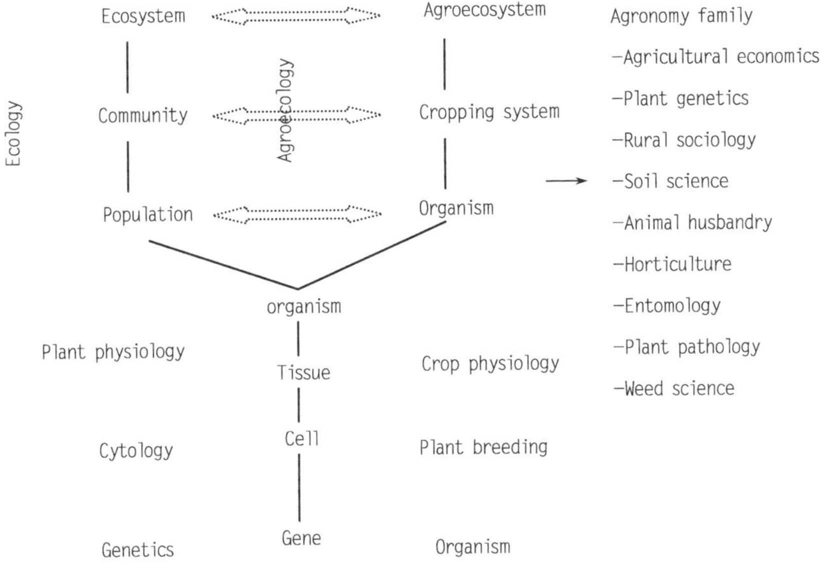

Fig. 2. 1 The niche of agroecology in agricultural sciences (Conway, 1986).

2. 1. 1 Agroecology: interdisciplinary approaches

Agroecology strives to bridge two fields, agronomy and ecology, and thus brings a holistic approach to agriculture, that can broaden the scope of perspective within an agroecosystem to consider everything from the field to the landscape level, or similarly, from a gene to biosphere level. The famous ecologist Eugene P. Odum considered the greatest advantage of ecology to be the use of holistic thinking. He championed this message and brought the ecosystem concept to life in his classic textbook "Fundamentals of Ecology" first published in 1953.

Fig. 2. 2 conveys the interdisciplinary traits of agroecology. Ecology is a science to understand nature and act as a bridge between the natural and social sciences (Odum, 1996). While agriculture is a specific industry that relies greatly on natural and social resources and, by definition is meant to meet the profit needs of society, it is still restricted by natural rules. Agroecology is a cross-discipline between ecology and agricultural sciences (e. g. crop cultivation, crop farming, plant nutrition, oil chemistry and rural sociology). Therefore, it is necessary to reconstruct the framework of agroecology by constructing the subject families of agroecology, in which general agroecology is further elaborated as that bridge between ecology, agricultural science and rural sociology (Fig. 2. 2). Such an interdisciplinary framework of Agroecology will harmonize the economic, social and environmental goals of systematic agriculture.

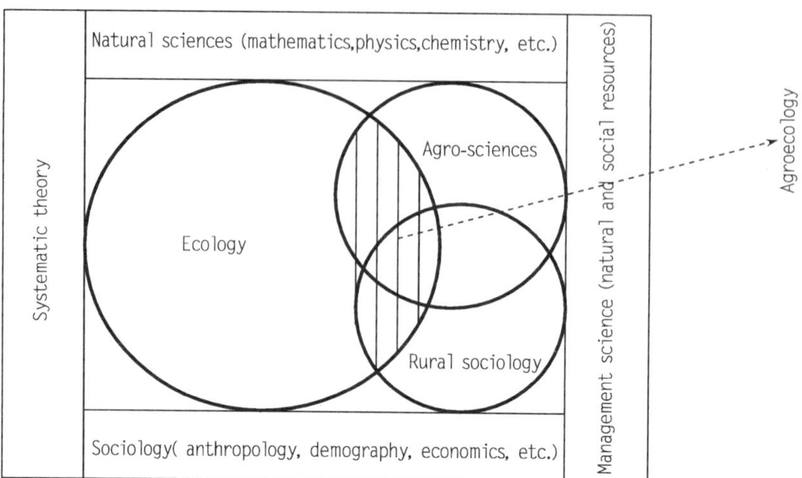

Fig. 2. 2 Discipline positioning of ecology and agroecology in modern academic disciplines.

2. 1. 2 Natural philosophies and premises of western thought: a prerequisite to agroecology

The scientific method followed in most modern sciences stems from Francis Bacon's early investigation of the origin, nature, methods and limits of human knowledge; Western conventional agriculture however, has manifested from the Newtonian mechanical worldview. Callicott (1988) postulates that the emergent agroecology movement is not so much of a long lasting fix for conventional agriculture, but rather, an indication of a global shift the natural philosophy of Western culture.

While the Newtonian mechanical worldview is no longer an acceptable model of natural philosophy, Isaac Newton's reductive viewpoint lingers in how we perceive and practice agriculture today. This mechanical perspective treats soil, nutrients, plants and even genetic information as if they are components to a machine that can be standardized for an assembly line (Callicott, 1988). These ideas are instilled in the educational system (Tab. 2. 1) .

Tab. 2. 1 The dominant premises of modern sciences and alternatives (Altieri, 1995)

Dominant premises in current agronomy	Alternate premises in ecology and agroecology
ATOMISM: Systems consist of unchanging parts and equal the sum of their parts.	HOLISM: Parts cannot be understood apart from their whole and wholes are different from the sum of their parts. Parts might evolve new characteristics and totally new parts can arise.
MECHANISM: Relationships between parts are fixed, systems move from one equilibrium to another, and changes are reversible.	SYSTEMATISM: Systems might be mechanical, but they might also be deterministic yet not predictable or smooth because they are chaotic or simply very discontinuous. System can also be evolutionary.
UNIVERSALISM: Diverse, complex phenomena are the result of underlying universal principles, which are few in number and unchanging over time and space.	CONTEXTUALISM: Phenomena are contingent upon a large number of factors, particularly over time and space. Similar phenomena might well occur in different times and space due to widely different factors.

Continued

Dominant premises in current agronomy	Alternate premises in ecology and agroecology
OBJECTIVIM: We can stand apart from what we are trying to understand.	SUBJECTIVISM: Social and most "natural" systems cannot be understood apart from our values, and how we have understood and hence acted upon these systems in the past.
MONISM: Our separate individual ways of understanding complex systems are merging into a coherent whole.	PLURALISM: Complex systems can only be known through multiple, different patterns of thinking, each of which isn't necessarily a simplification of reality. Different patterns are inherently incongruent.

Another somewhat related natural philosophy, Atomism, derives from the physical sciences and philosophy. Atomism theorizes all matter in the natural world in its ultimate divisible units is made up of atoms and empty space, call void. Atomism also conceived compound bodies as the uniting of multiple varieties of atoms. Modern chemistry developed from this natural philosophy and the development of modern physics as the science of these unions, dissolutions, and rearrangements (Callicott, 1988). Agriculture can be analyzed atomistically, seeing systems as simply the sum of their parts, in which case, controlled experiments in laboratories and plot field stations can be conducted to determine the constituents to a specific agricultural production (Altieri, 1995).

In biology, a mechanism is a function of an object or process. A mechanism relates parts of system that do not change; this condition allows for prediction and control (Altieri, 1995). The mechanical worldview is similarly conceptualized by Euclidean three-dimensional space and time, and atoms (Callicott, 1988). However, this philosophy states that all causal relations in a system are ultimately reducible to the motions and collisions of the elementary particles; accordingly, an organism became simply an elaborate assemblage of specialized cells, reducible to their molecular constituents and furthermore to several atomic building blocks (Callicott, 1988).

Universalism states that a relatively small number of universal principles can explain the world around us (England, 1994). The premise of universalism originated from Charies Dawin's theory of natural selection and was followed by Mendel's theory of genetic selection, which drives agricultural practices from plant breeding to hybrid selection.

Objectivism suggests we can separate our values, ways of knowing, and actions from the process of trying to understand the systems in which we are studying (England, 1994). The famous German soil chemist, Justus Liebig, characterized objectivism. His work on the replenishment of elements for soil fertility was based on the assumption that soil nutrients (such as N, P, K) were carried away in the produce, year after year; therefore, the farmer could replenish soil fertility for optimal field conditions. His work has been overemphasized in the chemical manufacturing industry since the industrial agricultural era started in the 18th century, promising bigger and better agricultural yields through unlimited increases in chemical input. As Karl Marx reviewed in his famous work "Capital", the overemphasis of Liebig and other agronomists directly led to the overuse of fertilizer on arable land and soil degradation. This inevitably fed into the agricultural productivity crisis.

Monism postulates that our separate disciplinary ways of knowing are constantly merging into a coherent whole (England, 1994). Traditional agronomy is a discipline that mixes the mono-atomic sciences into one in order to guide the agricultural production processes; the cartoon (Fig. 2.3) satirizes the monism scenario in the "blind men and an elephant." Individually, each blind man assesses the use of a specific part of the elephant, but none alone can determine that what they feel is part of a larger animal. If each blind man represents a specialty of modern agricultural science, we can infer that only when the discrete scientific topics merge can an agricultural system be assessed in its entirety. Unfortunately, the reductive, material, mechanical worldview described previously inspired, and continues to inspire modern industrial agriculture. Treating agriculture as industrial constituents like parts to a machine, fails to recognize agriculture in its wholeness. Without the ability to treat an agricultural system as such, managers will not be able to imitate the natural balance that occurs within nature, restoring the balance to the people-nature interface.

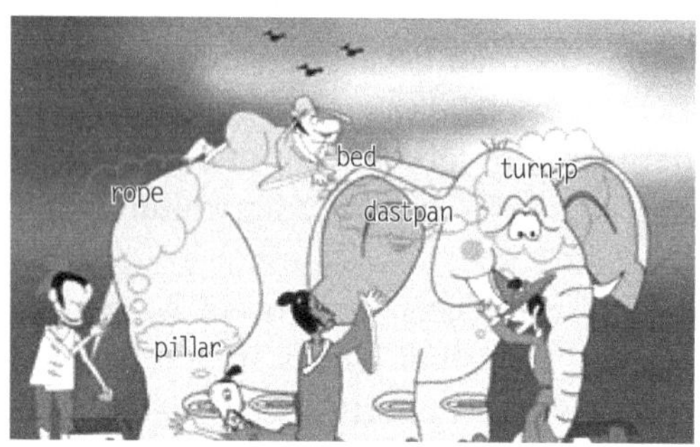

Fig. 2.3 Cartoon of the blind men and an elephant.

The alternate premises in ecology and agroecology offer a sharp contrast to the dominant western premises (*a*tomism, mechanism, universalism, objectivism and monism) in agriculture. The five new "ism's": Holism, Systematism, Contextualism, Subjectivism and Pluralism, are rooted in systematic or multidisciplinary thinking. **Agriculture is considered in its wholeness and cannot be disassembled into parts. In this regard, Agroecology can be interpreted as the science introducing structure and function to agroecosystems through applied ecology and a balance between the interface of natural and social science. Therefore, it is bound to integrate plant, animal, soil science and agricultural engineering to provide a comprehensive view of agriculture** (农业生态学是介绍农业生态系统的结构与功能的学科。而农业生态系统则是人参与下的自然与社会系统的共同部分，以农业生产为手段，以食物生产为动力的综合系统。农业生态学综合了动、植物科学、农业工程技术和土壤科学，提供一个系统的视野).

2.1.3 Agroecology is the economics of matter cycling through agriculture

There is no doubt that modern industrial agriculture is dependent upon capital. From an ecologists' standpoint, agriculture is reliant on natural capital and services such as air, water, land and biodiversity to sustain an agricultural environment. From an economists' standpoint, modern agriculture relies on huge material and energy inputs (subsidies) from outside the agroecosystems. The material and energy capital is traded with monetary and other man-made capital; we tend to discount natural capital, even though it is a key to sustainable success. Agroecology recognizes both types of capital and accounts for them simultaneously.

As an example to consider: research indicates that the ecological impact of a 50-year-old tree can be calculated economically to be more than 100 thousand dollars, including \$31,200 for producing oxygen, \$62,500 for preventing atmosphere pollution, \$31,250 for conserving soil erosion and increasing fertility, \$31,250 for water nurturance, \$2,500 for producing protein (Wang, 2005). However, if a farmer cut this tree for marketing, he may receive a mere $200 in return. This implies that the ecological productivity of a tree far exceeds its market value; it may be argued that this is true for whole agroecosytems.

Unfortunately, producers, consumers and other dealers in the chain, including researchers and educators from disciplines other than ecology and agroecology, tend to consider that the economic contribution of agriculture consists only in basic economic calculations of production costs and returns. This is the source of the current agricultural tragedy. Agroecologists, however, consider the economy of agriculture as matter and energy recycling, enabling agriculture growth without depleting agricultural resources (Fig. 2. 4).

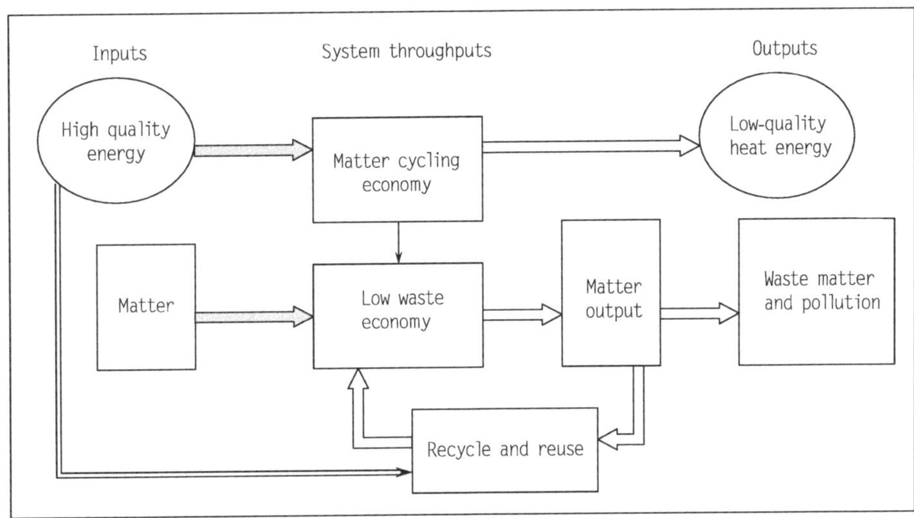

Fig. 2. 4 Agroecology viewing agricultural economic systems as matter and energy recycling and then low waste economic system.

In Agroecology, agroecosystems can represent loosely or closely coupled ecosystems and economic models. As demonstrated in Fig. 2. 5, both ecological and economic factors influence productivity. Therefore Agroecology is both the ecological and economical foundation of agroecosystem production (economic, biological and ecological). Agroecology is ultimately a scientific theory for sustainable agroecosystem management (Wang et al., 2006).

For most people in the world, food represents a way of life rather than just "food" itself (McMichael, 2000; Maguer, 2004; Hodges, 2005). Symbolically, food offers an intimate relationship between nature and society (Walther-Toews, 1991). It is also common to believe "we are what we eat" (Pretty, 2004). Such connections with food would promote, more and less, an environment fostering "sustainability" (in agriculture and rural development). However much desired, sustainability is a popular term that is interpreted as an allusive or infeasible illusion, highlighting the need for appropriate management of natural resources while contributing to human wellbeing (Pinstrup-Andersen, 2002).

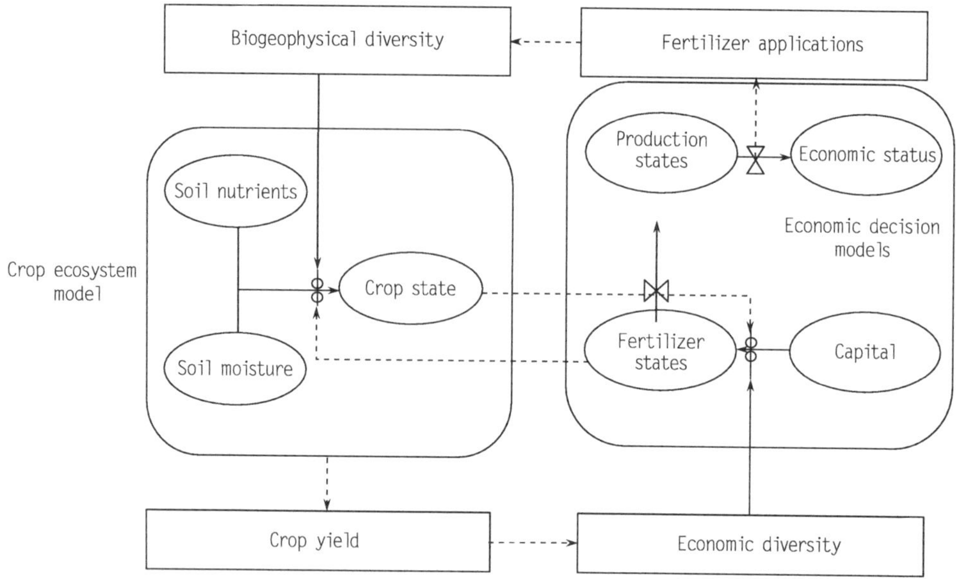

Fig. 2. 5　An agroecosystem represents as loosely or closely coupled ecosystems and economic models. Dotted connections represent feedbacks from system states to drivers in a loosely coupled model. Solid connecters represent feedback between processes in a closely coupled model（Antle et al.，2001）.

2. 2　Agroecology：The ecology of food systems

2. 2. 1　How is food produced?

As we all know，food supports human life. Agroecosystems are managed ecosystems that provide human needs，including food. There are an estimated 1400 million plant and animal species in earth's ecosystems，but only a tiny proportion of existing plant and animal species are part of the human diet. Wheat，rice and corn provide half of the calories that people consume. Two-thirds of the world's population survives primarily on these grains.

Traditional subsistence agriculture and intensive agriculture use human and animal labour for personal food production，and secondarily for market trade. Many traditional farmers rely on interplanting to increase crop diversity and overall agroecosystem yields. Common interplanting strategies include poly-varietal cultivation，intercropping，agro-forestry，and polyculture.

Current industrialized agriculture uses large amounts of input energy，from fossil fuels，oil and natural gas，water，commercial fertilizer and pesticides，to produce large quantities of crop and livestock for domestic and foreign sale. With the population explosion，particularly in developing countries，the yield per unit of land and gross output of food production has been the principal goal in agricultural production.

Since 1950，most of the increase in global food production has come from techniques developed during the "Green Revolution" . This technology originated with the breeding of dwarf high yield wheat and corn varieties in Mexico in 1962 by Dr. Norman Borlaug，after which a hybrid rice comedy was created in China in 1973. In most countries around the world，Green revolution techniques have included the use of inorganic fertilizers and pesticides, which have enabled farmers to more than double crop production without cultivating more land. As a result, world grain production nearly tripled between 1950 and 1990 before levelling off.

Besides crop production, there are several other ways to produce more food, one such option is producing more meat. Livestock can graze on rangeland or in pastures. Increasingly, farmers are raising animals in feedlots for meat, but there are problems that accompany these intensive livestock operations. Overgrazing results in rangeland degradation, desertification and contamination of the environment because of the lack of ability to utilize animal manures (Fig. 2.6). Also, Greenhouse Gas emissions are a major side-effect of livestock, especially ruminants.

Fig. 2.6 Manure contamination in a hog farm in Fuqing County, Fujian Province, China (pictured by S. Wang in 2003).

Another way to provide more food is to catch and raise more fish. Fish farming and fish ranching are forms of aquaculture. Use of aquaculture can boost seafood harvests, but it creates vast amounts of concentrated animal waste. Intensive aquaculture has increased as a result of overfishing, which has depleted many of the world's fisheries. In some cases, overfishing has led to commercial extinction of species.

Other possible methods of increasing the global food supply include introducing new foods into the diet, irrigating and cultivating more land and growing more food in urban areas.

Traditionally, farmers have used crossbreeding to improve crop strains and livestock. Today, genetic engineering can be used to produce genetically modified organisms (GMOs), however, the use of genetically engineered crops remains controversial.

2.2.2 Food is more than production

A sustainable food system is a complicated network consisting of food production, consumption, processing, distribution and resource use. A smooth food production process through the ecological circle depends as much on healthy soil, water and air as it does on good practices by farmers. The latter is affected by social market, the linking mechanism between an ecological circle and its social circle. A defective ecological circle usually results in food safety issues, which means many chemical and natural toxic materials accumulating in the food, which ultimately can be a menace to human and nature's health (Fig. 2.7).

Firstly, an ecological circle depends on natural renewable and non-renewable resources, and is limited by the abiotic environment (water, air and land). These are all needed in production, waste and residue handling. Energy input in production is another basic part of the system. Therefore, it is necessary to pay close attention to the cyclical nature of sustainable ecosystems. Agriculture is a production, consumption, recycles system whose sustainability is, in the long run, limited by the degree to which this circle is cultivated and maintained.

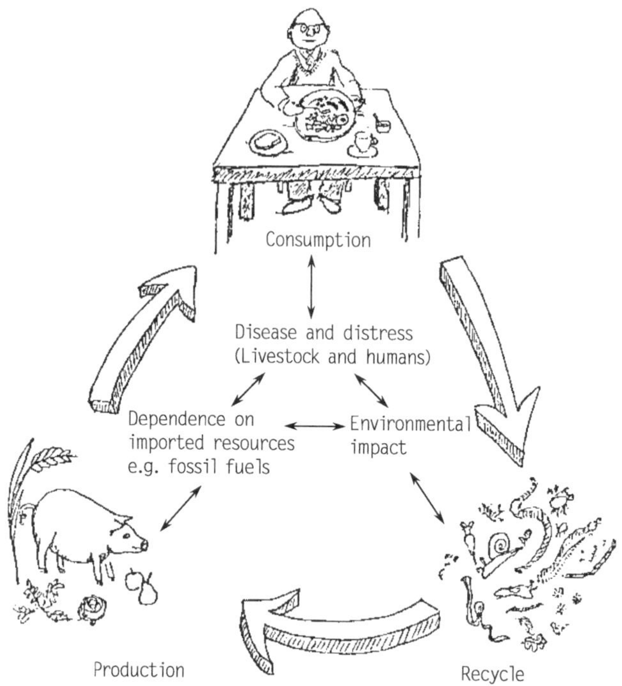

Fig. 2. 7 The ecological circle of human food system (Hill, 1985).

Secondly, food production is a process of a social circle. From a barn to a dining table, there are several procedures such as post-harvest disposition, processing, packaging, transportation, pricing and distributing that involve many shareholders (producers, retailer, wholesalers and consumers) and social resources (energy, technology and monetary capitals and so on). The primary goal of any food system should be the availability of food and resources for all people to achieve their optimal physical, mental and spiritual health through nourishing food. Other goals include fulfilment, justice, flexibility, evolution and sustainability. Therefore it is not enough to emphasize increased productivity and profit of modern food systems because that will eventually lead to the degradation of the very resources and environment upon which the food system relies. So, the social circle of the food system is extremely important to the ecological circle.

The pattern of food distribution and consumption in present food systems is not sustainable; to fulfil the need for sustainable systems, farmers need to be more reliant on people and knowledge, and less on imported chemicals and high-powered machines. As much as is possible, resources required to operate the farm should be generated on the farm or obtained within the region; the aim should be to avoid rather than control problems. Marketing should emphasize direct distribution to local populations; natural capital should build and maintain itself rather than erode; waste should be minimized and a greater number of components within such systems should be harvested for food. Rather than export our malfunctioning system of agriculture to other countries we should do everything in our power to promote the evolution of sustainable systems, first in our own gardens, farms, regions and countries, and then in those of others.

The modern fuel reliance food system has been resulting in tremendous food security and safety problems. In the 1990s, nearly 80% of malnourished children lived in countries with food surpluses. Poverty, not the lack of food production, is the real food problem for about one out of eight people. Between 1970 and 2000, the percentage of people suffering from chronic under nutrition or malnutrition fell from 35% to 17%. This decline is expected to continue. The two most common nutritional deficiencies are Marasmus and Kwashiorkor. About one out of three people suffer from micronutrient deficiencies, most commonly the lack of vitamin A, iron, and iodine. In the United States and other developed countries, over nutrition is a growing health problem.

In summary, food is more than production using land and labour, the basic framework of food includes energy consumption, water, soil, biodiversity and other ecosystem services. Accompanying these ecosystem services are some negative or unwanted natural risks like viruses, bacterial contamination events, distribution unavailability and break-downs in supply chains, corridors and gateways. This is due to insufficient social infrastructure, and dynamic sets of changes with time and space including increased demand, changing consumption preferences and changing land farming patterns (e. g. changes from crop production to biofuel production). Such complicated, interwoven process need to be taken into account and addressed under the umbrella of the Agroecology discipline.

2.2.3 Agroecology: The ecology of food systems

It is obvious at this point that our food producing systems must be operated in a sustainable way. As stated previously, Agroecology has been variously defined as the ecology of agriculture, the study of ecological functions in farming and the marriage of agriculture and ecology. More specifically, Agroecology is defined as the application of ecological concepts and principles to the design and management of sustainable agroecosystems. Agroecology can also be defined as the integrative study of the ecology of the entire food system, encompassing ecological, economic and social dimensions of food.

Because of the extreme importance of food for human beings, the application of agroecology principles expands our thinking beyond production practices and immediate environmental impacts at the various scales from field and farm level to the national, regional and global scales. This concept has captured the imaginations of farmers and academics that are searching for innovative ways to increase productivity in the short term and sustainability of agriculture in the long term in order to insure a reasonable quality of human life. To do so, we must expand the agroecology course teaching content in agricultural colleges in the future. This will address the complexity of improving today's food systems beyond the narrow components of agricultural production and their immediate environmental impacts; this supports the development of sustainable agroecosystems. Studying the ecology of food systems can provide insight into how to deal with questions at the systems level and contribute to development of sustainable societies.

2.2.4 Considering people and their food systems in agroecosystems

Current agricultural systems separate consumers from their sources of food and from the production environment; unlike in the past, producers and consumers do not know each other and have lost contact. There is a separation and lack of awareness on the consumers part about how and where food is produced and processed; this produces a lack of appreciation of the fact that what we produce is actually determined by what we consume. When such a connection is lost, everyone in this system works blindly, causing inefficiency, lack of trust and waste.

In addition, the global food system does not currently provide adequate food to the tables of the majority of people on the planet. This is particularly true when we consider global equity in terms of nutrition, health and food security with an increasing global human population. An interdisciplinary, integrated approach is essential to adequately address the complexities of interactions in the total food system. A broader, interdisciplinary focus on agroecology as the study of food systems will help us identify the real human costs and benefits of the current system and find a better way to design the global and regional food system. The development of a sustainable food system will require more attention to the efficiency of the entire process of converting natural resources to what reaches consumers' tables. This includes analysis of food production, processing, marketing, and consumption (Fig. 2.8). When agroecology is defined as the ecology of food systems, we are obligated to look beyond the efficiencies of resource use in production, the short-term environmental impacts of practices and annual enterprise economics (Francis et al., 2003).

2.2.5 Redesigning the food system for sustainability

If we examine the widespread problems with hunger and sustainability of food systems, there are three main tools to use when trying to reduce hunger and the harmful effects of agriculture. To meet the increased and changing demand we need to slow population growth, reduce poverty, and develop phases of sustainable agriculture systems (i. e. methods of growing crop and raising livestock based on natural fertilizers and pest control, soil and water conservation and limited use of non-renewable fossil fuel energy (Miller, 2009). The main elements of a sustainable agriculture consist of (Hill, 1985):

- Create new crop lands
- Increase productivity while decreasing damage to ecosystems
- Water systems management
- Energy systems management
- Adapting to climate change

2.3 Global food system: Two case analyses of basic agroecology

2.3.1 Case analysis 1: Let China harvests the sun and eat lower in the food chain

Who is feed China, a hungry dragon? With less than 7% of arable cropland and 22% of world's population, China has been surprisingly managed to feed itself without relying heavily on imports. However, with a rapid population growth rate and an economy quickly rising speed in the world, worries and discussion about China's food supply have aroused since the 1990s.

Lester Brown, who is the President of Washington's Worldwatch Institute, wrote a paper proposing a standpoint that China is rapidly losing the capacity to feed itself (Brown, 1994). According to Brown's thought, China's grain output had already reached its top notch and would only lower, declining by at least 20 percent by the year 2030. As China's economic growth moves the country up the food ladder, demand for more meat, requiring more feed grain, and also more plant oils and sugar rises while China's huge population continuing to increasing. Brown argued that as China loses its arable land, running out of irrigation water and exhausting opportunities for further major yield rises, it will no longer be able to satisfy the increasing need for food through domestic production. As a result, a richer China will have no way but to make up its food deficit by rising imports, casing an unbearable strain on the global food market. China's feed and food grain imports—potentially exceed today's global grain export capacity in a large extent—will lead to worldwide prices growth of nearly all major food commodities, making food dear for everybody. Considering the limited prospects for the expansion of grain exports from North America, Australia and Europe, Brown thought that China's purchases would soon cause such a tight seller's market for grain that major exporters could be forced to put limits on foreign sales in order to prevent skyrocketing domestic prices. On the other hand, if the global grain market can not supply China enough food for the coming generation, where will it get its grain after losing half of its farmland and at least a fifth of its harvests?

Lester Brown amplified this dismal scenario in "Who Will Feed China?" in 1995 (Brown, 1995). A slim volume subtitled "Wake-up Call for a Small Planet", that aroused suitably sensationalized and predictably superficial attention of mass media, always eager to report bad news. It caused worry about China's long-term prosperity among people and concerns among policy-makers trying to discern future patterns in the global food market. As is always the case with Brown's wake-up calls, they cannot be dismissed outright, but they also cannot be taken as straightforward fact. On the one hand, Brown describes the issues as an infuriating mixture of informed understanding and measured analyses. on the other hand, as an infuriating mixture of a slanted selective use of facts and utterly indefensible thought. According to Brown, China has to follow its neighbours, South Korea and Japan, relying on increasing food imports. However, it seems this is still not the problem for China, as the country still relies on its own grain production.

Although, there were many opposite views to Brown's point on Chinese food security, it is beyond all doubt that food has always been a central factor in the Chinese economy, its culture and its politics (Gale, 2006). The U. S. Department of Agriculture assessed that food accounts for the largest percentage in Chinese household budgets, including 38 percent of expenditures made by urban families and nearly half of rural household expenditures. This cultural food importance coupled with the many famines in China's history elevates the importance of remaining self-sufficient in food in the minds of Chinese policymakers (Gale, 2006).

The changes in Chinese eating habits make China the world's most dynamic market for food and perhaps the most important driver in world agricultural trade. The sheer size of the population means that changes in the Chinese market could have repercussions throughout global agriculture markets.

For decades analysts have been forecasting robust growth in Chinese agricultural import, but growth has failed to materialize until recently.

There are several reason that may explain a lower than expected level of Chinese food imports. Most notably, Chinese tend to eat low on the food chain: their diet exhibits high efficiency by eating more grain and less meat than North Americans. Ecologically speaking, the practice of low trophic level diet allows for a high conversion rate, directly harvesting the sun (Fig. 2. 8).

Roundly estimated, China has a total 150 million hectares of farmland according to LANDSAT (satellite) images; most of the southern and northeastern land grows rice, while north China grows wheat and corn. The yields per capita in China are higher than most other areas in world due to traditional practices, modern irrigation, fertilizing and pest control technologies. The total amount of grain production, never lower than 471 Mt since 1998 when severe flooding happened in the Yangzi basin for the whole year, makes the average 300 kg per capita sufficient to provide the recommended diet of protein and calories.

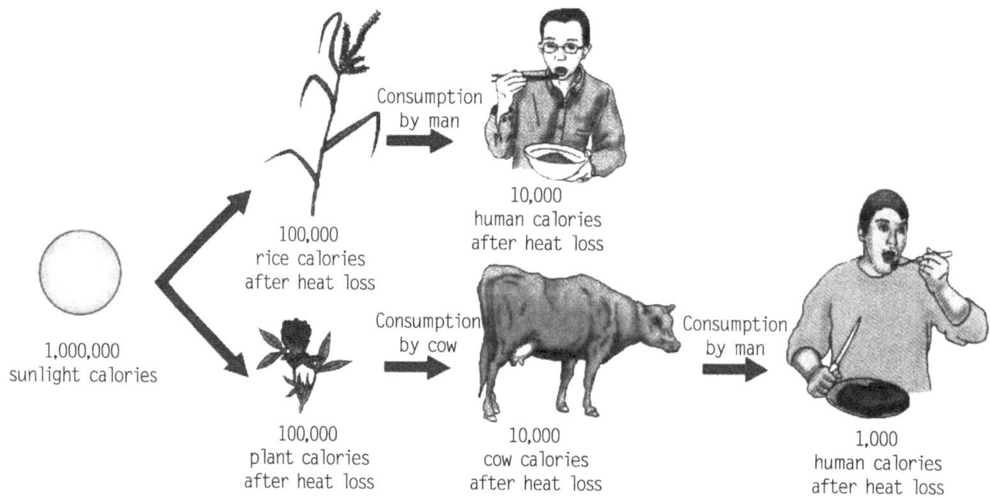

Fig. 2. 8 Should we feed grain to beef cattle or should we eat the grain?

On average people around the world get 1055 calories per day from eating grain directly—that's 45% of their total intake—the rest comes from meat, milk and eggs from animal that were fed grain in the low converting rate. Traditional Chinese eating habits should be encouraged throughout the world because of its high efficiency in accordance with the law of the ecological pyramid (Fig. 2. 8). The problem is that as the Chinese have become more prosperous, they too have started eating higher on the food chain.

For past decades, global demand for grain has been increasing faster than supply. While grain yields are increasing at 1. 1 percent per year, the world's population is growing slightly faster at 1. 2% per year, but that's just the start. Growing prosperity and increasing urbanization, especially in India and China, are driving up demand for animal-based food, putting further pressure on grain supplies. It takes 2 to 6 kilograms of grain fed to a cow, pig or chicken to make 1 kilo of meat, milk or eggs, both American poultry ranchers and Asian farmers recognize the efficiency of raising poultry for food. In this view, we strongly suggest that China and other developing countries change meat consumption from pork to chicken and choose higher conversion rate animal raising methods like poultry rather than beef, pork and milk because livestock and dairy farming consume large quantities of precious grain that has been fed in China for a long time. No other food source can make up for shortage of grain.

Meanwhile, in the past decade China has started to lose its capacity for higher food production after paying considerable attention to industrial methods of agriculture in order to pursue "the world factory." China has entered a fast urbanization stage; on the one hand, 6.70 M hm^2 of farmland has been occupied for industries and city building since 2003; on the other hand, agricultural infrastructure investment was cut and agroeocosystems were polluted dramatically, resulting in a decreased capacity for food production. It is a lesson in agroecological principles. The combination of staying self-sufficient by increasing grain production in China and maintaining the habit of eating low on food chain/high efficiency will rely on the increased yield per capita of the grain crop, but the question remains: Is it possible?

When you look at some other figures, you will notice that China still has 200 million people living in poverty, a figure second only to India. The population of China that does not have adequate food numbers is 23.65 million. The food security problem still remains, particularly in light of the energy shortage. More and more land is used to grow biofuel; energy and food are twins and surging oil prices are the catalysts for surging food prices.

In summary, agriculture, as the only life industry on earth is bound to be an "unprofitable" affair theoretically and in reality. This is why governments in developed economies have provided massive subsidies to farmers to keep society stable. The case of the food system in China demonstrates that following the ecological law is necessary, and good governance is also indispensable, in natural and human law. Again, agriculture is "the science, art, politics and sociology of changing sunlight into healthy, happy, people" (Caldwell, 1996; Wang, 2005).

2.3.2 Case analysis 2: Buying local in Canada

The Canadian agriculture and agro-food sector contributes an economic value of $95 billion per year with product exports above $21 billion each year; however, it only produces almost 10 percent of Canada's GDP (Agro-food Canada, 2001).

The Canadian food system has undergone radical change since World War II. There has been a coordinated effort by government and corporate interests to industrialize and rationalize the food production and delivery system. Such a system following the world trend treats food as a commodity generating profit, providing a variety of cheap food for urban dwellers. However, due to public attention to environment and food quality, food production, processing, and consumption in Canada in the past few decades, Canadians are more suited to the sustainable styles and thus decrease its negative impacts on environment and cultural maintenance.

The philosophy of Sustainable agriculture had been accepted in Canadian agriculture and food system extensively. Attempts to transition from conventional to sustainable agriculture had been conceived and implemented in 1990 through policy regulation and sound technologies, in which, efficiency, substitution and redesign (ESR) was proposed as the three inevitable stages (MacRae et al., 1990; 1993).

Recently, "Buying Local" or "Food Miles" has become a popular strategy in pursuing a Canadian sustainable food system. With the deep globalization, food system is more and more delocalized and embedded in the global scale, by the way of trade liberalization, information sharing, technology, or other observable routes. Many observers believe globalization can play a major role in accessing food sources for people, but many argue that it can also make matters worse, e. g. presenting more risks to farmers and further deteriorating the environment or further worsening the food and nutrition situation (Parrott et al., 2002; Pinstrup-Andersen, 2002). The local food system is widely regarded as more sustainable, at least from a theoretical viewpoint, local food systems preserve farmland and the farmer himself (Pinstrup-Andersen, 2002; Lapping, 2004). Hence, the emergence of small-scale, local production movements in industrialized countries like Canada and the United States (Lapping, 2004).

Canada's "Buying Local" strategies are advocated by some non-governmental organizations, like Woman's Institutes of Nova Scotia (WINS), who encourage residents to purchase local food products-firstly, by looking for food products produced inside the consumer's community; secondly looking to products produced in their county and then province. This strategy is called "Community, County, Province".

As implied by Fig. 2. 9, organic food may be considered to be the best food style in the world, but if all kinds of organic food on this Canadian household table are all coming from China, produced 10 thousand miles away and transported with fossil oil energy, are they really organic? Therefore, buying local in many ways equals to the pursuit of a sustainable Canadian food system.

Fig. 2. 9 Are those food organic? "Organic" food display in Canadian household dining table are transported from China, approximately 10 000 kilometres from Canada (Caldwell, 2009).

There are several ways for local consumers to buy local produce and even get involved in its production. One way is through Community Supported Agriculture (CSA), which is a process where the consumer buys shares in a farm's harvest and the farmer provides produce to that consumer on a regular basis. In the CSA arrangement, consumers get much of their weekly produce by picking up a box of organic, fresh-picked fruits and vegetables grown on a farm in their community. A farmer commits to growing food for a group of people (often called "members" or "shareholders"), and the people support the farmer by paying for their shares of produce ahead of time, often at the beginning of the season. CSA members ideally share both the risks and the bounty of farming.

The key word in Community Supported Agriculture is "community," as it builds a stronger sense of community by developing and strengthening the relationship between farmer and consumer. There are many benefits to this relationship for both the consumer and the farmer. The subscriber or shareholder knows where their produce is coming from and how it is grown. Customers also can have a say in what is produced as this benefits both the farmer and the consumer. Food miles have also been minimized and the quality is superior because of its freshness.

In many CSAs the customer pays a fee and produce is delivered on a weekly or bi-weekly basis. Mixed vegetables and fruit are the largest component of the basket of goods but it can also include meat, cheese, flowers, breads and recipes. A typical period to subscribe can run from spring to late fall and some farms offer subscriptions through the winter months.

CSA have been proliferated in Canada and elsewhere which provides a solution for the hopes and dreams of sustainable agriculture. The WTO agriculture section should be reviewed in depth under this advocation and the agroecological view as well.

Literatures cited in this chapter

Agriculture and Agrifood Canada. 2001. Agriculture in harmony with nature: Agriculture and Agri-Food Canada's Sustainable Development Strategy 2001-2004.

Altieri M. A. 1995. *Agroecology: The Science of Sustainable Agriculture*. 2nd ed. London: Intermediate Technology Publications.

Altieri M. A. and Nicholls, C. I. 2004. An agroecological basis for designing diversified cropping systems in the tropics. *Journal of Crop Improvement* 11: 81-103.

Antle J. M. et al. 2001. Research needs for understanding and predicting the behavior of managed ecosystems: Lessons from the study of agroecosystems. *Ecosystem* 4: 723-735.

Brown J. L. 1994. Who Will Feed China? *Newsletter of the Worldwatch* Aug: 24.

Brown J. L. 1995. *Who Will Feed China? Wake-up Call for a Small Planet*. New York: W. W. Norton & Company.

Caldwell C. D. 1996. IN100: Agroecology course resource manual. Nova Scotia Agricultural College: 215.

Callicott J. B. 1988. Agroecology in context. *Journal of Agricultural and Environmental Ethics* 1: 3-9.

China's Biodiversity Status Research Group. 1998. *China's Biodiversity Status Research Report*. Beijing: China's Environment Press.

Clements D. R. and Shrestha A. 2004. New dimensions in agroecology for developing a biological approach to crop production. *Journal of Crop Improvement* 11: 1-20.

Conway G. R. 1986. Agroecosystem analysis for research and development. Bangkok: Winrock International.

England R. W. 1994. *Evolutionary Concepts in Contemporary Economics*. Ann Arbor: The University of Michigan Press.

Foster J. B. 1997. The crisis of the earth: Marx's theory of ecological sustainability as a nature-imposed necessity for human production. *Organization & environment* 10 (3): 278-295.

Francis C., Lieblein G., Gliessman S., Breland T. A. Creamer N., Harwood R., Salomonsson L., Helenius J., Rickerl D., Salvador R., Wiedenhoeft M., Simmons S., Allen P., Altieri M., Flora C., and Poincelot R. 2003. Agroecology: The ecology of food systems. *Journal of Sustainable Agriculture* 22: 99-118.

Gale F. 2006. Trends in Chinese Food Demands and Trade Patterns. Agriculture Outlook Forum, United States

Department of Agriculture.

Hill S. B. 1985. Redesigning the food system for sustainability. *Alternatives* 12 (3/4): 32-36.

Hill S. B. 1998. Research Paper Redesigning Agroecosystems for Environmental Sustainability: A Deep Systems Approach. *Systems Research and Behavioral Science* 15: 391-402.

Hodges J. 2005. Cheap food and feeding the world sustainably. *Livestock Production Science* 92: 1-16.

Lapping M. B. 2004. Toward the recovery of the local in the globalizing food system: The Role of alternative agricultural and Food models in the US. *Ethics, Place and Environment* 7: 141-150.

MacRae R. J., Henning J., and Hill S. B. 1993. Strategies to overcome barriers to the Development of sustainable agriculture in Canada: The role of agribusiness. *Journal of Agricultural and Environmental Ethics* 6: 21-51.

MacRae R. J., Hill S. B., and Henning J. 1990. Policies, programs, and regulations to support the transition to sustainable agriculture in Canada. *American Journal of Alternative Agriculture* 5: 76-92.

Maguer M. L. 2004. Partnerships in food safety: How the interface between decision-maker and scientist affects policy. *Journal of the Science of Food and Agriculture* 84: 391-394.

Mcmichael P. 2000. The power of food. *Agriculture and Human Values* 17 (1): 21-33.

Miller T. G. and Spoolman S. 2009. *Sustaining the Earth: an integrated approach*. Belmon: Cengage Learning.

Odum E. P. 1996. Ecology: *Bridging science and society*. Sunderland: Sinauer Associates Inc.

Parrott N. Wilson N., and Murdoch J. 2002. Spatializing quality: Regional protection and the alternative geography of food. *European Urban and Regional Studies* 9: 241-261.

Pinstrup-Andersen P. 2002. Towards a sustainable global food system: What will it take? John Pesek Colloquium, Iowa State University.

Pretty J. 2004. We are what we eat. *New Scientist* 184: 44-47.

Waltner-Toews D. 1991. One ecosystem, one food system: The social and ecological context of food safety strategies. *Journal of Agricultural & Environmental Ethics* 4: 49-59.

Wang S. L. 2005. Information technology: toward the way to the sustainable management of agroecosystem. *Agriculture Network Information* 8: 4-12.

Wang S. L., Caldwell C. D., and Kilyanek S. L. 2006. A new framework for the study of agroecology: a case study from China. Montreal: Presented in Canadian Society for Ecology and Evolution (CSEE) Inaugural Meeting.

Unit 2 Basic Analysis of Agroecosystems

Chapter 3 Agroecosystem and its analysis

Learning objectives

1. Define an agroecosystem in a comprehensive context.
2. Describe the hierarchies of agrecosystems.
3. List and define the five basic properties of agroecosystems.
4. List the procedures for an agroecosystem analysis.

3.1 What is an agroecosystem?

The concept of an "agroecosystem" is fairly new; it is the most intensively managed ecosystem on earth (Fig. 3.1). Only 30% of the earth's surface is considered habitable land, and of that 30%, only 10% is used for cultivation (Reicosky, 1998). Perhaps agroecosystems have the greatest impact of any ecosystem type on our lives because they comprise a small percentage of Earth's total landmass, yet they provide us with food, fibre and largely impact the quality of our environment and thus our lives. To continue providing us sustenance, the emphasis of agricultural production is shifting from maximization to regeneration and optimization while increasing sustainability and limiting environmental damage (Elliott and Cole, 1989). Converging goals of ecologists and agricultural scientists within agroecosystem science will help provide insightful solutions concerning problems in production and the environment (Elliott and Cole, 1989).

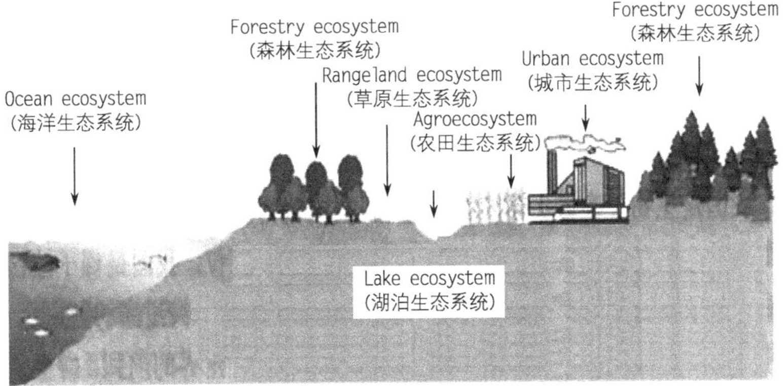

Fig. 3.1 Agroecosystems among the different kinds of ecosystems on earth.

These agroecosystems analyzing approaches are relatively neoteric work. Conway and Barbier (1990) put forward an Agroecosystem Analysis method (AeA), broadening the scale of conventional farm system analysis to embrace agroecosystem hierarchies. With the combination of natural and socioeconomic elements, the trade-offs between them are taken into account in AeA. Therefore, it is essential to understand the concepts, properties and hierarchies of agroecosystems. And interdisciplinary thinking and multidimensional approaches involving both natural and social science are necessary in AeA. This chapter aims to offer the agroecosystem profile and then provide a framework of AeA with several cases that illustrate how to use the AeA.

An agroecologist studies an agroecosystem in it's entirely, essentially seeing it as the most basic unit of their science. An agroecosystem is defined as a geographically and functionally coherent domain of agricultural activity, including all living and non-living components (the physical environment, the community and the economy), and the interactions among them (Kishk, 2003). Essentially, an agroecosystem can be viewed as a subset of any conventional ecosystem that is designed and managed for production purposes. At the core of an agroecosystem lays the human component of agriculture. As a result, an agroecosystem's boundaries go well beyond the immediate site of agricultural activity (e. g. the farm) to include the entire region impacted by human activity. Human agricultural activities usually affect the complexity of species assemblages, matter cycles, energy, information and economic flows. Traditionally an agroecosystem, particularly one managed intensively, is characterized as having a simpler species composition, energy and nutrient flow in relation to "natural" ecosystems. Additionally, agroecosystems often have elevated nutrient inputs. Runoff of excess nutrient inputs can lead to eutrophication in connected ecosystems not directly engaged in agriculture.

A typical home garden in rural China is an example of an agroecosystem. These agroecosystems consist of the crop plant components (forest trees, shrubs, fruit trees and herbs), livestock (cattle, goats and chickens), natural organisms (bacteria, fungi, pests and weeds) and sometimes product processing machines within a certain biophysical boundary. Within this boundary, typically defined by a fence or hedge, the basic, ecological processes remain: competition between the plants, consumption of the plants by livestock and pests and predation of pests by their natural enemies. Residents regulate the agricultural processes through cultivation, subsidy (fertilizers), control (of water, pests and diseases) and harvesting. Economic and social pressures outside the system further regulate these ecological processes. An interactive, natural-socio-economic system such as a rural home garden has both biophysical and socioeconomic boundaries; having to deal with material cycles, energy, information and most importantly, monetary flows significantly differentiates an agroecosystem from a natural ecosystem. This complex, agro-socio-economic-ecological system, bounded in several dimensions, is an agroecosystem—a system of an assemblage of elements contained within a boundary interacting with each other both in structure and function (Conway, 1993).

Agroecology promotes a style of management that narrows the gap between agroecosystems and "natural" ecosystems, both by increasing the biological and trophic complexity of agrecosystems and decreasing the nutrient inputs/outflow. For example, traditional Chinese polyculture or buffer strips offer a certain complexity to a cropping system for wildlife habitat maintenance. By using ecosystem-based farming methods, farmers can reduce mechanical tillage, nutrient and other chemical inputs. These methods reduce soil degradation, nutrient runoff and leaching from the agricultural lands that feed into lakes and groundwater, with the aim of avoiding eutrophication and reducing groundwater contamination.

3.2 The hierarchies of agroecosystems

This definition and depiction of efficient agroecosystems offer many options for sustainable management. Firstly, the definition fosters genuinely interdisciplinary approaches to farming systems research, insisting biologists and social scientists work together for a holistic picture of the system. Secondly, agroecosystems exist with intrinsic hierarchies differing in scales of organizational levels, spatially, temporally, biogeographically and social-economically. In fact, agroecosystems usually exhibit political dimensions too (Fig. 3.2).

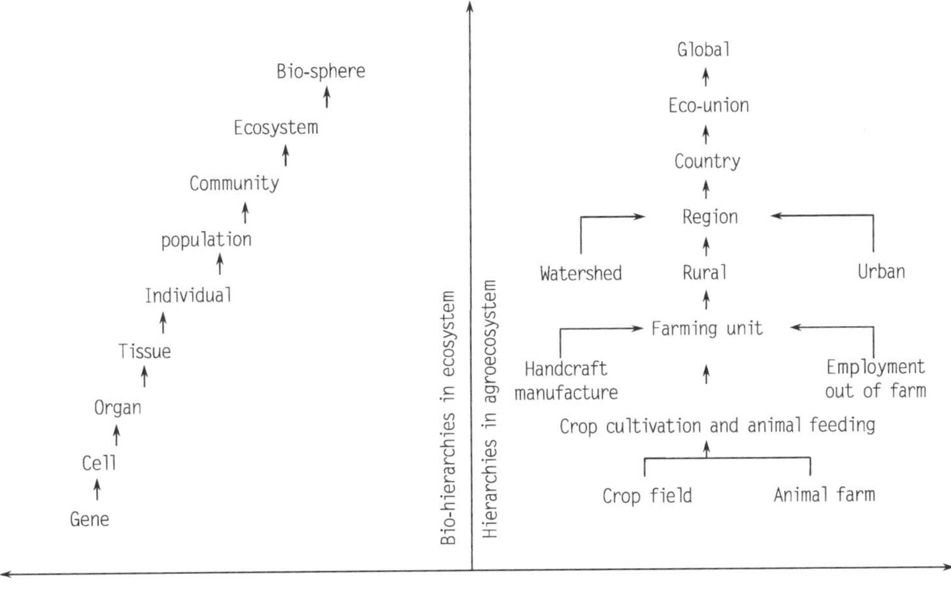

Fig. 3.2 Hierarchies of ecosystems and agroecosystems (Left: Odum, 1971; Right: Conway, 1987).

As shown in Fig. 3.2, we can conceive of natural ecosystems as nested hierarchies from gene to ecosystem and further to biosphere. In the process of agricultural development, these strata are modified for the purpose of food or fibre production and other ecosystem services creating hybrid hierarchies within agroecosystems. Genes and cells make up the basic levels of an agroecosystem hierarchy. Above that is the agroecosystem's microenvironment followed by the people who tend and harvest that environment. Some recognizably distinct systems where this occurs include: a lone fruit tree in a farmer's garden, a milk cow in a stall, an individual plant in a crop population and a single animal in a herd. The next level, the field or paddock, adds to the complexity of the hierarchy, just as each consecutive level continually makes the agroecosystem more intricate. Each level forms a component of the agroecosystem in the next, higher level. Hence, the global agroecosystem consists of national agroecosystems from around the world, linked together by international trade with the present globalization initiative in the background. Each national agroecosystem composes itself of regional agroecosystems linked together by national markets. Understanding how these hierarchies levels bridge together, while understanding the complexities within each hierarchical level is crucial for AeA.

3.3 The properties of agroecosystems

Ecology and evolutionary biology characterizes individual organisms by the basic properties of growth and reproduction, maintenance and survival. The "goal" of an organism is increased fitness, achieved through some combination of high and/or low values for each of these properties. The particular combination present in an organism can be regarded as its life history strategy. For natural populations, communities and ecosystems it is possible to define a similar set of ecosystem properties, consisting of productivity, stability (constancy) and resilience. In each case these properties refer to the numbers or biomass of individuals or species, or some combination thereof. Unlike individual organisms, though, there is no obvious "goal" for a population, community or ecosystem and these properties are simply the outcomes of co-evolution. However, one might consider individual goals of fitness (i. e. surviving and passing beneficial genes to offspring) as a larger goal of maintaining the population, community or ecosystem (Holling, 2001).

Despite theirs complexity, agroecosystems can be characterized by five system properties: productivity, stability, sustainability, equitability (Conway, 1985), and homogeneity, which are relatively easy to define although not equally as easy to measure.

3.3.1 Productivity

Productivity is the output of valued product per unit of resource input (land, labour, energy or capital), commonly measured as annual yield, net income per hectare, man-hour, unit of energy, investment or total production of goods and services per household or nation (Conway, 1986, 1987). Yield of consumable and marketable products can be measured in kilograms (i. e. kg of grain, tubers or fish), or alternatively, as calories, proteins, vitamins or simply the product's market value. Frequently however, yield calculations must include factors that are typically difficult to measure. These factors include labour generation, items of convenience or aesthetic value or value added to social, psychological and spiritual well-being (Conway, 1987).

The efficiency of productivity can be measured through comparison between two or more agroecosystems. Efficiency assessments may look at productivity at every hierarchical level in the agroecosystem, and over time productivity of an individual agroecosytem may vary (Conway, 1987). These comparisons need not be made on similar agroecosystems.

3.3.2 Stability

Stability is the constancy of productivity in the face of small disturbances from normal fluctuations and cycles in the surrounding environment (Conway, 1987). These disturbances may occur inside or outside the system from climate and environmental processes, or from social and economic variables. Climate and environmental disturbances might affect the physical and biological processes that occur in an agroecosystem. Social and economic variables can occur as a result of changing market demands. Since productivity is variable, stability refers to the long-lasting trends that define an agroecosystem (Conway, 1987).

3.3.3 Sustainability

Sustainability of an agroecosystem in relation to productivity means maintaining set productivity when subject to a major disturbing force (Conway, 1987). Disturbing forces include stresses and perturbations. Stresses generally occur on a regular basis and can be small and predictable, whereas perturbations are irregular occurrences, large and unpredictable. Thus, increasing soil salinity is a stress while droughts or floods are considered perturbations. One can measure this type of sustainability, the ability of an agroecosytem to withstand disturbances whilst productivity persists, in inertia (resistance), elasticity, amplitude, hysteresis and malleability of the agroecosystem in response to a disturbing force (Conway, 1987). An agroecosystem manager may attempt to maintain sustainability through inputs (often fertilizers or pesticides). However, these inputs may inherently cause some disturbances in the system, causing stress or increased organism resistance eliciting the need for continuous inputs to sustain productivity.

3.3.4 Equitability

Equitability measures how evenly the productivity (level of equity generated) of the agroecosystem is distributed among its human beneficiaries (Conway, 1987). The equity generated consists of the total production of goods and services in an agroecosystem. Equitability is difficult to measure because it reflects personal value judgements, however, methods such as the Lorenz curve and Gini coefficient attempt to definitively measure equitability.

3.3.5 Homogeneity

The agricultural industry can be divided into crop farming, forestry, fisheries and processing. Homogeneity is defined as the fitness and connectivity of those sectors. In other words, homogeneity equates to the degree an agroecosystem relies on an outside ecosystem, particularly the social marketing system. For example, homogeneity within a sector would refer to different crop varieties planted on the same crop field living in a symbiotic relationship to reduce pest exposure and pesticide use.

Homogeneity can be represented by (one minus) the Shannon-Wiener diversity index (Spellerberg, 2003), which measures species biodiversity in an ecosystem.

$$\text{Shannon-Wiener diversity index} = H\ (x) = -\sum p_i \log p_i$$

$$\text{Homogeneity index} = 1 - \sum p_i \log p_i$$

In this equation p_i represents one of the following: ① percentage of GDP in a certain sector among an entire industry, ② percentage of GDP in a subsector within a sector in field ecosystem, or ③ a species percentage in a planting area.

These five properties can be quantified by tracing the historical evolution of agroecosystems. Due to complex interactions, significant trade-offs usually exist between agroecosystem properties (Conway, 1993). High productivity often occurs at the expense of sustainability. For instance, new forms of land use or new technologies may immediately increase productivity, but lower the long-term value of one or more of the other properties in the agroecosystem. Depending on the people managing the agroecosystem, one may choose to value productivity more highly than sustainability or equitability more highly than productivity. Therefore, the manager can determine what trade-offs he or she is willing to accept.

The manager may choose to emphasize different needs over time, altering the properties' assumed importance due to relative changes in the agroecosystem. Thus, agricultural development typically involves a progression of changes in the relative values of these properties, with successive phases of development requiring an adaptation of priorities.

These properties and trade-offs may be used as performance indicators of agroecosystems. Traditional agricultural systems with shifting cultivation generally have low productivity and stability, but high equitability and sustainability (pattern A in Tab. 3. 1). Traditional Chinese multi-cropping systems tend to be productive, stable and retain a high degree of sustainability and a lesser degree of the equitability (pattern B in Tab. 3. 1). However, the introduction of new technology, while greatly increasing the productivity, is likely to lead to lower values of other properties (pattern C in Tab. 3. 1). This happened with the introduction of new high yielding rice varieties such as IR8 and relatives in the 1960's Green Revolution. Yields fluctuated widely while generally declining, due in part to growing pest and disease attacks. More recent rice varieties combine high productivity with stability, but still have poor sustainability (pattern D in Tab. 3. 1). The ideal goal should be pattern E or pattern F on marginal lands, where there is a conflict between productivity and sustainability.

Tab. 3. 1 Properties of different agroecosystems (Conway, 1985)

Types	Agricultural patterns	Productivity (生产力)	Stability (稳定性)	Sustainability (可持续性)	Equitability (均衡性)	Homogeneity (协调性)
A	Swidden shifting cultivation	low	low	high	high	high
B	Chinese traditional cropping system	medium	medium	high	medium	high
C	Improved	high	low	low	low	low
D	Improved	high	high	low	high	low
E	Ideal (best land)	high	medium	high	high	high
F	Ideal (marginal land)	medium	high	high	high	high

In Canada, the potato production system can have very high productivity, but the stability is often low due to pest and disease attacks, and the sustainability is low as a result of erosion and pesticide use. In a Chinese agroforestry system, interplanting trees with cereal cropping, a common practice in the northern province of Hebei, usually restores some stability and sustainability due to the buffering effect produced by greater diversity of cropping. Increasing equitability usually costs the system lowered overall productivity compared with single cash crops. In theory, such a system is encouraged but, unfortunately, is seldom realized in practice.

3.4 Agroecosystem analysis

The agroecosystem analysis framework is based upon the concepts of agroecosystem hierarchies and properties that were addressed above. Agroecosystem analyses usually consist of the following objectives and procedures.

3.4.1 Objectives of analysis

The objectives for an Agroecosystems Analysis are:

(1) to provide a developing criteria for farm comparisons and for a strategy to collect needed information.

(2) to conduct interviews and make observations to collect relevant information during farm visits.

(3) to compare and contrast production, economic, environmental, and social characteristics of different farms.

(4) to develop skills appropriate to small group processes and practice these skills in analyzing and evaluating the farm interview information.

(5) to integrate and understand the multiple goals of farm families and explore how these are being achieved.

(6) to practice oral and written communication skills in presenting results of farm analysis.

3.4.2 The procedure of analysis

The agroecosystem analysis procedure has evolved from one originally designed for the analysis of natural ecosystems. It relies on the five property concepts described earlier and four assumptions described below:

(1) One can produce a realistic and useful analysis without knowing all aspects of the agroecosystem in question.

(2) Understanding a few key functional relationships will offer a greater knowledge of the behaviour and other important properties of an agroecosystem.

(3) A few key management decisions may produce significant improvements in agroecosystem performance.

(4) Defining and answering a few appropriate key questions can lead to identification and understanding of these key relationships.

Fig. 3.3 graphically displays and describes the analysis procedure steps. The procedure is best followed in a seminar or workshop environment in which group meetings are interspersed with intensive work sessions of smaller groups (Conway, 1985). Tab. 3.2 suggests an appropriate timetable for a one-week agroecosystem analysis workshop, day-by-day.

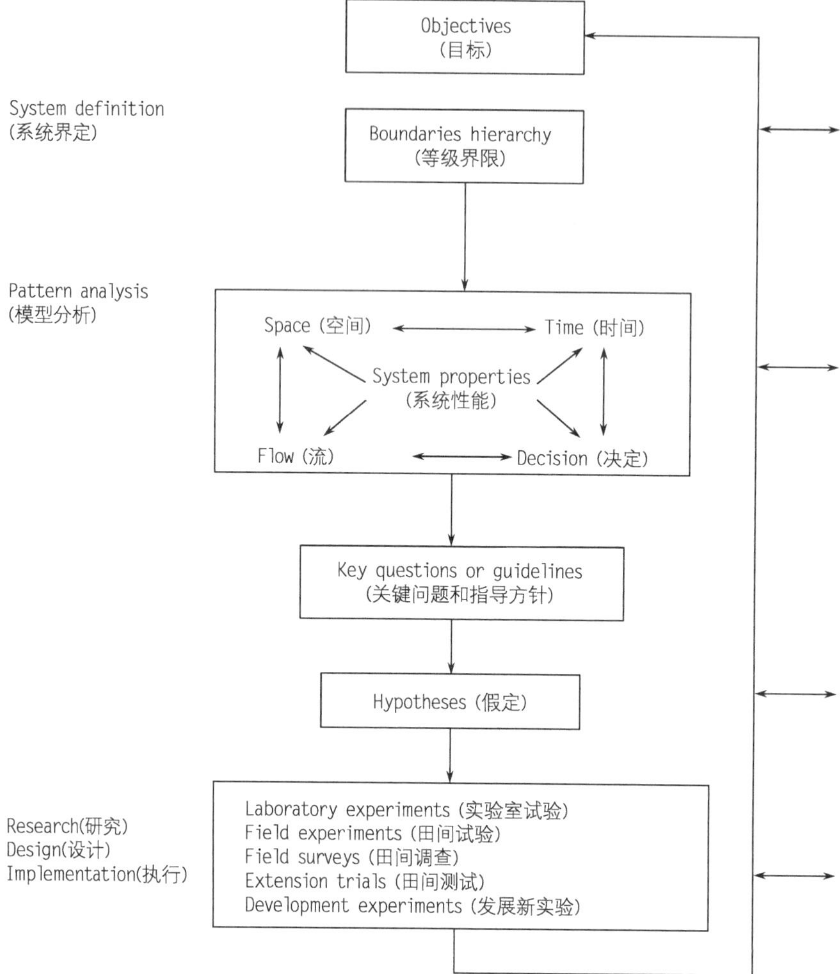

Fig. 3. 3 Basic steps of the procedure for agroecosystem analysis (Conway, 1985).

3. 4. 3 Precise definition of objective agroecosystem

In order to achieve high quality results from an agroecosystem analysis, one must precisely identify objectives and outline those objectives to the entire team. Explicit objectives defining agricultural goals will foster discussions about the most appropriate changes for yielding the desired results. An example of explicit objectives, taken directly from Conway (1985):

(1) To identify research priorities that will lead to improvements in the level and stability of net income of farm households in the x region.

(2) To identify tentative guidelines for improving agricultural productivity of the poor farmers in y village.

3. 4. 4 System definition

Exploring key functional relationships can help distinguish systems, system boundaries and system hierarchies to determine properties of ecological systems. Four patterns are important for understanding ecological system properties: space, time, flows and decisions. Space, time and flows generate insight for natural and social scientific analyses, while decisions reflect human contributions to agroecosystem management.

Tab. 3. 2 Timetable for a week-long workshop about Agroecosystem analysis (Conway, 1985)

Day 1	Participant introduction (参观者简介). Conceptual basis and details of procedure (生产的感念基础和细节流程). Introduction to study area or theme (介绍研究领域或主题).
Day 2	Briefing on case study data (简介案例研究资料). System definition by whole workshop team (整个团队参与界定系统定义). Break into groups, each assigned a level in the system hierarchy (e. g. field plot-farm-village-region) or one of a series of agroecosystems (e. g. different farms or villages): each group carries out Pattern Analysis (进行分组，每一组分配农业生态系统的一个等级 (如田间小区-农场-村庄-地区) 或作为农业生态系统中的同类部分 (如不同的农场或村庄): 每一组进行模式分析.
Day 3	Continuation of Day 2 in groups; analysis of system properties and key question identification (与第二天的团体进行交流，对系统的组分关键问题进行分析).
Day 4	Field visits to case study sites (走访作为案例点的田间实地).
Day 5	Presentation by groups of their findings (各组发表各自的发现).
Day 6	Whole team discussion of key questions and research design and implementation (整个团体内讨论关键问题和重新设计与执行问题).
Day 7	Writing of draft report by editorial team (团队进行报告草稿的撰写).

(1) Space

Spatial patterns disclose potentially significant functional relationships, these patterns can be discovered with the use of maps and transects. For instance, in a typical Chinese terrace rice field, analysis of the irrigation system may lead farmers to suggest triple cropping as appropriate management, thereby allowing farmers to have a more reliable water supply. Recognizing the most suitable practices for a particular agroecosystem through spatial pattern analysis will allow a farmer to generate a stable production flow.

(2) Time

Time patterns for agroecosystems appear as seasonal changes and long-term changes. Seasonal changes account for crop sequences, labour and credit peaks while long-term changes include factors of price, production, climate and demographics. Graphic displays most commonly depict both seasonal and long-term changes.

(3) Flows

Flows, including transformations of energy, materials, money and information within an agroecosystem, indicate feedback mechanisms. Flows should be depicted in a simple diagram, expressing major causes and effects in an agroecosystem.

(4) Decisions

Decision patterns occur within every hierarchical level in the agroecosystem and can range in importance from affecting one practice of an individual farmer to affecting national agricultural policy. Two patterns of decisions are important for the ecological system: choices made in a single agroecosystem and the patterns where spheres of influence affect the decision of the decision maker.

(5) Key questions

Many key questions may emerge about system definitions, pattern analysis and system properties. These questions may range from easily answerable to solutions that will require experimentation on testable hypotheses. For examples of specific key questions about an agroecosystem in Thailand, or more information about the properties of agroecosystems and procedures and definitions of agroecosystem analysis refers to "Agroecosystem Analysis" by Gordon Conway (1985).

Literatures cited in this chapter

Conway G. R. 1985. Agroecosystem analysis. *Agricultural Administration* 20: 31-55.

Conway G. R. 1986. *Agroecosystem analysis for research and development*. Bangkok: Winrock International.

Conway G. R. 1987. The properties of agroecosystems. *Agricultural Systems* 24: 95-117.

Conway G. R. 1993. In *Economics and Ecology: new frontiers and sustainable development*. London: Chapman and Hall.

Conway G. R. and Barbier E B. 1990. *After the Green Revolution: Sustainable agriculture for development*. London: Earthscan.

Elliott E. T. and Cole C. V. 1989. A perspective on agroecosystem science. *Ecology* 70: 1597-1602

Holling C. S. 2001. Understanding the complexity of economic, ecological, and Social systems. *Ecosystems* 4: 390-405.

Kishk F. M., Gaber H. M., and Abdallah S. M. 2003. Environmental Health Risks Reduction in Rural Egypt: A Holistic Ecosystem Approach. Environmental Data and Reports: Egypt.

Odum E. P. 1971. *Fundamentals of ecology*. Philadelphia: W B Saunders Company.

Reicosky D. C. and Forcella F. 1998. Cover crop and soil quality interactions in agroecosystems. *Journal of Soil and Water Conservation* 53 (3): 224-229.

Spellerberg I. F. and Fedor P. J. 2003. A tribute to Claude Shannon (1916-2001) and a plea for more rigorous use of species richness, species diversity and the 'Shannon-Wiener' Index. *Global Ecology and Biogeography* 12 (3):117-179.

Chapter 4 Energy flow and matter cycle in agroecosystems

Learning objectives

1. Define the following terms:
   - Ecology
   - Food chain
   - Food web
   - Ecological efficiency
2. Describe the energy flow in agroecosystems.
3. Describe matter cycle in agroecosystems.

4.1 Energy flow and matter cycle in a natural ecosystem

Ecology is a study of the connections among organisms and their living and non-living environment. An ecosystem is a living community with complex interactions between biotic factors (different scales of organisms) and abiotic factors (including physical and chemical factors). Simply, in an ecosystem, solar energy flows into and through the system, powering the nutrient cycles that maintain system stability (Fig. 4.1). Solar energy initiates photosynthesis by plants (producers), converting solar energy from its radiant state to stored chemical energy (carbon-based matter). Several trophic levels of consumers use the stored chemical energy in the food chain and food web; decomposers recycle the remaining waste material. Decomposed organic chemicals are converted into inorganic chemicals that producers in the next life cycle absorb and release as carbon dioxide back into the atmosphere. The amount of energy converted depends on the efficiency of plants, consumers and their abiotic factors. Producers can use the cycled matter and the inorganic building blocks of the living system over and over again if they are not washed away or removed from the ecosystem.

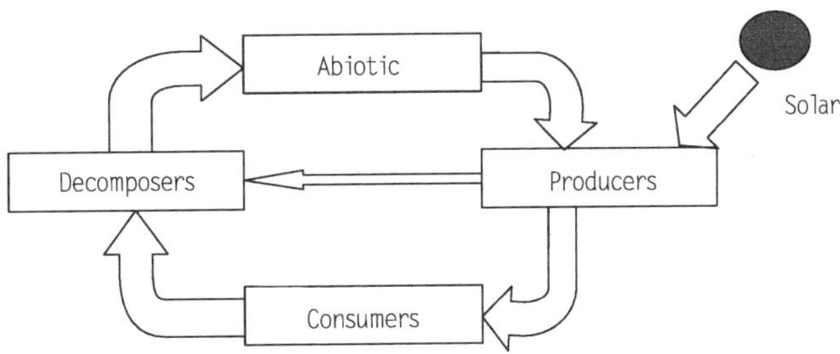

Fig. 4.1 The energy flow and mater cycle in a natural ecosystem.

In a food chain, "food" contains the base group of materials in the ecosystem. Organisms get their essential nutrients by participating in a food chain. A food chain diagram describes the transfer of energy and matter from primary producers to consumers to decomposers via a series of organisms that eat and are eaten (Fig. 4. 2). Various food chains can link together to form a food web (Fig. 4. 3). Each organism in an ecosystem can be assigned to a trophic level within its food chain or food web. Each trophic level contains a certain amount of biomass; that total biomass decreases as we travel up the food chain. The transfer of energy between these levels has a certain ecological efficiency.

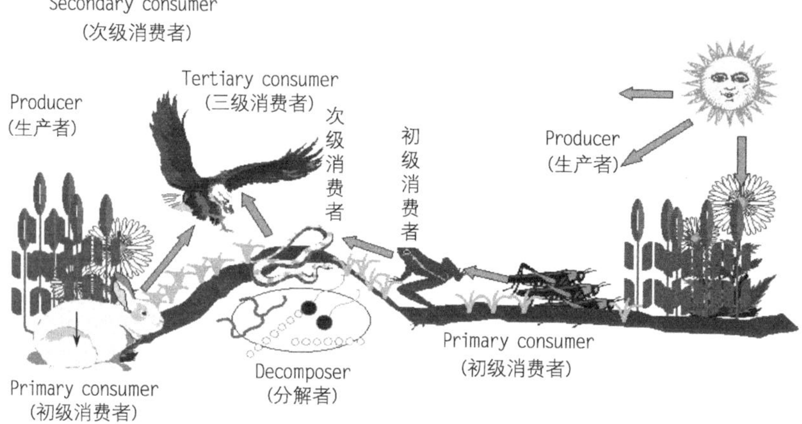

Fig. 4. 2　A universal food chain in ecosystems (Lin, 2007)

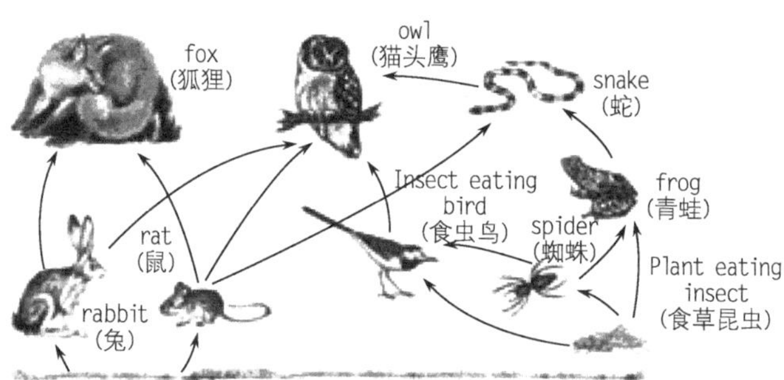

Fig. 4. 3　A food web in terrestrial ecosystems (Lin, 2007).

Food chains can be represented as an energy flow pyramid (Fig. 4. 4). A food chain or web pyramid mass will represent biomass storage in each trophic level. A number pyramid can represent the number of organisms within each trophic level in a food chain or web. According to Lindeman's research (1942), the trophic-dynamic model explains the major loss of energy as you move up each trophic level due to respiration and an inefficient transfer of energy. The ratio is generally referred to as the law of one-tenth (Fig. 4. 5). This is a rough "rule of thumb" since some agricultural systems are actually considerably more efficient (e. g. broiler chickens).

Fig. 4. 4 The pyramid of energy flow in ecosystem representing ecological efficiency of the intertrophic levels of food chain.

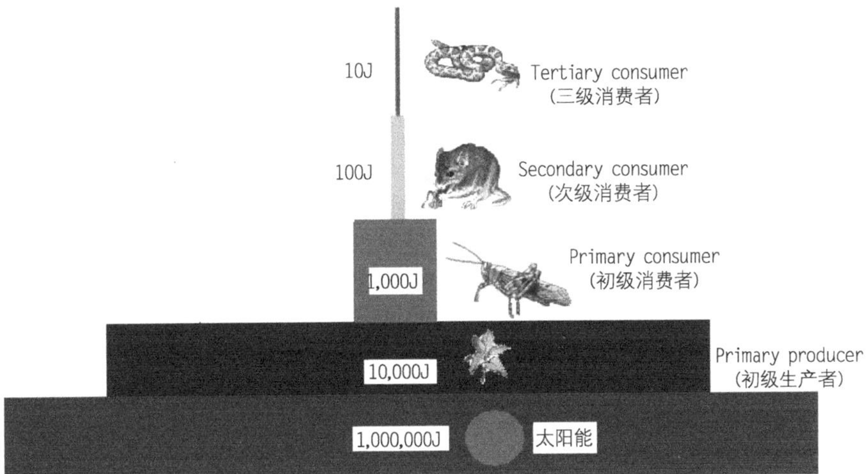

Fig. 4. 5 The ecological efficiency of energy conversion in natural ecosystems (Lin, 2007).

Complex trophic interactions within a natural ecosystem result in energy flows where certain amounts of energy are dissipated at different stages along the food chain and the greatest amount of energy within the system ultimately moves along the detritus pathway (Gliessman, 2005). Annual system production corresponds with energy content and can be calculated in net primary productivity or biomass (Gliessman, 2005). In Fig. 4. 4, gross primary productivity is the rate at which producers photosynthesize to make more biomass. Net primary productivity affects the number of consumers in an ecosystem and varies across Earth. The planet's net primary productivity (NPP) ultimately limits the number of consumer organisms (including humans) that can survive on the earth. Humans now use, waste, or destroy about 27% of the earth's total NPP and 40% of the NPP of the planet's terrestrial ecosystems, and these numbers are expected to rise.

The efficiency of nutrients entering and cycling through an ecosystem is based on hydrogeochemical processes, biological components and the maturity of the system (Gliessman, 2005). A natural ecosystem tries to regulate nutrients by recycling and replacing losses with local inputs. Nutrients, atoms, ions, and molecules are continuously cycled in nutrient cycles or biogeochemical cycles. The hydrologic cycle collects, purifies, and distributes Earth's water. Other examples include the carbon cycle, nitrogen cycle, phosphorus cycle and sulfur cycle. In an agroecosystem, human activities alter these cycles to regulate or enhance or improve nutrient balances, sometimes even destroy them.

Let's assess the best-known nutrient cycle, the carbon cycle that relates mostly to global climate change. Annually, 61. 4 billion net tons of carbon are fixed worldwide by primary production and 60 billion tons are released by respiration. The burning of fossil fuels and other industrial activities add another 5. 5 billion tons of carbon to the atmosphere. Changing land use (e. g. cutting down forests) further increases the atmospheric content for 1 billion tons per year. However, the main process is mass exchange of carbon dioxide between oceans and atmosphere. CO_2 is easily dissolved by water, and levels in atmosphere and ocean are in a dynamic equilibrium. Currently, more carbon dioxide is dissolved than released. This process can absorb some of the excess CO_2 in air.

The main pool for carbon dioxide is not the atmosphere, but rather the ocean. More than 90% of carbon dioxide is stored there, most of it stored in the deep sea (carbon containing rocks not considered).

The carbon cycle, involving photosynthesis of primary producers (plants) and respiration of all organisms, tends to reach a balance in space and time maintaining a constant global concentration of CO_2 in the atmosphere. However, human activities such as agricultural and industrial development, over combustion of fossil fuel and dramatic increases in CO_2 concentration is leading to global climate change via the green house effect (Chapter 5 explores this topic in detail).

4. 2 Energy flow in agroecosystems

Human manipulation and alteration of land for the purpose of establishing agricultural production differentiates agroecosystems from natural, un-managed ecosystems. Therefore, although energy flow initially generates from solar radiation in both systems, human-driven agroecosystems have much greater energy subsidies from the societal economic systems. Human inputs derive primarily from unsustainable, man-made sources. Predominantly open agroecosystems direct considerable amounts of energy out of the system during each harvest rather than storing energy in biomass that could otherwise cycle within the system.

While solar radiation remains as the major source of energy, managed ecosystems tend to rely on human-derived and manufactured input sources. Agroecosystems using vast amounts of fossil fuel inputs while directing most energy out of the system during harvest can be considered flow-through systems. For self-sustainability, agroecosystems should optimize solar energy and fuel internal trophic interactions to maintain system function (Bacon et al. , 2008). To illustrate this point, there has been significantly different in input and output energy between pre and post industrialized agriculture (Tab. 4. 1).

Tab. 4. 1 Energy flow comparison among different developmental stages (Luo et al. , 2009)

Agricultural developing stages	Appearing times	Energy output in biomass [kJ/(hm^2 · a)]	Energy input in organic type ($\times 10^9$ J/hm^2)	Energy input in inorganic type ($\times 10^9$ J/hm^2)
Historical agriculture	10000-7000BC	0. 836-41. 8	0. 418-4. 18	0
Pre-industrialized agriculture	700BC-300BC	104. 5-4180	4. 18-41. 8	0－0. 836
Industrialized agriculture	1700s	4180-41800	8. 36-83. 6	0. 836-83. 6

In the USA agricultural development, the evolution of energy subsidies in food production systems has greatly changed since the beginning of 20th when Industrial agriculture started to prevail. With energy subsidies, US agriculture has been getting 1 unit of food energy by expending 10 units of fossil energy since the 1970s (Odum, 1989).

4. 3 Matter cycle in agroecosystems

Through complex sets of inter-connected cycles, micro and macronutrients circulate within the ecosystem where they are most often bound in organic matter. Biological components of each system become very important in determining nutrient movement efficiency, ensuring that a minimum amount of nutrients are lost from the system (Bacon et al. , 2008). Annual nutrient loss can be devastating from harvesting, leaching and erosion due to improper practices. Agroeecosystems are nutrient leaky systems and need to be carefully managed in order to keep the losses to a minimum. Nutrients can be "leak" from an agroecosystem through exposed soil between crop plants and between cropping seasons (Gliessman, 2005). Modern agriculture relies on human inputs to replace the lost nutrients and sustain the system so it can continue to produce.

Subsidized fertilizers, pesticides and machinery-based inputs allow nutrients to cycle in agroecosystems, increasing the total carbon foot print of the system. In more developed countries, increased input bears more crop yield per capita. For example, Japan and the USA have both the highest fertilizer and additional inputs, and the greatest crop yield per ha in world. In contrast, Indian agriculture represents the lowest input pattern in the world. These yield results encourage developing countries to increase their man-made inputs in order to fulfil the food production pressure of growing populations. However, tremendous problems described previously accompanied these massive crop productions. Therefore, low matter input and higher efficiency should be a key to managing sustainable agroecosystems.

In summary, present industrialized farming practices are energy and matter intensive. Of all the energy used in industrialized countries, the food sector accounts for 10%～15%; approximately two-fifths of that energy is used for food processing, packaging, and distribution, two-fifths is used for refrigeration and cooking by final users and only one-fifth is actually used on the farm—half of that in the form of chemicals application (Hawken, et al. , 1999). Today, energy used to produce food far exceeds the energy received from consuming food. Reducing the need for man-made sources of energy to balance natural nutrient cycles in agroecosystems will spare humanity from using an exorbitant amount of energy, money and resources in food production.

Literatures cited in this chapter

Bacon C. M., Mendez E. V., and Gliessman S. R. 2008. *Confronting the Coffee Crisis: Fair Trade, Sustainable Livelihoods and Ecosystems in Mexico and Central America*. Boston: MIT Press.

Conway, G. R and Barbier E B. 1990. *After the Green Revolution: Sustainable agriculture for development*. London: Earthscan.

Gliessman S. R. 2005. In The Earthscan Reader in Sustainable agriculture. London: Earthscan.

Hawken P., Lovins A., and Lovins L. H. 1999. *Natural Capitalism: Creating the Next Industrial Revolution*. Boston: Little Brown and Company.

http://www. authorstream. com/Presentation/post2m-532557-ecosystem-components/.

http://www. whrc. org/carbon/carbon. htm.

Lin W. X. Ed. 2007. *Ecology (in Chinese)*. Beijing: Science Press of China.

Linderman R. L. 1942. The trophic-dynamic aspect of ecology. *Ecology* 23: 399-418.

Luo S. M. 2009. *Agroecology*. Beijing: China Agriculture Press.

Odum E. P. 1971. *Fundamentals of ecology*. Philadelphia: Saunders Publishing.

Odum E. P. 1989. Input management of production systems. *Science* 243: 177.

Odum H. T. and Odum E. P. 2000. The Energetic Basis for Valuation of Ecosystem Services. *Ecosystems* 3: 21-23.

Chapter 5 Agroclimate and agriculture's roles in global climate change

Learning objectives

1. Define the following terms:
   - Greenhouse Gases
   - Greenhouse Effect
   - Global Climate Change
2. Use an example to illustrate the impact of climate change on agriculture.
3. Use an example to show the impact of agriculture on climate change.
4. Describe methods agricultural producers can use to adapt to and mitigate the effects of climate change.

5.1 Climate change, global warming and its trends

Weather describes the short-term properties such as wind, temperature, moisture and atmospheric pressure occurring in the troposphere (对流层) at a particular time and place. Climate refers to the long-term weather status.

Climate changes primarily result from global air-circulation patterns and solar energy. Air circulation is influenced by uneven heating of the earth's surface, tilt and rotation of the earth's axis, long-term variations in the amount of solar energy reaching the earth and properties of air and water that transfer heat and water from one area to another in cyclical convection cells.

Solar energy from the sun in the form of heat and light is either reflected back into space or absorbed by clouds, land and oceans in the atmosphere. Ocean currents redistribute heat, which influences climate and vegetation. Ocean upwelling brings deep, cool water to the surface further transferring the absorbed heat. The El Nino-Southern Oscillation (摆动) causes a change in normal flows of wind and surface water causing unusual warming and cooling across the Pacific Ocean in approximately five-year intervals. This can suppress coastal upwelling, decrease some fish populations and trigger widespread weather changes.

Earth can absorb and re-radiate light as thermal radiation. When atmospheric greenhouse gases absorb this thermal radiation and re-radiate it back into the atmosphere in all directions the process is called the "Greenhouse Effect". Greenhouse Gases (GHG's) are gases distributed in the earth's lower atmosphere (troposphere) such as carbon dioxide, chlorofluorocarbons, ozone, methane, water vapour, and nitrous oxide. Under normal conditions in the atmosphere, these gases act somewhat like panes of glass in a greenhouse to regulate the temperature of the troposphere. These gases allow the passage of long wavelength radiation from the sun to the surface of the earth; however, the re-radiated wavelengths are longer and the GHG's tend to reflect these wavelengths back to the earth, acting like the glass panes in a greenhouse. Fig. 5. 1 shows the principles of the greenhouse effect. When water vapour, carbon dioxide, ozone and several other gases absorb heat from the earth's surface in the troposphere, the gas molecules vibrate and transform absorbed energy into longer-wavelength infrared radiation. If natural processes do not remove the increased atmospheric concentration of greenhouse gases, global warming results.

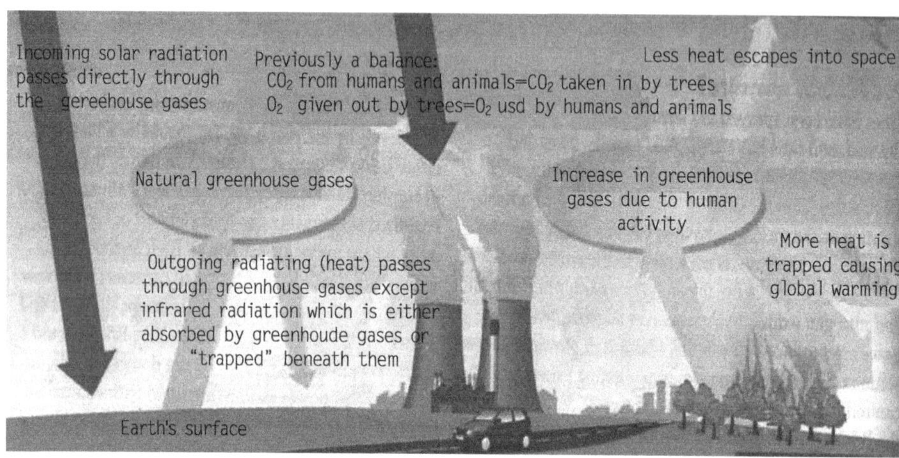

Fig. 5. 1 The schematic principles of greenhouse effect and global warming.

Human activities generally having an economic interest usually involve the use of fossil fuels, which have contributed greatly to the Greenhouse Effect and global warming. Agricultural practices are one of the major human activities that contribute to global warming.

Earth's average temperatures have naturally been changing throughout its history, and numerous research papers indicate a strong correlation between atmospheric CO_2 and earth's temperature. Research on atmospheric CO_2 measured from Antarctic ice cores has shown that the earth's climate had been cyclically stable over the past 400, 000 years, but has experienced a rapid 30% increase in 250 years (1750-2000) from 280 ppmv CO_2 to 367 ppmv CO_2 (Lal, 2004). Ground truth research has shown that in the last 60 years, the global CO_2 concentration has quickly climbed from 310 to 370 ppmv CO_2 with an average global temperature elevated by 1. 5℃ on earth's surface (Fig. 5. 2).

Since the 1750s atmospheric greenhouse gases concentrations have sharply increased, mainly as a result of human activities (Tab. 5. 1). These activities include the widespread use of fossil fuels, deforestation, burning of grasslands and the agricultural use of nitrogen fertilizers (TIEE, 2009). Climate scientists speculate that increased GHG concentrations have led to global warming. Global warming refers to earth's atmosphere warming due to increases in GHG concentrations, primarily from human activities.

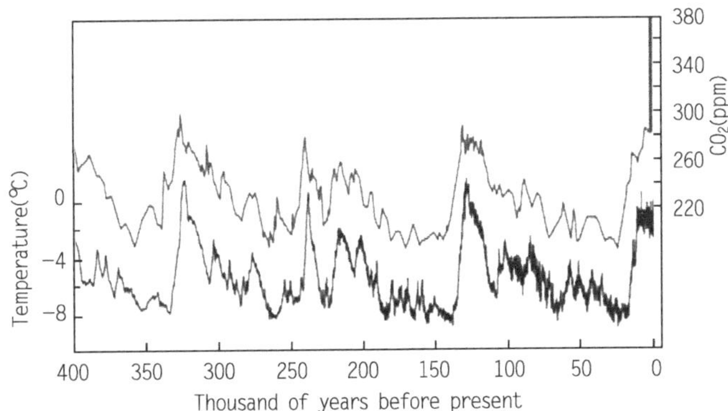

Fig. 5. 2 Changes in CO_2 and temperature in last 400, 000 years. The blue bar illustrates inferred temperatures and carbon dioxide concentrations from Antarctic ice-core records over the past 400, 000 years. The red bar indicates increased atmospheric CO_2 levels during the last 200 years (Fedorov, 2006).

Tab. 5. 1 Change in atmospheric concentration of trace gases since the industrial revolution circa 1750 (Lal, 2004 modified from IPCC, 2001)

Types of GHGs	Present concentration*	Percent increase since 1750 (%)	Present rate of increase (%/a)
Carbon dioxide (CO_2)	379ppm	31	0. 4
Methane (CH_4)	1745ppb	151	0. 4
Nitrous oxide (N_2O)	314ppb	17	0. 25
Chlorofluorocarbons (CFCs)	268ppt	α	Decreasing

* ppm = parts per million, ppb = parts per billion, ppt = parts per trillion

The relatively hot temperatures of the past 1,000 years, specifically during the 1990's, has made global warming a top priority of scientists. Some possible indicators of global warming occurring in particular places around the world include: melting sea ice and glaciers, rising ocean temperatures and tundra soil giving off more CO_2 than it retains. However, many of these global warming indicators are debatable. For instance, while we see rising temperatures in the Antarctic cause melting of some ice sheets, we also see other ice sheets thickening in these conditions.

Many scientists use models projecting future atmospheric GHG concentrations to predict the ecological and economic effects of global warming to warn society. However, other scientists still believe these models are based on insufficient data, possibly overestimating the affect humans have on their environment. Predicting the future through mathematical models does require making many assumptions about unknown changes that may occur and how those changes may influence feedback mechanisms. For instance, if ice continues to melt, the ice's albedo may alter the reflectance of incoming solar energy, further influences the amount of energy earth absorbs. This process will continue to change the rate of ice melt, change in albedo and then again, the change in solar reflectance.

The long-term impacts of global warming might include changes in the distribution of water, plants and animals, in addition to major shifts in ocean currents, sea levels, disease spread and economies.

The time has come to take necessary measures to decrease human GHG emissions. The Intergovernmental Panel on Climate Change (IPCC) gave several scenarios of CO_2 concentrations according to different levels of control on human practices [Fig. 5. 3 (a)].

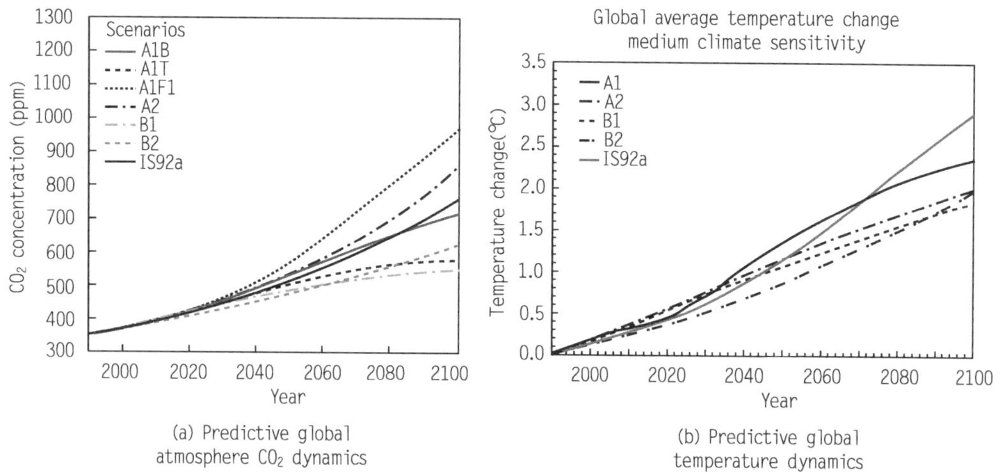

Fig. 5. 3 The predictive global atmosphere CO_2 (a) and temperature (b) dynamics (Smith et al., 2004).

Fig. 5. 3 (b) describes five emissions scenarios (four from IPCC) of global average temperature change using a central climate sensitivity value. This measurement accounts for differences in land-ocean climate and a slowing for the global ocean circulation system (thermohaline circulation [THC]). A1 and A2 account for higher carbon dioxide emissions and increased fossil-fuel use, while B1 and B2 scenarios account for more realistic carbon dioxide emissions reduction possibilities. Using the IPCC parameters, the IS92a scenario measures an updated model for halocarbons and radioactive forcing parameters, resulting in a warming less than the IPCC second assessment model scenarios. A key feature to note from this diagram is that scenarios mostly differ due to socio-economic conditions and regardless of the small differences in underlying assumptions we are unlikely to distinguish among the scenarios until late in the next century (Smith, et al., 2004).

There are two likely strategies to deal with global warming. One strategy suggests continuing to depend on fossil fuels but looking for alternatives to emissions storage such as in the deep sea or deep underground, however, many unknown effects financially and ecologically exist with this option. The more sustainable strategy would require adopting new energy forms from renewable sources such as solar, wind and hydrogen and shifting consumer practices by using less water, growing less water dependent crops, expanding wildlife reserves and using sustainable urban planning to prepare for natural hazards.

Global efforts have started shifting ideas and practices towards the more sustainable, effective strategy. The Kyoto Protocol was adopted in 1997 aiming to reduce four greenhouse gas emissions and two groups of gases: carbon dioxide, methane, nitrous oxide, sulfur hexafluoride, hydrofluorocarbons and perflouorocarbons, respectively. Initially, 37 "Annex I countries" signed and ratified these reductions, but as of July 2010, 191 countries have committed themselves to this agreement. A new trading market regime has emerged from these commitments, where treaty participants can buy and sell greenhouse-gas emission allowances. However, emissions trading have sparked some debate as the idea essentially allows richer countries to continue producing over their emissions caps by buying-off the poorer countries. This prevents developing countries from financially competing with more developed areas of the world, creating a further socio-economic divide and only offsetting emissions rather than reducing the practices that cause them.

The Copenhagen conference, the 5th meeting to the parties of the Kyoto Protocol, occurred during December 9-17, 2010 to establish stronger imperatives for reducing global emissions. This conference determined that both developed and developing countries are responsible for decreasing GHG emissions, and the former have a duty to assist the latter by developing a "Low Carbon Economy" that can cut down the GHG emissions. China has promised to cut down 40%-45% of their carbon emissions per capita GDP before 2020, based on 2005 levels. These goals will be challenges for both developed and developing nations.

5.2 Agroclimate and climate change related to agriculture

5.2.1 Agroclimate

As stated above, the meteorological terms climate and weather greatly differ from each other even though they are sometimes used as synonymous. Climate is a pattern of variation in meteorological factors over a large area formed over many years, while weather is used to describe the short term or the instant condition of climatic factors. In agricultural terms, overall crop production is mostly determined by the regional climate. From an agricultural standpoint, regional climate determines major crop productions and must be thoroughly understood for efficient agroecosystem management. Both macroclimatic and microclimatic variation affects agricultural and natural resource management. Macroclimatic and microclimatic features affect crops in terms of their water requirements, cultivation times, economic viability, pest and disease tolerance and the total yield and product quality (Hadid, 2002). Furthermore, animal production is mainly affected by climate via crop (forage) production.

5.2.2 Climate and crop production

The amount and rate of growth in any plant depends on the energy difference between gross and net photosynthesis. This process provides the energy for organic metabolism (growth and development) and for forming the building blocks from which

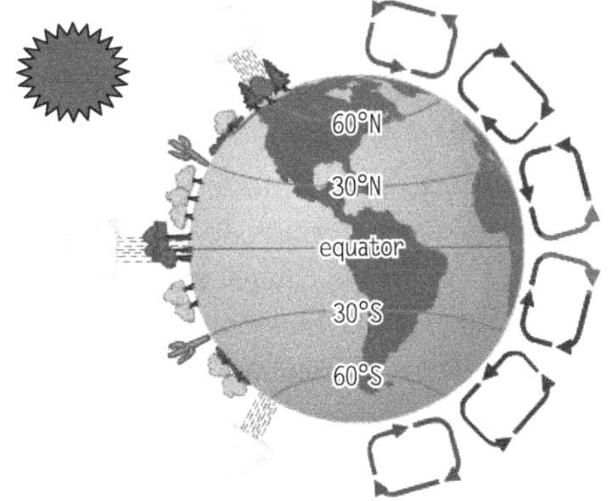

Fig. 5.4 The relative position between the sun and earth's location determines the distribution of crop species via the dynamic of temperature and light.

protein and fats are eventually synthesized. Climatic factors include CO_2, temperature and radiation (light or heat energy) that determine crop potential productivity. These two fixed factors depend on the relative position between the sun and the crop's location on earth (Fig. 5. 4), thus the sun and climate determine the distribution of crop species.

In addition to climatic defining crop production, crop yield is also limited by restricting factors such as water, N, P and K availability. These factors are also influenced by the movement of earth orbiting around the sun, but can be reduced by pests, weeds and diseases that likewise are influenced by climatic factors (Fig. 5. 5).

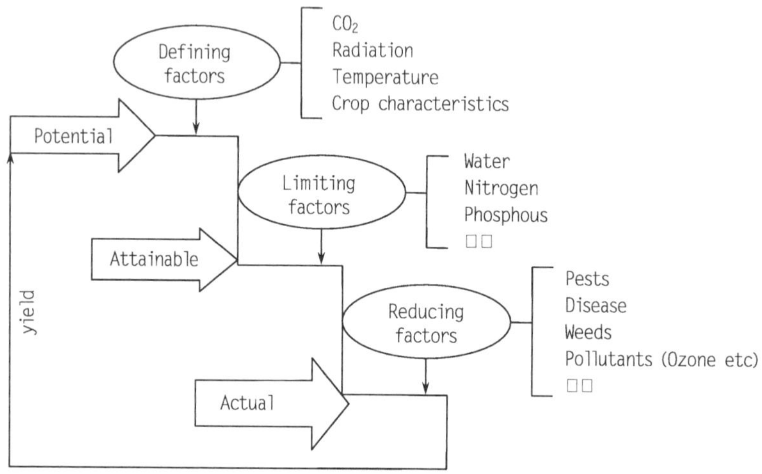

Fig. 5. 5 Crop production levels depending on defining, limiting or reducing factors driven by regional and global climatic factors (Fuhrer, 2003).

Crops do adapt to these defining factors to some degree. For example, there are three differentiated physiological metabolic pathways for carbon fixation, namely the Carbon 3 (C_3, Calvin Cycle), the Carbon 4 (C_4), and Crassulacean Acid Metabolism (CAM). These pathways adapted to different CO_2, water stress and light intensity situations, under different long-term abiotic environments. In addition, there are several photoperiodic differentiations in crops according to the adaptation of light durations call "short day", "long day", and "day neutral" crops. While long day crops are limited to high latitudes, the cultivation of short day and day-neutral crops may be restricted to low latitudes and high latitudes only in areas where spring or autumn seasons are warm enough to allow their complete harvest cycle.

5. 2. 3 Climate change related to agriculture

The interrelatedness of climate and agriculture are beginning to significantly impact each other. Global warming, causing changes in temperature, precipitation and levels of carbon dioxide, affect agricultural production and the world's carrying capacity, limiting the ability to provide enough food to support the need of humans and domesticated animals. At the same time, greenhouse gas emissions and land alteration from agriculture contributes to the changing climate. Altering agriculture land for crops through deforestation and desertification influences the ability of Earth's surface to absorb solar radiation and in the process, emits large amounts of GHGs into the atmosphere.

5.2.4 Impact of climate changes on agriculture

The impacts of climate change on crop yields are depicted in Fig. 5.6. Although finite details may differ from region to region, changes in CO_2 concentration, temperature and soil moisture strongly affect crop yields. CO_2 fertilization refers to increasing a crop yield as a result of increased atmospheric CO_2 increasing biomass generation through photosynthesis (Faisal and Parveen, 2004). Increased temperatures stimulate photosynthesis during plant emergence and formation and photorespiration causing a shift from C_3 to C_4 plants. Increased temperature also accelerates development, shortens duration of plant growth, increases evapotranspiration and stresses root zones with soil moisture loss, depleting plant organic matter (Faisal, 2004). Inundation and increased salinity, due to sea level rise and inward water movement respectively, will also affect crop yield (Fig. 5.6).

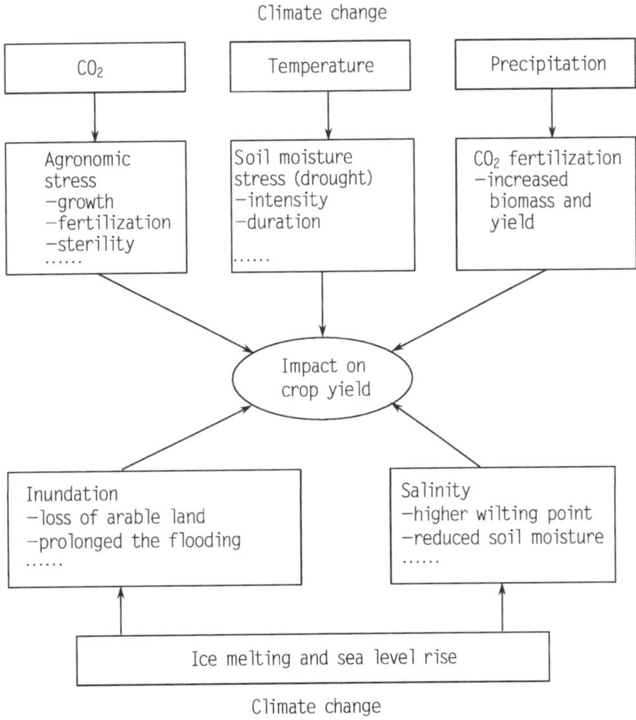

Fig. 5.6 Conceptual diagram of climate change impacts on crop yields (Faisal, 2004).

5.2.5 Agriculture's roles in global climate change

Agriculture and climate change are indiscerptible—climate change will influence agricultural crop production while agriculture continues to pollute the environment with emission. The agricultural sector drives climate change through gas emissions and altering land. In addition to using a significant amount of land and consuming fossil fuels, agriculture contributes directly to greenhouse gas emissions through practices such as rice production and the raising of livestock. According to the Intergovernmental Panel on Climate Change (IPCC), the three main causes of increased greenhouse gases observed over the past 250 years were fossil fuels, land use and agriculture.

(1) Land use

Four types of agricultural land use that contributes to increased GHGs (IPCC):

- Net deforestation releasing Carbon dioxide (CO_2)
- Rice cultivation releasing methane (CH_4)
- Enteric fermentation of cattle releasing CH_4
- Fertilizer application releasing Nitrous oxide (N_2O)

According to an IPCC Special Report on Emissions Scenarios, together these agricultural processes comprise roughly 53% of methane emissions, 80% of nitrous oxide emissions and virtually all carbon dioxide emissions tied to land use.

(2) Livestock

Livestock production covers 70% of all land used for agriculture and contribute excessively to land-use effects, since crops such as corn and alfalfa are grown as livestock feed (FAO, 2006). 18% of human-made GHG emissions come from livestock and livestock-related activities, releasing (FAO, 2006):

- 9% of global carbon dioxide emissions
- 35%-40% of global methane emissions (mainly from enteric fermentation and manure)
- 64% of global nitrous oxide emissions (mainly from fertilizer use)

(3) Cultivation leading to soil carbon losses and greenhouse effect

Cultivation of undisturbed soils results in the loss of soil carbon. Great Plains (prior to European colonization) contained relatively high, possibly more than 50,000 kg, of organic carbon per hectare stored in the topsoil; this is equivalent to the amount of carbon found in 20,000 gallons of gasoline (calculations based on 2.5% soil carbon, 20 cm deep topsoil and soil bulk density of 1 g/cm^3). Research has shown that crop cultivation decreases soil carbon storage.

(4) Methane emissions from agriculture

This chapter has already presented the amount of atmospheric carbon dioxide and methane that exists and some major sources contributing to those emissions. While carbon dioxide concentrations are much higher than methane concentrations, per kilogram methane is over 20 times more powerful than carbon dioxide at trapping heat in the earth's atmosphere. This number becomes increasingly significant since methane concentrations have more than doubled since 1750, meaning human activities have contributed much more methane into the atmosphere than natural sinks (TIEE, 2009). The doubling of atmospheric methane since pre-industrial times can be greatly attributed to agricultural processes. Domestic animal digestion, rice growing and animal waste among many other agricultural practices produces 210×10^{12} g of methane per year, leaving 84 Tg of methane in excess after natural oxidation processes (TIEE, 2009).

As you can see in Tab. 5.2 nearly all methane emissions on Canadian farms come from livestock. Methane is released into the atmosphere from livestock after getting produced in the tracts of ruminant animals during digestion. In addition to livestock releasing methane in China, methane also comes from rice paddies. Cultivating ride paddies is a very important practice in Chinese agriculture; however, rice cultivation occurs in wetlands where soil has little oxygen availability. In an anaerobic environment such as a wetland, decomposition of organic matter produces methane rather than carbon dioxide. Agriculture is one of the most necessary practices in modern culture, but it also produces nearly half of all methane emissions on earth.

Tab. 5.2 CH_4 from Canadian livestock production ($\times 10^9$ g) (Wang et al., 2010)

Animal production types	Manure	Livestock	Total
Dairy	70	200	270
Beef	10	580	590
Hogs	120	15	135
Poultry	10	n/a	10
Sheep	1	10	11
Total	211	805	1016

(5) Nitrogen Fertilizers Increase Nitrous Oxide Emissions

Nitrous oxide (N_2O) is an important greenhouse gas because of its relatively high radiative effectiveness, meaning a molecule of N_2O stays in the atmosphere for 114 years, much longer than carbon dioxide or methane (TIEE, 2009). Nitrous oxide is 310 times more effective at trapping heat in the earth's atmosphere compared to carbon dioxide (U.S. EPA). Similar to carbon dioxide and methane, human activities have increased atmospheric nitrous oxide concentration by 10% since pre-industrial time periods (TIEE, 2009). Agriculture contributes globally 70%-80% of N_2O. Most N_2O is produced in soil; however, excess nitrogen fertilizer contributes to the increased amount of N_2O in GHG levels.

Naturally occurring nitrogen helps plants and soil grow and gives soil microorganisms energy. Soil bacteria fixate on nitrogen in the nitrification and denitrification processes, releasing nitrous oxide as a byproduct. Introducing nitrogen fertilizer to agricultural soils to increase plant growth and food production has led to the overuse and excess emissions of nitrous oxide.

Most likely, over-cultivated soils in temperate regions around the world have lost most carbon to the atmosphere and over produces nitrous oxide. However, sustainable agroecosystem management practices can actually increase soil carbon content and reduce nitrous oxide emissions. Some strategies would include conservation tillage, perennial crop growth, reducing fertilizer or cover crop planting. With these methods taken into consideration, net global warming potential may strongly decline. Adaptation and mitigation of harmful agricultural practices will make a huge difference in the fight against climate change.

5.3 Adaptation and mitigation to the climate change in agriculture

5.3.1 Adaptation actions

Agroecosystem management can improve a great deal, adopting new, more suitable agricultural practices to keep soil healthy and provide clean water. For example, one can use groundwater and surface water more efficiently, conserve rainfall, explore new technology and create public policy to maintain production in the face of a more variable and less hospitable environment.

5.3.2 Mitigation actions

Mitigation actions are as important as adaption. Agricultural mitigation options using micro-practices in managing agroecosystems and can be broadly divided into two categories: ① strategies to maintain and increase stocks of organic carbon in soil and biomass, and ② reductions in fossil carbon consumption, including reduced emissions by the agricultural sector itself and substituting fossil fuel with biofuel in agricultural production.

The following macro view recommendations are encouraged to mitigate climate change in managing the global scale agroecosystems:

Proactively addressing the Kyoto Protocol recommendations, both on a national and international level.

Decreasing food transportation and trade distances through localized food production systems and strategies such as Canada's "buying local campaign" . Such as eating low food chain (see Chapter 2).

Improving farming and animal husbandry practices toward sustainable agriculture to lower greenhouse gas emissions and maximize carbon sequestration.

Literatures cited in this chapter

Abou-Hadid A. F. 2002. "*The Agro-Climate Application Information System for Crop Production and Protection in Egypt" in International Symposium on Mediterranean Horticulture: Issues and Prospects*. Cairo, Egypt: ISHA Acta Horticulture.

Faisal I. M. and Parveen S. 2004. Food security in the face of climate change, population growth, and resource constraints—implications for Bangladesh. *Environmental management* 34 (4): 487-498.

Fedorov A. V., Dekens P. S., McCarthy M., Ravelo A. C., deMenocal P. B., Barreiro M., Pacanowski R. C., and Philander S. G. 2006. The Pliocene Paradox (Mechanisms for a Permanent El Nino). *Science* 312 (5779):1485-1489.

Food and Agricultural Organization of the United Nations (FAO). 2006. *Livestock's long shadow-environmental issues and options*. UN: FAO.

Fuhrer J. 2003. Agroecosystem responses to combinations of elevated CO_2, ozone, and global climate change. *Agriculture, Ecosystems and Environment* 97: 1-20.

IPCC's Working Groups. 2001. *Chapter 3: Scenario Driving Forces' in IPCC Special Repot on Emissions Scenarios*. The Hague: GRID-Arendal.

Lal R. 2004. Soil carbon sequestration to mitigate climate change. *Geoderma* 123: 1-22.

Smith S. J., Wigley T. M. L., Nakicenovic N., and Raper S. C. B. 2000. Climate Implications of Greenhouse Gas Emissions Scenarios. *Technological Forecasting and Social Change* 65: 195-204.

Wang S. L., Caldwell C. D., and Zhu W. F. 2010. Low carbon agriculture: origins, principles and strategies (in Chinese). *Journal of agricultural modernization research* 31 (5): 604-607.

Chapter 6 Water in agroecosystems

Learning objectives

1. Discuss the significance of water for people and in relation to agroecosystems.
2. Describe the hydrologic cycle and its relationship to the social aspects in agroecosystems.
3. Define and describe the major aspects of managing water in agroecosystems.

6.1 Water resources in the global ecosystem

Water covers about 71% of the earth's surface; however, only 2.5% of the water on earth is fresh water. Most of the freshwater on earth is locked in glaciers or too deep in the ground to be used, leaving less than 1% of water on earth available for human consumption. Important freshwater resources, such as groundwater, would diminish within a short time period without replacement via the hydrologic (water) cycle (Tab. 6.1). The hydrologic cycle refers to the continuous movement of water throughout the earth, purifying, recycling and replenishing reservoirs (Fig. 6.1). Groundwater is often used for agricultural, commercial, and industrial and personal uses when the water flows to the surface naturally forming springs, seeps, oases and wetlands (or into man-made wells).

Tab. 6.1 Water in the global ecosystem (Dyck and Peschke, 1995)

Reservoir	Area (km^2)	Volume (km^3)	percentage of all (%)
Oceans	361, 300, 000	1, 338, 000, 000	96.5000
Groundwater	134, 800, 000	23, 400, 000	1.7000
Soil water	82, 000, 000	16, 500	0.0010
Ice and snow	16, 227, 500	24, 364, 100	1.7700
Fresh water lakes	1, 236, 400	91, 000	0.0070
Salt water lakes	822, 300	85, 400	0.0060
Swamps	2, 682, 600	11, 470	0.0008
River water		2, 120	0.0002
Water in biota		1, 120	0.0001
Water in atmosphere		12, 900	0.0400

Approximately 1.2 billion people do not have access to safe drinking water and over 10 million people dwelling in mega-cities throughout the developing world heavily depend on groundwater (Kante, 2004; Datta, 2001, 2005). While 500 million people live in water-scarce and water-stressed countries, even in locations where water is plentiful many poor people cannot afford a safe supply of drinking water (Kante, 2004). Prolonged droughts and water scarcities kill more than 24 000 people a year and have created millions of refugees since the 1970s.

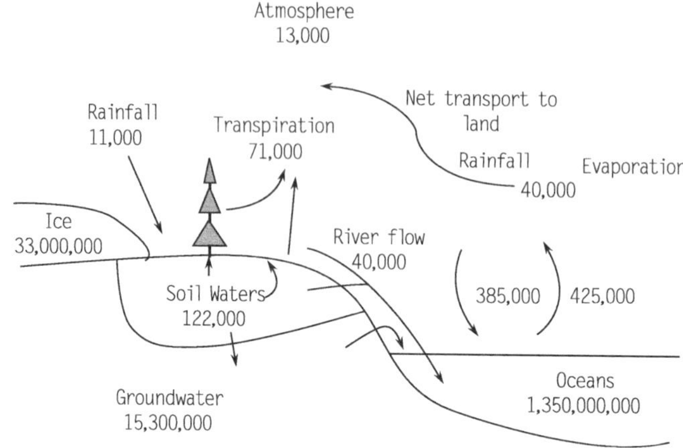

Fig. 6. 1 The global water cycle. Pools (km^3), Fluxes (km^3/a) (Schlesinger, 1997).

The three main pressing water related problems are: ① groundwater overuse, ② water pollution and ③ inefficient water use (causing water cycle imbalance):

(1) Overusing groundwater has caused water table imbalances and ecological and health issues. To produce electrical power and reduce flooding people build dams with powerful technology. These dams often increase the annual runoff available for human use, but also reduce downstream flow drastically and can prevent rivers from reaching the sea, thereby radically changing the region's entire ecosystem. Transferring water through tunnels, aqueducts, and underground pipes often draw groundwater faster than it can be renewed. These practices change the water table levels and create serious ecological and health disasters in the ecosystem.

(2) Worldwide water pollution occurs as both surface and underground contamination due to industrial wastes and overuse of agricultural chemicals. Water pollution refers to a physical, chemical or biological change, from a point or non-point source pollutant that reduces water quality. Some major categories of water pollutants include oxygen-demanding wastes, inorganic chemicals, organic chemicals, plant nutrients, radioactive material and heat. Measuring biological oxygen demand or taking a chemical analysis can indicate pollutants from point sources. Once identified, point sources can be monitored and regulated. Unfortunately, it is more difficult to control non-point source pollutants. Lakes and ponds are quite vulnerable to pollution because they have little flow. However, flowing bodies of water such as streams may rapidly recover from pollution through dilution and bacterial decay, so long as they are not inundated with contaminants. Laws concerning water-pollution control have significantly improved stream water quality in most developed countries, but political infrastructure in developing countries has not been able to enforce pollution control and stream water quality remains poor in those places. In China, there is a serious water pollution issue with the paper-industry dumping toxic chemicals and waste in rivers. In 2004, one-third of factories lining the Huai River, which supplies one-sixth of the nation with

drinking water, still did not meet waste dumping government standards (Rothman, 2006). Many areas such as the Huai Lakes in southern China are facing this problem (Liu and He, 1998).

(3) Using water inefficiently is another major area of concern and only amplifies the problems to overexploit the land for more water. In the USA alone, the world's largest water users, loses nearly half of the water it withdraws. In China, especially in the west of the country, irrigation systems are unchanged from what was used 6000 years ago for a much smaller population.

Solving these problems will require an integrated approach to fixing each of these issue areas. The first step will require using water more efficiently. Redesigning national water-use policies will provide incentive for water conservation and higher efficiency. Exploring more efficient irrigation system technologies for use in the world's croplands will also conserve water long-term. A "blue revolution" will initiate and encourage more sustainable water management in the future. Improving water quality will be an important facet of sustainable water management, preventing pollutants from reaching the surface or groundwater.

6.2 Water in agroecosystems

Agriculture uses the most freshwater of any industry sector, generally for the purpose of irrigation. In fact, irrigation for agricultural purposes accounts for 85% of worldwide freshwater consumption (Villers, 2005). In some developing countries irrigation takes up to 90% of the national water withdrawn, while slightly less, water withdrawal for irrigation in developed countries, it is still a significant proportion (e.g., in the USA 30% of freshwater usage is for irrigation).

Irrigated water in agriculture gets used for growing crops, weed control, frost protection and chemical applications. Usually irrigated water comes from a higher percentage of surface water than groundwater, however in the U.S. groundwater withdrawals for irrigation has risen from 23% to 42% from 1950 to 2000 (the USA Department of the Interior). Worldwide agriculture accounts for the largest water withdrawals and can be considered the main "culprit" of water scarcity when water supplies cannot satisfy all demands (Sinha, 2008).

6.2.1 Water cycle in agroecosystems

Fig. 6.2 shows a very general conceptualization, embracing most possible inputs and outputs to the water flows in an agroecoystem. **Maintaining a healthy agroecosystem requires a balance among fluxes, however in reality, balancing fluxes is quite complex. Agroecosystems, considered as parts of watershed ecosystems, can self-regenerate water resources via micro-cycles, which include multiple landscapes and biodiversity aggregations. In these micro-cycles, rainfall water represents the basic water resource, partially assimilated by plants, partially evaporated at the water surface forming the "Green Stream" (65% of total). This is potentially very high quality water without human interference, which is available for the next water cycle. The remaining water flow is called the "Blue Stream" (35% of total) and it flows to aquifers underground, or runs off via the soil surface to rivers and the sea. This Blue Stream also has the possibility of intervention and exploitation by human activity outside the watershed] (Fig. 6.3, Fig. 6.4)** [在实际中,农业生态系统可看作是管理的流域生态系统。流域内定期的降雨代表着流域的真正水资源,其中一

部分被植物消耗了，一部分从含水表面蒸发，它们形成“绿色水流”（占65%），干净地得到储备以供下一次循环使用；而余下的部分则补充含水层（地下水）和进入河流之中，形成“蓝色水流”（占35%），可供系统外的人类社会和水生生态系统使用，但可能存在不确定的人为污染]。

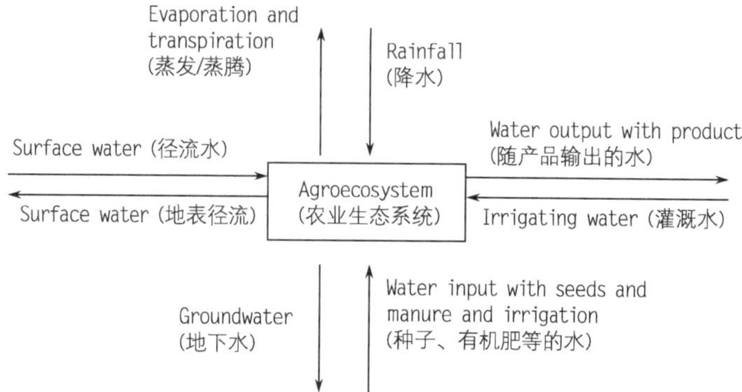

Fig. 6. 2 The general pattern of water cycle in agroecosystems.

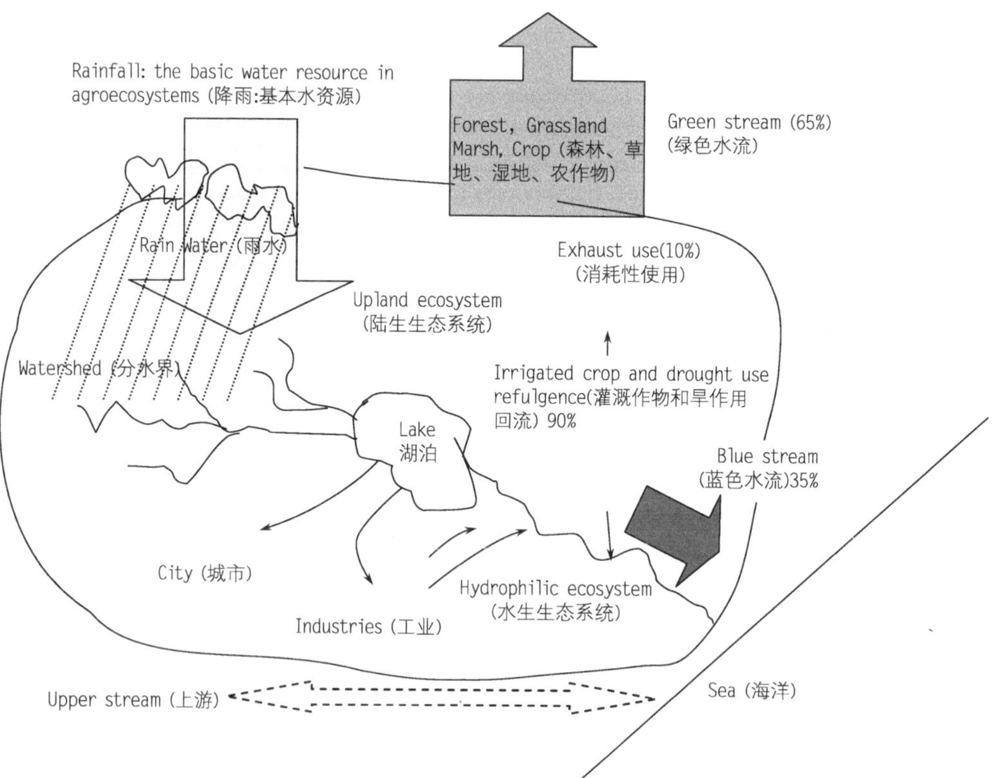

Fig. 6. 3 Water cycle in agroecosystems (Falkenmark et al., 1996).

Water cycles in agroecosystems are changing due to global warming, groundwater overuse and contamination and field temperature increases. Global warming is changing the water cycle routes in all ecosystems, including agroecosystems. Increasing CO_2 concentrations has globally and regionally changed the rainfall distribution in

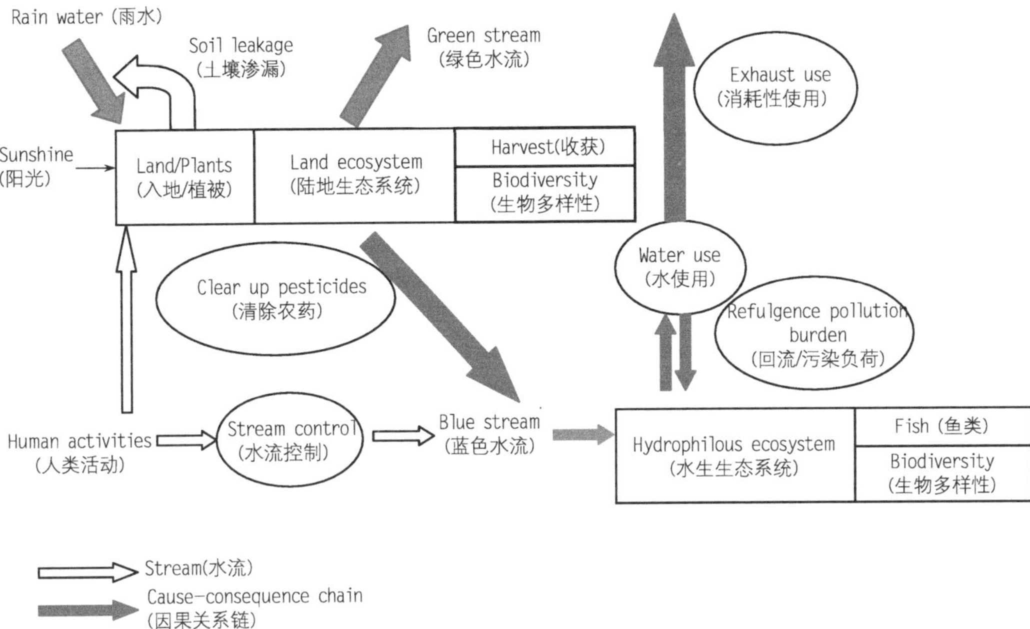

Fig. 6.4 The blue stream with human intervence in agroecosystems. Human activities on the geomorphology change the blue stream directly by means of water controls in building and exhaust use of water, and indirectly by control of land and plants.

time and space. Rainfall has become more variable and erratic, causing a greater incidence of droughts and flooding. In the meantime, industrialization and urbanization, especially in developing nations, has increased the acidity of rainwater, destroying water quality. Another characteristically changing aspect of the water cycle is groundwater overuse and pollution. Groundwater has been overdrawn and heavily contaminated, decreasing its availability to agroecosystems. Finally, increasing field temperatures have led to higher evaporation rates, which increase water loss in agroecosystems.

6.2.2 Social aspects of water from agroecosystems

Human social systems act as sub-systems of agroecosystems. Human activities are driven by demand for ecosystem services, including water. Society anticipates a sustainable supply of such services because of the importance of water in agroecosystems both as a human need in itself and in its role in producing sufficient healthy food for sustaining human life. While agricultural water services are just one of the many crop production inputs, it is a critical lead input without which intensification and diversification of agricultural production would be impossible. In addition, agroecosystems rely greatly on water to maintain its sustainability and water misuse by humans may elicit many negative effects on the natural cycle of water in agroecosystems and then lose its sustainability. In turn, this results in social deterioration such as hunger and poverty, disease and even political instability that exacerbates the natural degradation in water (Fig. 6.5). People are dependent upon water yet they tend to degrade that very resource upon which society is built.

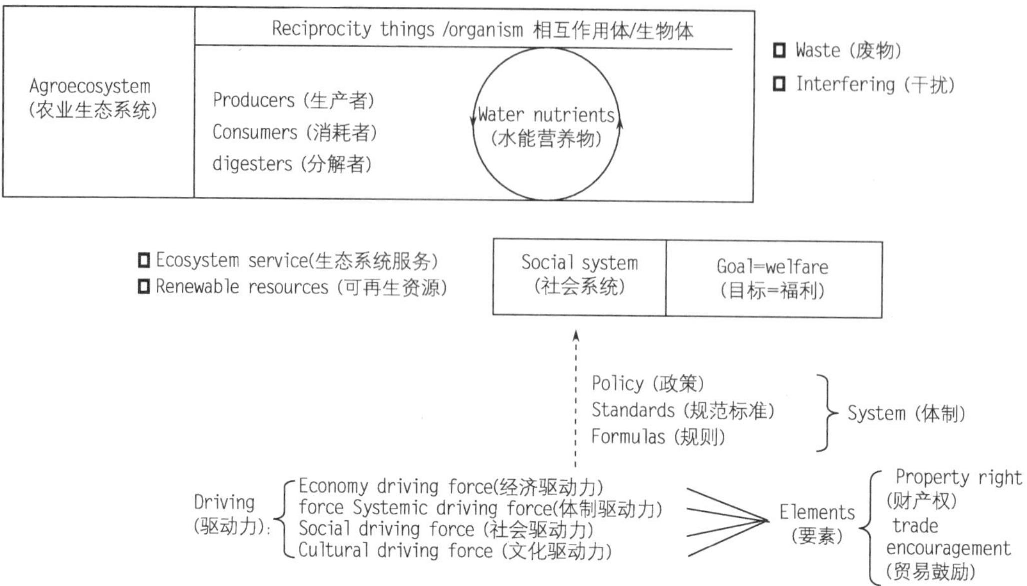

Fig. 6.5 Agroecosystem reliance on water to maintain its sustainability. Human beings greatly rely on the acquirements of renewable resources and ecosystem services on earth. Activities that improve welfare are driven by social elements and affected by the system. However, waste and human interfering affects the ecosystem functions generated in these activities. (人类极大地依靠全球生态系统提供可更新资源和获取生态系统服务。人类改善福利的活动是由社会所驱动并受制度体制的影响，但却产生了废物和其他干扰而影响了生态系统的功能).

6.3 Aspects of water management in agroecosystems

Ecosystems naturally function as water purifiers, however, when precipitation falls on agricultural lands with altered hydrology, the water cleansing process suffers. The intensified processes of fertilization, pesticide application, irrigation and animal production only further stresses the ecosystem and prevents it from working properly. Better management of agroecosystems to protect water supplies would include understanding quality control of soil, crop nutrients, pesticides, animal and other residues, and incorporating principles of hydrology, plant cover and stress maintenance (Keeney, 1999). Here we propose a framework with four aspects for managing water in agroecosystem.

6.3.1 Improving on-farm water management

Managing root zone water application and procuring high over productivity is contingent upon a number of factors such as soil fertility, cultivar selection, cropping density, disease and pest management and post-harvest controls (FAO, 2007). With water restrictions on post-harvest controls, efficient water management practices become critical. With technologies that schedule irrigation, biotechnology and geographic information systems, agricultural improvements can maximize the use of a limited water supply.

6.3.2 Improving the performance of irrigation system

Farmers need a reliable supply of water from irrigated systems to prepare crops in a timely manner and in the right volume. While these irrigation systems were initially designed to alleviate problems of food scarcity, poverty and unemployment, now they benefit the farmers and communities alike. Irrigation management fulfils multiple objectives, from recharging local aquifers to maintaining shelterbelts and orchards to mitigating environmental externalities associated with waterlogging and salinity (FAO, 2007).

6.3.3 Using non-conventional waters

Increasing water supply through the reuse of drainage water has become a good option for arid, semi-arid areas and water scarce countries. The FAO (2007) has provided guidelines covering many aspects of water conservation at the field level, water reuse at the scheme level and safe disposal and treatment of drainage effluent. Other non-conventional uses of water to increase supply includes treating wastewater, saline water and greywater to increase water use efficiency, reduce water losses and pollution, increase recycling and access to high quality water for water scarce countries.

Water harvesting refers to the process of capturing, collecting and concentration runoff and rainwater for an available resource. Water harvesting can ease pressure on existing available resources to supply crops with rain fed irrigation water.

6.3.4 Recycling the water

Using recycled and rain fed water in agriculture will allow for the allotment of more raw water for other higher utility uses. These uses include municipal supplies, environmental reserves and hydropower generation (FAO, 2007). Addressing global water scarcity in the long run requires the emergence of new policies. These policies will rely on the pursuit of food security, investment in water related activities and relieving agricultural reliance on irrigation. Most evidently, government expenditures will have to focus on irrigation, flood control, dams and trade and exchange rates with a focus on food exports.

Literatures cited in this chapter

Datta P. S. 2000. Water: Key Driving Force. In Advances in Land Resources Management for 21st Century, Proceedings of the International Conference on Land Resource Management for Food, Employment and Environmental Security, November, 2000, Soil Conservation Society of India, New Delhi, 471-479

Datta P. S. 2005. Groundwater ethics for its sustainability. *Current science* 89 (5): 812-817.

Dyck and Peschke. 1995. Grundlagen dev Hydrologie. Berlin: Evnst & Sohn.

Falkenmark M. 1996. UN World Food Summit, Report 7. Rome: FAO

Food and Agriculture Organization (FAO). 2007. Agriculture and Water Scarcity: a Programmatic pproach to Water Use Efficiency and Agricultural Productivity. Work paper of Committee on Agriculture Twentieth Session, In website of the United Nations: www. fao. org

Kante B. 2004. Local capacities for Global Agendas; Impact of Cities on the Global Environment. Second World Urban Forum Dialogue on Urban Sustainability: United Nations Environment Programme. Barcelona.

Keeney D. 1999. Linking Soil Quality, Water Quality, and Agroecosystem Health. A Life Cycle Approach to Sustainable Agriculture Indicators, Ann Arbor, Michigan.

Liu C. M., and He X. W. 1998. Water problem strategy for China's 21st century. Science Press, China.

Rothman A. and Zhu J. 2006. Thirsty China. CLSA Asia-Pacific Markets Investment Strategy.

Sinha B. and Hyung T. 2008. Status and Challenges in Water Infrastructure in Asia and the Pacific. The First Regional Workshop on the Development of Eco Efficient Water Infrastructure for Socio-Economic Development in Asia and the Pacific Region. Seoul: 10-12.

Villers M. D. 2005. *Water*. Toronto, Canada: Stoddart publishing Co. Limited.

Chapter 7 Cultivated soils and soil organisms

Learning objectives

1. What is soil? Explain the concept that soil is a dynamic and open, three phase system.

2. How does soil form and what are the key contributing factors?

3. Using the USDA soil textural triangle, what soil classification is 20% clay, 20% sand and 40% silt?

4. What are the five ecological functions of soil in an ecosystem? For each of these ecological roles, suggest one way in which interactions occur with one of the other five functions.

5. Consider the volume composition of a loam surface soil in ideal conditions for plant growth as a pie chart. What might the situation look like after soil compaction from heavy traffic? Draw a new pie chart.

6. What are some of the major differences between "non-harvested soils" and "harvested soils?"

7. What are the important nitrogen processes in soil?

8. What is the relationship between photosynthesis and (cellular) respiration? What are their differences in terms of energy strategies?

9. What are the major processes that drive the soil carbon cycle? Sketch a diagram illustrating the inputs and outputs of carbon, energy and oxygen.

10. What are the major ecological classes of soil organisms and what are their roles in the carbon cycle?

11. In the soil nutrient cycle, what are the three distinct stores of nutrients, potential losses and inputs of nutrients from/to the soil ecosystem? Sketch a diagram.

12. What are the differences in nutrient cycling between harvested (agricultural) and natural (non-harvested) soil ecosystems?

13. What are the problems associated with managing the soil nutrient cycle in specialized production (i. e. cash cropping and concentrated livestock rearing)?

7.1 Formation, classification and functions of soils

7.1.1 What is soil?

Soil is the biologically active, unconsolidated minerals and organic matter on the surface of the earth. Soil is comprised of 50% pore space and 50% plant detritus and broken rock particles that have been altered by chemical and physical weathering (Fig. 7.1). Soil properties differ from those of its parent material and can be classified by its layers (soil horizons). Soil constituents are simultaneously in solid, gaseous and aqueous states. The pores within the solid soil particles contain soil solution (liquid) and air (gas). Therefore, soils are often treated as a three phase system.

Soil's upper boundary lies between the soil and depending on the location, air, shallow water, living plants or plant materials; the lower boundary separates soil from hard rock and earthy materials destitute of animals, roots and other biological activity (NRCS). A deeper understanding of soil formation and utilization is beneficial for agricultural purposes.

Fig. 7. 1 Soil is the unconsolidated mineral or organic material on the earth's surface.

7. 1. 2 Soil forming factors

(1) Parent material

Soil rarely develops directly from its underlying rocks, in which case this "residual" soil has the same general chemistry as its underlying bedrock. More often, soil forms from parent material. Parent material includes a combination of weathered bedrock, transported secondary materials, organic and sometimes anthropogenic materials. Weathering refers to the process of rocks breaking up, generally bedrock with greater concentrations of silica (e. g. granite and pegmatite) weather more easily (Ashman, 2002). Weathering can be divided into physical weathering and chemical weathering, both of which can further be separated by internal processes. Physical weathering includes thermal weathering and mechanical weathering. Thermal weathering refers to the fracturing of rocks due to heat expansion (mineral expansion or exfoliation). Mechanical weathering refers to the fracturing of rocks due to the expansion of freezing water in rock cracks (frost shattering, swelling and shrinking, and biological weathering). Chemical weathering can be divided into the following processes: hydrolysis (水解), carbonation, hydration, dissolution, oxidation and reduction. While both physical and chemical weathering break rocks into smaller fragments, chemical weather also alters the chemical properties of the rock itself. The chemical weathering processes stated above indicate the chemical alterations that occur from the interaction between the rocks and water molecules, soil organisms or atmospheric minerals. Secondary materials, transported from other locations by moving wind, water or ice, generally come from mixed old soil formations such as colluvium and alluvium. Transported materials can travel long distances; windblown "loess" is common in both the North American Midwest and Central Asia, while glacial till generally travels to southern latitudes (NRCS). Transported sediments from slow and fast moving water take on very different textures as well, such as a clay or silt. Organic materials include plant detritus, peat and humus; the main residual compounds include cellulose, hermicellulose, proteins, amino acids, lignin, fats and waxes (Ashman, 2002). In contrast, anthropogenic materials include particulates from human waste (e. g. from landfills and mines).

(2) Climate

Soil properties greatly depend on two climate factors: moisture (from precipitation, evaporation and transpiration) and temperature. Therefore, soil properties show distinct characteristics in different regions. The amount, timing and type of precipitation influences how particles and ions flow through the soil-ultimately this affects soil profile formation. Precipitation, specifically in the form of rainfall, affects soil-erosion rates as well. Evaporation and transpiration affects moisture conditions in regard to plant growth and soil formation, both processes also depend on temperature (Jenny, 1994). Moisture effectiveness, biological activity, chemical reaction rates and vegetation type varies with seasonal and daily temperature changes.

(3) Topography

Topographical features such as slope and aspect affect moisture and temperature content, thereby influencing soil properties. Slope refers to the angle of the landscape, while the horizontal direction the landscape faces is called aspect (typically when referring to a mountain). Steep slopes facing the sun may lose their topsoil more easily and face long term erosion, while more level, shaded soil (e. g. at the bottom of a mountain face) should have deeper, darker, richer soil.

(4) Biological factors

Plants, microorganisms (fungi, bacteria) and many higher animals (including humans) affect soil formation (Welbaum et al., 2004). Vegetation can shade soil, slow evaporation and prevent erosion. Decomposing plant leaves and shrubs add organic matter to topsoil. Plant roots affect soil in a multitude of ways. For instance, grass roots add organic manner when they decompose and taproots clear channels through dense soil layers for microorganisms to move through. Microorganisms can help chemical exchanges between plant roots and soil, which humans then combine and compact—so effectively in fact, it can sometimes be considered parent material again.

(5) Time

The soil formation process requires time to allow all the other factors to evolve and develop together. Many of these features interact with each other and change properties as they become buried as soil horizons. Extended periods of time also allow for stability in the system, since soil is dynamic and constantly changed by winds, weather and human activity. Soil also faces the less frequent, larger disturbances of floods, droughts and cyclones. Soil formation may re-start due to both small and large disturbances; therefore we may consider soil formation a continuous process because it never finishes.

7.1.3 The characteristics of soil

(1) Soil Colour

Soil colour is a good indicator of how well a soil absorbs and transmits water, aeration status, mineral content, temperature, vegetation and position in a soil profile (NESC, 2002). Soil colour should be identified through observations using the universally accepted Munsell colour system. Typically, soil colour depends on the presence of iron minerals. The colour distribution along a soil profile occurs as a result of chemical and biological weathering, specifically from reduction and oxidation (redox). Generally, red, brown or yellow colours indicate well-drained soils that allow air to enter and iron to oxidize. The Yellow River in China gets its name from the well-draining yellow sediment eroding from loessal (黄土的) soil. Dark colours indicate high organic content with cooler conditions where water drains and soil remains saturated. For example, the dark, organic matter enriched soil in the Great Plains comes from mollisols (软土) soil. A spotty gray colour indicates poorly drained soil. Many soils indicate some combination thereof, for instance, acidity and leaching gives podsols (灰土) in boreal forests highly contrasting colours between soil layers.

(2) Soil Structure

Soil structure describes how soil particulates arrange themselves as aggregates soil alignment influences water movement and aeration within the soil, plant growth and erosion resistance. Compressed or compacted soil from agricultural and commercial machinery affects soil drainage properties. Soil structure can indicate the content of organic matter, biological activity and human use. Soil porosity and permeability depend on soil structure and affects soil behaviour and its ability to retain water and nutrients.

(3) Soil Texture

Soil texture refers to the relative amounts of different sized soil particles (sand, silt and clay). Texture describes the fineness or coarseness of the soil mineral particles. Sand particles feel coarse and gritty to touch, can usually be seen with the naked eye and range in size from 0.05mm to 2.0mm; silt particles feel smooth and floury when pressed between fingers, must be seen under a microscope and range between 0.05mm and 0.002 mm; and clay particles, the finest particle class, are moist and sticky when wet and must be seen with an electron microscope (Daniels, 2006). Clay particles are finer than 0.002mm and commonly determined by forming a long ribbon between the fingers. Tab. 7.1 shows the range of soil texture classifications in finer detail.

Tab. 7.1 Soil texture classification (Gliessman, 2007)

Category	Diameter range (mm)
Gravel	>2.00
Very coarse sand	2.00-1.00
Coarse sand	1.00-0.50
Medium sand	0.50-0.25
Fine sand	0.25-0.10
Very fine sand	0.10-0.05
Silt	0.05-0.002
Clay	<0.002

Fig. 7.2 is the most commonly used tool to determine soil texture. To use this diagram you will need to know the percentage of sand, silt and clay in your soil. To use this diagram, first draw a line horizontally from your clay percentage across the triangle. Then, find the percentage of sand along the bottom and draw a line between that point and your percentage silt. The location where your lines intersect determines the soil textural class. For example, if you have a soil that contains 20% clay, 60% sand and 55% silt, you have a loam.

Soil textures develop from different weathering conditions and are more suitable

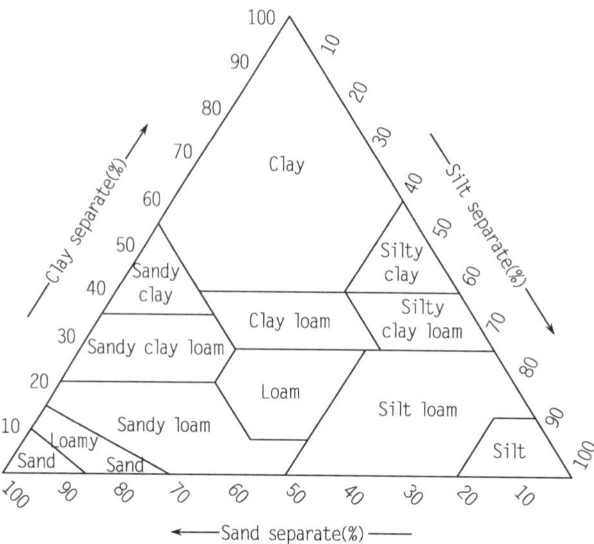

Fig. 7. 2　USDA soil textural triangle.

for certain activities. Sand and silt generally come from physical weathering while clay results from chemical weathering. Loam soils are especially good for growing crops. Approximate soil texture can be easily determined in the field by rubbing soil aggregates together between fingers and can be particularly useful for land use planning.

(4) Soil horizons

Soil horizons describe the different layers of soils formed from additions of organic matter and leaching. The vertical sequence of soil horizons is referred to as the soil profile. While many soil horizons exist within a soil profile, there are four key soil horizons in agricultural fields: A horizon, B horizon, C horizon and R layer (rock). The A horizon, or Ap horizon in plowed fields, contains surface or topsoil. The B horizon contains the subsoil, the C horizon contains some portion of weathered parent material and R layer, or rock, contains unconsolidated parent materials. A photograph in Fig. 7. 3 shows an actual soil profile from Kansas, the USA, and its correponding spectrum of soil horizons within a soil profile.

(5) Soil organic matter (SOM)

Soil organic matter comprises of fresh and decomposing plant and animal residues such as littler, leaf drop, root exudes, dead roots, insects, worms and humus, the fully decomposed stable organic matter. A specific SOM content will depend on the type of vegetation, soil texture, drainage and tillage. SOM is a critical aspect of soil functionality and important for most agricultural landscapes throughout the world. Soil organic matter improves soil structure and enhances water and nutrient holding capacities. SOM acts as a reservoir for nutrients, recycling an essential portion of a plant's

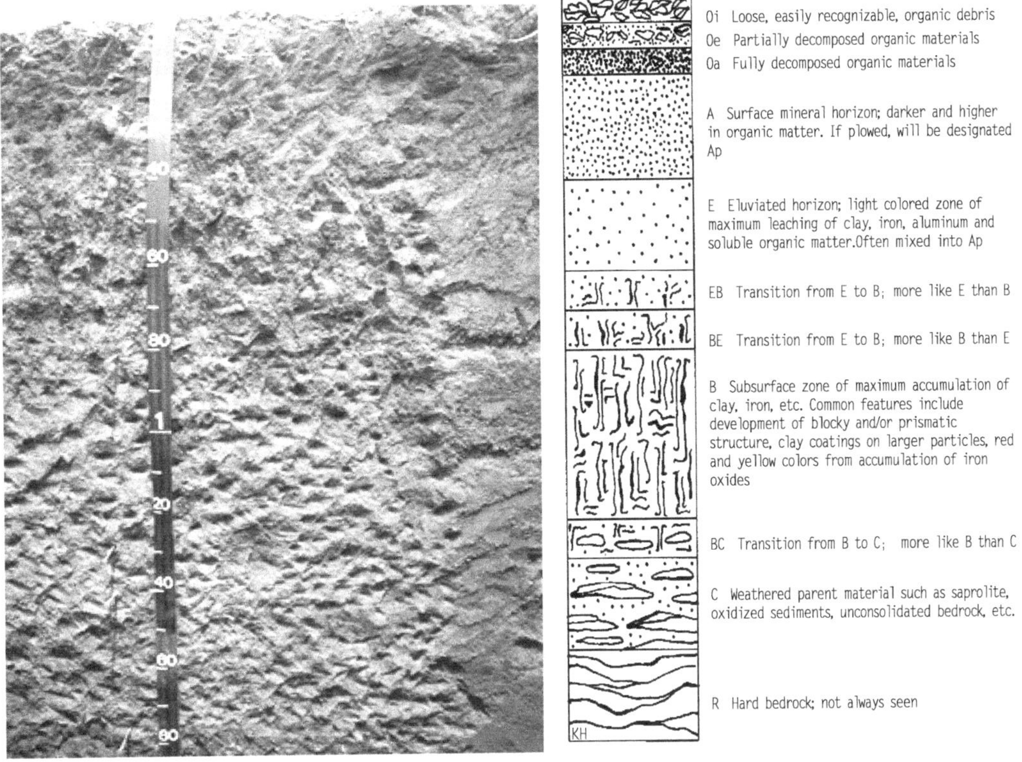

Fig. 7. 3 The Milan series soil profile horizons (Daniels, 2006).

nutrient needs. The humus in SOM has a high cation exchange capacity (CEC) that functions as a buffer again pH changes. SOM also chelates micronutrients, frees up micronutrient metals for uptake by complex formations between soluble organic compounds and the metals to keep them in solution (Balakrishna, 2007). Increasing soil organic matter and managing soil carbon content can enhance productivity and environmental quality by reducing atmospheric CO_2, and reduce the severity of natural disturbances such as drought, flood and disease.

7.1.4 Soil Functions

Healthy soil provides us with ecosystem services such as clean air and water, bountiful crops and forests, diverse wildlife and beautiful landscapes. Soil has five essential functions, which provide us with these ecosystem services (Fig. 7. 4).

(1) Sustaining plant and animal life

Soil supplies essential nutrients for plant growth and provides a medium and physical support for plant roots. Soil provides plants with 13-15 of the 16 required elements for normal plant growth and life cycle completion (Hodges, 2000). Air and water provide plants with the large quantities of the non-mineral elements, carbon, hydrogen and oxygen. The remaining 13 essential nutrients come from soil or fertilizers in depleted soils. The macronutrients soil provides for plants includes nitrogen, phosphorus, potassium, calcium, magnesium and sulfur Tab. 7. 2. The micronutrients, elements taken up by plants in smaller quantities, consist of boron, copper, chlo-

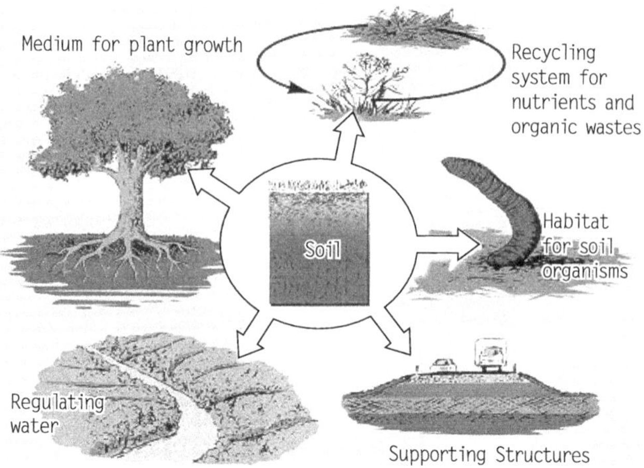

Fig. 7. 4 The five ecological functions of soil.

rine, iron, manganese, molybdenum and zinc (Hodges, 2000). A deficiency in any of these elements will limit plant productivity.

Tab. 7. 2 Soil supplies the elements essential for plant growth (Gliessman, 2007) *

Macro-nutrient elements (>0. 1% of dry plant tissue)		Micro-nutrient elements (<0. 1% of dry plant tissue)
Mostly from air and water	Mostly from soil solids	From soil solids
Carbon (CO_2)	Nitrogen (NO_3^-, NH_4^+)	Iron (Fe^{2+})
Hydrogen (H_2O)	Phosphorus ($H_2PO_4^-$, HPO_4^{2-})	Manganese (Mn^{2+})
Oxygen (O_2, H_2O)	Potassium (K^+)	Boron (HBO_3)
	Calcium (Ca^{2+})	Zinc (Zn^{2+})
	Magnesium (Mg^{2+})	Copper (Cu^{2+})
	Sulfur (SO_4^{2-})	Chlorine (Cl^-)
		Cobalt (Co^{2+})
		Molybdenum (MoO_4^-)
		Nickel (Ni^{2+})

* The chemical firms most commonly take in by plant are shown in parentheses, with the chemical symbol for the element in bold type

Humans indirectly receive these nutrients provided by the soil through the nourishment of plants. In essence, human health, global food and fibre production depend on productive, usable soils throughout the world. Soil composition also determines the nature of plant distribution and biodiversity.

(2) regulating water

Soil acts a buffering system and moderates the hydrological cycle by regulating drainage, temporarily storing water, cleaning water and overall watershed protection (Knowler, 2004). Soil accounts for three major functions needed when water reaches a soil surface: allows some water to infiltrate the aquifer, retains water for use in plant growth and organisms living in the soil, and cleans the remaining water before it runs into lakes and rivers. Overcultivation of soil can lead to a degraded system with a lower water-holding capacity, field capacity and plant-available water (permanent wilting percentage). For instance, tilling soil with a very fine sand content may compact the soil when moist, damaging the moisture content and subsequently the ability of the soil to foster optimal crop growth.

(3) Filtering potential pollutants

Soil naturally filters pollutants out of organic waste and water. Within the soil, mineral nutrients from humus are converted into a usable form for plant and animal uptake. Soil minerals and microbes filter, buffer, degrade, immobilize and detoxify both organic and inorganic waste materials. Soil also removes 99% of pollutants in water in unadulterated land. However, climate change, altered land use, new technologies, pesticides and fertilizers reduce the efficiency of soil filtering potential and increase contamination with toxic metals, hormones, nanoparticles and pathogens.

(4) Supporting structures

Soil plays an important role in engineering. Soil properties such as weight, porosity, void ratio, permeability, compressibility and shear strength determine building structure, location, strategies and materials used. Whether engineers are building a single family home or a skyscraper, they use soil mechanics to measure features such as total stress, pore water pressure and capillary action to accurately design and build the structure.

(5) Cycling nutrients

Nutrient recycling essentially keeps plants and animals nourished while removing waste that would otherwise build up and suffocate the system. The central role of soil organic matter is to cycle nitrogen, phosphorus, sulfur and micronutrients, closely followed by the Carbon Cycle (Balakrishna, 2007). In addition, soil organisms such as earthworms, bacteria and fungi help certain species release nutrients from organic matter while other organisms help release plant growth hormones, improve soil structure, fight root disease and detoxify the soil. Soil and the millions of organisms living within the soil play a pivotal role in storing, transforming and releasing nutrients through various nutrient cycles. Fertile soil benefits the tiniest of microorganisms to the masses of people, who require healthy soil for food, fibre and other ecosystem services.

A sustainable ecosystem depends on soil implementing all five functions just described to provide us with essential ecosystem services. Beyond needing these crucial services for the functioning natural ecosystem we live in, they also constitute an important component of sustainable agricultural production.

7.2 Soil nutrient cycling

7.2.1 Nutrient cycles

(1) Nitrogen cycle

The nitrogen cycle is the biogeochemical cycle where N_2 converts to N compounds and from N compounds back into N_2. Most nitrogen found in the soil comes in the organic form (amino acids, proteins and amino sugars), however most plants absorb N in ammonium forms. Inorganic sources of nitrogen include N_2, NO_x, NH_3, NH_4^+, NO_2^- and NO_3^-. These compounds are unstable and constantly return to the atmospheric as a gas.

Soil nitrogen can also go through fixation where nitrogen and oxygen combine to form NO_3. Plants or animals can use nitrates, while lightening, fertilizer or nitrogen-fixing bacteria can fix nitrogen gas into nitrites (Balakrishna, 2007). Nitrites can be fixed back into nitrogen gas by denitrification. Meanwhile, the nitrogen consumed by plants and animals gets disposed of and changed into ammonia. Soil bacteria can turn ammonia into nitrates, which is then usable in denitrification as well.

Additionally, soil nitrogen can also go through immobilization, mineralization, aminization, ammonification and nitrification (Hodges, 2000):

• Immobilization: plants and microbes absorb forms of plant-available N and transform them into amino acids and proteins

• Mineralization: decomposition and liberation of mineral forms of nitrogen (NH_4^+, NO_2^- and NO_3) from plant tissues

• Aminization: hydrolysis of simple proteins to form amines and amino acids

• Ammonification: release of amines and amino acids, which are used by heterotrophs and further broken down into ammoniacal compounds

• Nitrification: converting ammonium to nitrite by soil microorganisms

Agricultural systems can easily lose nitrogen through volatilization, leaching, runoff and crop removal by multiple or one-time heavy applications of sludge, manures or N fertilizer, improperly timed use of N fertilizer, lack of soil conservation measures, extended periods of heavy rain or exported crop removals.

(2) Phosphorus cycle

The phosphorus cycle is the biogeochemical cycle through the lithosphere, hydrosphere and biosphere (Balakrishna, 2007). Phosphorus is naturally found in abundance as part of a phosphate ion PO_4^{3-} as salt in rocks; however, plant available phosphorus is limited mainly to solution HPO_4^{-2} and $H_2PO_4^{-2}$ (Hodges, 2000). Plants take up the phosphorus and then herbivores consume the plants, after which carnivores consume the herbivores. When the animal or plant decomposes, phosphates return to the soil.

Phosphorus primarily serves as an important biological component of nucleotides, storing energy within cells (ATP) or forming nucleic acids (Balakrishna, 2007). While phosphates move quickly through plants and animals, they have incredibly low mobility in soil and strongly reacts with soil solutions and solids. Phosphorus is strongly bound in the soil and generally moves through diffusion. Although most forms of phosphorus are unavailable, the plow layer of soil contains the most phosphorus and must be conserved. Removal of phosphorus can pollute surface water, enhance soil erosion and decrease productivity and fertility of soil causing a myriad of agricultural problems in an ecosystem.

(3) Sulfur cycle

The sulfur cycle is a biogeochemical cycle with four essential steps: ① organic sulfur mineralizes to the inorganic form, hydrogen sulfide (H_2S), ② sulfide and elemental sulfur reduce to sulfate (SO_4^{2-}) and other related compounds, ③ sulfate reduces to sulfide, and ④ sulfur compounds go through microbial immobilization into the organic form of sulfur (Balakrishna, 2007).

Sulfur is a constituent of plant biochemicals such as proteins, vitamins and hormones, which regulate plant growth, an essential component in chlorophyll synthesis and photosynthesis reactions (Hodges, 2000).

(4) Carbon cycle

The global carbon cycle includes exchanges among the land, ocean and atmosphere. Carbon cycling within soil is an essential component to the global carbon cycle because the process of decomposition takes place in the soil and large concentrations of carbon are stored in soil. In fact, carbon concentrations contained in the organic matter of terrestrial soils is three to four times greater than the carbon content in the atmosphere (Stevenson, 1999). The carbon cycle is driven by two principal complementary reactions: respiration and photosynthesis. Respiration combines carbohydrates and oxygen to produce carbon dioxide, water and energy. Photosynthesis uses the water and carbon dioxide from respiration to produce carbohydrates and oxygen. The products of one reaction form the inputs, or reactants, of the other in a continuous chemical cycle. Photosynthesis captures energy from the sun and stores it in carbohydrates (as carbon-carbon bonds), while respiration releases that energy. Plants and animals can carry out respiration, but only producers, primarily plants, can carry out photosynthesis.

$$\text{Photosynthesis: sunlight (energy)} + H_2O + CO_2 \rightarrow \text{carbohydrates} + O_2$$

$$\text{Respiration: carbohydrates} + O_2 \rightarrow \text{energy} + H_2O + CO_2$$

Understanding the role of soil in the carbon cycle is necessary in agroecosystem management. Changes in land use and agricultural practices can significantly affect how much carbon soil organic matter releases into the atmosphere. Using soil conservation methods can help reduce the amount of carbon dioxide released into the atmosphere.

Bacteria, actinomycetes and fungi are an indispensible component to the decomposition process, utilizing carbon from decaying plants and animals for the synthesis of microbial cell components or turning it into humus. Soil organisms, classified as producers, consumers and decomposers, play a key role in the carbon cycle.

Producers, or autotrophs, create complex organic compounds (carbohydrates, fats and proteins) using inorganic compounds or energy captured from the sun (photosynthesis). Producers include plants, algae and bacteria. For example, the photosynthetic producer algae, forms a long chain of individual cells. Scientists believe algae converted a reducing atmosphere to an oxidizing atmosphere early in earth's history. Fig. 7.5 shows a microscopic view of blue-green algae (cyanobacteria) grown in a laboratory.

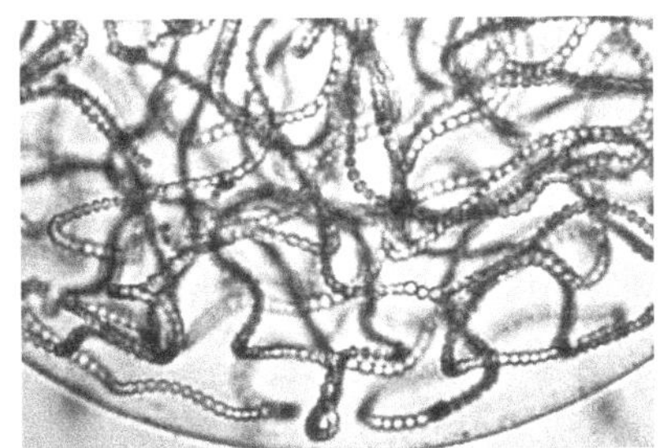

Fig. 7.5 A microscopic view of lab-grown cyanobacteria, a primary producer.

Consumers, or heterotrophs, cannot produce their own complex organic compounds and fix carbon. However, they consume plants or animals and use their energy for growth and activity. Consumers can be categorized based on their digestive abilities of plant and animal materials as herbivores, omnivores and carnivores. Another way to categorize consumers is by their position in the food chain. Primary (1°) consumers, such as parasites and diseases, eat producers directly. Nematodes are 1° consumers, parasitizing plant roots and stems (Fig. 7. 6). Secondary (2°) consumers eat primary consumers. Centipedes, 2° consumers, prey on soil insects and consume their tissue (Fig. 7. 7). The levels continue (3°, 4°, etc.) but the energy efficiency decreases as you move up the food chain.

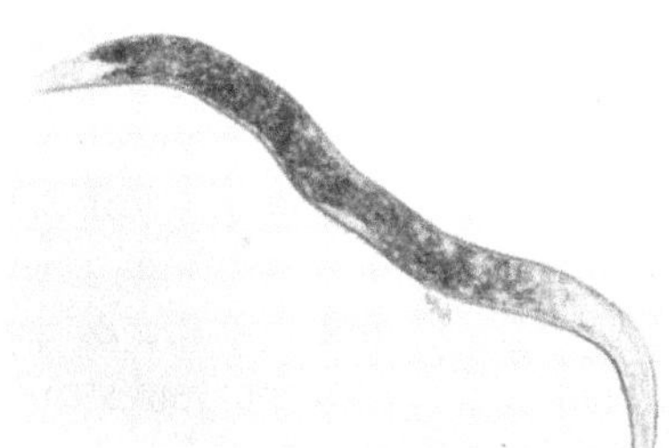

Fig. 7. 6 A microscopic photo of a nematode, a primary (1°) consumer often found in wet soil. Nematodes are parasitic roundworms.

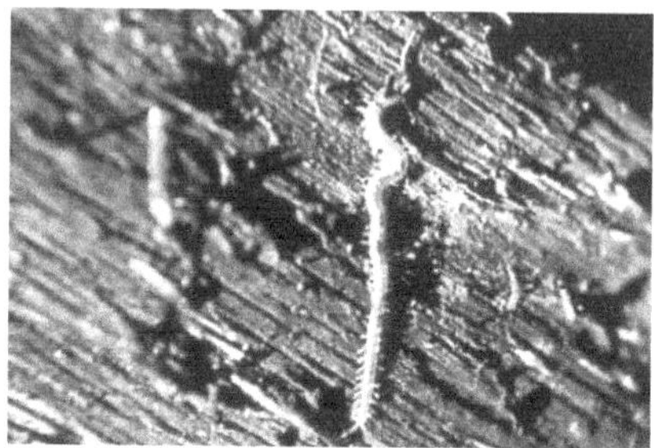

Fig. 7. 7 A centipede is a secondary (2°) consumer that lives in soil. Centipedes are merciless to their prey, but beneficial to mankind because they keep crop pests under control.

Fig. 7. 8 Earthworms are decomposers in soil, ingesting organic matter, mineral particle and excrete castings.

Decomposers (腐生物) break down the organic layer and provide nutrients for plant growth, converting CO_2 from waste while consuming O_2 produced by photosynthesis. Decomposers include insects, fungi, algae, bacteria and earthworms (Fig. 7. 8).

The carbon cycle is summarized in Fig. 7. 9.

7. 2. 2 Nutrient transformations

The Soil Nutrient Cycle refers to the continual, dynamic biogeochemical processes and transformations taking places among all the nutrient cycles within the soil. As nutrients go through the recycling process, they undergo chemical transformations changing their chemical makeup (often multiple formation changes). Nutrients generally form and transform through absorption, death, excretion, exudation, and mineralization (Fig. 7. 10). Throughout these cycles nutrients get lost and added, sometimes because of human activity.

(1) Absorption

Decaying rocks and minerals release inorganic ions that plants and soil organisms can absorb. Plants absorb their essential nutrients (non-mineral and mineral elements) through root systems, however not all nutrients in soil are available for plant uptake. The form and chemical properties of the element, soil pH, soil colloidal interactions and microbial activity (i. e. aeration, compaction, temperature, moisture) determine the availability of nutrients to plants (Hodges, 2000).

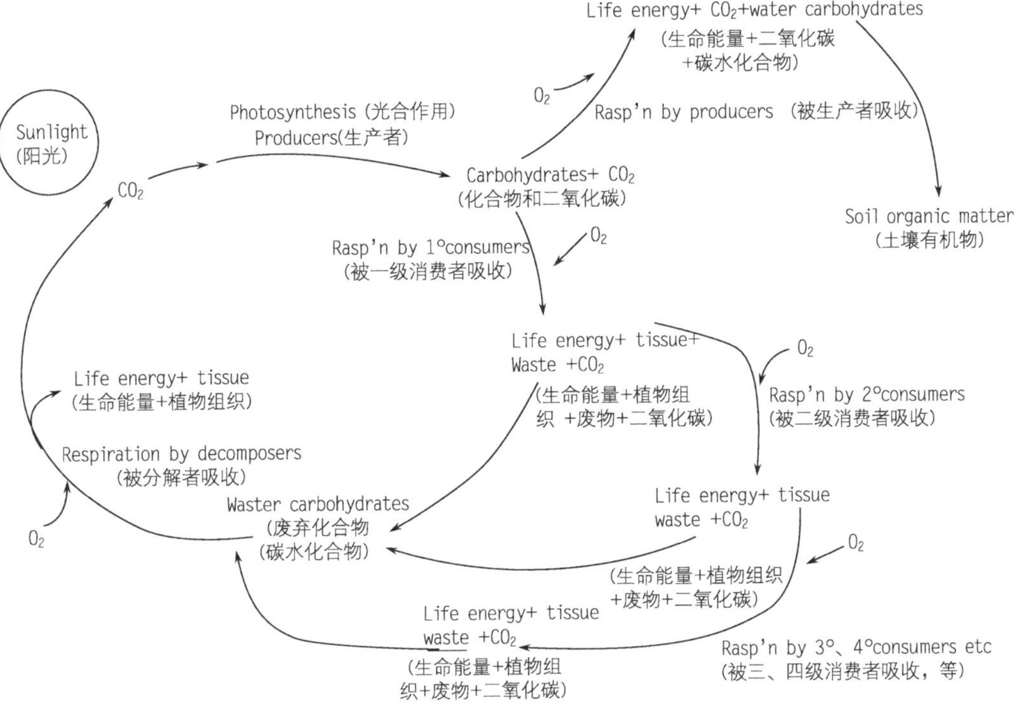

Fig. 7. 9 The soil carbon cycle (Wang et al., 2010).

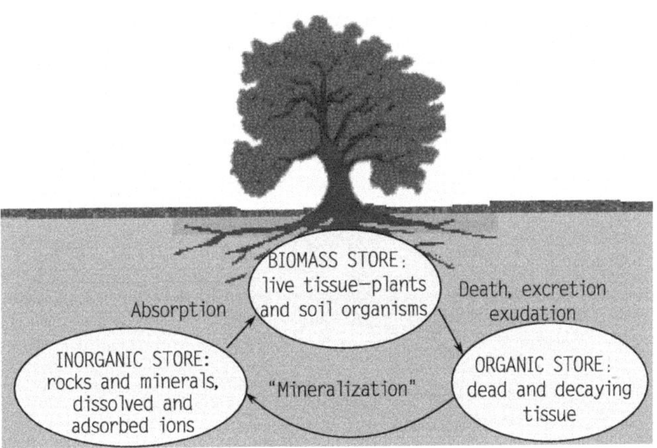

Fig. 7. 10 The nutrient cycle where nutrients form, store and transform.

(2) Death, excretion, cell leakage

Living organisms excrete nutrients as waste or through leakage in damaged cells. Decaying tissue from dead organisms directly adds nutrients to the soil organic matter. Soil "humus" decays very slowly, because it is more resistant material.

(3) Mineralization

In the decomposition process of organic matter (mineralization), complex organic compounds become simpler organic compounds, release their carbon and become inorganic. In soil humus, mineralization significantly influences micronutrient availability and releases organic forms of nitrogen, phosphorus and sulfur. Mineralization rates can drastically change according to temperature and moisture conditions, and poor aeration can slow or stop the mineralization process altogether.

(4) Losses

The soil nutrient cycle loses nutrients through erosion, leaching and gaseous losses. During erosion, water and wind carry away nutrients in eroding soil particles. Leaching allows dissolved nutrients to percolate through the soil beneath the reach of plant roots. Nitrogen, sulfur and other volatile forms of nutrients can also be released as gas into the air.

(5) Inputs

Nutrients can enter the soil nutrient cycle through natural precipitation, acid rain and nitrogen fixation. Precipitation carries dust particles and dissolved gases with stored nutrients, acid rain from industrial pollution deposits nitrogen and sulfur, and nitrogen fixation converts N_2 gas (in the air) to ammonium (NH_4^+) ions, for use by plants and other soil organisms. Certain microbes, such as legume root-nodule bacteria, carry out nitrogen fixation.

7.3 Soil management in agriculture

7.3.1 Harvested versus non-harvested Soils

(1) Non-harvested soils

In most natural soil ecosystems, nutrient inputs and outputs reach an equilibrium state. The diagram below (Fig. 7.11) shows data from nutrient cycling studies in a non-harvested, balanced forest soil ecosystem. It demonstrates the balance in a natural ecosystem between uptake and leaf fall and between losses and inputs.

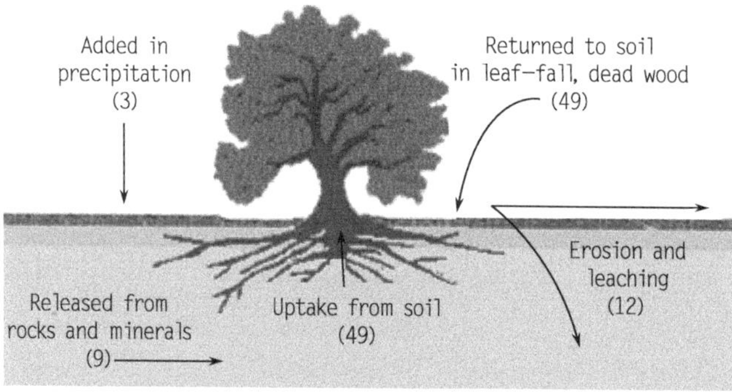

Fig. 7.11 Calcium cycling in a New Hampshire hardwood forest soil. Numbers in brackets represent yearly flux, in kg Ca/hm^2 (Borman and Likens, 1970).

(2) Harvested soils

In contrast to non-harvested soils, harvested crops and animal products remove nutrients from farmed soils and alter soil texture, structure and nutrient cycles. Some farm management practices further increase soil nutrient loss by not counteracting mechanisms such as erosion, leaching, runoff, gaseous loss and crop removal. Over time, physical, biological and chemical tillage clear the topsoil and subsoil layers, distinctively changing the soil profile by blurring soil horizons and reducing soil productivity.

Soil erosion, the removal of nutrients attached to soil particles by wind or water, is considered one of the most serious global environmental problems we face. Erosion has led to the loss of cultivated soil 13-40 times faster than the rate of renewal and sustainability (Pimentel, 1998). Erosion results in lower productivity, fertility, water quality, nutrient storage and richness of soil organic matter. Erosion also plays into ecological economics, because investing in soil conservation can result in farm net returns up to 64% (Knowler, 2004). Consequently, soil conservation has gained international attention about its macroeconomic power, and has led to political intervention to reduce soil degradation.

(3) Farm soil management

To maintain soil fertility for crop production, farm management must pay special attention to soil conservation, specifically focussing on replenishing nutrient losses. Farmers seek to reduce or replace nutrient losses with good soil husbandry, recycling crop residues (non-harvested plant material and livestock manure) and taking advantage of natural inputs (e. g. using legumes in crop rotations to increase nitrogen fixation). Continuous harvests may still require the application of additional nutrient inputs. These mainly come from fertilizers and lime, but can also come from off-farm livestock manure, sewage and food-processing wastes. Fig. 7. 12 shows the altered nutrient cycle in harvested soils.

Fertilizers refer to soluble nutrient sources with high concentrations and come in a variety of chemical forms, although most often as simple inorganic salts. The positive attributes of commercial fertilizers include their high water solubility, immediate availability to plants and their precise composition and application rates, whereas organic fertilizers have great variability because of physical and biological conditions (Balakrishna, 2007). Knowing the fixed nutrient composition in commercial fertilizers allows farmers to measure precise rates for optimal plant growth and soil productivity. However, unanticipated heavy rains or applications in excess can make these highly soluble nutrients leach, increasing the soil cation exchange capacity. Using fertilizers appropriately requires a deep knowledge of the physical and biological properties of the farm soil and the chemical nutrient capacities of the fertilizer. Planning the timing and amount of fertilizer application can also help reduce or eliminate leaching and runoff issues.

Liming, rather than raising soil pH, neutralizes toxic elements in acidic soils through the addition of hydroxide, decreasing Al^{3+}, Mn^{2+} and Fe^{3+} solubility and causing them to precipitate. The benefits of liming include (Hodges, 2000):

- Supplying soil with calcium and manganese
- Increasing phosphorus, molybdenum and boron availability
- Creating more favourable conditions for microbial mediated reactions (i. e. nitrogen fixation and nitrification)
- In some cases, improving soil structure and increasing herbicide effectiveness

Liming materials are relatively immobile in soil and inefficient when not incorporated throughout the plant root zones, so soil management prior to lime applications

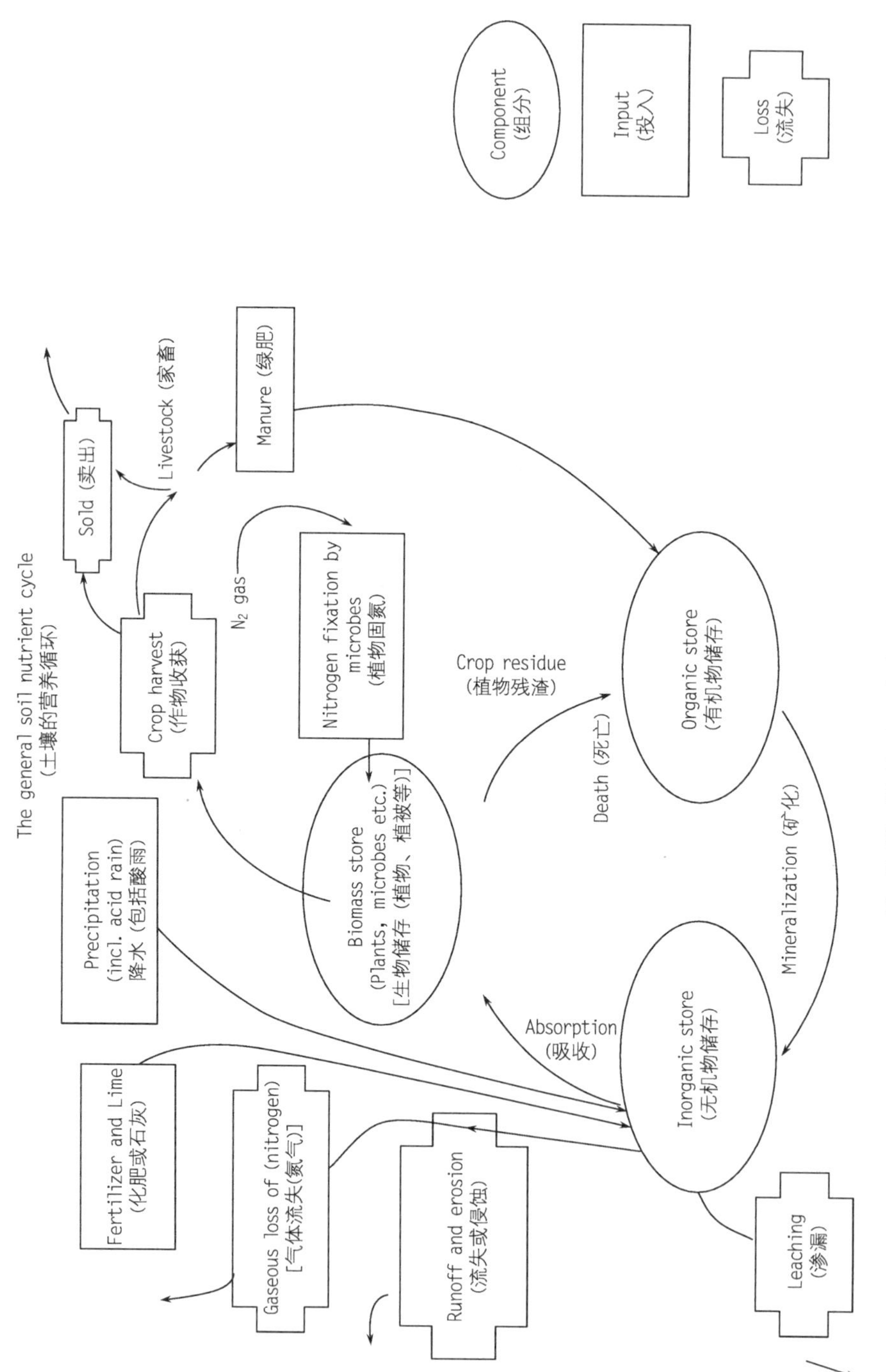

Fig. 7. 12　Nutrient cycle in cultivated soil.

is important. While many benefits exist for liming, overliming can significantly damage soils, reducing the availability of micronutrients and entailing unnecessary expenses and time for the soil to recover. When lime is not recommended, alternatives include using calcium, manganese, gypsum, magnesium, sulfate and/or potassium-magnesium-sulfate (Hodges, 2000).

7.3.2 Agricultural management: soils and nutrient cycling within different farm systems

(1) Mixed Farms

The traditional method of mixed farming in Eastern Canada involves forage production to feed livestock on-farm. Nutrients from the feed are later excreted onto the soil by the animals. The following year, crops are supplied with these manure-stored nutrients. Combined with nitrogen fixing legume forages, manure nutrients may provide most of the crop requirements.

(2) Specialized agriculture: cash cropping

Cash cropping refers to specialized farms that produce crops exclusively for selling purposes. These systems rely on off-farm nutrient supplies each year because they have no livestock to produce a manure nutrient supply. Generally specialized agriculture must rely on commercial fertilizers, which can lead to problems in over concentrated and highly soluble nutrients.

(3) Concentrated Livestock Production

At the other extreme, concentrated livestock production systems exclusively raise animals. These systems rely on purchased crop for feed and end up with an excess of manure nutrient supplies on a limited amount of land. The surplus of manure nutrients often become a disposal problem.

(4) Production problems

Both cash cropping and concentrated livestock production cannot function without off-farm supplies. While the solution of supplying cash cropping with the excess manure, and likewise, supplying the concentrated livestock production with crops seems simple, in reality these farms may be separated by long distances and transport problems may arise. These systems can lead to soil productivity problems, nutrient cycle issues, nutrient deficiencies or surpluses if not closely managed. Serious environmental issues arise in all harvested farms that cannot replenish the soil to its natural, stable state.

(5) Better Management Practices (BMPs)

BMPs reduce negative environmental impacts through soil conservation and a reduction in nutrient losses with waste utilization plans and nutrient management plans. BMPs include (Hodges, 2000):

- Sediment and erosion control
- Reduction in soil movement and runoff into streams and adjacent fields (grassed waterways, buffer strips, riparian buffers)
- Incorporation of nutrients to reduce off-site movement, volatile losses and odours
- Cover crop use to scavenge remaining nutrients in application site soil

In summary, agroecosystem function is highly dependent upon healthy soil. Soil undermines all agricultural practices, from plant and animal nutrient supply and water regulation to supporting the silo and housing structures on the farm itself. The complex processes that take place within the soil must be studied for good farm management. Soil erosion and degradation is an increasing problem around the world. Incorporating soil conservation practices into agroecosystem management will benefit microorganisms living within the soil, crop production at the farm level and macroeconomics at the international level. Failure to do so could actually lead to declining populations and a reduction in biodiversity.

Literatures cited in this chapter

Ashman M. R. and Puri G. 2002. *Essential Soil Science: a clear and concise introduction to soil science*. Victoria: Blackwell Publishing.

Balakrishna A. N. 2007. Meaning of soil biological quality and methods of characterizing demonstrations. CSM-BGBD internal project report. Bangalore.

Coleman D. C., Odum E. P., and Crossley D. A. J. 1992. Soil biology, soil ecology, and global change. *Biology and Fertility of Soils* 14: 104-111.

Daniels W. L. and Haering K. C. 2006. 'Chapter 3. Concepts of Basic Soil Science' in The Mid-Atlantic Nutrient Management Handbook. USDA Mid-Atlantic Water Program (MAWP).

Hodges H. F. and Reddy K. R. 2000. *Climate Changes and Global Crop Productivity*. Oxon: CABI Publishing.

Jenny H. 1994. *Factors of Soil Formation: A System of Quantitative Pedology*. Toronto: General Publishing Company, Ltd, 1994.

Knowler D. J. 2004. The economics of soil productivity: local, national and global perspectives. *Land Degradation & Development* 15: 543-561.

Pimentel D. and Kounang N. 1998. Ecology of Soil Erosion in Ecosystems. *Ecosystems* 1: 416-426.

Stevenson F. J. and Cole M. A. 1999. *Cycles of soil: carbon, nitrogen, phosphorus, sulfur, micronutrients*. Toronto: John Wiley & Sons, Inc.

Wang S. L., Cladwell C. D., and Zhu W. F. 2010. Low carbon agriculture: origins, principles and strategies. *Journal of agricultural modernization research* 31 (5): 604-607.

Welbaum G. E., Sturz A. V., Dong Z. M., and Nowak J. 2004. Managing Soil Microorganisms to Improve Productivity of Agro-Ecosystems. *Critical Reviews in Plant Sciences* 23 (2): 175-193.

Chapter 8 Agrobiodiversity and agroecosystem stability

Learning objectives

1. List and describe the three main classifications of biodiversity.
2. Compare and contrast biodiversity in natural ecosystems and in agroecosystems.
3. Explain the key principles of managing biodiversity for agro-ecosystem stability.
4. Explain the problems and causes of agrobiodiversity loss.
5. Describe the ways to enhance agroecosystem stability and increase biodiversity within agroecoystems.

Agroecosystems depend on the presence of biodiversity for internal functions. However, many human activities such as the indiscriminate killing of wildlife, have resulted in the loss of precious gene pools and a reduction in ecosystem services such as food production, nutrient cycling, microclimate and hydrological regulation, suppression of diseases and detoxifying of chemicals (Altieri, 1999; Alkorta, 2003). Biodiversity loss joins a litany of anthropogenic interdependent ecological "crises": global warming, ozone layer depletion, acid rain, disappearance of tropical rainforests, dwindling varieties of wildlife, marine pollution, trans-boundary movements of hazardous waste and desertification (Alkorta, 2003). Pollution, rapidly growing in developing countries, promises to act as a catalyst for biodiversity loss on a catastrophic level. Threats to agroecosystem biodiversity require increased attention to avert and mitigate the collapse of biological complexity.

8.1 Biodiversity

Biodiversity refers to the assemblage of all the species of plants, animals and microorganisms living and interacting within species, between species and of ecosystems. Scientists estimate that upwards of 10 million—and some suggest more than 100 million—different species inhabit the earth.

While five major mass extinctions have occurred in earth's history, biodiversity loss has never before been human induced. Many recent conservation measures concentrate on "hotspots", areas with exceptional concentrations of endemic species and high rates of habitat loss, to stem the mass extinction of species that is now underway (Myers, 2000). Agriculture has been a major contributor to biodiversity loss through monocropping, species domestication, selective breeding and hybridization. However, supporting biodiversity in agroecosystems can actually benefit the overall function and productivity in nature while still providing agricultural production.

8.1.1 Classifications of biodiversity

During the "Convention on Biological Diversity", biodiversity officially became defined as diversity on three levels: genetic, species and ecosystem (habitat). In practice, biodiversity conservation measures generally focus on an individual species in a natural or semi-natural setting.

(1) Genetic biodiversity

Genes determine which traits an organism exhibits; genetic biodiversity refers to all the genetic information contained in every plant, animal and microorganism on Earth. Genetic biodiversity helps ensure a species can evolve or respond to diseases, predators, parasites, pollution and climate change (Kearns, 2010). Many agricultural crops grow in monocultures, genetically homogenous species. While this practice usually consists of high-yield varieties that can be economically valuable, a single pest, disease or environmental disruption can ravage the entire crop.

(2) Species biodiversity

Species biodiversity refers to all the variety of plants, animals and microorganism species on earth, including the tiniest single-celled microbes to the largest organism on earth, the blue whale. The greatest species diversity can be found among prokaryotic organisms (eubacteria and archaea). Prokaryotic organisms provide our environment with a multitude of functions, deriving energy from both organic and inorganic chemicals; recent discoveries show that many can survive in extreme conditions. However, even with an estimated 15,000 new species (big and small) described each year; scientists believe we are losing organisms at a faster rate than we can identify them.

(3) Ecosystem biodiversity

Ecosystem biodiversity relates to the variety of habitats, biotic communities and ecological processes that influence morphology, behaviour and interactions among species in an ecosystem (FAO, 2007). Pristine ecosystems preserve support systems and biological processes that maintain life; these processes include nutrient and water cycling, photosynthesis, energy flow through the food web and patterns of plant succession (Kearns, 2010).

Natural biodiversity provides ecosystem services such as food, medicine, goods or environmental protection. Protected areas generally consist of a heterogenous matrix, with many microhabitats for different species, but all associated with the same system. Conservation measures usually aim to increase ecological resilience, biological control and cultural or traditional values based on intrinsic or aesthetic values.

Agroecosystems exist to produce food, feed, goods (timber, fibre) and other natural products for use or sale. Any conservation efforts mainly focus on sustaining production processes. The first interest in agroecosystems is to increase functionality of productive species; in the past, this has led to a reduction in diversity. Agroecosystem biodiversity can be categorized into three intermingled and strongly interacting sub-systems: managed fields (productive sub-system), semi-natural habitats surrounding those fields and the human sub-systems consisting of settlements and infrastructures (Moonen, 2008). Conservation typically focuses on the semi-natural sub-system to increase regional species pools and genome diversity, habitat diversity at all levels and to serve as a buffer against large-scale pest invasion and increase multi-functionality of direct economic returns. Recently, projects have considered the possibility of using agroecosystems to remediate environmental pollution from industrial activities to serve the purposes stated above.

8.1.2 The value of biodiversity

While intrinsic values for biodiversity exist, most of the reasons we value biodiversity are homocentric. Biodiversity provides us with (FAO, 2007):

- Food, fuel, fibre, shelter and building materials
- Purification of air and water
- Detoxification and removal of wastes
- Stabilization and moderation of climate, floods, droughts, temperature extremes and wind forces
- Generation and recycling of soil fertility and nutrient cycling
- Pollination of plants and crops
- Control over pests and diseases
- Maintenance of genetic resources and the ability to adapt to change
- Cultural, aesthetic and spiritual values

Furthermore, future gene adaptations may provide high value crops; biota may contain cures for emerging diseases and ecosystem services can be accessed for changing human needs (FAO, 2007). The current loss of ecosystems, species and gene pools can lead to the loss of critical ecosystem services.

Tab. 8.1 Putting a price on biodiversity goods and services (Zedan, 2005)

Ecological functions	Economic values (USD)
Ecosystem services worldwide	$ 18－61 trillion per year
Soil microbial services	$ 33 billon per year
Global benefits from coral reefs	$ 30 billion per year
Insect pollination of over 40 commercial crops (in the USA)	$ 30 billion per year
Sales of prescription drugs containing ingredients from wild plants (in the USA)	$ 15 billion in 1990
Genetic traits from wild crop varieties introduced into domestic agricultural crops (in the USA)	$ 8 billion per year
Total seed－sector activities worldwide	$ 45 billion per year
Global market for herbal drugs	$ 47 billion in 2000

Biodiversity directly accounts for 40% of the world economy estimated at US $ 18-61 trillion per year (Tab. 8.1, Zedan, 2005). The ecological value of biodiversity far exceeds its economic market value. Accounting for just 17 ecosystem services for 16 biomes for earth ecosystem, the minimum estimated value equalled approximately $ 33 trillion per year (Costanza, 1997). The annual market for products derived from genetic resources, including pharmaceuticals, botanical medicines, agricultural produce, ornamental horticultural products, crop protection products, biotechnologies and cosmetic products is between US $ 500-800 billion (European Commission, 2004). Likewise, the total estimated value of ecological services from biodiversity in China is more than 37.1×10^{12} Yuan RMB, far more than its traditional economic value of 1.72×10^{12} Yuan RMB in 1998 (see Tab. 8.2, China's Biodiversity

Status Research Group, 1998).

Tab. 8. 2 Values of biodiversity in China (China's Biodiversity Status Research Group, 1998)

Value classified (价值分类)	Value types (价值类别)	Economic values (经济值) ($\times 10^{12}$ Yuan)
Direct use value (直接使用价值)	Marketing products (产品及加工品年净价值)	1. 02
	Other direct use (其他直接服务价值)	0. 78
	Sum of subclass (小计)	1. 80
Indirect use value (间接使用价值)	Organic matter enhancement (有机质生产价值)	23. 3
	CO_2 sequestration CO_2 (固定价值)	3. 27
	O_2 release O_2 (释放价值)	3. 11
	Nutrient cycle and deposit (营养物质循环和储存价值)	0. 32
	Soil conservation (土壤保护价值)	6. 64
	Water preservation (涵养水源价值)	0. 27
	Pollutant absorption (净化污染物价值)	0. 40
	Sum of subclass (小计)	37. 31
Potential use value (潜在使用价值)	Selecting use value (选择使用价值)	0. 09
	Preserving values (保留使用价值)	0. 13
	Sum of subclass (小计)	0. 22
	Sum total (总计)	39. 33

8. 1. 3 Threats to biodiversity

Recognition of decreasing biodiversity has increased in recent years; however the rate of biodiversity loss has not declined. For example, even with the widespread public awareness over global deforestation, the world lost nearly 200 million hectares of forested land between 1980 and 1995 (WRI). Biodiversity loss goes far beyond deforestation. Biodiversity is currently depreciating worldwide from the degradation of tropical rainforests, coral reefs, wetlands, grasslands and soil. Closely related problems include habitat destruction and invasive species outcompeting native species. Atmospheric pollution will only accelerate these global extinction rates.

Biodiversity loss combined with the loss of traditional knowledge will limit options for human adaptation to a changing environment. Decreased biodiversity will limit nutrition, food production and job opportunities.

The World Conservation Union-Conservation Measures Partnership (IUCN-CMP) has classified direct threats to biodiversity into 11 categories, beginning with the highest level of threat (2008):

- Residential and commercial development
- Agriculture and aquaculture
- Energy production and mining
- Transportation and service corridors
- Biological resource use
- Human intrusions and disturbance
- Natural system modifications

- Invasive and other problematic species and genes
- Pollution
- Geological events
- Climate change and severe weather

8.1.4 Global biodiversity

While global biodiversity includes millions of species, they are unevenly distributed in terms of location and threats. Tropical rainforests and coral reefs are the pinnacles of biodiversity. 90% of described terrestrial species live in rainforests, and 34%-53% of total described species live in coral reefs, while they only cover 5% of the area of global rainforests (Reaka-Kudla, 1996). Human activities have accelerated species extinction rates 1000 fold by eroding environmental services, responding only to crisis at the local and national level, and spending 90% of conservation funding in economically rich countries that are biodiversity minimal (Brooks, 2006). Conservative estimates suggest we lose 5,000 species a year, while less conservative estimates raise that number to 150,000 species extinctions per year (Goodland, 1992).

8.2 Biodiversity in agroecosystems

8.2.1 Agrobiodiversity loss

Replacing natural biodiversity with a limited number of cultivated plant varieties and domesticated animals in modern agriculture has simplified the structure of the environment. On the 1440 million ha of cultivated land around the world, around 70 crop species are planted (approximately 12 grain species, 23 vegetable species, 35 fruit and nut species) whereas just 1 hm^2 of tropical rainforest typically contains 100 species of trees alone (Altieri, 1999). In particular, agriculture has become increasingly dependent on a few bean, maize, wheat, corn, rice and cotton varieties. Tab. 8.3 and Tab. 8.4 show the extent of genetic loss in crops and the reduction in diversity of fruits and vegetables. Scientific research has expressed concern time and time again over the great danger associated with genetic uniformity. While industrial agriculture and the Green Revolution have significantly increased global food production, with it came significant biophysical and socio-economic costs and disadvantages to many parts of the world.

8.2.2 Problems increasing agrobiodiversity loss

The threat of erosion of agrobiodiversity has manifested in many different ways within farming systems, off farms, in natural habitats and throughout communities worldwide. These threats derive from conflicting policies and inappropriate production practices. For example, livestock suffers from genetic erosion; as farmers concentrate on new breeds of chickens, sheep, pigs and cattle, traditional strains disappear. The FAO estimates that globally every week at least one traditional breed of livestock dies (FAO, 2001). 16% of breeds of cattle, water buffalo, goats, pigs, sheep, horse and moneys have become extinct and another 15% are rare. These losses weaken breeding programs and risk the ability of livestock to adapt in the future. As consumers of animal products, we also lose nutrition, knowledge and cultural diversity.

Tab. 8. 3 Extent of genetic loss in selected crops (Thrupp, 2000)

Crop	Country	Number of varieties loss
Rice	Sri Lanka	From 2000 in 1959 to fewer than 100 today, 75% descend from a common stock
Rice	Bangladesh	62% descend from a common stock
Rice	Indonesia	74% descend from a common stock
Wheat	United states	50% of crop in 9 varieties
Potatoes	United	75% of crop in 4 varieties
Soybean	United	50% of crop in 6 varieties

Tab. 8. 4 Reduction of diversity in fruit and vegetables in 1903-1983 (Thrupp, 2000)

Crop	1903	1983	Loss
Asparagus	46	1	97. 8
Bean	578	32	94. 5
Beet	288	17	94. 1
Carrot	287	21	92. 7
Leet	39	5	87. 2
Lettuce	497	36	92. 8
Onion	357	21	94. 1
Parsnip	75	5	93. 3
Pea	408	25	93. 9
Radish	463	27	94. 2
Spinach	109	7	93. 6
Squash	341	40	88. 3
Turnip	237	24	89. 9

8. 2. 3 Underlying causes of agrobiodiversity loss

The proximate causes to the erosion of diversity are tied to unsustainable technologies, land-degrading practices and overuse of chemicals. Yet, these proximate causes have developed in close association to underlying ideologies, policies and education, business, demographic and socio-economic pressures (Thrupp, 2000). The relationship among the problems, proximate causes and underlying causes to agrobiodiversity loss can be seen in Tab. 8. 5.

Agricultural systems can be classified by four parameters: biological diversity, intensity of human management, net energy balance and management responsibility; if we think of ecosystem management as a continuum, Fig. 8. 1 expresses wilderness on one end of the spectrum and intensively managed ecosystems on the other (Tivy, 1990). Agroecosystems range within this continuum, but try to closely adapt to the wild, ecological conditions with high biodiversity and lower management inputs. Tivy (1990) stated that in the intensively managed systems, "man's technical expertise is such that the physical environment is no longer a significant variable in determining or influencing the type of agroecosystem" . The typical consequence of agrobiodiversity loss is examplified by "*The Great Irish Potato Famine*" in the following knowledge box.

Tab. 8. 5 Addressing problems and causes of agrobiodiversity loss linked to agriculture (Thrupp, 2000)

Problems	Proximate causes	Underlying causes of all problems
Erosion of genetic resources (livestock and crops/plants) -threatens food security -increases risk -prevents future discoveries	Dominance of uniform high yield varieties (HYVs) and monoculture, biases in breeding methods, weak conservation efforts	Industrial/Green Revolution paradigm that stresses uniform monoculture Inequitable distribution of land and resources Policies that support uniform HYVs and chemicals (e. g. subsidies, credit policies and market standards) Pressures and influence of seed/agrochemical companies and extension systems Trade liberalization and market expansion polices that neglect social and ecological factors Lack of awareness of agroecology in R&D and in education institutions Disrespect for local knowledge Demographic pressures erosion of insect diversity
Erosion of insect diversity -increases susceptibility -ruins pollination and biocontrol insect	Heavy use of pesticides, use of monoculture/uniform species, degrading habitats harbouring insects	
Erosion of soil diversity -leads to fertility loss -reduces productivity	Heavy use of agrochemicals, degrading tillage practices, use of monoculture	
Loss of habitat diversity including wild crop relatives	Extensification in marginal lands, drift/contamination from chemicals	
Loss of indigenous methods and knowledge of biodiversity	Spread of uniform "modern" varieties and technologies	

The Great Irish Potato Famine-a Case Study in Biodiversity

The Great Famine in Ireland was a natural catastrophe caused by a potato disease between 1845-1852. Over that time period, the population of Ireland reduced by 20%-25%. Approximately one million people died of starvation and epidemic disease, and another two million people emigrated.

The potato was initially introduced to the gentry of Ireland as a garden crop, became a widespread supplementary food by the late seventeenth century and a staple of the lower societal classes by the early eighteenth century. In fact, a third of the population depended on potatoes for their entire sustenance.

As potato acreage expanded, the variety of potato species did not increase and diversify. Potato blight, the fungus *Phytophthora infestans*, attacked in successive blasts ravishing most of the potato population for four to five consecutive years. Although the exact origin of blight is unknown, it was probably introduced through cargo ships, coming from Peru, Baltimore, Philadelphia or New York. Between 1728 and 1851, the Census of Ireland Commissioners recorded 24 widespread crop potato failures. Although actions and inactions of the Whig government, specifically concerning food security and housing regulations intensified the magnitude of the situation, agricultural practices that include greater biodiversity may have ameliorated the situation or prevented the extensive ravishing of Irish farmland. The effects of the Great Famine have permanently shaped the demographic, political and cultural landscape in Ireland.

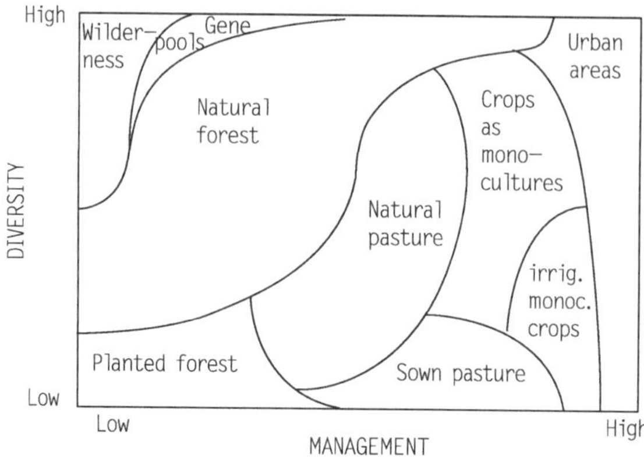

Fig. 8. 1 The relationship between the degree of management and biodiversity in different agroecosystems (Tivy, 1990).

8. 3 Regenerating biodiversity in agroecosystems

8. 3. 1 Enhancing agroecosystem stability

Enhancing biodiversity in agricultural systems will play a key role in creating sustainable agroecosystems. Perhaps we should examine farming practices in third world countries, where agricultural land is marginal and therefore, practices are more risky. Traditional multiple cropping systems, traditional agroforestry systems, intercropping, shifting cultivation and other traditional farming methods generally mimic natural ecological processes, promoting species richness, production stability, efficient labour use and reduced pest and disease incidences while offering a diversified diet and maximum economic returns with little technological input. Traditional, multiple cropping systems alone can provide up to 15%-20% of the world's food supply (Altieri, 1999). Fig. 8. 2 describes the integration of resources, components, and functions for multiple-use farm systems which all help regenerate biodiversity in agroecosystems.

Agroecosystems benefit from resources in their natural habitats. According to Ann Lee Thrupp (2000), agrobiodiversity encompasses the following biological resources:

- Genetic resources
- Edible plants and crops
- Livestock and freshwater fish
- Soil organisms
- Insects, bacteria and fungi
- "Wild" resources (species and other elements)

8. 3. 2 Regenerating the Soil biodiversity

High soil quality plays a crucial role in agroecosystem stability; however, some agricultural practices make it difficult to maintain an ecologically balanced and productive soil environment. Frequent tillage and chemical overuse reduce soil biodiversity and increase the dependence on a few key crops.

As Chapter 7 discusses in more detail, soil biodiversity regulates a host of activities in the soil ecosystem, which directly affect the fertility and ability of the soil to support plant and animal growth. Rich soil biomass may contain thousands of organisms, fungi and bacteria for decomposition and nutrient cycling. Soil microbes influence plant nutrient availability and increase soil tolerance to disturbances. Tab. 8. 6 summarizes key influences of soil biota on soil processes. Increasing topsoil and soil organic matter will improve biological processes without human input. Managing soil quality will stabilize crop production and nutrient cycling in an agroecosystem and minimize risk of disease and losses on the farm.

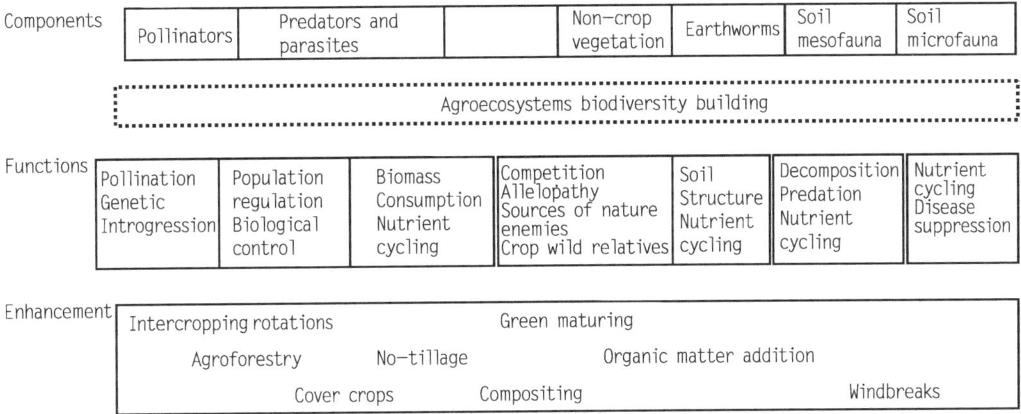

Fig. 8. 2 The integration of resources, components and functions for multiple-use farm systems (Altieri, 1995).

Tab. 8. 6 Influences of soil biota on soil processes in ecosystems (Altieri, 1999)

Types of soil biota	Functions in nutrient cycling	Functions in maintaining soil structure
Microflora (fungi, bacteria, actinomycetes)	Catabolize organic matter; mineralize and immobilize nutrients	Produce organic compounds that bind aggregates; hyphae entangle particles onto aggregates
Microfauna (Acarina, Collembola)	Regulate bacterial and fungal populations; alter nutrient turnover	May affect aggregate structure through interactions with microflora
Mesofauna (Acarina, Collembola, enchytraeids)	Regulate fungal and microfaunal populations; alter nutrient turnover; fragment plant residues	Produce fecal pellets; create biopores; promote humification
Macrofauna (isopods, centipedes, millipedes, earthworms, etc.)	Fragment plant residues; stimulate microbial activity	Mix organic and mineral particles; redistribute organic matter and micro-organisms; create biopores; promote humification; produce fecal pellets

8. 3. 3 Increasing the Landscape biodiversity

Since millions of microbes exist on earth and perform extremely important functions, many studies focusing on biodiversity regeneration in agroecosystems have been conducted at the field level, rarely considering any larger scale. However, large scale fragmented landscapes produced by crop monocultures have significantly affected agroecosystem biodiversity and reintroducing a mosaic structure can lead to the creation of multiple habitats for shelter, feeding and reproduction (Altieri, 1999). Some options for regenerating biodiversity at the landscape level include diverse vegetation field margins, head rows, wetlands, woodlots, fence rows and farmyards. In particular, corridors can modify microclimates and air currents, influence nutrient, water and material flows, and interrupt disease dispersion. Landscape level biodiversity helps stabilize these processes in the agroecosystem for greater control over the system and minimizing human dependence on technology, labour and other resource rich materials.

8.3.4 Reconstructing biodiversity in agroecosystems

Restoring biodiversity to agroecosystems can be executed in numerous ways. Identifying the desirable type of biodiversity to carry out specific, intended ecological services will help one determine the best management practices. Well planned strategies can enhance desired functional components of biodiversity in the agroecosystem and implement synergisms through polycultures, agroforestry systems and crop-livestock mixture arrangements (Atlieri, 1999). Fig. 8.3 demonstrates different agricultural designs and practices that can enhance functional diversity or negatively affect it. This diagram is most helpful when used in conjunction with a specific agroecosystem goal for enhancing or regenerating biodiversity.

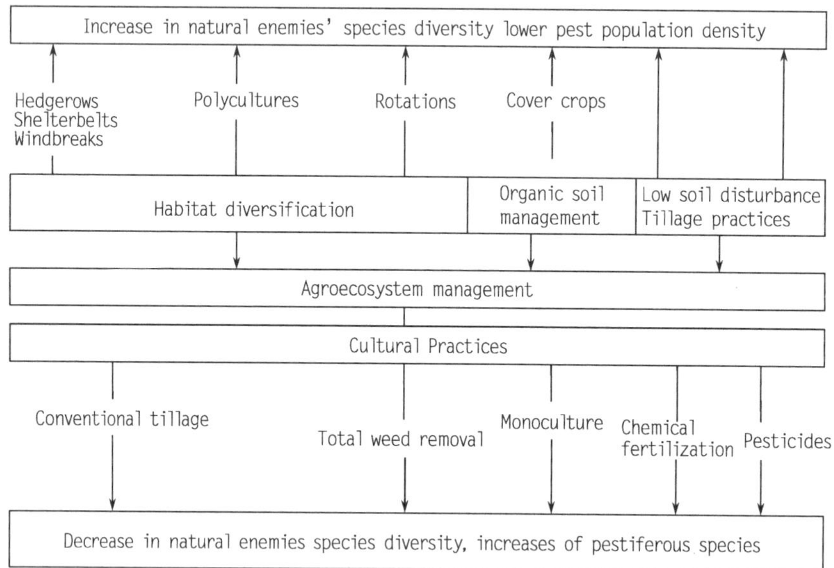

Fig. 8.3 The effects of agroecosystem management and associated cultural practices on the biodiversity of natural enemies and the abundance of insect pests (Altieri, 1999).

Evidence suggests some farm-management practices addressed in Fig. 8.3 have already successfully made space for wildlife in agroecosystems. These practices include: ① establishing conservation-tillage systems, ② minimizing herbicide application, ③ leaving uncultivated strips within crop fields as habitat for weedy relatives of crop plants, ④ windbreaks, ⑤ border plantings or live fences between plots or paddocks, or between farms, ⑥ irrigation bunds, ⑦ vegetative barriers to soil and water movement within crop fields (Alkorta, 2003).

(1) Using multicropping to restore the landscape biodiversity

The use of multicropping can turn a once heavily eroded hill valley in Southern China into restored land focusing on watershed management and agricultural production (Fig. 8. 4). This photograph depicts interlaced crop species forming forested land, orchards and herbaceous plants. Animal rearing takes places in the valley providing manure for the plants. Through indigenous knowledge, these plants provide medicines and a religious sanctuary for the local people, in addition to food and fibre.

Fig. 8. 4 An agro-landscape in a hill valley in southern China (Luo, 2007).

Fig. 8. 5 demonstrates another field conversion strategy in the Pearl River Delta, or Guangdong, China. "Sangji yutang" refers to the system of mulberry fields and fishponds, where paddy fields are converted to fishponds and surrounded by mulberry plants, sugarcane, grasses or miscellaneous vegetables on elevated land. Typical land use relied on mulberry leaves feeding silk worms to produce enormous quantities of silk for export to Europe and the United States. Excess mulberry fed the pond fish or fertilized the mud below. This well-established field conversion system distinguished the delta regions in south-eastern China, allowing this traditional, family oriented, labour intensive, value-added industrial processing system to survive the Depression, several wars, and political upheavals and through the post-Mao years (Hsieh, 2000).

Fig. 8. 5 "Sangji yutang" landscape in the Pearl River Delta or less commonly known as Guangdong, China. This system has evolved over 1,000 years (Luo, 2007).

(2) Managing the field

Using diversifying methods, such as intercropping and agroforestry, to mimic naturally ecological processes while optimizing natural inputs of sunlight, soil nutrients and rainfall will help to create a sustainably manageable, complex agroecosystem. Assembling a diverse array of functional components in an agroecosystem will initiate synergisms to naturally activate and substantiate ecosystem services. Using different combinations of crops, trees and animals will activate soil biological processes, nutrient recycling and immunity reinforcement. Strategies to restore agrobiodiversity should exhibit the following features (Altieri, 2005):

- Crop Rotations: to provide temporal diversity, crop nutrients and to break pest, disease and weed life cycles
- Polycultures: to introduce competition or complementation to enhance yields
- Agroforestry Systems: to enhance complimentary relations between functional components for multiple uses within the agroecosystem
- Cover Crops: to improve soil fertility, biological control of pests and to modify orchard microclimate
- Crop/Livestock Mixtures: to aid in the achievement of high biomass output and optimal recycling

Fig. 8. 6 demonstrates a rice-fish paddy ecosystem in China. In a traditional paddy field, fish eat weeds and insects reducing the need for pesticide use around the rice. This also diminishes GHG emissions from the paddy soil.

Fig. 8. 6 A rice-fish paddy agroecosystem in China (Luo, 2007).

(3) Managing the soil

Using an ecosystem approach to the application of production techniques and land use practices can enhance soil biodiversity management. According to the FAO, the following techniques can enhance soil biodiversity functions in the production of basic grains. To broaden agroecosystem resilience and improve yields, use crop rotations, leguminous cover crops, improved local seed varieties and diversified crop associations. To reduce disturbances of soil structure and biota, use low-impact tillage methods. To produce organic fertilizers, use stubble, harvest residues, livestock manure and green manure. Finally, to main soil structure and moisture content, use conservation measures.

The FAO also describes the following land management practices that favour plant and animal diversity associated with soil biological activity. The methods include: mosaics of various crops and land uses; capturing and conserving rainwater for plants, animals and people; incorporating backyard animals using their manure for soil organic matter in home gardens; and restoring agricultural biodiversity by planting native crops, medicinal plants and tree species.

(4) Managing crops

To reverse genetic agrobiodiversity loss from monocultures, multicropping such as intercropping can provide field integrated pest management and increased disease resistance in crop production in addition to improved genetic diversity. An experiment comparing monocultures with intercropping 24 traditional and hybrid rice varieties in the Yunnan Province, China, resulted in a significantly more resistant rice field to epidemic disease when using mixed planting, eliminating the need for pesticide use in these plots (Zhu, 2000). Fig. 8. 7 shows this ecologically sound approach for disease control and decreased pesticide use.

Fig. 8. 7 24 varieties of rice intercropping in Yunnan Province, which decreased pesticide use (Luo, 2007).

Literatures cited in this chapter

Akem C., Ceccarelli S., Erskine W., and Lenné J. 2000. Using genetic diversity for disease resistance in agricultural production. *Outlook on agriculture* 29 (1): 25-30.

Alkorta I., Albizu I., and Garbisu C. 2003. Biodiversity and agroecosystems. *Biodiversity and Conservation* 12: 2521-2522.

Altieri M. A. 1999. The ecological role of biodiversity in agroecosystems. Agriculture, *Ecosystems and Environment* 74: 19-31.

Altieri M. A. 2005. Agroecology: principles and strategies for designing sustainable farming systems. Biosafety infomation center, Url: http: //www. biosatety-info. net/article php? aid=41, 2011-11-13.

Altieri M. A. and Nicholls C. I. 2004. *Biodiversity and pest management in agroecosystems*. Binghamton, NY: Hayworth Press.

China's Biodiversity Status Research Group. 1998. *China's Biodiversity Status Research Report*. Beijing: China's Environment Press.

Costanza R., d'Arge R., de Groote R., Farber S., Grasso M., Hannon B., Limburg K., Sutton P., and van der Belt M. 1997. The Value if the World's Ecosystem Services and Natural Capital. *Nature* 387: 253-260.

Food and Agriculture Organization (FAO) of United Nations. 1997. State of the World's Forests. Rome.

Goodland R. 1992. The case that the world has reached its limits: more precisely that the current throughput growth in the global economy cannot be sustained. *Population and Environment: A Journal of Interdisciplinary Studies* 13 (3) 6: 167-182.

Hsieh W. 2000. "Rural Entrepreneurs in the Canton Delta Region: Shift of Silk to Sugarcane in the 1930s," a paper presented at the annual meeting of the annual meeting meeting of the Association for Asian Studies, San Diego.

Kearns C. 2010. Conservation of Biodiversity. *Nature Education Knowledge* 1 (9): 7.

Mansur E., Bakker L. and Ndeso-Atanga A. 2007. The Value of Biodiversity. Food and Agricultural Organisation of the United Nations (FAO).

Moonen A. C. and Barberi P. 2008. Functional biodiversity: An agroecosystem approach. *Agriculture, Ecosystems and Environment* 127: 7-21.

Myers N., Mittermeler R. A., Mittermeler C. G., da Fonseca G. A. B., and Kent J. 2000. Biodiversity hotspots for conservation priorities. *Nature*, 403: 853-858.

Pimm S. I., Russell G. J., Gittelman J. L., and Brooks T. M. 1995. The Future of Biodiversity. *Science* 269: 347-350.

Reaka-Kudla M. L., Wilson D. E., and Wilson E. O. 1996. *Biodiversity II: Understanding and Protecting Our Biological Resources*. Washington, DC: Joseph Henry Press.

Salafsky N., Salzer D., Stattersfield A. J., Hilton-Taylor C., Neugarten R., Butchart S. H. M., Collen B., Cox N., Master L. L., O'Conner S., and Wilkie D. 2008. A Standard Lexicon for Biodiversity Conservation: Unified Classifications of Threats and Actions. *Conservation Biology* 22 (4): 97-911.

Thrupp L. A. 2000. Linking agricultural biodiversity and food security: the valuable role of agrobiodiversity for sustainable agriculture. *International affairs* 76 (2): 265-281.

Tivy J. 1990. *Agricultural Ecology*. Harlow: Addison Wesley Longman Ltd.

World Resources Institute, World Resources. 2000. *Deforestation: The global assault continues*. 1998-1999.

Zedan H. 2005. The role of the convention on biological diversity and its protocol on biosafety in fostering the conservation and sustainable use of the world's biological wealth for socio-economic and sustainable development. *Journal of Industrial Microbiology Biotechnology* 32: 496-501.

Zhu Y., Fen H., Wang Y., Li Y., Chen J., Hu L., Mundt C. C. 2000. Genetic diversity and disease control in rice. *Nature* 406: 718-772.

Unit 3 Agroecosystematic Processes and Their Anthropocentric Problems

Chapter 9 Land preparation

Learning objectives

1. Define succinctly the following terms:
   - Primary tillage
   - Secondary tillage
   - Zero tillage
   - Tilth
   - Conservation tillage
2. List and describe the purposes for tillage.
3. Describe the advantages and disadvantages of conservation tillage.

9.1 The functions of land preparation

To ensure the long term success of a crop rotation, land preparation should be done prior to planting or transplanting of the plant material. The purpose of land preparation is to provide the necessary soil conditions for seeding or to ensure the successful establishment of the young offshoots or the tissue culture plants received from the nursery.

9.2 The procedures of land preparation

Some forms of Land preparation are undertaken before field seeding, seedbed preparation is critical to crop productivity. The way soil is managed depends on:

- the cropping system
- soil amendment
- soil tillage system

The first step in preparing virgin land for crop production is clearing it to remove existing vegetation. Once the original vegetation is cleared to the desirable extent, the land is ready to be prepared for seeding. One of the land preparation activities that are undertaken on virgin land is terrain modification, the purposes of which are:

(1) Levelling. The land may require leveling to improve surface drainage, leveling should be done professionally to conserve the fertile topsoil.

(2) Terracing. Land preparation involving terrain modification through reduction in slope, designed to prevent accelerated erosion and to facilitate the use of the land for cropping.

(3) Improving the drainage. Poor drainage may be corrected before planting; this may be accomplished by surface methods or underground methods.

Methods of land preparation include the use of equipment such as the tractor and ploughing implements, animal traction and hand tools.

9.3 Tillage system

Tillage is the agricultural preparation of the soil by ploughing, ripping, or turning it before seeding.

9.3.1 The objectives of tillage

(1) Land levelling. Land may be levelled again for seedbed preparation, as well as for other purpose described above.

(2) Seed bed preparation. In order for proper germination to occur, the seed must make good contact with soil to be imbibing moisture. Seed bed preparation is done according to the requirements for tilth. Tilth is the physical condition of soil as related to the ease of tillage, fitness as a seedbed and its impedance to seedling emergence and root penetration that meets the needs of different seeds. A soil with good tilth can be described as one that has good aeration, takes water readily, drains well, and works down to a good, loose, seedbed. This is one of the functions of tillage seedbed preparation. Tillage to prepare a seedbed after the land has been ploughed is accomplished with disks, harrows or field cultivators. Disk plows should be used in soils that have been ploughed and left with rough surfaces, in preparation of a good seedbed. There is little reason why disking should not replace completely plowing in soils that have relatively little or fine crop residues. Once over with a disk plow nearly completes seedbed preparation. At this time, most of the trash and residues are worked into the soil. Overworking a field with a disk can be disastrous as it leaves the soil surface fine, and loose. Overworked soil easily loses moisture and the lower half of the ploughed soil layer may end up as hard as before it was ploughed because it gets compacted with the machinery. It needs to be considered that the disk does not function well in fields with large stones, it could be damaged.

(3) Mixing organic matter and soil amendments into the soil. The crop and weed biomass residue can be incorporated into the soil with tilling processes, as well as basic manure and fertilizer input to improve the physical and chemical (nutrient) characteristics prior to seedling. In addition to these practices, a good fertilizer program promotes greater crop growth. Crops, in turn, contribute to soil improvement by protecting the soil against the impact of falling rain, by holding the soil in place with extensive plant root systems, and by providing soil nutrients from organic matter of decomposing plant residues.

(4) Weed control. Weeds may influence seedling growth by competing with the crop and harbouring diseases and insect pests, so they need to be controlled before sowing. Farmers probably already know that plowing is the most effective tillage method for weed control. Before planting, plowing completely cuts off perennial weed shoots and exposes many root stocks to sunlight so they dry out and die. Also, the plow leaves the surface rough and porous, increasing the amount of water that enters the soil and helping to control erosion. Soil runoff can also be reduced if furrows are ploughed opposite to the way water would flow. Good contact between the

seed and soil is needed in order for the seed to take on enough water to swell and germinate.

(5) Improve soil physical conditions. Soil texture and structure are important in crop production. Tillage can be explored to loosen the compact soil for crop root growth and development. Because of the possible damage to soil structure from overworking the soil, one modern approach to soil conservation is to use only as much tillage as is required to produce a good crop. The kind and amount of tillage is determined according to crop, soil and field conditions. No one set of guiding standards is appropriate for all situations. Tillage must be done in a way that will assure adequate protection of soil and water resources. A good soil surface will prevent crust formation and allow rapid rainfall penetration.

(6) Erosion control. Tillage may be conducted in a certain way to provide a rough soil surface to impede the actions of agents of soil erosion, particularly when conservation tillage is utilized. Other management practices, such as contouring, strip planting, cover cropping, alley cropping, reduced tillage, terracing and leaving some crop residue on the land help to eliminate or minimize the loss of soil from water and wind erosion. Using good erosion control practices such as terracing and contour preserves not only the soil, but also many nutritional elements needed for plant growth (Fig. 9. 1) .

Fig. 9. 1 Diagram for terracing and contour farming preventing from erosion.

(7) Shaping soil. Tillage is used to create raised beds for plant or to created furrows for irrigation.

Another critical concept is the best time for seedbed preparation. Marginal moisture supply is critical at plowing time because the soil must be dry enough for tillage without causing excessive compaction or creating clods in fine-textured soils. As soon as the crop has been taken out, the land can be tilled and preparations can be started for next cropping season. In areas where there is more than one cropping season per year, land can be prepared once a year, using the same crop furrows for subsequent crops. The best time to work the land will be just before planting time making sure the land is not too wet or too dry. Under most conditions, a smooth, finely pulverized seedbed should not be prepared until just before a crop is to be planted.

9. 3. 2 The types of tillage

There are two types of tillage: primary and secondary tillage.

(1) Primary tillage

Primary tillage is the first working after the last harvest and normally the most aggressive tillage operation. It is normally undertaken when the soil is wet enough to allow the field to be ploughed and strong enough to give reasonable levels of traction. This can be immediately after the crop harvest or at the beginning of the next wet season. When there is sufficient power available some soil types are ploughed dry. The objectives of primary tillage are:

• Till the soil to attain a reasonable depth (15-36cm) with varying clod sizes, and stirs up the topsoil

• Kill weeds by burying or cutting and exposing the roots, and chop, bury vegetation and debris from the soil surface

• Soil aeration and water accumulation. Depending on the soil type and the plough the soil will normally be inverted aerating the deep layers and trapping water during a rainfall event. Usually primary tillage does not produce a suitable seed bed due to rough nature of soil (large clods)

Equipment used to break and loosen soil may be called primary tillage equipment. It includes moldboard, disk, rotary chisel and subsoil plows. The moldboard plow is adapted to the breaking of many soil types. It is well suited for turning under and covering crop residues. There are hundreds of different designs, each intended to function best in performing certain tasks in specified soils. The part that breaks the soil is called the bottom or base; it is composed of the share, the landside, and the moldboard. The implement most commonly used with an animal powered system is the moldboard plough (Fig. 9. 2). In clay soils, the fields often have to be fully saturated before tillage can be undertaken. In lighter texture soils such as loam or sand, tillage can be undertaken at moisture levels below field capacity. In 2-wheel powered systems, both moldboard and disc ploughs are used. The disc is usually the preferred system as it takes less power and can handle obstacles much easier. When traction is a problem, cage wheels need to be fitted to the tractor.

Fig. 9. 2 Using mouldboard plough and its result *in situ* in Canada.

In a 4-wheel tractor system, three-disc, and seven-disc and offset ploughs are the most common. Tined ploughs are preferable in the upland systems but as yet are not widely available in Asia. Moldboard ploughs are also not commonly used in tractor based systems.

Care needs to be taken when using the moldboard and disc plough as a large cut-out furrow left in the middle of the field causes major problems with field levelness. For moldboard and disc ploughs, fields are best ploughed in deep soil so drainage channels are left at the outer edges of the field.

When a bottom turns the soil, it cuts a trench, or furrow, throwing to one side a ribbon of soil that is called the furrow slice. When plowing is started in the middle of a strip of land, a furrow is plowed across the field; on the return trip, a furrow slice is lapped over the first slice. This leaves a slightly higher ridge than the second, third, and other slices. The ridge is called a back furrow. When two strips of land are finished, the last furrows cut leave a trench about twice the width of one bottom, called a dead furrow. When land is broken by continuous lapping of furrows, it is called flat broken. If land is broken in alternate back furrows and dead furrows, it is said to be bedded or listed.

Different soils require different-shaped moldboards in order to give the same degree of pulverization of the soil. Thus, moldboards are divided into several different classes, including stubble, general-purpose, general-purpose for clay and stiff-sod soil, slat, blackland, and chilled general-purpose. The blackland bottom is used, for example, in areas in which the soil does not scour easily; that is, where the soil does not leave the surface of the emerging plow clean and polished.

The share is the cutting edge of the moldboard plow. Its configuration is related to soil type, particularly in the down suction, or concavity, of its lower surface. Generally, three degrees of down suction are recognized: regular for light soil, deep for ordinary dry soil, and double-deep for clay and gravelly soils. In addition, the share has horizontal suction, which is the amount its point is bent out of line with the landside. Down suction causes the plow to penetrate to proper depth when pulled forward, while horizontal suction causes the plow to create the desired width of furrow.

Moldboard plow bottom sizes refer to width between share wing and the landside. Tractor-plow sizes generally range from 10 to 18 inches (25 to 45 centimetres), although larger, special-purpose types exist.

On modern mechanized farms, plow bottoms are connected to tractors either as trailing implements or integrally. One or more bottoms may be so attached. They are found paired right and left occasionally (two-way), with the advantage of throwing the furrow slice in a constant direction as the turns are made. A variation is the middle breaker, or lister, which is a bottom equipped with both right- and left-handed moldboards.

The disk plow employs round, concave disks of hardened steel, sharpened and sometimes serrated on the edge, with diameters ranging from 20 to 38 inches (50 to 95 centimetres) . It reduces friction by making a rolling bottom in place of a sliding one. Its draft is about the same as that of the moldboard plow. The disk plow works to advantage in situations where the moldboard will not, as in sticky non-scouring soils; in fields with a plow sole; in dry, hard ground; in peat soils; and for deep plowing. The disk-plow bottom is usually equipped with a scraper that aids in pulverizing the furrow slice. Disk plows are either trailed or mounted integrally on a tractor.

The rotary plow's essential feature is a set of knives or tines rotated on a shaft by a power source. The knives chop the soil up and throw it against a hood that covers the knife set. These machines can create good seedbeds, but their high cost and extra power requirement have limited general adoption, except for the small garden tractor.

The chisel plow is equipped with narrow, double-ended shovels, or chisel points, mounted on long shanks. These points rip through the soil and stir it but do not invert and pulverize as well as the moldboard and disk plows. The chisel plow is often used to loosen hard, dry soils prior to using regular plows; it is also useful for shattering plow sole.

Subsoil plows are similar in principle but are much larger, since they are used to penetrate soil to depths of 20 to 36 inches (50 to 90 centimetres). Tractors of 60 to 85 horsepower are required to pull a single subsoil point through a hard soil at a depth of 36 inches. These plows are sometimes equipped with a torpedo-shaped attachment for making subsurface drainage channels.

(2) Secondary tillage

Secondary tillage is any working completed after primary tillage and is undertaken for:

- Follows primary tillage and produces a finer tilth for seeding, done to a shallower depth of 5-15 cm
- The implements break up the clods, reducing ped size
- weed control
- incorporation of fertilizers
- levels of soil surface

Secondary tillage is usually shallower and less aggressive than primary tillage. The final workings are then completed using peg tooth harrows to puddle the soil and leave the surface level and ready for planting.

Fig. 9. 3 Disking.

In 2-wheel tractor systems, the mold-board, the disc and the rotovator are used for second tillage. In some instances, peg tooth harrows are also used if rotovators are not available. Cage wheels on the tractor are needed for traction in all soil types and these also help puddle the soil (Fig. 9. 3).

In 4-wheel tractor systems, seven-disc ploughs, offset disc ploughs and rotovators are the most commonly used equipment for second workings. In this system, fields are either mechanically puddled with tractors using a rotovator and leveling board or by tractors fitted with large cage wheels and harrows.

It is common in many countries for the first two workings to be undertaken using tractors and the final working done by animals and harrows.

Problems of flotation and traction are a major concern in most soil types after the second working and during land leveling. In some of the sandy soils, flotation is a problem when excessive wheel slip causes the tires to break through the firmer surface layers and the tractor sinks.

9. 3. 3 Conservation tillage

Another basic tillage strategy is called Conservation tillage, which entails crops being grown with minimal cultivation of the soil. Conservation tillage is any tillage and planting system in which at least 30% of the soil surface is covered by plant residue after planting to reduce soil erosion by water (Uri, 1999); or where soil erosion by wind is the primary concern of at least 1 000 pounds per acre of flat small grain residue equivalent are on the surface during the critical erosion period (Nyakatawa et al. , 2001).

The chief goals of this tillage practice are to reduce soil erosion and conserve moisture.

(1) Methods of Conservation tillage

The common types of Conservation tillage include no-tillage, mulch tillage, strip tillage, minimum tillage and ridge tillage; they differ from each other mainly in the degree to which the soil is disturbed prior to planting

- No tillage

No tillage also called zero tillage or no-till; it is the tilling practice in which the soil is opened by coulters, row cleaners, disc openers, in-row chisels or rototillers prior to planting the seed. Weeds are controlled by herbicides prior to seedling.

- Mulch tillage

The common objectives of a mulch tillage system are to leave crop residue to serve as mulch; some equipment is used to incorporate crop residues into the soil, the rest remains on the surface (Fig. 9. 4).

Fig. 9. 4 Mulch tillage.

- Strip tillage

In strip tillage systems, narrow strips are tilled and then planted with standard equipment. Where soils are compacted but subject to erosion, strip tillage is a good compromise because crops can be planted efficiently and grows well in the loosened soil of the tilled strips while the untilled portions of the field conserve soil and water and control weeds.

- Minimum tillage

Minimum tillage is a tillage type that leaves 15%-30% residue cover after planting or 500 to 1 000 kg/hectare of small grain residue equivalent throughout the critical wind erosion period. It involves considerable soil disturbance, though to a much lesser extent than conventional tillage; some crop residues are left on the soil surface and this is sometimes called reduced tillage.

- Ridge tillage

In ridge tillage, a small band of soil or ridge is tilled; the soil from the top of the ridge is mixed with crop residues between ridges and makes debris reducing soil erosion and water retention.

The differences between conventional and conservation tillage (including reduced and no-tillage) are best shown in Fig. 9. 5.

(2) Advantages and Disadvantages

Conservation tillage practices in agronomic crops were introduced over 50 years ago to conserve soil and water.

Crops grown without tillage use water more efficiently, the water-holding capacity of the soil increases, and water losses from runoff and evaporation are reduced (Fig. 9. 5). For crops grown without irrigation in drought-prone soils, this more efficient water use can translate into higher yields.

In addition, soil organic matter and populations of beneficial insects are maintained, soil and nutrients are less likely to be lost from the field and less time and

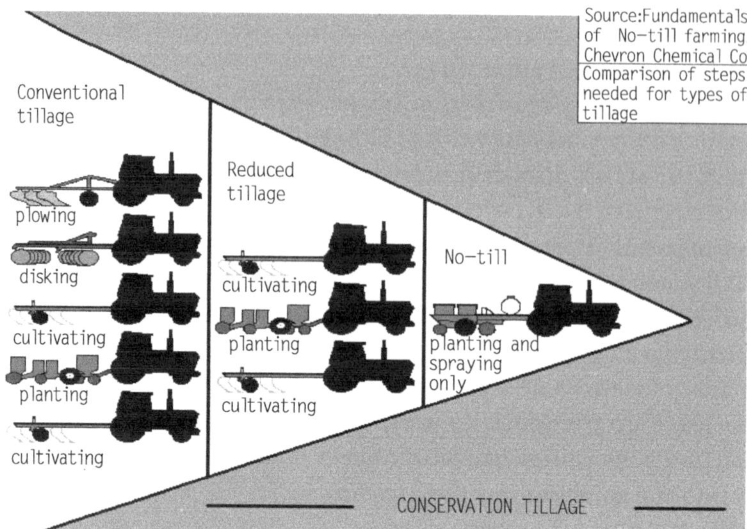

Fig. 9. 5 Comparison of conventional, reduced and no-tillage.

labor is required to prepare the field for planting. In general, the greatest advantages of reduced tillage are realized on soils prone to erosion and drought.

There are also disadvantages of conservation tillage. Potential problems are an increased possibility of soil compaction, flooding or poor drainage, delays in planting because fields are too wet or too cold, and carryover of diseases or pests in crop residue

Additional problems from residues may be caused by allelopathy and high C : N ratios. Allelopathic effects are most often seen when small-seeded vegetables, such as lettuce, are planted directly into rye residues. When the residues are incorporated, as in strip tillage, allelopathic substances break down relatively quickly and are usually not a problem.

When the amount of tillage is reduced, the stubble or plant residues are not completely incorporated, and most or all remain on top of the soil rather than being ploughed or disked into the soil. The new crop is planted into this stubble or small strips of tilled soil. Weeds are controlled with cover crops or herbicides rather than by cultivation. Fertilizer and lime are either incorporated earlier in the production cycle or placed on top of the soil at planting. Because of this increased dependence on herbicides for weed control and to kill the previous crop, the inclusion of conservation tillage as a "sustainable" practice could be questioned.

In vegetable crops, the difficulty of controlling weeds and the need for custom-built equipment have slowed the acceptance of conservation tillage practices. Commercial seeders which plant well into stubble have been developed for most agronomic crops, but are only now becoming available for vegetable crops.

Other relative disadvantages of conservation tillage in vegetables relate to the intensive nature of vegetable production. Since inputs are high in terms of seeds or transplants, fertilizers, pesticides and harvest expenses compared to agronomic crops such as corn and soybeans, the economic return must also be high.

Literatures cited in this chapter

Nyakatawa E. Z. , Reddy K. C. , and Lemunyon J. L. 2001. Predicting soil erosion in conservation tillage cotton production systems using the revised universal soil loss equation (RUSLE). *Soil & Tillage Research* 57: 213-224.

Tivy J. 1990. *Agricultural Ecology*, Harlow: Addison Wesley Longman Ltd.

Uri. N. D. 1999. An evaluation of the economic benefits and costs of conservation tillage. *Environmental Geology* 39 (3-4): 238-248.

Chapter 10 Erosion and soil degradation: "Keep your soil covered"

Learning objectives

1. Define the following terms accurately and succinctly:
   - Erosion
   - Geological erosion
   - Accelerated erosion
   - Cover crop, catch crop, break crop, smother crop
   - Underseeding
   - Crop rotation
   - Living mulches
2. Explain the differences among: sheet, rill and gully erosion.
3. Discuss the benefits and drawbacks of underseeding cereals with forages.
4. List and briefly describe the factors which contribute to the soil loss. Which of these can we control to limit soil loss?

Soil, the thin layer of the earth, fulfills fundamental functions in terms of life in general and particularly in terms of need and well-being of human societies. However, as the contradiction between the population on one hand, and the economy, society, resources and environment on the other has become gradually apparent, more and more demands are being imposed upon the soil by different human activities. As a result, land degradation is becoming more and more serious worldwide in the last decades. It is estimated that nearly 2 billion hectares of soil resources of the world have been degraded, and most (about 85%) soil degradation stems from soil erosion. Globally, soils are degraded in a variety of forms such as soil erosion, chemical deterioration and physical degradation.

The causes of land degradation are mainly anthropogenic and mainly agriculture related, such as excessive herding, reckless deforestation, agricultural mining, urban conversion, irrigation and pollution Additionally, soil degradation is root in the absence of any soil awareness, in all spheres of society, and the ignorance on conservation of soil. It is necessary for us to fully understand the types, development rules and consequences of soil degradation, so as to seek countermeasures to control soil degradation and improve soil quality.

10.1 Soil erosion

Soil erosion is detachment and transportation of soil from one place to another place and its deposition by the action of such natural agencies such as rainfall, flowing water, wind, glaciers, winds, temperature change, gravity, waves, and ice, or other natural forces, and anthropogenic factors. It is normally a natural process occurring over geological timescales, but it is increased by land misuse.

10.1.1 Causes of soil erosion

Soil erosion has many underlying factors, some induced by nature and some by humans. The major natural factors that can cause soil erosion can be stated as follow: Climatic factors include precipitation, evapotranspiration, temperature, wind speed & direction and seasonality, storm frequency. Geologic factors include gradient of the slope the sediment or rock type, its porosity and permeability, and whether the rocks are tilted, faulted, folded, or weathered. Biological factors include ground cover, its nature and extent, the type of organisms inhabiting the area. Besides natural causes of soil erosion, there are a lot of human causes of erosion as well. Human activities, such as faulty farming systems, deforestation caused by overgrazing, exploiting irrationally, clearance of land for agricultural purposes and construction, dam construction and mining activities and diversion of the natural course of river, are just a few among the various human activities is perhaps the most hazardous cause of soil erosion, which has increased over the last decade.

Generally, if in the similar vegetation and ecosystems, high-intensity precipitation, more frequent rainfall, more wind, or more storms are expected to lead to more erosion. Meanwhile, high sand or silt contents in soils and steep slopes in an area contribute to erodibility of soil, as do areas with highly fractured or weathered rock in an area. Porosity and permeability of the soil affects the speed with which the water can percolate into the ground. The more water moves underground, the less runoff is generated, reducing soil and water loss soils containing more clay contents are less easily to erode than those with sand or silt. However, it should be mentioned that atmospheric sodium has a huge impact on erodibility of clay.

The amount and type of ground cover factor is most subject to change. In an undisturbed forest, ground cover shelters soil from raindrop impact and slow surface runoff by a litter layer and an organic layer. In the forest, these two layers and the underlying soil are porous and highly permeable to rainfall. In generally, only large hailstorm events and the most severe rainfall will cause overland flow in a forest. If the trees are removed logging or by fire, infiltration rates become high and erosion low to the degree, the forest floor remains intact. Severe fires can lead to significantly increased erosion if followed by heavy rainfall. In the case of road building, the susceptibility of the soil erosion is easily increased. When the litter layer is removed or compacted.

Although erosion is a noticeable natural process, it is increased by human activities. For example, construction of roads increases impermeable of surfaces, which lead to soil streaming and ground loss. Fault agriculture system also accelerates soil erosion. Such as increase of field size, correlated to hedges and ditches removal. Meadows are in regression to the profit of ploughed lands; Spring cultures (sunflower, corn, and beet) surfaces are increasing and lead to more naked ground in winter; both use of herbicides and fertilization also increases the risks of erosion as well as new cultural practices. It is observed a gradual decrease of soil organic matter content in soils is in relation to chemical uses, as well as a decrease of soil biological activity. Lastly, Agriculture increases the risk of erosion through its disturbance of vegetation by way of tilling or plowing, overgrazing of animals, planting of a monoculture, land-use conversion row cropping and crop removal.

It is found that land that is used for agricultural crops production generally experiences an obviously greater rate of erosion than that of land under natural vegetation. It is more noticeable if tillage is used. Tillage not only reduces vegetation cover on the surface of the soil, but also disturbs both soil structure and plant roots, leading to detachment and transportation of soil. However, improved land use practices could reduce erosion in a certain extent. Using techniques in an area, such as terrace, cover crops, conservation tillage practices, and tree planting could prevent run down of the topsoil, being generally less erosive.

Vegetation removing from an area oriented by human activities, making the soil easily eroded. Logging can cause increased erosion rates due to soil compaction, exposure of mineral soil, for example roads and landings. However it is the removal of compromise to the forest floor that can lead to erosion rather than the removal of the canopy, because rain drops striking tree leaves coalesce with other rain drops creating larger drops. These larger drops fall again, reaching terminal velocity and strike the ground with more power, and the fall in the open. Terminal velocity of rain drops is up to about 8 meters. Forest canopies are usually higher than this, so leaf drop can regain terminal velocity. However, impact of the rainfall can be absorbed by the intact forest floor, with its layers of leaf litter and organic matter.

Overgrazing can diminish the ability of the vegetation to protect soil, causing increaseof erosion. Changes in the varieties of vegetation in an area also take an important role in erosion rates. Different kinds of vegetation cause different infiltration rates of rain into the soil. Forested areas have higher infiltration rates, so precipitation will result in less surface runoff, which erode. Instead much of the water will keep in subsurface flows, which reduce erosive action. Both leaf litter and low shrubs play important parts in the high infiltration rates of forest systems, the decrease of which can lead to higher erosion rates. Leaf litters also protect the soil from the impact of falling raindrops, which is a significant agent of erosion. What is more, the speed of surface runoff flows can be changed by vegetation. For instance, grasses and shrubs can also be instrumental in this aspect. Shifting cultivation such as slashes and burn method contribute to soil erosion in a large amount arras in the world. In generally, this causes the decline in fertility and lead to soil degradation.

According to research on soil erosion, rainfall amounts and intensities growth will causing rates of erosion increasing. Thus, erosion will increase, when rainfall amounts and intensities increase in many parts of the world as expected, only if we take action to keep up with soil. It is predicted that soil erosion will change if climate changes much for a variety of reasons. The most direct reason is the change in the erosive power of rainfall. Other reasons include: ① shifts in plant biomass production associated with moisture regime cause changes in plant canopy; ② temperature and moisture dependent soil microbial activity as well as plant biomass production rates cause changes in both plant residue decomposition rates, leading to changes in litter cover on the ground; ③ shifting precipitation regimes and evapo-transpiration rates cause changes in soil moisture, varying infiltration and runoff ratios; ④ soil erodibility changes due to soil organic matter concentrations loss in soils that lead to a soil structure more susceptible to erosion and runoff increasing due to increased soil surface sealing and crusting; ⑤ increasing winter temperatures casing a shift of winter precipitation from non-erosive snow to erosive rainfall; ⑥ melting of permafrost made changes between a previously non-erodible soil state and an erodible soil state; and ⑦ It is necessary to accommodate new climatic regimes due to shifts in land use.

10.1.2 Types of soil erosion

There are several ways to classify soil erosion. One distinction is between accelerated and geologic erosion. Another distinction is between gravity erosion, water erosion wind erosion and ice erosions.

(1) Geological erosion and Accelerated erosion

• Geological erosion

Geological erosion is natural levelling process that takes place without the influence of human activities. It usually occurs where soil is in its natural environment surrounded by its natural vegetation without human disturbance, being due to detachment and transportation by wind, water, or ice; by down-slope creep of soil and gravity; or by living organisms in the case of bio-erosion. It's a relatively a slow continuous process that often goes on unnoticed.

• Accelerated erosion

Soil erosion that occurs when people disturb the soil or natural vegetation (include grazing livestock, cutting forests for agriculture use, tearing up land for construction of mines, roads and buildings, or plowing hillsides, or other human activities) is called accelerated erosion. Accelerated erosion is often 10 to 10,000 times as destructive as geological erosion in many places, especially on sloping lands. Accelerated erosion is the most dangerous type and it needs concerted efforts through careful planning and implementation of appropriate control measures.

(2) Gravity erosion, Water erosion Ice erosions and Wind erosion

• Gravity erosion

Mass wasting, which also called mass movement is also considered to be one form of soil erosion. It is the natural process by which soil, rock and other material move downslope under the influence of gravity. As mass material moves from higher elevations to lower elevations, under effect of other eroding agents such as streams and glaciers, the materials moves even lower elevations. Mass-movement processes usually take place continuously on all slopes; some mass-movement processes are a slow moving, others are a slow moving, often with disastrous results. Any perceptible downslope movement of rock or sediment is considered to be in general terms as a landslide. However, landslides can be classified in a much more detailed way that reflects the mechanisms responsible for the movement and the velocity at which the movement occurs. One of the visible topographical manifestations of a very slow form of such activity is a screed slope.

Slumping on precipitous hillsides, which are occurring with distinct fracture zones, included materials like clay, once released, may move quite rapidly downhill. They will often show a spoon-shaped isotactic depression, in which the material has begun to slide downhill. In some cases, the slump is the result of water beneath the slope weakening it. In many cases it is simply caused by poor engineering along highways where it is a regular occurrence.

Surface creep is the slow movement of soil and rock debris due to gravity. And it is hard to observe except through extended observation. However, the term can also describe the rolling of dislodged soil particles 0.5 to 1.0 mm in diameter by wind along the soil surface.

• Water erosion

Removal and detachment of surface material due to the action of water is water erosion. The most ubiquitous form of erosion is water erosion. Water erosion is fundamentally a two-part process involving the detachment and transport of soil particles from the soil mass. There are several types of water erosion that can cause difficulties for topsoil.

Soil moves a few inches and usually is redistributed back over the surface soil. Rill erosion happens when runoff forms small channels that are several inches deep. Construction sites and sloping fields often show signs of rill erosion. Gully erosion starts when water accumulates and repeatedly flowers through narrow channels for long periods of time. Channels become deeper as the water removes the soil. Sheet erosion occurs when runoff travels over ground and moves particles that are dislodged by splash erosion. It is a gradual process and difficult to detect until it turns into rill erosion. Stream channel erosion begins as flows cut into the channel and make it deeper and continues until the channel reaches a slope. The channel will deepen further and the sides will begin to slough off, resulting in stream bank erosion. Controlling water erosion is done by maintaining proper plant growth, reducing tillage and direct seeding. Extreme measures for reducing water erosion are grassed waterways, a channel that is dug to help move water away down a slope. Grassed waterways are usually used on farms.

Rain splash erosion is the detachment and airborne movement of small soil particles due to the rain falls with high intensity. Behaving as little bombs, rain drops fall on exposed or bare soil, casing soil particles redistributed soil structure destroyed, resulting in surface crusting and lower infiltration. In generally, it is the first stage in the erosion process.

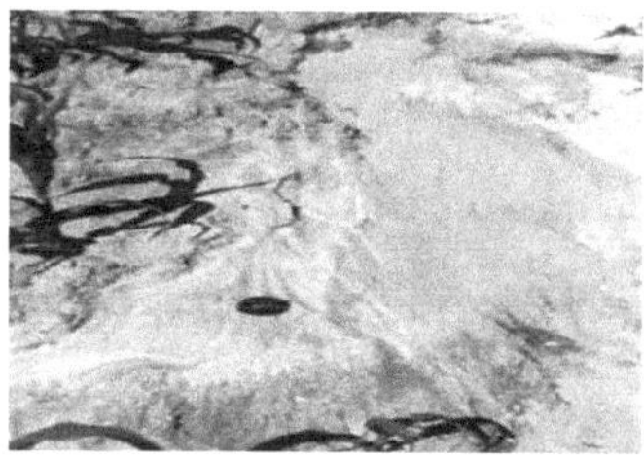

Fig. 10.1 Sheet erosion.

Sheet erosion refers to the detachment of soil particles by raindrop impact in both cultivated and non-cultivated environments, and their removal downslope by a shallow "sheet" of water flowing instead of in definite channels (Fig. 10.1). Sheet erosion accounts for large volumes of soil loss, although rarely seen.

In a sheet erosion process, soil particles are only transported, rather than detached. Particles of clay, silt and sand fill the soil pores, leading to infiltration reduction. Then overland surface flow of water begins due to the lowering of infiltration rates. When rainfall intensity is greater than infiltration, soil runoff takes place. Sheet erosion is a two-steps process. In the first stage, raindrop knocked soil particles into the air. The second is sheet floods-erosion, in which the loose particles are moved downslope by broad sheets of rapidly flowing water filled with sediment known as sheet floods. Sheet erosion is generally induced by cloudbursts, sheet floods commonly travel short distances and last only for a short time. Sheet erosion results in the loss of the finest soil particles which contain large amount of the available nutrients and organic matter.

Rill erosion refers to the development of ephemeral, small concentrated flow paths, which function as both sediment source and sediment delivery systems for erosion on hill slopes (Fig. 10. 2). Generally, where water erosion rates on disturbed upland areas are greatest, rills are active. When surface water (sheet erosion) concentrate into deeper, faster-flowing channels, the flow becomes deeper the velocity increases detaching soil particles and scouring channels up to 30cm deep. Flow depths in rills are typically on the order of a few centimeters or less and slopes may be quite steep. These conditions compose a very different hydraulic environment than typically found in channels of streams and rivers. Eroding rills evolve morphologically in time and space. The rill bed surface changes as soil erosion take place, which in turn alters the hydraulics of the flow. It is the hydraulics that is the driving mechanism for the erosion process, and therefore dynamically changing hydraulic patterns lead to continually changing erosion patterns in the rill. Thus, the process of rill erosion involves a feedback loop between flow detachment, hydraulics, and bed form. Flow velocity, width, depth, hydraulic roughness, friction slope, local bed slope, and detachment rate are time and space variable functions of the rill evolutionary process. Superimposed on these interactive processes, the sediment load, or quantity of sediment in the flow, has a huge effect on soil detachment rates in rills. As sediment load aggrandize, the ability of the flowing water to detach more sediment reduce. Rill erosion can be described as the intermediate process between sheet and gully erosion.

Fig. 10. 2 Rill erosion.

Gully erosion is an advanced stage of rill erosion where surface channels have eroded to the point where they cannot be removed by tillage operations. Gully erosion is responsible for removing vast amounts of soil, irreversibly destroying farmland, roads and bridges and reducing water quality by increasing the sediment load in streams. Gully initiation is thought to be a response to excessive water in the local environment caused by the removal of perennial vegetation.

Gully erosion, also called ephemeral gully erosion, an advanced stage of rill erosion where surface channels have eroded to the point where they cannot be removed by tillage operations. It often happens when water accumulates and repeatedly flowers through narrow channels for long periods of time. Channels become deeper as the water removes the soil. This is particularly noticeable in the formation of hollow ways, where, prior to being tarmacked, an old rural road has over many years become significantly lower than the surrounding fields (Fig. 10. 3).

Gully is enough deep that it would not be erased by cultivation, whereas rill erosion is easily smoothed by ordinary farm activities. The narrow gullies, or channels, ranging from 1 to 2 feet to as much as 75 to 100 feet, may be of considerable depth. In generally, gully erosion is not accounted for in the revised universal soil loss equation (USLE).

Fig. 10. 3 Gully erosion.

• Ice erosion

The movement of glaciers predominantly erodes by abrasion/scouring and plucking. In the abrasion process, debris in the basal ice scrapes along the rock surface, polishing and gouging the underlying rocks, while in the process of plucking glaciers cause pieces of bedrock to crack off and be incorporated in the flowing ice. These processes usually combine erosion and transport by a water network beneath the glacier.

Ice erosion is caused by movement of ice, typically as glaciers. Snow has potential energy when it is deposited in higher elevations. When ice and flows converted into energy of motion, a glacier that flows down slope becomes a powerful erosive agent. Plucking, abrasion and freeze thaw are three main process of glacial erosion Plucking takes place when melt water from a glacier freezes around lumps of cracked and broken rock. Glaciers can also cause pieces of bedrock to crack off, when the ice moves downhill. Abrasion takes place when rock frozen to the base and the back of the glacier scrapes the bed rock. As the bed rock surges forward, it moves large sheets of frozen sediment at the base along with the glacier. Freeze-thaw is when melt water or rain gets into cracks in the bed rock, usually the back wall. Combined with erosion and transport by the water network beneath the glacier, these processes leave moraines, drumlins, eskers, ground moraine (till), kames deltas, kames, moulins, and glacial erratics in their wake, especially at the end or during glacier retreat.

Cold weather leads to water trapped in tiny rock cracks to freeze and expand, breaking the rock into several pieces. Then, gravity erosion generally is induced to take place on steep slopes. The screed which forms at the foot of a steep mountainside is mostly formed from pieces of rock (soil) broken away by this means. It is a common engineering problem Morning thaws can drop hazardous rock pieces onto the road. So, rock cliffs are always alongside roads, because In some places, water seeps into rocks during the daytime, then freezes at night. Ice expands and causes the crack to get larger. Eventually, when the repetition in the forming and melting of the ice causes fissures the rock will break away.

• Wind erosion

Wind erosion is the physical wear and tear done to the earth's surface by wind. There are two main effects. First, wind causes small particles to be lifted and therefore moved to another region. This is called deflation. Second, these suspended particles may impact on solid objects causing erosion by abrasion (ecological succession) . Wind erosion generally occurs in areas, when there is reduction of vegetation, when soil surface crust is broken and organic matter in soil has decreased. It is hard to measure wind erosion, however drifts, bare soil, exposed plant roots and dust clouds can be seen as sighs of wind erosion. Although wind is a natural force of nature, there are strategies that minimize wind erosion. Vegetation conservation is necessary, without plants bare soil is vulnerable. Over-grazing and deforestation must be limited as soon as possible. Besides, trees and tall grasses can be made into field shelter belts, so as to provide some extra protection against wind erosion by reducing the wind velocity.

10.1.3 Effects

Soil erosion results in land infertility and eventually leads to desertification and devastating flooding. It is estimated that during the past half century, 5 billion hectares, 43% of the world's vegetated land, approximately 40% of the world's agricultural land is seriously degraded. Among them 3.6 billion hectares is of desertification mostly as a result of overgrazing. In the world, more and more, original topsoil has been displaced, mostly due to over cultivation, overgrazing, and deforestation. As more soil erosion occurs, a serous of undesirable effect has been place in agroecosystem. And the damage of soil erosion may be not immediately apparent, they are real and grow with time flying. When soil erosion happens very gradually it has minimal effect on the land as enough time would be there for the replacement with new soil. But accelerated erosion leads to detrimental effects. In general, soil erosion effects can be divided into two sides:

(1) On-site effects

The most obvious effect of soil erosion is the removal of valuable topsoil. Crop sowing, growth and harvest are directly affected through the loss of natural nutrients and applied fertilizers with the soil. Seeds and plants can be disturbed or completely removed from the eroded site. And the quantity of essential nutrient loss of eroded soil is unmoral high. Erosion selectively removes organic matter and fine mineral particles, while leaving behind mainly relatively less active, coarse fractions. It is shown the organic matter and nitrogen in the eroded soil to be 5 times as high as in the original top soil. Pesticides may also be carried off the site with the eroded soil. What is worse, erosion can spread plat disease organism from the soil to plant foliage and from a higher- to a lower-lying field. Besides, Soil erosion can cause great damage to environment as increased loss of soil can affect the growth of natural vegetation and in turn this leads to conversion of fertile land into a desert. The loss of soil has a vital effect on soil quality, structure, texture and stability. The breakdown of aggregates and the removal of smaller particles or entire layers of soil or organic matter can weaken the structure and even change the texture. Textural changes can in turn affect the water-holding, water infiltration; water ran out, capacity of the soil, making it more susceptible to extreme condition such a drought.

(2) Off-site effects

Off-site effects of soil erosion are not always as apparent as the on-site effects. Eroded soil, deposited down slope can inhibit or delay the emergence of seeds, bury small seedling and necessitate replanting in the affected areas. Sediment can be deposited on down slope properties and can contribute to road damage.

In addition, soil erosion brings a huge amount of economic loss. Sediment movement in soil erosion which reaches streams or watercourses can accelerate ban erosion, clog drainage ditches and stream channels. Silt in reservoirs, reduce downstream water quality, cover and fish spawning grounds. Pesticides and fertilizers, frequently transported along with the eroding soil can contaminate or pollute downstream water sources and recreational areas. Besides, due to huge amount of suspended soil particles in water it retains the heat and raises the water temperature, which affects the living organisms. Finally, blowing sands in wind erosion may bring damages to roads, drainage ditches, municipal water system and other essential expensive maintenance and buildings, as well as fruits and foliage of crops in neighbouring field.

10. 2 Land degradation

Human's devastating exploitation on land leads to its degradation and pollution, which may result in land degradation. According to researches, land degradation will remain an important global issue for the 21st century because of its adverse impact on agronomic productivity, the environment, and its effect on food security and the quality of life. The importance of land degradation among global issues is enhanced because of its impact on world food security and quality of the environment.

Land degradation refers to a human-induced or natural process with reduction or loss of potential ecological functions or potential production capacity of soil, resulting from land uses or from a process or combination of human activities and habitation patterns. These functions or potential production capacity refer to bio-mass production (nutrient, air, heat and water supply, root support for plants) to filtering, buffering, storage and transformation. Land degradation not only affects soil quality for agriculture, but also has implications for the urban environment, pollution and flooding. Land degradation results from mismanagement of land and thus deals with two concatenate, complex systems: the natural ecosystem and the human social system. The success or failures of resource management programs depend on interactions between the two systems determine.

10. 2. 1 Types of land degradation

Acidification, contamination, desertification, erosion, or salination are major forms of land degradation.

While soil acidification of alkaline soils is beneficial, it leads to land degradation when soil acidity lowers crop productivity and increases soil vulnerability to contamination and erosion. Soil acidification is a naturally occurring process in humid climates that has long been the subject of research, whose findings suggest acid precipitation effects. Soils are often initially acid because their parent materials were acid and initially contain less basic cations (calcium, magnesium, potassium and sodium) . Acidification happens when these elements are removed from the soil profile by normal rainfall or the harvesting of forest or agricultural crops. Soil acidification is accelerated by the use of acid-forming nitrogenous fertilizers and by the influences of acid precipitation.

Soil contamination or soil pollution is caused by the presence of xenobiotic (human-made) chemicals or other alteration in the natural soil environment. Soil contamination at low levels is always within soil capacity to treat and assimilate. Many waste treatment processes rely on this soil capacity of treatment and assimilate. Exceeding treatment capacity can soil biota damage and soil function limitation. Derelict soils occur where industrial contamination or other development activity damages the soil to a certain degree that the land cannot be used safely or productively. Remediation of derelict soil uses principles of geology, physics, chemistry, ecology, and biology to degrade, attenuate, isolate, or remove soil contaminants and to restore soil functions and values. Techniques involve leaching, air sparging, chemical amendments, phytoremediation, bioremediation, and natural attenuation.

Desertification is an environmental process of ecosystem degradation in arid and semi-arid regions, often due to various factors: including climatic variations and human activities. Desertification is one of the world's most serious global environmental problems. It takes place worldwide in dry lands. It is estimated that some 10%-20% of dry lands are already degraded, the total area influenced by desertification being between 6 and 12 million square kilometers. However, it is droughts that cause desertification are a common misconception. Droughts are common in arid and semiarid lands. Well-managed lands can recover from drought when the rains return. Soil management tools, which include maintaining soil nutrient and organic matter levels, reduced tillage and increased cover, help to control erosion and maintain productivity during periods when moisture is available. While continued land abuse during droughts is obviously increases land degradation. It is found that desertification is accelerated by increased population and livestock pressure on marginal lands.

Soil erosion is caused by wind, water, ice, movement in response to gravity, and human activities. Although these processes may be simultaneous, erosion is distinguished from weathering. Erosion is an intrinsic natural process, but in generally it is accelerated by human land use. Poor land use practices include deforestation, overgrazing, false farming activities and improper construction activity. However, Soil erosion also can be limited and controlled by improved management environmentally friendly technologies techniques like limiting disturbance during construction, avoiding construction during erosion prone periods, terrace-building, intercepting runoff, use of erosion suppressing cover materials and planting trees or other soil binding plants.

Soil salination is the accumulation of soluble mineral salts near the surface of soil that it leads to degradation of soils and vegetation. Consequences include corrosion damage, reduced plant growth, Soil salination happens due to a combination of natural and human caused processes. It usually caused by the capillary flow of water from saline ground water. Arid conditions are easier to induce salt accumulation. This is especially obvious when soil parent material is saline. Irrigation of arid lands is the most problematic part in salination. Where the rate of surface evaporation is high, the problem by moistening soil will deteriorate by the irrigation and causing water to be drawn from deeper levels as water evaporates from the surface. The evaporation of pure water leaves the salts behind, allowing them to accumulate. When they reach a certain concentrations, they are toxic to many plants thus sterilizing the land. And, rapid salination occurs when the land surface is within the capillary fringe of saline groundwater. Soil salinity control includes flushing with higher levels of applied water in combination with tile drainage.

Deforestation has led to a severe shortage of fuel wood and building materials in many areas. Crop residues and animal manure, which were previously returned to the soil to add valuable nutrients, are having to he burnt for fuel.

The region's grasslands are also being destroyed. A matter of great economic importance since grazing is the largest land use in Asia. Grasslands are under attack from over-intensive grazing and from the incursion of marginal agriculture which often fails and then leaves a residue of degraded land. In a converse of logic, as grazing areas decrease, livestock numbers often increase. Grazing areas are often located at the source of important catchment areas, influencing downstream agricultural and settlement so the cost of their deterioration is high.

The problem of the "vanishing grasslands" is particularly serious in countries where grazing lands are used communally, but livestock are private property. It is virtually impossible to stop overgrazing in areas where grazing rights are not defined. No nation in the region has an effective plan of action to meet this challenge.

Land degradation is also altering hydrological conditions where vegetative cover is removed, the soil surface is exposed to the impact of raindrops which causes a sealing of the soil surface. Less rain then infiltrates the soil. Runoff increases, stream flows fluctuate more than before, flooding becomes more frequent and extensive, and streams and springs become ephemeral. These conditions encourage erosion, as a result, sediment loads in rivers are increasing, dams are filling with silt, hydro-electric schemes are being damaged, navigable waterways are being blocked and water quality is deteriorating. In several parts of India, the potential life of reservoirs has been more than halved by sedimentation rates that are ten times higher shall those assumed by the designers.

10.2.2 Consequences of land degradation

Recently, increasing human population has caused a great strain on the world's soil systems. The combination of large population, fast industrializes and concentrated agriculture has led to serious deterioration of soil, along with disaster effects.

(1) Yields impact

The most important on-farm effects of land degradation are declining potential yields.

Many soils suffer from various types of degradation that can ultimately result in reduction of their productive potential. The threat of degradation may also be reflected in the need to use a higher level of inputs in order to maintain yields. Serious degradation sometimes results in temporary or permanent abandonment of some plots. In generally, degradation is one of the most important factors in inducing farmers to convert land to lower-value uses, for example, less-demanding cassava may be replace for maize, fallow periods may be lengthened, cropland converted to grazing land, or grazing lands converted to shrubs or forests.

(2) Natural disasters

Mud flows, floods are responsible for the death of many living beings each year's. In addition to reduced land fertility, land degradation may also results in sediment-loading of rivers and lakes, of reservoirs, smothering of wetlands and coral reefs, and clogging of water intakes and waterpower turbines. It makes rivers unnavigable, increases the destructiveness and frequency of floods, health problems or property damage caused by wind-eroded soil, and loss of habitat due to devegetation or degradation of agricultural lands. On the other hand, nonfarm groups may also create externalities that contribute to farmland degradation through their use and management of natural resources. Examples include urban sprawl, soil pollution from industry or waste management, diversion of local water sources to distant or non-agricultural users, and rules to protect biodiversity that restrict agricultural land use and management.

(3) Deterioration of the water quality

Contamination of drinking water by agricultural chemicals; diversion of water sources from other users by irrigation.

The contribution of nitrogen and of phosphorus and the increase in the turbidity of water can lead to eutrophication. Soils particles in surface waters are also contaminated by agricultural chemicals and by some pollutants of industrial pollution source, urban non-point source pollution and road source pollution (such as heavy metals) . The ecological impact of agricultural inputs (such as chemical fertilizers and pesticides) is known but not easy to evaluate because of the mass of the products and their broad spectrum of action.

(4) Biological diversity loss

According to some study, the term degradation or desertification also refers to irreversible decrease in the biological potential of the land. Sometimes, overgrazing, and nutrient loss, mainly causing environmental problems and loss of biodiversity. Soil degradation often involves the disappearance of the climax vegetation, the decrease in animal habitat, thus directly and indirectly results in a biodiversity loss and animal extinction.

10.3 Keep your soil covered

Problems of soil erosion can be fought, and certain practices can result in soil enhancement and rebuilding. Even though methods for reducing erosion are simple, they are often not chosen because these practices outweigh the short-term benefits. Rebuilding is hardly needed through the improvement of soil structure, addition of organic matter and limitation of runoff. However, these techniques will never totally succeed to restore a soil (and the fauna and flora associated to it) that took more than 1000 years to build up.

Conservation-tillage farming is one of the most effective technologies of soil conservation. Conservation tillage is especially suitable for erosion-prone cropland. In some agricultural areas it has become more common instead of traditional mouldboard plowing. Conservation tillage methods include no-till, strip-till, ridge-till and mulch-till. Terracing, contour farming, strip cropping, alley cropping, establishing windbreaks, and gully reclamation are also ways to soil conservation.

Soil erosion can dramatically and quickly destroy soil productivity. Thus the most important soil management issue is preventing soil erosion. There are many ways to conserve soil and manage moisture. Organic agriculture is concerned with using proper rotations, nourishing the soil, and building nutrients and organic matter using on-farm resources. For instance, in a Pennsylvania, organic rotations with forage and green manure legumes added soil organic matter to levels 3 to 5.5 times higher than levels found in commonly-used conventional corn and soybean rotations. According to some studies, organic agriculture can increase soil organic matter dramatically and quickly. Organic agriculture makes for increase the health of the soil and its moisture-holding capacity. Some other conventional agriculture, using minimum-tillage and direct seeding, can also help increase soil fertility and protecting scarce moisture.

Serious consequences to land degradation call for improved incentives for farmers to take care of their land and improving knowledge to ground management. It is crucial to keep your soils covered. Why? Avoid the downward spiral of soil degradation. How to prevent land degradation erosion by soil cover? How does that help? It provides a barrier between the wind and the rain that might be coming to move the soil. The following recommendations frequently aim to protect and improve agricultural lands.

10. 3. 1 Cover crops

Cover crops, a category of green manure, are the crops that are grown for the herbaceous material, and serve to manage soil fertility, soil quality, water, weeds, pests, diseases, biodiversity and wildlife in agroecosystems, realize the goal of soil erosion reduction, nutrients conservation, and organic matter maintenance. Cover crops are of interest in sustainable agriculture as many of them not only improve the sustainability of agroecosystem attributes, but also indirectly improve qualities of neighbouring natural ecosystems. A cover crop is often grown when a cash crop is not being grown or it might be grown between the rows of a cash crop. Cover crops can also be catch crops, smother crops, break crops, allelopathic crops, bee habitats and nitrogen-fixing crops. One of the best cover crops is perennial forage. Forages are crops like clover, timothy, alfalfa. Having good soil cover with forage crops is a generally clever way to conserve soil.

10. 3. 2 Catch crops

In agriculture, a catch crop is a fast-growing crop, acting to "catch" nutrients to protect soil from erosion and minimizes nutrients loss through leaching, which is grown simultaneously with, or between successive plantings of a main crop. It is grown after a crop like wheat or potatoes are harvested; instead of leaving the ground bare, a catch crop enriches the soil by adding organic matter. By using catch crops, such as grain (millet) one can catch nutrients and maintains them in the root zone available for the next cash crop that is grown.

10. 3. 3 Break crops

A break crop is a green manure grown in order to break either life cycle of weed, pest or the disease in a crop rotation, aiming is to optimize yields of the primary crops and to reduce the use, and cost of pesticides. For example, if you were to grow oats and then you want to grow corn the next year, crops might catch similar diseases. However grow a different crop in between those two, the disease cycle will be broken. Another common example is maize (corn) as a break crop, which is typically rotated with cotton plantations. What is more, a break crop can help achieve nitrogen fixation, playing an important role in agriculture land.

10. 3. 4 Smother crops

Smother crops is a term refers to green manure used to reduce weed germination in succeeding crops. For this purpose, smother crops are usually characterized by its extremely vigorous and rapid growth and is usually chosen with specific weeds in mind. The straw residue from smother crops (i. e. rye, ryegrass, etc.) can inhibit early season germination of weeds such as common lamb's quarters, common purslane and redroot pigweed by 75% or more. Another smother crops are crops like buckwheat that grow quickly with big leaves and it will smother weeds i. e. , it will inhibit weed growth. Ryegrass and fall rye are also very good smother crops. Smother crops are also effective in suppression of many winter annual weeds such as henbit and chickweed.

10. 3. 5 Allelopathic crops

An allelopathic crop produce natural chemical toxins can be used to inhibit the growth of weeds and plants that don't want in the system. Allelopathic crops can provide significant weed control in no-till cropping systems. They compete with them for light, moisture, and nutrients, to suppress weeds during the growing season such as rye and yellow sweet clover.

10. 3. 6 Bee habitats

Cover crops, especially the nitrogen-fixing legumes provide good bee habitats. In any region, they produce honey, which is very helpful to crop growing. Bee habitats supply habitual residence where bees can go and pollinate. Forages, with lots of flowers, are an excellent habitat, encouraging the living conditions for bees and you want lots of bees to pollinate fruits and other crops. Besides, other examples are sweet clover and buckwheat.

10. 3. 7 Nitrogen-fixing crops

Legumes cover crops are almost the most important green manure crops, especially the forage legumes such as clovers. These crops fix nitrogen from the air, add organic matter to the soil and make it available to succeeding crops. It should be noted that a crop like red clover can be classified as several categories of cover crop; i. e. , break crop, catch crop (has a deep taproot, N-fixing crop, and bee habitat. Good nitrogen-fixing crops, such as deep-rooted alfalfa, vetch or sweet clovers are able to loosen compacted subsoil.

10. 3. 8 Underfeeding

Underseeding is when you have a cereal crop such as oats or barley and it is seeded with a perennial forage mix that might be something like clover or timothy at the same time with the same equipment. Why is it called underseeding? In General, the term of underseeding can be stated as follows: The annual crop such as barley or oats grow quickly, produce ground cover quickly and shelter the developing perennial crop as it emerges. While the growing speed of perennial crops are much more slowly and appeared to be underneath the annual crops. When the annual crop is harvested, the perennial forage mix will continue to grow, at a time when the soil would otherwise be vulnerable to erosion and weed encroachment.

10. 3. 9 Rotation

Rotation is an agricultural practice of growing different crops each successive season (year) on a same acreage in sequence. Rotation is found to be the most successful agricultural practice in limiting the impact of biotrophic pathogens. Potatoes, as such a valuable crop, tend to be grown in a close rotation, and grow year after year in a few cases. However, most farmers use this anymore. Sometimes potatoes are grown one year and something else the next year, so that it is a two-year rotation. According to researchers, crop rotations usually lead to high crop production that is far superior to what is reached when planting the same crops in the same location year after year. Crop rotation is also helps to minimize the impact of pests on the various crops, as well as to promote sustainability and biodiversity by avoiding synthetic fertilizers, pesticides and herbicides.

10.3.10 Living mulches

Living mulch is referred to as cover crops, but they grow at least part of the time simultaneously with the crop. Cover crops are generally under sown with a main crop or crop interplant with the primary purpose of improving soil structure, aiding nutrition or avoiding pest attack, and weed suppression, and regulation of soil temperature. Living mulches grow for a long time with the main crops, whereas cover crops are always included into the soil or killed with herbicides. Living mulch, as a suitable way of maintaining vegetation cover is important for preventing soil erosion, nitrate leaching and weed emergence in slowly developing crops like maize. Perennial crops are especially suited to Living mulches use such as fruit where self-reseeding is an advantage.

Literatures cited in this chapter

Coleman D. C., Odum E. P., and Crossley D. A. J. 1992. Soil biology, soil ecology, and global change. *Biology and Fertility of Soils* 14: 104-111.

Eswaran H., Lal R., and Reich P. F. 2001. "Land degradation: an overview". Responses to Land Degradation. Proc. 2nd International Conference on Land Degradation and Desertification. New Delhi, India: Oxford Press.

He X. B. and Jiao J. R. 1998. The flood and soil erosion in Yangtze River. *Water Policy* 1: 653-658.

Johnson, D. L., Ambrose S. H., Bassett T. J., Bowen M. L., Crummey D. E., Isaacson J. S., Johnson D. N., Lamb P., Saul M., and Winter-NelsonA. E. 1997. Meanings of environmental terms. *Journal of Environmental Quality* 26: 581-589.

Lu Y. C., Watkins K. B., Teasdale J. R., and Abdul-Baki A. A. 2000. Cover crops in sustainable food production. *Food Reviews International* 16: 121-157.

Omafra S., Wall G., and Baldwin C. S. 1978. Soil Erosion-Causes and Effects, Queen's Printer for Ontario [EB/OL] http: // www. omafra. gov. on. ca/english /engineer /facts /87-040. Htm. 2011-05-07.

Pimentel D. and Kounang N. 1998. Ecology of Soil Erosion in Ecosystems. *Ecosystems* 1: 416-426.

Scherr S. J. and Yadav S. 1996. Land degradation in the developing world. Implications for food, agriculture, and the environment to 2020. Food, Agriculture and the Environment Discussion Paper 14, International Food Policy Research Institute, Washington.

Snapp S. S., Swinton S. M., Labarta R., Black J. R., Leep R., Nyiraneza J., and O'weil K. 2005. Evaluating cover crops for benefits, costs and performance within cropping system niches. *Agronomic Journal* 97: 1-11.

Chapter 11 Resources and wastes in agroecosystems

Learning objectives

1. Understand the differences between agroecosystem resources and wastes.
2. Identify the different composition and uses of animal and plant manures.
3. Discuss the uses of biogas.
4. Explain the process, factors affecting and techniques for managing compost.
5. Describe four agricultural uses of compost.

11.1 What are resources and wastes in agroecosystems?

Chapter 3 describes agroecosystems in great detail, as shaped by biotic and abiotic factors. These relatively open systems produce a flow of materials (outputs) for human use. In order to maintain ecological processes and an energy balance while simultaneously increasing the conversion efficiency of energy, an agroecosystem requires tremendous amounts of energy subsidies from society. From an energy flow analysis standpoint, wastes and by-products accompany every production process in agroecosystems, by way of resource utilization (Fig. 11.1). The ecological (biotic and abiotic) determinants along with human energy subsidies (ecological and economic) act as resources for agroecosytems. These resources, listed in Tab. 11.1, can be categorized into physical, biological, socioeconomic and cultural inputs. The wastes and by-products of the production system are almost all the same (i. e. respiration gives off CO_2 and wastes, and CO_2 accompanies fossil fuel burning, Fig. 11.1).

11.1.1 Resources in agroecosystems

(1) Genetic resources

Genetic resources of crop plants and microorganisms play an integral role in sustainable agriculture. Agriculture almost always results in a loss of genetic diversity, through natural and human selection, and more so in high-income countries. Unforeseen problems may include a reduced germplasm base and genetic pollution in crops. However, efforts to combat the loss of genetic resources can be seen all around the world. For example, Japan is experimenting with agri-aquaculture and other countries have focused on improving methods of nutrient recycling.

(2) Soil resources

Soil resources, another important aspect to sustainable agriculture, require good nutrient management. Correcting micronutrient deficiencies and promoting compost production and use help match the nutrient supply to the nutrient needs of the crop. The use of information technology and remote sensing in precision agriculture helps farmers make precise measurements of field conditions and record any changes that may occur. Precision agriculture is useful on a broad scale, and therefore most suitable for large, capital intensive, individual farms in countries such as the USA. Like-

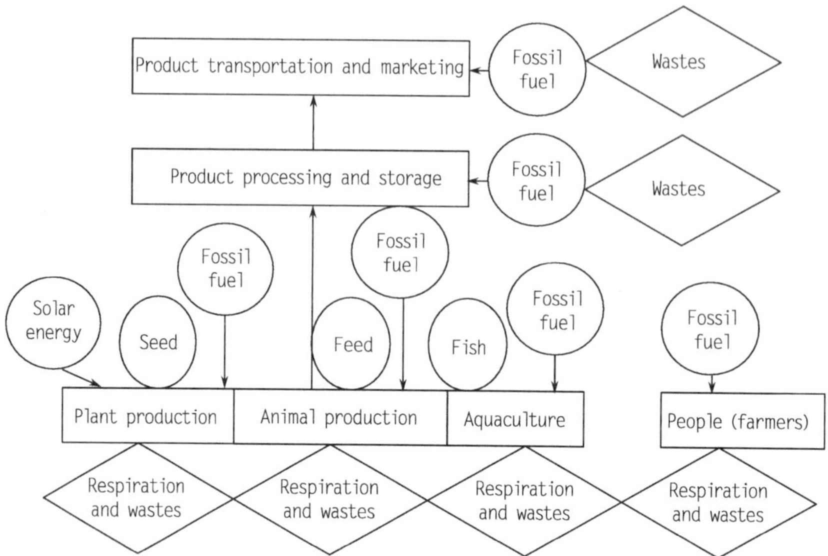

Fig. 11. 1　Agroecosystem processes are dependent on various resources producing wastes.

wise, precision agriculture can detect overall environmental stress over many small farms around Asia.

Tab. 11. 1　Resources in agroecosystems

Types of resources	Classification of resources
Physical	Radiation (solar energy)
	Temperature (heat)
	Rainfall, water supply (moisture)
	Soil condition
	Slope
	Land availability
Biological	Natural vegetation and interaction amongst
	Soil biota and interaction amongst
	Agrobiodiversity (crop, livestock and poultry and other domesticated microorganisms) and their interactions
Socioeconomic	Labour and draft forces
	Fertilizer and manure
	Pesticides, insecticide and herbicides
	Burning fossil energy
	Monetary capital
Cultural	Traditional knowledge
	Ideology in agroecosystem management
	Historical events

(3) Water resources

Sustainable agriculture demands the on-going availability of water resources. In many countries water is considered a scarce resource, limiting the food supply available to those countries. Currently in high-income countries, little incentive exists for farmers to adopt water-saving strategies because the cost of water and the cost of wasting water costs very little to the user. However, in poorer, more densely populated countries, irrigation is needed for agriculture and costs too much for poor farmers on small farms. Scientists and policy makers in many Asian countries realize that water availability will help alleviate poverty and malnutrition, typical goals in national development. Government subsidies or reducing water fees for low-income users can give poor farmers an advantage to sustain themselves, which in the long term should cost less to the government and its people.

11.1.2 Waste in agroecosystems

Ecologically, every production process produces wastes. However, recycling and reuse can extend supplies of some non-renewable resources, such as metallic minerals. True waste and environmental degradation occurs when the rate of use of a renewable resource exceeds the sustainable yield. Therefore, recycling economics is an essential component of managing agroecosystems.

11.1.3 Resource and waste managing issues

Success of agroecological initiatives that improve resource and waste management depends on farm diversification, better use of local resources, emphasis on human capital enhancement and community empowerment, better access to markets, credit and income generating activities (Altieri, 2002). Underlying factors for successful agroecological improvements of activities demonstrated in Fig. 11.2 include (Altieri, 2002):

- Appropriate technology adapted by farmers' experimentation
- Social learning and participatory approaches
- Good linkages between farmers and external agencies, together with the existence of working partnerships between agencies
- Presence of social capital at local level. In most cases, farmers adopting agroecological models achieve significant levels of food security and natural resource conservation

11.2 Animal and plant manures

Manure is organic matter that adds fertility to soil through the addition of nutrients such as nitrogen and bacteria, for use as organic fertilizer in agriculture. In this section we will discuss three main classes of manures used in soil management: animal manure, plant manure and biogas.

11.2.1 Animal manures (brown manures)

Typically, animal manure refers to feces used for organic fertilizer. Manure from different animals may have different qualities, nutrient content and composition according to animal diet and maturity of the animal, and therefore require different application rates. Farm slurry and farmyard manure refer to common forms of animal manure. Farm slurry, or liquid manure, occurs as a result of more intensive livestock rearing that uses concrete or slats rather than straw bedding. Farmyard manure uses

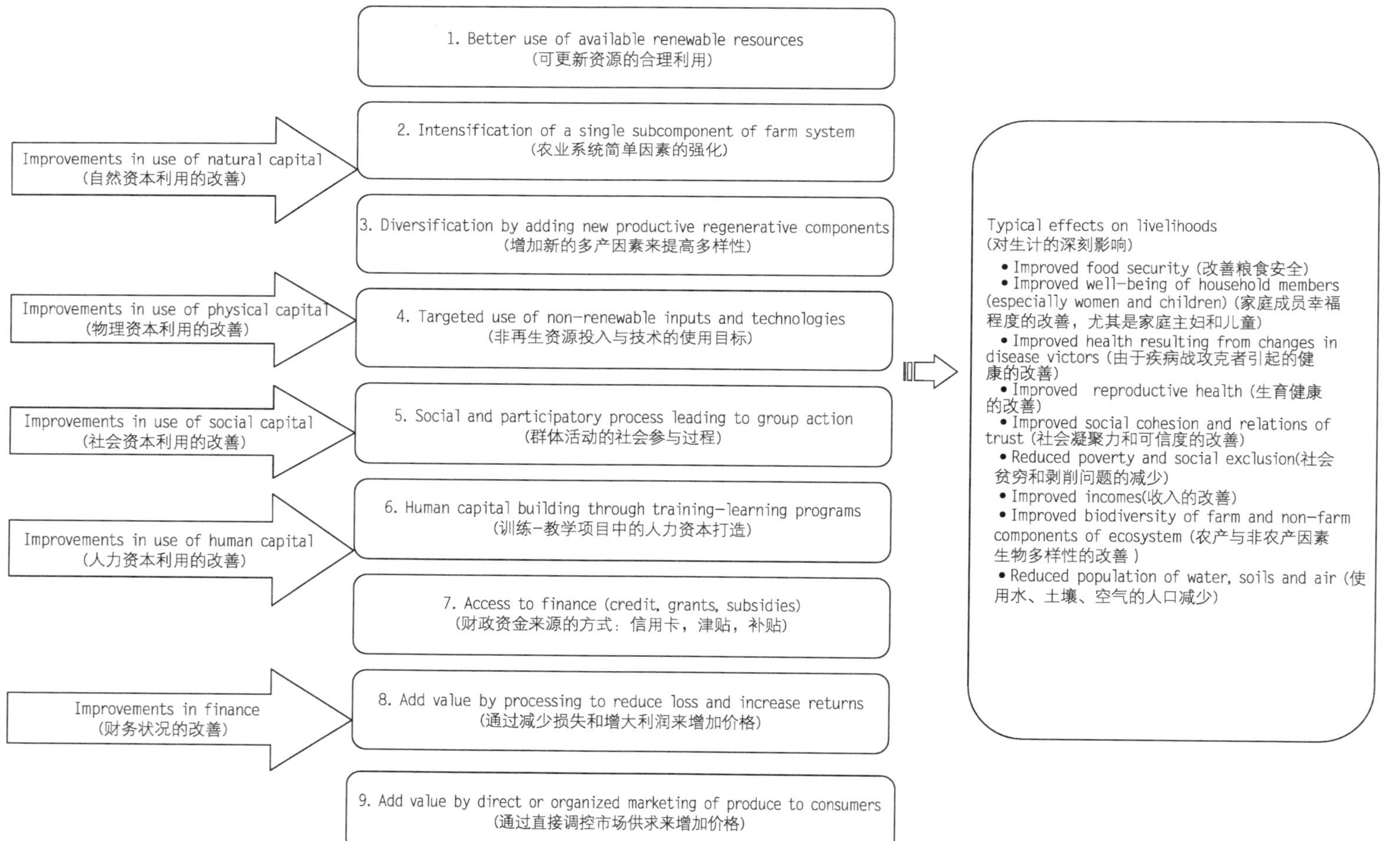

Fig. 11.2 Resource entry points for sustainable agroecosystem improvements (Altieri, 2002).

straw bedding to absorb feces and urine, and therefore may contain plant material. Many types of animal manures also contain other animal products such as wool shoddy (and other hair), feathers, blood and bone.

Animal dung is an example of animal manure that has been used for agricultural fertilizer for centuries. Animal dung improves soil structure to hold more nutrients and water, promotes soil microbial activity to improve plant nutrition, and adds nitrogen and other nutrients to assist in plant growth.

Generally farmers spread manures from pigs and cattle across a field with a manure spreader. However, manures from human sewage or intensive pig farming slurry may have particularly unpleasant odors. In these cases, manure is usually knifed (injected) directly into the soil to reduce release of the odor.

11.2.2 Plant manures (green manures)

Plant manure refers to crops grown for the sole purpose of increasing soil fertility through ploughing them into the soil, incorporating nutrients and organic matter. Different plants incorporate different nutrients into the soil. Leguminous plants such as clover for instance, fix nitrogen using Rhizobia bacteria in specialized nodes in the root structure. Other plant manures may include the contents of the rumens of slaughtered ruminants, spent hops (left over from brewing beer) and seaweed.

11.2.3 Biogas (marsh gas in Chinese)

Biogas, or marsh gas in China, is a biofuel produced from the biological breakdown of organic material in the absence of oxygen. Biogas is a useful resource for both agricultural production and producing energy, linking an ecological gap between waste and resource.

A biogas plant is effective manure for fertilizing crops, found in both liquid and solid form. Biogas manure may be a good substitute for fertilizer or raw animal manure, which contains pathogens and odours. Often marsh gas facilities are constructed in combination with other agricultural enterprises in northern areas of China, producing so-called "four in one" patterns. Such facilities are encouraged by the Chinese government in rural areas for multiple utilizations, living energy substituting for coal, nature gas and electricity and good manure for fertilization.

Biogas undergoes anaerobic digestion or fermentation of biodegradable materials such as plant biomass, manures, sewage sludge, living waste (mostly food waste), green waste and energy crops. Biogas, comprised primarily of methane (55%-75% depending on the facilities) is 21 times more potent as a greenhouse gas than carbon dioxide. Fortunately, methane can be combusted with oxygen in the air for agricultural production and for producing hydrogen and carbon dioxide in rural areas. This release of energy can be used as a low-cost fuel source in any country for heating purposes, in waste management facilities to run heat engines, or to generate either mechanical or electrical power. Biogas can be compressed, much like natural gas, and used to power motor vehicles. Biogas is also a renewable fuel, so it may qualify for renewable energy subsidies in some parts of the world.

In the USA, methane biogas from cow manure would be sufficient to produce 99 million metric tons of greenhouse gas emissions, 4% of the greenhouse gases produced by the USA (Cuellar, 2008). The digester, an airtight circular pit made of concrete with a pipe connection, directs manure into the pit, usually directly from the cattle shed. Wastewater fills the pit to a required quantity and the gas pipe connects to the kitchen fireplace through control valves. The simplicity in implementation and use of cheap raw materials in villages makes this facility one of the most environmentally sound energy sources for rural needs. Vermiculture (the use of worms to produce compost) compliments this process to further enhance the slurry produced by the biogas plant for use as compost, but is also a popular practice worldwide.

11.3 Compost: Making and using it

11.3.1 What is compost?

Composting refers to the natural process of organic matter decomposing by microorganisms under controlled conditions (FAO) . The stabilized compost product serves as humus, a soil amendment or fertilizer (Fig. 11.3). In a farm setting, compost usually consists of a combination of food waste and animal waste undergoing aerobic decomposition.

Fig. 11.3 A final compost product from a student group on the campus of Fujian Agriculture and Forestry University (picture by Wang, 2007).

Compost improves the physical, chemical and biological properties of soil, resulting in the following improvements. The soil ① becomes more resistant to stress (i. e. drought, disease and toxicity), ② improves the crop's ability to uptake plant nutrients, and ③ has vigorous microbial activity, enhancing the active nutrient cycling capacity. These improvements ultimately help farmers reduce cropping risks, produce higher yields and spend less capital on inorganic fertilizers. Compost offers other on-farm benefits. Compost reduces mass, volume and doors, destroys pathogens, kills weed seeds, improves transportability and nutrient qualities, decreases pollutants, available for land application when convenient and acts as a saleable product. A few disadvantages of on farm compost exist as well. Compost also increases the loss of ammonia, involves time and labour, and requires initial and operating costs for equipment and marketing for sale.

11.3.2 The composting process

Composting may be categorized according to the type of decomposition process undergone. Anaerobic composting refers to decomposition in the absence, or in limited supply, of oxygen. Biofuel, discussed earlier, engages in anaerobic decomposition. Anaerobic composting has strong odors, phytotoxicity, leaves weed seeds and pathogens intact and often takes a long time to complete the process. While anaerobic composting requires little labour and loses very few nutrients, the drawbacks just mentioned often outweigh the merits. Generally, people chose to adopt aerobic composting methods.

Aerobic composting takes place in the presence of ample oxygen and occurs in two stages: an active stage and a curing stage. During the active stage microorganisms feed on organic matter and consume oxygen while producing heat, carbon dioxide, ammonia and water vapour. A management plan for maintaining proper temperature, oxygen, moisture and other factors affecting the composting process is important in the active composting stage to achieve complete decomposition of all the biodegradable matter. During the curing stage microbial activity slows down and nearly stops as the process reaches completion, resulting in a relatively stable, organic end product.

Tab. 11.2 Basic composting methods (Manure Composting Manual, Government of Alberta, 2005)

	Bin	Passive windrow	Active windrow	Aerated static windrow	In-vessel channel
General	Low technology, medium quality	Low technology, quality problems	Active systems most common on farms	Effective for farm and municipal use	Large-scale systems for commercial applications
Labour	Medium labour required	Low labour required	Increases with aeration frequency and poor planning	System design and planning important. Monitoring needed	Requires consistent level of management/product flow to be cost efficient
Site	Limited land but requires a composting structure	Requires large land areas	Can require large land areas	Less land required given faster rates and effective pile volumes	Very limited land due to rapid rates and continuous operations
Bulking agent	Flexible	Less flexible, must be porous	Flexible	Less flexible, must be porous	Flexible
Active period	Range: 2-6 months	Range: 6-24 months	Range: 21-40 days	Range: 21-40 days	Range: 21-35 days
Curing	30+ days	Not applicable	30+ days	30+ days	30+ days
Height	Dependent on bin design	1-4 metres	1-2.8 metres	3-4.5 metres	Dependent on bay design
Width	Variable	3-7 metres	3 - 6 metres	Variable	Variable
Length	Variable	Variable	Variable	Variable	Variable
Aeration system	Natural convection and mechanical turning	Natural convection only	Mechanical turning and natural convection	Forced positive/negative airflow through pile	Extensive mechanical turning and aeration
Process control	Initial mix or layering and one turning	Initial mix only	Initial mix and turning	Initial mix, aeration, temperature and/or time control	Initial mix, aeration, temperature and/or time control, and turning
Odour factors	Odour can occur, but generally during turning	Odour from the windrow will occur. The larger the windrow the greater the odours	From surface area of windrow. Turning can create odours during initial weeks	Odour can occur, but controls can be used, such as pile insulation and filters on air systems	Odour can occur. Often due to equipment failure or system design limitations

Composting processes range from extremely simple methods practiced by individuals at home, semi-intensive methods practiced by farmers on their land, to large-scale operations practiced industrially in cities. Composting systems use low technology as well highly sophisticated, automated technology. Tab. 11.2 describes five basic composting methods: bins, passive windrows, active windrows, aerated static windrows and in-vessel channels. People practice composting primarily as a waste management strategy or to produce a soil amendment, but these two objectives complement each other.

11.3.3 Factors affecting aerobic composting

(1) Aeration

Aerobic composting requires large amounts of oxygen, ideally an oxygen concentration greater than 10% to avoid anaerobic conditions with suppressed aerobic microorganism growth. Aeration is indispensable to the composting process, adding fresh air throughout the material, reducing odours, removing excess heat, and encouraging complete decomposition of carbon to release carbon dioxide rather than methane. Heat removal is particularly important in warm climates where the risk of overheating and fire exist. While less than 5% oxygen concentration will lead to anaerobic conditions, too much aeration can lead to other consequences. Namely, excessive oxygen concentrations will result in ammonia loss with high nitrogen (and therefore low C : N ratio).

(2) Moisture

Moisture content supports the metabolic activity of microorganisms and indirectly supports the supply of oxygen. Composting materials should maintain moisture content between 45%-65% by weight to ensure adequate moisture without limiting aeration. Bacterial activity slows down with moisture content below 40% and ceases entirely below 15%. Moisture content over 60% leads to leached nutrients, reduced porosity, increased odours and a slowed decomposition rate. In practice, desirable compost pile moisture content would start around 50%-60% and finish around 30%.

(3) Nutrients

The composting process requires adequate levels of carbon, nitrogen, phosphorus and potassium. Composting converts these nutrients from raw farm organic materials (i. e. manure, livestock mortalities) to stable forms with a lower likelihood of nutrient loss through volatilization and leaching. The C : N ratio is especially important among the required nutrients. An optimal C : N ratio of raw materials ranges from 25 : 1 to 30 : 1 with an acceptable range between 20 : 1 and 40 : 1, because microbes need at least 20-25 times more carbon than nitrogen to remain active. Microorganisms use carbon for energy and nitrogen for protein and reproduction. Ratios higher than 40 : 1 limit microorganism growth slowing the decomposition process. Ratios less than 20 : 1 underutilize nitrogen potentially losing nitrogen to the atmosphere as nitrous oxide or ammonia. The stable end product of composting should contain a C : N ratio between 10 : 1 and 15 : 1.

(4) Temperature

Temperature changes in composting piles indicate changes in microbial activity. To destroy pathogen viability, temperatures should remain above 55°C for minimum two weeks. To eliminate weed seeds the temperature should remain above 62°C, however microorganisms will begin to die around 70°C. During the active composting stage higher temperatures result from vigorous microbial activity. With each 10°C increase in temperature, biochemical reaction rates nearly double. To regulate temperature, regularly turn and aerate compost piles.

(5) Lignin content

The complex chemical structure of lignin, one of the main constituents of plant cell walls, makes it highly resistant to microbial degradation (FAO). Lignin enhances porosity thereby improving conditions for aerobic composting and reducing nitrogen loss. However, lignin may also higher the C : N ratio worsening porosity and prolonging composting time. Maintaining an adequate lignin content can create more favourable composting conditions if managed correctly.

(6) pH value

Adequate pH levels for microorganisms range between 6.5 and 7.5. Most animal manures pH ranges between 6.8 and 7.4 before major changes occur in the decomposition process. Lowered pH (higher acidity) may result from the temporary release of organic acids. Heightened pH (higher alkalinity) may result from the production of ammonia from nitrogenous compounds.

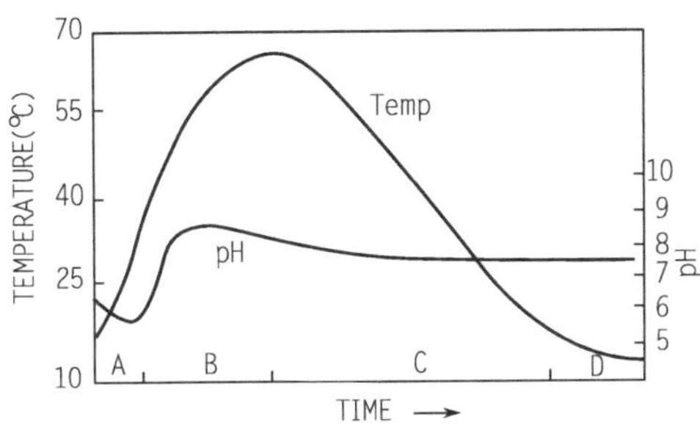

Fig. 11.4 Temperature and pH phases of composting. A: Mesophilic, 10-40℃; B: Thermophilic, 40-65℃; C: Cooling, 65℃ to ambient; D: Maturing (curing)

Of all the factors listed above, regulating temperature and pH are the most important (Fig. 11.4).

11.3.4 Techniques for managing the composting process

Composting under different climatic and material conditions with varying biological, physical and chemical properties requires different technical applications. Every compost pile needs different handling, whether the composition differs slightly or significantly. The following section provides you with techniques for effective aerobic composting, but keep in mind to alter specifications to each pile's needs.

(1) Improved aeration

As stated above, compost must receive sufficient oxygen to allow aerobic microorganisms to turn raw materials into a stable end product. Pile size, porosity of material, ventilation and turning practices all help improve compost aeration.

In high piles, anaerobic zones occur near the centre, slowing the overall composting process. In small piles, heat loss occurs quickly and sometimes fails to achieve adequate temperatures to kill pathogens and weed seeds. Porous materials should be kept in loose piles, limiting heavy weight on top in larger piles. Climate must also be taken into consideration; in cold climates minimize heat loss by creating larger piles, in warm climates reduce pile sizes to avoid overheating and potential fires.

Incorporating ventilation techniques complements efforts to optimize pile size. Ventilation holes supply more air to oxygen deficient areas of the pile, generally in the centre. The Chinese rural method of compost ventilation employs bamboo poles deep into the pile for 24 hours.

The technique of turning the compost pile results in a uniform distribution of air, prevention of overheating and killing of microbes. The Chinese rural composting pit method reduces a composting time of six to eight months to three months by turning

Fig. 11.5 Turning the pile at FAFU (pictured by Wang, 2007).

the pile three times throughout the maturing process. Worldwide, different methods include turning just once to turning once every day. However, too frequent turning may lower temperature and slow the composting process altogether. (Fig. 11.5)

(2) Inoculation

Some compost piles require inoculum organisms to enhance microbial activity, even after improving pile aeration. Inoculation, commonly using fungi, allows for rapid composting and composting of weeds. "Effective microorganisms" or EM, offers an affordable choice for resource-poor farmers.

(3) Other measures

Supplemental nutrition, shredding the pile and adding lime to compost piles are other methods that facilitate aerobic composting. Supplementing nitrogen, phosphorus, sugar or amino acids often compliment the techniques mentioned above, boosting microorganisms initial activities. In particular, modifying a high C : N ratio can significantly improve the composting process. Shredding the pile to downsize increases the surface area available for microbial action whilst providing better aeration. Adding lime weakens the lignin structure enhancing the microbial population, but can also result in a higher pH value.

(4) Vermicomposting

Another type of low temperature composting is vermiculture. Vermiculture means artificial rearing or cultivation of worms (earthworms) and the technology is the scientific process of using them for the betterment of human beings. Vermicompost is the excreta of earthworm, which is rich in humus. Earthworms eat cow dung and other farm wastes, pass it through their bodies and convert them into vermicompost. The municipal wastes: non-toxic solid and liquid waste of the industries and household garbage's can also be converted into vermicompost in the same manner. Earthworms not only convert garbage into valuable manure, but also keep the environment healthy. Conversion of garbage by earthworms into compost and the multiplication of earthworms are simple processes and can be easily handled by the farmers (http: //agri. and. nic. in/vermi _ culture. htm).

11.3.5 Agricultural uses of compost

The stabilized product from composting serves as a rich and important source of nutrients commonly used in modern agriculture. The organic material is used as a soil amendment, growing medium component, organic mulch, topsoil replacement or an amendment for soil blending.

(1) Soil amendment

Incorporating compost into the soil as a soil amendment may be used for topdressing crops such as turf. Principally, compost as a soil amendment is valued as a soil conditioner rather than a fertilizer. Most compost has a fertilizer ratio in the range of 1-1-1; that means it is 1% nitrogen, 1% phosphate and 1% potash-a very low analysis fertilizer. Typically, commercial fertilizers such as soluble chemical fertilizers, have a much higher analysis, such as 10-10-10 or 10-15-30. Although compost is a very low analysis fertilizer, the value lies in its slow release. Nutrients in a slow release fertilizer are not very soluble and do not release rapidly, therefore, they do not leach or get lost easily. Soil may benefit from a slow release fertilizer by having the ability to retain more nutrients in the soil. A slow release fertilizer is very advantageous in certain situations, but it is unable to provide the same effects as quickly as most commercial fertilizers. However, compost has tremendous value as a soil conditioner; it improves the physical properties of the soil by improving the soil's water-holding capacity, tilth, water infiltration and nutrient holding capacity.

(2) Growing medium component

Using compost as a growing medium, potting mix and potting soil is the second major use of compost in modern agriculture. This product may be bagged for commercial sale as a growing medium for plants. Compost provides a loose, friable (separate texture and structure), moisture retentive, high water-holding capacity, good growing medium for plants while suppressing or inhibiting plant diseases. Using compost to suppress diseases is particularly attractive to organic farmers, who by definition cannot use fungicides, insecticides or herbicides, and has become a very active area of research right now. Compost, also used as organic mulch, offers the benefits of suppressing weeds, conserving moisture and adding organic matter to the soil.

(3) Topsoil replacement/amendment for soil blending

An increasingly popular use of compost employs compost as a component of topsoil replacement, a soil blending mix. Compost has a very high volume market, as it can accept large amounts of compost around construction sites. Significant soil disruption occurs when building a house, restoring a dilapidated building or other industrial activities. Compost can help restore vegetation, a very difficult task, to those locations where soil has been stripped and removed.

In summary, resources and wastes continuously flow into and out of agroecosystems. Diversity is an important aspect of resources, especially when pertaining to genetic, soil and water resources. However, this chapter focuses mostly on the handling of wastes, and furthermore how to turn wastes into resources. Using animal and plant manure as organic fertilizer adds fertility to soil through the addition of nutrients such as nitrogen and bacteria. Biogas is a useful resource for both agricultural production and producing energy, acting as a low-cost fuel source. Finally we discuss composting raw materials, outlining the process, factors affecting the process, and techniques to improve aerobic composting. Composting offers huge benefits as a source of nutrients and waste control for home gardening to a farmyard to an industrial operation.

Literatures cited in this chapter

Alberta Agriculture, Food and Rural Development. 2005. *Manure Composting Manual*. Alberta, Canada.

Altieri M. A. 2002. Agroecology: the science of natural resource management for poor farmers in marginal environments. *Agriculture, Ecosystems and Environment* 93: 1-24.

Cuellar A. D. and Webber M. E. 2008. Cow power: the energy and emissions benefits of converting manure to biogas, Environmental Research Letters, (3): 1-8.

Food and Agricultural Organization. 2004. On-farm composting methods 'Composting process and techniques'. Rome.

Chapter 12 Natural capital accounting: Ecological footprint and emergy analysis

Learning objectives

1. Explain the need for natural capital accounting.
2. Identify the key differences between ecological footprint and emergy analysis.
3. Discuss a national ecological deficit in terms of EF and available bio-capacity.
4. Explain the term carrying capacity.

Society depends on earth's natural capital for ecological services and natural resources. Earth has a specific carrying capacity, a maximum population size (of all species) that its natural capital can sustain indefinitely. Society can achieve sustainability when humanity can maintain the planet's natural capital stocks and live within earth's natural carrying capacity. A natural capital accounting framework allows society to calculate the difference between earth's natural capital production (on many scales) and human consumption. We will discuss two major accounting frameworks recognized globally: the ecological footprint concept introduced by Rees and Wackernagel (1996), and emergy analysis introduced by H. T. Odum (1988, 1996, 2000).

12.1 Ecological footprint (EF): concept and calculation

12.1.1 The EF concept

An ecological footprint uses existing data to track national economies of energy and resource throughput, translated into biophysical units. Every person on Earth depends upon and occupies a certain amount of nature to live. Ecological footprints measure the quantity of a natural capital required to live, at an individual, regional, national or global scale. The ecological footprint of over 52 nations has been calculated, representing the critical point between natural capital requirements of a defined population or economy and its biologically productive areas (Holmberg, et al., 1999; Wackernegal, et al., 1996). Calculations of ecological footprint rely on two key assumptions: ① people can track most resources consumed and wastes generated, and ② flow of resources and wastes can translate into biologically productive areas.

12.1.2 Methods for calculation

Ecological footprint calculations assess ecological productivity, resource production and trade previously measured by national statistical institutes. National assessments generally use data available through the United Nations. Footprint measurements are expressed as biological productive areas with world average productivity, allowing for comparable footprints among nations and contrastable measurements with the globally available biological capacity.

EF calculations analyze resource and energy flows on spreadsheets, composed of three main sections: consumption of biotic resources and its sub products, commercial energy analysis, and footprint and ecological capacity. Consumption of biotic resources and its sub products consists of over 19 resource types, yield, production, import, export and waste between production and final consumption. Detailed flow trade analyses mitigate duplication errors from raw materials to processed trade items. The second section focuses on the footprint of commercial energy consumption, separately analyzed from other resources. Energy consumption accounts for a significant portion of a country's footprint and detailed, accurate data usually exists for each country separate from UN statistics. Fossil gas, liquid fossil fuel, solid fossil fuel, firewood and hydropower contribute to the overall commercial energy consumption footprint of a nation. Afterwards, the national energy balances are corrected for trade. The third section identifies national footprint and ecological capacity. Arable land, pasture, forest and seas make up bio-productive areas. Results are presented as per capita figures; this number multiplied by the population gives the total national footprint. A national ecological deficit refers to an area where the ecological footprint exceeds the available ecological capacity. 35 of the 52 countries analyzed run on a national ecological deficit, meaning the available natural capital that people rely on will not sustain those people forever, under existing behaviour and technologies.

12.1.3 Analysis

EF offers an inexpensive, quick natural capital appraisal of a country's ecological footprint. This measure helps nations determine the magnitude of need to improve sustainability. However, limitations of data do exist. Increasing the accuracy of freshwater area use, absorption of waste products and contaminants along with incorporating areas of extreme environments may create an even more accurate account of the global ecological footprint.

12.2 Emergy analysis

Emergy measures the work of nature and humans in generating products and services with a science-based evaluation system that produces a common measurement representing both environmental values and economic values (Odum, 1996). Emergy refers to the amount of one type of energy directly or indirectly used up in transformations to generate a flow and storage (Zhao et al., 2005). A high emergy value of a product or service implies high-energy requirement to make that produce or service. An "emjoule", or emergy joule refers to a unit of emergy. Generally, emergy is expressed in solar emjoules, or seJ.

$$\text{Emergy} = \text{available energy of item} \times \text{transformity}$$

Emergy analysis determines how items transform from raw units to solar emergy, the total number of input flows and the total emergy driving a process. Different indices can be evaluated and applied to aspects of sustainability. Tab. 12.1 offers an expression and significance of four emergy-based indices: emergy investment ratio, emergy yield ratio, environmental loading ratio and index of sustainability.

Tab. 12. 1 Emergy-based indices (Zhao et al. , 2005)

Indices	Expression formula	Signification
Emergy investment ratio (EIR)	$F/(N+R)$	The ratio of emergy F fed back from outside the system to the indigenous emergy inputs (N + R)
Emergy yield ratio (EYR)	Y/F	The ratio of the emergy of the output Y divided by the emergy of those inputs F to the process that are fed back from outside the system under study
Environmental loading ratio (ELR)	$(F+N/R)$	The ratio of purchased F and non-renewable indigenous emergy N to free environmental emergy R
Index of sustainability (ESI)	EYR/ELR	The emergy yield ratio divided by environmental loading ratio

12. 3 Modified method of natural capital accounting

Ecological footprints compare human demands with nature's available capital through an inexpensive and quick natural capital appraisal. EF offers a measure of ecological consumption for use as a tool to promote policy and planning for sustainability, as well as an assessment of progress. Emergy analysis links ecological and economic systems, giving a quantitative measure of resources used to develop a product. The emergy method analyzes flows in an ecosystem, evaluating rational use of natural resources (Zhao et al. , 2005). A modified method of natural capital accounting enhancedecological footprint calculations with emergy analysis. In this method, emergy assessments are converted into space equivalent numerical values. This three-step method translates the demand of natural resources and supply of natural services into more understandable and quantifiable terms.

Step 1: Calculate human consumption based on ecologically productive areas and amount of natural supplies.

Step 2: Translate human consumption amounts with emergy analysis into common emergy units. Five sources of renewable emergy are considered in calculating total emergy of a region, including sun, wind, chemical energy in rain, geopotential energy in rain and earth cycle energy (Zhao et al. , 2005).

Step 3: Divide emergy amounts by emergy density to derive ecological footprint and carrying capacity.

In summary, natural capital accounting provides a framework to measure ecological flows and services on a regional and national scale. Quantifying human consumption and ecological space provides a common language for society to work towards sustainability. Ecological footprint calculations, emergy analyses and methods of some combination thereof are important for simplifying complex resources and patterns into understandable terms. While limitations exist for each method of calculation, these techniques provide a strong foundation for humanity to begin to determine Earth's carrying capacity and the rate at which ecological services are depleting.

Literatures cited in this chapter

Holmberg J. , Lundqvist U. , Robèrt K. , and Wackernagel M. 1999. The Ecological Footprint from a Systems Perspective of Sustainability. *International Journal of Sustainable Development and World Ecology* 6: 17-33.

Odum H. T. 1988. Self-Organization, Transformity, and Information. *Science* 242: 1132-1139.

Odum H. T. 1996. *Environmental Accounting: Emergy and Environment Decision Making*. New York: John Wiley & Sons, Inc.

Odum H. T. 2000. *Handbook of Emergy Evaluations Folios: A Compendium of Data for Emergy Computation Issued in a Series of Folios; Folio #2: Emergy of Global Processes*. Gainesville, FL: Center for Environmental Policy.

Wackernagel M. and Rees W. E. 1996. *Our Ecological Footprint: Reducing Human Impact on the Earth*. Gabriola Island, BC: New Society Publishers.

Wackernagel M., Onisto L., Bello P., Linares A. C., Falfan I. S. L., Garcia J. M., Guerrero A. I. S., and Guerrero M. G. S. 1999. National natural capital accounting with the ecological footprint concept. *Ecological Economics* 29: 375-390.

Zhao S., Li Z. Z., and Li W. L. 2005. A modified method of ecological footprint calculation and its application. *Ecological Modelling* 185: 65-75.

Unit 4 Sustainable Production Systems

Chapter 13 Domestic livestock systems

Learning objectives

1. What difficulties did hunter-gatherers face?
2. What is domestication?
3. How did domestication allow for an increase in human population?
4. Is domestication exploitation? What's your opinion?
5. Discuss at least five recent examples of domestication (or "part-domestication?") .
6. Define the following terms:
   - Meat
   - Feedlot
7. Discuss the reasons for and against the consumption of meat by humans.
8. List the nutritional benefits and deficiencies of meat in a human diet.
9. Describe the production methods used in producing:
   - Ranched cattle
   - Beef on mixed farms
   - Beef in dairy herds
   - Pork
   - Meat chickens
10. Explain the effect of size of meat production businesses on the economy, environment and rural society.
11. List the most popular forms of meat in the retail system.
12. What was the original role of salting, smoking and curing of meats?

13.1 Domestication and evolution of agriculture

Domestication (from Latin "Domesticus")or taming is the process whereby a population of animals or plants, through a process of selection, becomes accustomed to human provision and control. A defining characteristic of domestication is artificial selection by humans. Domestication is also defined as the process of establishing a relationship between people and a plant or animal in which the plant or animal is no longer "wild" but instead lives in association with people, for at least part of its life cycle, and provides some benefits to people. By contrast, exploitation is defined as a relationship between two organisms in which only one organism benefits, while the other is harmed in some way.

Plants domesticated primarily for aesthetic enjoyment in and around the home are usually called house plants or ornamentals, while those domesticated for large-scale food production are generally called crops. A distinction can be made between those domesticated plants that have been deliberately altered or selected for special desirable characteristics and those domesticated plants that are essentially no different from their wild counterparts (assuming domestication does not necessarily imply physical modification). Likewise, animals domesticated for home companionship are usually called pets while those domesticated for food or work are called livestock or farm animals.

There were not any domestic animals 10,000 years ago as we understand them today, nor probably any domestic crops or field or garden crops. The human population of the earth was much smaller than it is now. It is more than six billion now; comparatively, in those days it is estimated that there were approximately one million people total on the earth.

What would people have been eating at that time? Because they existed in the wild, our remote ancestors probably lived by hunting and gathering. In other words, they would gather wild fruits, wild berries and vegetables growing in nature. They would also be hunting wild land animals; they would fish for fish if they could catch those; they would probably raid birds' nests for eggs. What might be a difficulty making a living in that way? One thing is that they would probably have to keep moving because they would soon eat up all that was available in their vicinity. Finding enough food would be a problem, thus producing the necessity of having to keep moving. When they moved, they would sometimes encounter plants and animals with which they were not familiar; some would be toxic or just not good for health. How did they determine what was good and what was bad? Mostly it was by trial and error. It was probably safer to try a new animal food than to try a new plant type due to the propensity for plants to produce toxins for defense against predation.

It would be natural to attempt to develop an alternative technique. In a hunter-gatherer society, probably hunger would have been the main limiting factor to numbers; people would often have been close to starvation and died thus limiting the size of the human population. Coming forward from that time, probably two of the most important inventions, the domestication of crops and animals were made in those times. The scenarios could be imagined as following, one of our distant ancestors, probably a woman, trying to get an edible plant to grow in a convenient place, a garden she set up for example in a greater quantity than it did naturally. Domestication of crops was one of the most important discoveries or inventions ever. Again another of our distant ancestors perhaps was taking pity on a young animal that had become separated from its mother. At first maybe this was a kind of pet, but later some of these pets would have developed maturely, that must be a start of domestication of animals. Over the centuries there must have been many unsuccessful attempts of such kinds of domestications, more and more plants and animals became adapted to being domesticated. Some of those attempts did work and those lucky tries gave us the crops and the domestic animals that we have today. An obvious example would be the cereal crops. Cereals are grasses and they were developed from wild grasses in Asia and Central America. These domesticated grasses are now our most important food sources.

Some domestication of plants and animals was done in prehistoric times, some have been done more recently; e. g. , many ornamental plants are fairly recent selections from wild species and people are still developing new ornamentals today.

As for domesticated animals, probably the dog was the first domestic animal anywhere in the world. Some farm animals have only recently been persuaded to adapt to human control. One example of recent domestication for farming is the eland. The eland is the largest species of antelope and in Kenya and some other east African countries there are now large eland ranches where the eland was captured from the wild and persuaded to at least put up with being controlled by humans. In the former Soviet Union, some of the southern areas, there are also some eland ranches. In Atlantic Canada, there are a number of deer farms and most of those deer on deer farms are fairly recent domestications, perhaps white-tailed deer. In New Zealand, there are many recently domesticated red deer farms or ranches. Two other examples of recent domestication took place in Prince Edward Island of Canada around 1900 are mink and fox. The first successful farming of mink and fox were done by a couple of pioneers in 1900.

Domestication of plants and animals led to agriculture. One consequence of domestication of plants and animals was a big increase in the human population. The relationship between domestic animals and people can be explained by the ecological terms of words "symbiosis" and "exploitation", "symbiosis" means benefits to both sides by living together , while, "exploitation" means only benefit to humans. Consider cattle for an example; people eat cattle and take milk from them, and use their skins for jackets or shoes or purses. Meanwhile people do give them something in return by protecting them from other predators, giving them food, growing crops for them and giving them shelter by building them barns or windbreaks.

Socially, many farmers have a close relationship with their animals; for example, the relationship between people and horses or dogs in those kinds of relationships, it may be a bit unequal but there is give and take on both sides. Dogs and humans get on particularly well; for some reason, these two species suit each other and they can develop close bonds. The dog is a very versatile animal; there exists an avalanche dog or drug-sniffing dogs at airports, or sheep dogs or seeing-eye dogs. Dogs can do a lot of things very well and people make use of their superior abilities, superior to us in many of these situations. Most dogs seem satisfied with the trade-off in terms of their care and the relationship with their owner.

Some "domestic" animals are wild animals that have only a casual contact with humans. Sometimes people who enjoy sport fishing stock a lake with fish, trout or some other fish that are good to catch; people can perhaps scarcely claim that they are domestic but they are in a closer relationship than the wild fish, albeit not a relationship to the liking of the fish. Those fish are not domestic but stepping away from being wild fish and toward being domestic species. Consider another example of Eiderdown; eiderdown comes from the eider duck that lives in Iceland and a number of other places. This bird eats shrimp and small fish in the sea and it nests on the shore. The duck will line its nest with down, the fluffy feathers plucked from its own body and these eider feathers, this material is one of the lightest and best heat insulators known. Eiderdown is very high on the list of materials with a very high heat insulation value. People use eiderdown from these ducks in products like parkas, sleeping bags and comforters. In Iceland people go and steal some of the down from the birds' nests and the birds then replace it. If people get too greedy and steal too much then the birds move away. People are exploiting the ducks but in return we are offering them something; in Iceland, humans mount a 24-hour guard on the nesting grounds complete with rifles to keep away other predators, mainly foxes. It is an arrangement with some benefits in both directions. It's not pure "exploitation" but a form of symbioses.

Another instance of animals that are domestic but only barely so is mussels. There are quite a few mussel farms in Prince Edward Island and many of them are family businesses run with a small boat. The mussel is a shellfish; it's a type of filter-feeding mollusc. It draws a current of sea water through it and filters out tiny particles (plankton) which it then eats. Mussel farmers hang plastic socks in the sea, kind of a net that stays down in the water most of the time, the baby mussels attach to net and then they grow, a nice surface to settle on. Eighteen months later they have grown into big mussels, and they are ready for harvest. The farmer hoists the nets up and takes off the mussels.

Oysters are also filter-feeding shellfish. Oyster farmers do more for the oysters than the mussel farmers do. Oyster farmers rear the young oysters as well as growing the bigger ones, therefore it is said that farmed oysters are more domestic than the mussels. Oysters feed on algae and the oyster farmers grow algae to feed the young shellfish. Baby oysters are grown in tanks, with water circulating and as they grow they are put into pearl nets, these are mesh bags. These are put into the sea and then they filter feed naturally. As the oysters grow, farmer eventually move them to a different container called a lantern neck, it looks a bit like a lantern and again is lowered into the sea and again the animals will filter feed. The oysters reach market size in three or four years.

Another recently domesticated animal is the pine marten for utilizing the high quality fur. They are cute but they also have very sharp teeth . They are semi-wild animals; you have to wear heavy gloves and take a lot of precautions dealing with them. Getting wild animals like pine marten to breed in captivity is often difficult and is often one of the main obstacles to domestication. People may find out what the animals like to eat in order to feed them successfully; however, it is most important to find the way their breed, otherwise one cannot keep domestic animals on an ongoing basis. Only recently can people manage to get the marten bred indicating that they are adapting well to domestic life in captivity.

What do people feed the fur animals, what would they be eating typically? Fur animals are quite often fed waste from fish plants or slaughterhouse by-products or eggs which are cracked and broken. To a large extent the fur industry is a recycling industry in Atlantic Canada; they are usually near places where there is or was quite a lot of fishing. In Nova Scotia, dig by County is the main fur-growing area because that is also a fishing area. The fish by-products, the heads and guts go to feed mink or other fur animals.

Many of the domesticated animals are either birds or mammals. Sometimes they are very highly domesticated and some of them cannot survive by themselves in the wild; a domesticated turkey has been selected for traits that make it unsuitable for survival outside the barn. They don't have the skills and the physical conformation to survive by themselves.

However, some domesticated animals actually can survive in the wild. There are a number of animals which were once domestic but have returned to the wild and we call these feral animals. For example, there are feral horses on Sable Island, south of Nova Scotia in Canada. Sable Island has wild horses which were originally domestic and have gone wild. In many places there are islands with feral goats on them. These goats were originally put there by people, now they take care of themselves. While the horses are standard bred and are used mostly for harness racing. There are horses which were developed for doing heavy work, land cultivation, pulling heavily loaded carts. Most of those applications have been superseded by trucks and tractors but the Clydesdale and other draught breeds still exist, some for work purposes and some for display.

What is the common use of animal urine? It is usually used as a fertilizer to supply N, P and K for crop needs. Urine is normally a way in which nitrogen is cycled back from animals to plants, most of time the horse urine is being collected for much more specialized purpose, namely extracting hormones; this is a mare that has just given birth to a foal. There are mares in the barn with ropes attached to the rear end of the mare and a rubber tube coming down collecting urine from the mare. When she urinates it goes into that rubber tube. When mares are pregnant they excrete estrogen in their urine, a hormone. Pregnant humans don't do that, pregnant cows don't do that, pregnant dogs don't do that but pregnant horses do. It is a peculiarity of horses. This estrogen is actually a useful medical drug and some farms collect urine from the pregnant mares and send it to a chemical company where the estrogen is extracted and used for medical uses.

In Canada most poultry are kept indoors partly because for protection against predators, partly because there is less labor required feed and managing them, and also the farmers can supply extra light. If we supply extra light to the birds, in the case of egg-laying birds, they will lay eggs for longer periods of the year. Birds in natural situations will lay eggs in summer when the days are long, in the winter when the days are short, they stop lying. Human usually don't want them to stop lying; instead people would like them to lay all year round and the easiest way to that is to have them in the barn with lights. Chickens, despite their name, are not "chicken" at all. They are actually very aggressive animals and they can sometimes turn on each other and tear each other to shreds. Sometimes that has unfortunately been used in cock fighting and chicken fighting.

13. 2 Animal production and products

Raising animals (animal husbandry) is an important component of modern agriculture. It has been practiced in many cultures since the transition to farming from hunter-gatherer lifestyles. Usually animal production includes livestock rearing, poultry raising and aquaculture.

13. 2. 1 Livestock rearing

Livestock refers to one or more domesticated animals raised in an agricultural setting to produce commodities such as food or fiber, or labor. Livestock generally are raised for subsistence or for profit. Livestock includes cattle, water buffalo, sheep, goats, pigs (red meats). Products of livestock include:

(1) Meat

Meat is the muscles and other tissues of a livestock that provide a useful form of dietary protein and energy human need (Fig. 13. 1); the protein in meat is of high quality, providing a good match for human needs. Meat also provides the following:

- Many vitamins, including B12
- Many minerals especially iron (red meats), Zn
- Omega-3 fats from oily fish (sardine, salmon, others)
- Conjugated linoleic acid, CLA

What meat cannot provide are dietary fibre, vitamin C and calcium.

Fig. 13. 1 Meats of livestock.

(2) Dairy products

Mammalian livestock can be used as a source of milk, which can in turn easily be processed into other dairy products such as yogurt, cheese, butter, ice cream, kefir, and kumis. Using livestock for this purpose can often yield several times the food energy of slaughtering the animal outright.

(3) Fibre

Livestock produce a range of fibres/textiles. For example, sheep and goats produce wool and mohair; cows, deer, and sheep can make leather; and bones, hooves and horns of livestock can be used.

(4) Fertilizer

Manure can be spread on fields to increase crop yields. This is an important reason why historically, plant and animal domestication have been intimately linked. Manure is also used to make plaster for walls and floors, and can be used as a fuel for fires. The blood and bone of animals are also used as fertilizer.

(5) Labor

Animals such as horses, donkey, and yaks can be used for mechanical energy. Prior to steam power, livestock were the only available source of non-human labor. They are still used for this purpose in many places of the world, including ploughing fields, transporting goods, and military functions.

(6) Land management

The grazing of livestock is sometimes used as a way to control weeds and undergrowth. For example, in areas prone to wild fires, goats and sheep are set to graze on dry scrub which removes combustible material and reduces the risk of fires.

Many secondary products have arisen in an attempt to increase carcass utilization and reduce waste. For example, animal offal and non-edible parts may be transformed into products such as pet food and fertilizer. In the past such waste products were sometimes also fed to livestock as well. However, intra-species recycling poses a disease risk, threatening animal and even human health (such as bovine spongiform encephalopathy (BSE), scrapie and prion). Due primarily to BSE (mad cow disease), feeding animal scraps to animals has been banned in many countries, at least in regards to ruminants and pigs. Farming practices vary dramatically worldwide and between types of animals. Livestock are generally kept in an enclosure, are fed by human-provided food and are intentionally bred, but some livestock are not enclosed, or are fed by access to natural foods, or are allowed to breed freely, or any combination thereof. Livestock raising historically was part of a nomadic or pastoral form of material culture. The herding of camels and reindeer in some parts of the world remains unassociated with sedentary agriculture. The transhumance form of herding in the Sierra Nevada Mountains of California still continues, as cattle, sheep or goats are moved from winter pasture in lower elevation valleys to spring pasture and summer pasture in the foothills and alpine regions, as the season's progress. Cattle were raised on the open range in the Western United States and Canada, on the Pampas of Argentina, and other prairie and steppe regions of the world.

The enclosure of livestock in pastures and barns is a relatively new development in the history of agriculture. When cattle are enclosed, the type of "enclosure" may vary from a small crate, a large fenced pasture or a paddock. The type of feed may vary from natural growing grass, to highly sophisticated processed feed. Animals are usually intentionally bred through artificial insemination or through supervised mating. Indoor production systems are generally used only for pigs and poultry, as well as for veal cattle. Indoor animals are generally farmed intensively, as large space requirements would make indoor farming unprofitable and impossible. However, indoor farming systems are controversial due to the waste they produce, odour problems, the potential for groundwater contamination and animal welfare concerns.

Other livestock are farmed outside, although the size of enclosure and level of supervision may vary. In large open ranges animals may be only occasionally inspected or yarded in "round-ups" or a muster (livestock) . Working dogs such as sheep dogs and cattle dogs [citation needed] may be used for mustering livestock as are cowboys, stockmen and jackaroos on horses, or with vehicles and also by helicopters. Since the advent of barbed wire (in the 1870s) and electric fence technology, fencing pastures has become much more feasible and pasture management simplified. Rotation of pasturage is a modern technique for improving nutrition and health while avoiding environmental damage to the land. In some cases very large numbers of animals may be kept in indoor or outdoor feeding operations (on feedlots), where the animals' feed is processed, offsite or onsite, and stored on site then fed to the animals.

Livestock, especially cattle, may be branded to indicate ownership and age, but in modern farming identification is more likely to be indicated by means of ear tags than branding. Sheep are also frequently marked by means of ear marks and/or ear tags. As fears of mad cow disease and other epidemic illnesses mount, the use of microchip identification to monitor and trace animals in the food production system is increasingly common, and sometimes required by governmental regulations.

Modern farming techniques seek to minimize human involvement, increase yield, and improve animal health. Economics, quality and consumer safety all play a role in how animals are raised. Drug use and feed supplements (or even feed type) may be regulated, or prohibited, to ensure yield is not increased at the expense of consumer health, safety or animal welfare. Practices vary around the world, for example growth hormone use is permitted in the United States, but not in stock to be sold to the European Union. The improvement of health, using modern farming techniques, on the part of animals has come into question. Feeding corn to cattle, which have historically eaten grasses, is an example; where the cattle are less adapted, the rumen pH changes to more acidic, leading to liver damage and other difficulties.

13.2.2 Poultry raising

Poultry is the category of domesticated birds including Chicken, Duck, Emu, Goose, Turkey and so on that people keep for the purpose of collecting their eggs, or killing for their meat and/or feathers. These most typically are members of the super order Galloanserae (fowl), especially the order Galliformes (which includes chickens, quails and turkeys) and the family Anatidae (in order Anseriformes), commonly known as "waterfowl" (e.g. domestic ducks and domestic geese). Poultry also include other birds which are killed for their meat, such as pigeons or doves or birds considered to be game, like pheasants. The term also refers to the flesh of such birds.

The meatiest parts of a bird are the flight muscles on its chest, called breast meat, and the walking muscles on the first and second segments of its legs, called the thigh and drumstick, respectively.

White meat has less oxygen-carrying myoglobin than the dark meat, and is thus lighter in color. Dark meat comes from muscles more heavily exercised, which therefore have more fat stored in them. This accounts for both dark meat's reputation as being unhealthier, and yet more flavourful. Birds that fly rarely (domestic turkey) or sporadically (chicken) have white meat breasts, and birds that fly frequently or long distances (ducks, geese and doves) have dark meat breasts. Quail breast meat is intermediate in color.

13.2.3 Aquaculture

Aquaculture, the farming and husbandry of freshwater and marine organisms finishes about 12% of the food people obtains from the waters of the globe. It is most important in Asia and has grown rapidly since 1970s (Bardach, 1985), and will be grown even quickly in 21st century with the demand of animal protein by increasing world population particular in developing nations (see chapter 14 in details).

13.3 Efficiency in animal production

Let's review the basic theory of food chain in ecology (see chapter 4 in detail). Organisms get the food and nutrients they need by participating in a food chain that means in basic ecology series of organisms in which each eats or decomposes the preceding one. The concept was founded by the famous ecologist Lindeman in 1940. Various food chains can link together to form a food web that means a complex network of many interconnected food chains and feeding relationships. Each organism in an ecosystem can be assigned to a trophic level in its food chain or food web. Each trophic level contains a certain amount of biomass. The transfer of energy between these levels has a certain ecological efficiency.

Ecological efficiency is percentage of energy transferred from one trophic level to another in a food chain or web. Between the levels, the energy could not be transformed in 100% due to losses as the metabolic heat and other ways (Fig. 13. 2).

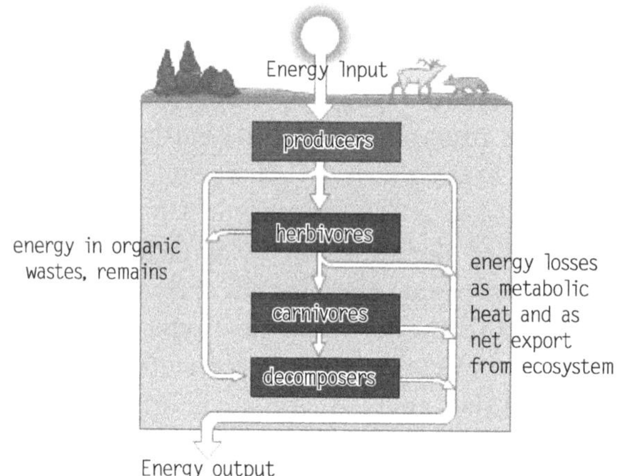

Fig. 13. 2 The energy flows with trophic levels in ecosystems with energy losses as metabolic heat and as net export from ecosystem.

Ecological efficiency with each trophic level in food chains can be descriptively represented as a pyramid termed Ecological pyramid (Fig. 4. 4) first proposed by Lindeman after the food chain concept. There exist 3 types of Ecological pyramids: Biomass storage in various trophic levels of a food chain or webs can be represented by a pyramid of biomass; the number of organisms at each trophic level in a food chain or web can be represented by a pyramid of numbers and the energy storage in various trophic levels of a food chain or webs can be represented by a pyramid of energy.

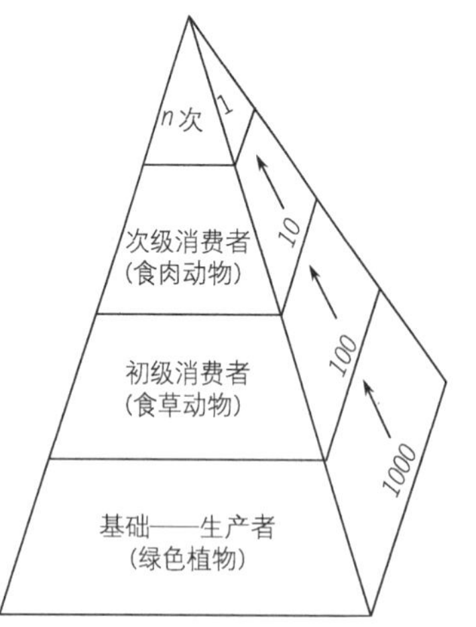

Fig. 13. 3 The one-tenth law in ecosystem.

In the food chain, gross primary productivity is the rate at which producers use photosynthesis to make more biomass. It varies across the earth. Net primary productivity affects the number of consumers in an ecosystem. Therefore, because the planet's net primary productivity (NPP) ultimately is limited by resource that limits the number of consumer organisms (including humans) that can survive on the earth. Humans now use, waste, or destroy about 27% of the earth's total NPP and 40% of the NPP of the planet's terrestrial ecosystems. This share is expected to increase and thus threaten the habitats and food supplies of other species. Subsequently, Lindeman developed the one-tenth law quantifying the ecological efficiency in energy which means that there is only 1 unit energy transformed from 10 units energy between the trophic levels (Fig. 13. 3).

So does in an agroecosystem, a single food chain and its transformation efficiency in energy is showed in Fig. 13. 4, there is only 1.49×10^7 kcal energy transformed by primary producer (here alfalfa) via the photosynthesis from total amount of 6.30×10^{10} kcal sun radiation energy, Calves can only transform 1.19×10^5 kcal energy when they consume above amount of alfalfa, a boy can get 8.3×10^5 kcal out of such amount of Calves. Very often on average, only 1% of total solar radiant energy is converted to primary production via photosynthesis, 10%-20% plants to animals, 0-20% animals to animals in agroecosystem much higher in ecosystem (Tab. 13. 1).

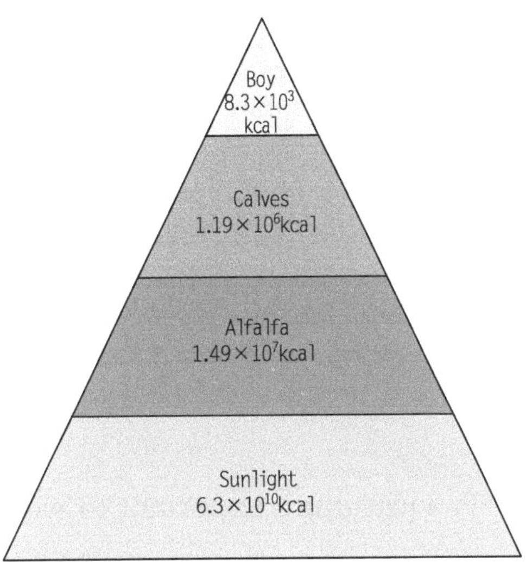

Fig. 13. 4 Energy Ecological Pyramid in agroecosystem.

Tab. 13. 1 Estimate of relative % feed nutrient conversion into edible product (Caldwell, 2008, personal communication.)

Animal product	Energy conversion (%)	Protein conversion (%)
Milk	20	30
Broilers	10	25
Eggs	15	20
Pork	15	20
Turkey	10	20
Beef	8	15
Lamb	6	10

Literatures cited in this chapter

Bardach J. E. 1985. The role of aquaculture in human nutrition. *Geo-journal* 10 (3): 221-232.

Gliessman, S. R. 2005. *Agroecology : The ecology of sustainable food system*. Boca Raton: CRC Press.

Chapter 14 Aquaculture systems

Learning objectives

1. Define aquaculture and explain its role in world food production.
2. Name the most commonly farmed species in China and Canada.
3. Explain the principles of IAAS.
4. Explain the differences between aquaculture in the developed and developing world.
5. Discuss energy efficiency and how aquaculture should grow in the 21st century.
6. List 5 aquaculture systems and an advantage and disadvantage of each.

14.1 Is aquaculture important to world food production?

Aquaculture, defined as the farming and husbandry of freshwater and marine organisms, has steadily increased in importance for global food production (Bardach, 1985). In addition to providing protein for human consumption, the aquaculture industry produces aquatic species for sport fishing, ornamental activities, the production of chemicals and education.

14.1.1 The purposes of aquaculture

Fish stocking as a practice supports commercial, tribal or recreational fishing while supplementing natural populations of fish species or restoring dilapidated populations. Fish stocking refers to the release of juvenile fish into rivers, lakes and the ocean from hatcheries that raise millions of fish from the egg stage of fish lifecycles. Aquaculture also supports the multi-million dollar ornamental fish industry by producing fish as a product that people can buy and sell in the aquarium fish trade.

Above all else, the rationale for the management and culture of aquaculture has remained unchanged for centuries: to produce food intended for immediate human consumption (FAO, 2010). This traditional approach to aquaculture remains extremely important in global food production today.

People have exploited the seas for centuries and we now find ourselves in a situation with a multitude of endangered fish species and collapsed fisheries around the world. For example, the collapse of the cod fishery of the Grand Banks in Newfoundland, Canada and the diminishing fish populations around China's inshore fishery area. Likewise, the wild catch from the global seas and oceans continues to decline, with an estimated 32% of world fish stocks already overexploited. What is going to happen to fish stocks over the next 100 years? Most of the projections are not positive. To compensate for declining wild fisheries, aquaculture outputs have increased. Over the last 40 years modern technology has led to extremely rapid development in aquaculture practices. Between 1987 and 1997 aquaculture output nearly doubled both in value and weight, contributing to over one quarter of fish consumed worldwide (Naylor, 2000). According to the FAO report, State of the World Fisheries and Aquaculture 2010, aquaculture output is increasing above the 6.6% annual output each year and accounts for 46% of the world's food-fish supply. Aquaculture is now overtaking cattle ranching in terms of production of protein. However, researchers remain skeptical about whether aquaculture enhances or diminishes available fish supply to support a growing population worldwide. A meeting held in Norway indicated that 90% of the future of world aquaculture depends on production in developing countries; among them, China already dominates global aquaculture output producing 47.5 million tonnes in 2008 alone (FAO, 2010).

14.1.2 The history of aquaculture

The origin of aquaculture developed in China dating back some 4000 years ago between 2000-1000 B.C. Initial husbandries of *Cyprinus carpio*, or common carp, have been passed down in narrative form from generation to generation. In 500 B.C., Fan Lai wrote the famous and historically significant book "*The Classic of Fish Culture*", the first written evidence of aquaculture. Aquaculture practices have remained an unbroken tradition in China to present day. Independent aquaculture developments arose in many other areas of the world thereafter; some of the oldest countries to develop aquaculture after China include French Indonesia, India, Indonesia, Japan, Korea and some countries in Europe. North America, Africa and Latin America developed aquaculture practices around the early 19th century, varying by continent and country.

14.1.3 Integrating aquaculture and agriculture

Globally, the production of animal protein from capture fisheries is near its limits and land availability constrains the further development of some forms of agriculture. However, an annual population increase of world population means that the world needs to produce more animal protein. What approach is the most effective way? Certainly aquaculture is not the only way to resolve this problem, but is a very good one, especially when ecologically based culture is introduced, it can be extended to low income farms to produce effective protein in low cost with high return for the poor farmers.

Integrating aquaculture and agricultural practices can maximize synergisms and reduce antagonistic interactions through concurrent production activities. Recycling of nutrients, integrated pest management (IPM) and optimal use of water resources results in synergistic interactions between agriculture and fish production practices; whereas antagonistic interactions, for instance the altering of fish habitats and fish stocks, arise when fisheries and agriculture competes for land and water resources (FAO). With increased farmer knowledge of agriculture and aquaculture cropping patterns, farmers can adopt a system most suitable and economically advantageous for increased food production with minimized environmental impacts.

14.2 The role of aquaculture in human nutrition

Aquaculture differs substantially in the developing world and the developed world. In the developing world, the growing of fish for food through aquaculture helps people stay alive. Fish is the primary source of animal protein for one billion people in 58 countries. In the developed world, namely North America, Europe and Japan, where there is an overabundance of food available, people choose to eat fish over other food products for the health benefits. Therefore, growing and selling fish in the North American market offers increasingly prosperous economic opportunities. The desire to live longer and eat more healthily drives the demand for more fish in the developed world. The developed and developing world's differ in both rationales for fish consumption and where aquaculture production places in the food chain. In high value developed countries, aquaculture is based on raising carnivorous fish such as Atlantic salmon and trout; these fish are fed a feed that is based on fishmeal; i. e. , we feed fish to fish. This means people in those wealthy countries are eating high on the food chain. Developing country aquaculture is based on herbivorous fish such as carp and tilapia. This is a cheaper, more sustainable type of aquaculture since it places people lower on the food chain.

14.3 The fish species from east to west

Pond culture, inherited from the ancient Chinese fish farm, has become a popular form of fish farming in China today. Considered the most important source of inland aquaculture, Chinese fish farms produce as much as 60% of global aquaculture. Silver carp (*Hypophthalmichthys molitrix*), grass carp (*Ctenopharyngodon idellus*) and common carp (*Cyprinus carpio*), displayed in Fig. 14. 1, account for the three most commonly farmed species in Asia. This large, warm water, slow-moving fish do well in ponds. The most common farmed species after carp are Japanese prawn (*Macrobrachium nipponensis*) and soft-shelled turtle (*Trionyx sinensis*) . Seaweed production is another important aspect of aquaculture in Asia.

Fig. 14. 1 Silver carp, grass carp and common carp fish species grown in Asia.

In contrast, cold-water Atlantic salmon accounts for 85% of Canadian aquaculture (Fig. 14. 2). The most commonly farmed fish after salmon in Canada includes trout, steelhead and other finfish. In addition, Canadian aquaculture also produces high volumes of bivalves and crustaceans. Much controversy exists over environmental issues related to aquaculture in Canada. In particular, a strong environmental movement against aquaculture has arisen in British Columbia. The spread of sea lice has been a main driver of this backlash. The spread of disease and parasites in crowded pens to wild fish is fairly common in aquaculture. In addition the combination of uneaten food pellets with the abundance of faeces from high concentrations of fish pollutes the surrounding water, plants and animals. However, onshore "closed" fish farms and experimental recirculation systems offer alternatives for containing waste problems. Consumer concerns and public outcry has led the Canadian aquaculture industry to seek more sustainable options for food production with less of an impact on the environment.

Fig. 14. 2 Canadian Atlantic salmon.

14. 4 Methods and energy efficiency of aquaculture

Aquaculture practices take place in three environments: freshwater, brackish water and marine. Freshwater practices take place in fishponds, pens, and cages and in rice paddies (limited). Brackish water practices occur in fishponds generally in coastal areas. Marine practices employ fish cages or substrates (for molluscs and seaweeds).

14. 4. 1 Culture systems

Degree of management, level of inputs and stocking density ranges from extensive to intensive to semi-intensive culture systems. For instance, we can categorize a culture system in terms of external energy inputs. Extensive aquaculture relies solely on natural food, semi-intensive aquaculture relies on a combination of natural food and added fish food, and intensive culture systems rely entirely on human provided food.

Chinese polyculture falls in between extensive and semi-intensive culture, for fish living in tanks will die without any human added food. Canada and most of the developed world depend on intensive aquaculture, hoping to profit from their investments. Famers let fish mature in high stocking densities while feeding them a diet of pellets. Fig. 14. 3 displays the rapidly developing technology of semi-intensive culture and intensive culture in aquaculture industries with various feeding patterns.

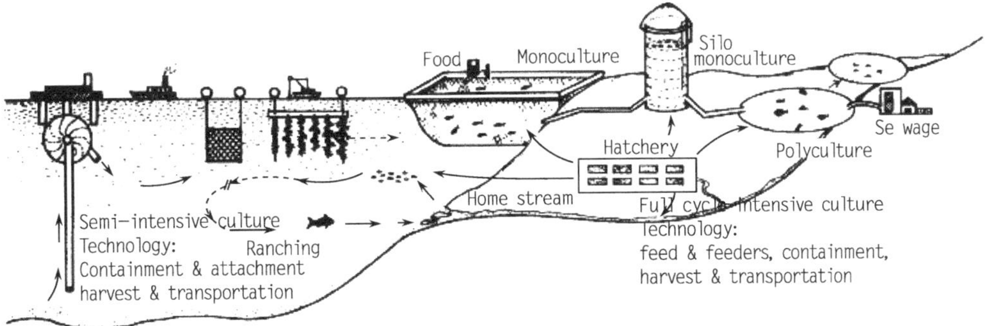

Fig. 14. 3 Scheme of various modes and intensities of aquaculture and their technologies (Bardach, 1985).

14. 4. 2 Energy efficiency

Energy efficiency is an important issue in choosing profitable and environmentally appropriate methods for aquaculture. Herbivorous fish, such as carp, catfish and tilapia, turn plant protein into meat for human consumption. From the energy standpoint, carp and catfish are the most energy efficient with diets low in cost and high in plant content. Herbivorous fish are much more efficient than salmon considering one tonne of salmon requires five tonnes of fish feed. Presently, farmers catch herring and turn them into brown pellets for salmon feed. Energetically, the process of farmers catching fish for feed is inefficient, however, until herring prices raise, this method is profitable. With respect to livestock efficiencies, salmon are still more efficient than beef, which requires seven kilos of grain for every one kilo of gain in body weight.

Other carnivorous fish include halibut and cod. Halibut and cod aquaculture are well developed in Norway and Canada. A significant investment in cod aquaculture exists in Newfoundland, Canada. Cod diets, inefficient and unsustainable as a practice, consist of high cost, high protein fishmeal. Animal nutritionists from around the world have been spending money and time researching the option of feeding carnivorous fish a soybean based diet. The method of feeding fish a soybean-based diet should be approached with caution since carnivorous fish cannot easily digest soybean meal. This could lead to a myriad of nutritional problems in addition to a more intensive demand for soybean in agriculture.

14. 5　Sustainable aquaculture systems

14. 5. 1　Sustainable aquaculture

The conceptual framework for a more sustainable approach to aquaculture systems is expressed in Fig. 14. 4, as an interdisciplinary approach considering production technology, socio-economics and environmental aspects. An aquaculture farming system must be a productive operation and more attractive to alternative or competing uses of resources (i. e. land, water, capital, labour and farm by-products). A sustainable aquaculture must also be socially viable and environmentally compatible.

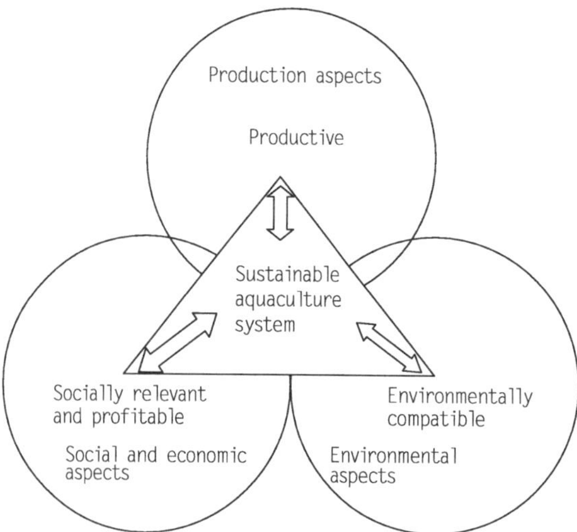

Fig. 14. 4　A system approach to promote sustainable aquaculture (Edwards, 1994).

(1) Production technology

Production technology includes species considered for culture, culture facility and husbandry needed for production. The culture species influences the type of culture facility. Together, the culture species and facility determine the type of husbandry needed for the various stages of production (hatchery, nursery and grow-out). More than 200 species globally are aquaculture farmed in facilities such as rice fields, static or running water ponds, and cages and pens. Improved breeding programmes produce better strains of some species and husbandry may involve various methods of stock management (monoculture or polyculture; single or multiple, stocking and harvesting strategies), use of different feeds (natural, supplementary or complete feed), management of substrate and water quality, and disease prevention and therapy.

(2) Social and economic aspects

Socioeconomic factors must be considered at the micro-level and the macro-level. Micro-level issues may be resolved at the community and farm or household level, generally concerning alternative uses of resources. Macro-level issues may involve regional, national or international cooperation. Macro-level socioeconomic factors include global trade, national development goals, government policy, social characteristics and cultural attitudes (Edwards, 2003).

(3) Environmental aspects

The internal environment of an aquaculture system may be defined as part of the husbandry of production technology. The external environment may be generally considered to include any resource with a two-way interaction between itself and the culture system. The natural environment and aquaculture exert both positive and negative influences on each other. A positive interaction may be a small-scale fishpond that traps nutrients and provides water for irrigation. Whereas an example of a negative interaction might be an area where agriculture pollutes an aquaculture environment through misuse of chemicals or by reducing biodiversity.

14.5.2 Sustainable agri-aquaculture

To increase food production on small-scale farms with limited resources, Integrated Agri-Aquaculture Systems (IAAS) developed in China. Initially, IAAS recycled on-farm wastes and by-products in a closed system. As IAAS evolved to an agro-industrial scale in China and the rest of the world, this practice has become a source of environmental pollution and eutrophication (Edwards, 2003) . These systems integrate aquaculture fish polycultures with agricultural livestock rearing and vegetable cropping. This occurs on rotational cycles within the bond environment, largely relying on bacteria and algae nutrient absorbing capabilities. The philosophy behind IAAS and linking adjacent aquaculture and agricultural systems is the utilization of wastes, feeds, natural irrigation and fertilization (pond residues), ultimately reducing costs, producing sufficient quantities of food and increasing profits.

The Chinese method of carp polyculture has been around for 2,000 years. Carp polyculture, the growing of more than one species together (Fig. 14.5), is displayed in the diagram below. Common carp eat insects, worms and snails; grass carp and silver carp eat plankton. Different species of carp will consume different food items in the pond. Thus the fish may have similar spatial niches and quite different functional niches.

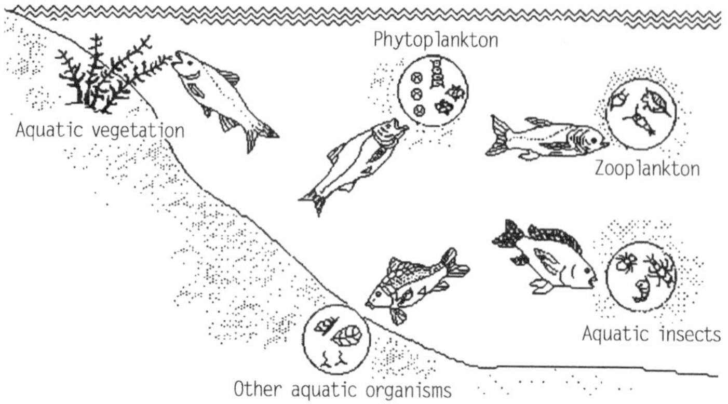

Fig. 14.5 Carp polyculture in early China.

The agri-aquaculture dyke-pond system in the Pearl River (Zhujiang in Chinese) is another example of successful Chinese polyculture. This closed system tightly manages inputs, recycling of materials and the circulation of organic matter within the system (Zhong, 1990). Fig. 14.6 displays a diagram of sustainable agri-aquaculture based on traditional Chinese methods.

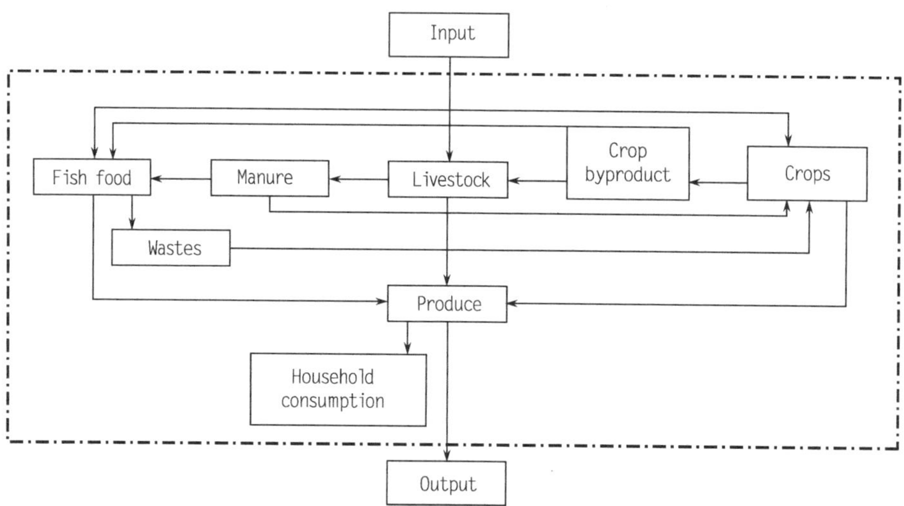

Fig. 14.6 A diagram of Chinese traditional Integrated-agriculture-aquaculture systems (Edwards, 1994).

In summary, Aquaculture is an important facet of global food production, complementing agricultural production. Today, we depend on farmed fish for a substantial portion of worldwide food consumed. Species of fish farmed and methods of aquaculture differ throughout the world, but all practices occur in freshwater, brackish and marine water, as extensive, intensive or semi-intensive cultures. Herbivorous fish are more energy efficient than carnivorous fish. However, people in the developed world prefer carnivorous fish, whereas herbivorous fish are more available in the developing world. A sustainable approach to food production integrates aquaculture with agriculture. Although IAAS can lead to pollution and eutrophication, if practiced correctly it can enhance a production system and reduce wastes and inputs. Plenty of research is currently taking place to improve upon agri-aquaculture practices.

Literatures cited in this chapter

Bardach J. E. 1985. The role of aquaculture in human nutrition. *GeoJournal* 10 (3): 221-232.

Chen G. L. 1993. Aquaculture, Ecological Engineering: Lessons from China. *Ambio* 22 (7): 491-494.

Edwards P. 1994. A Systems Approach for the Promotion of Integrated Aquaculture. Paper presented at Integrated Fish Farming International Workshop, 11-15 October 1994, Wuxi, People's Republic of China.

Edwards P. 2003. Chapter Two: Philosophy, Principles and Concepts of Integrated Agri-Aquaculture Systems. In: Gooley G. J. and Gavine F. M. Integrated Agri-Aquaculture Systems: A Resource Handbook for Australian Industry Development. Kingston, Australia: Rural Industries Research and Development Corporation.

FAO Fisheries and Aquaculture Department. 2010. *The State of the World Fisheries and Aquaculture*, Rome.

Li S. 1987. Energy structure & efficiency of a typical Chinese integrated fish farm. *Aquaculture* 65 (2): 105-118.

Naylor R. L., Goldburg R. J., Primavera J. H., Kautsky N., Beveridge M. C. M., Clay J., Folke C., Lubchenco J., Mooney H., and Troell M. 2000. Effect of aquaculture on world fish supplies. *Nature* 405: 1017-1024.

Pant J., Demaine H. and Edwards P. 2004. Assessment of the aquaculture subsystem in integrated agriculture-aquaculture systems in Northeast Thailand. *Aquaculture Research* 35 (3): 289-298.

Pant J., Demaine H. and Edwards P. 2005. Bio-resource flow in integrated agriculture-aquaculture systems in a tropical monsoonal climate: a case study in Northeast Thailand. *Agricultural Systems* 83 (2): 203-219.

Watson R. and Pauly D. 2001. Systematic distortions in world fisheries catch trends. *Nature*, 414: 534-536.

Zhong G. F. 1989. The structural characteristics and effects of the dike-pond system in China. *Outlook on Agriculture* 18 (3): 119-123.

Zhong G. F. 1990. The types, structure and results of the dike-pond system in South China. *GeoJournal* 21 (1-2): 83-89.

Chapter 15 Cereal-based cropping systems

Learning objectives

1. Define succinctly the following terms:
   - Paddy rice
   - Converted rice
   - Indica rice
   - Japonica rice
   - IRRI
2. Describe the role of cereals in:
   - Livestock-based rotations
   - Cash-crop systems
3. Name the principal cereal crops in the world and their major uses.
4. Explain the importance of rice in world agriculture and compare its use and importance between North America and Asia.

15.1 Why are seeds of cereal so great?

World hunger is an overarching issue and will remain a major concern during most of the 21st century. To a significant degree, advances in crop production will determine whether the hunger problem can be solved or not. Wild (2003) estimated that the annual food production in developing countries must be increased at the rate of 2.5% per year (or an additional 778 million tonnes/year) to meet the food demands and projected change in diet. This will greatly depend on improvements in crops and cropping methods in the 21st century under stresses of decreasing arable land and increasing soil degradation.

There are a huge number of plants in the world; there are approximately 35, 000 species of flowering plants and among them a large number which are economically important plants. However, people are dependent on 12 plants for almost all our food. Of those 12, 7 are cereal plants (Tab. 15.1 and Fig. 15.1). The food supply for humankind has a very narrow genetic base, a low diversity production base to support more than six billion people in the world. There is some fragility around that. From an ecological perspective, stability of an ecosystem is directly proportional to diversity; i. e. , the more genetic diversity people can maintain, the more stable that ecosystem is. Therefore, we now have a problem in the world of a narrow crop genetic base.

Crops are often classified by the type of organ that is harvested; i. e. , seed legume, tubers, vegetables, fruits and cereals. Eight plants, all cereals, provide 56% of the food energy and 50% of all protein in the world diet. Cereal grains were domesticated first by nomadic peoples because they are easy to harvest, store well, are a good source of energy, can be easily transported (quite light with a low water content), do not need much effort to process and can be planted easily. These remain some of the main reasons why seeds are so prominent in world agriculture.

Cereals, grains, or cereal grains are grasses (members of the monocot family Poaceae or Gramineae) cultivated for the edible components of their fruit seeds (botanically, a type of fruit called a caryopsis): the endocarp, germ, and bran. Cereal grains are grown in greater quantities and provide more food energy worldwide than any other type of crop; they are therefore staple crops.

In their natural form (as in whole grain), they are a rich source of vitamins, minerals, carbohydrates, fats, oils, and protein. However, when refined by the removal of the bran and germ, the remaining endocarp is mostly carbohydrate and lacks the majority of the other nutrients. In some developing nations, grain in the form of rice, wheat, or maize (in American terminology, corn) constitutes a majority of daily sustenance. In developed nations, cereal consumption is moderate and varied but still substantial and many cereal grains are fed to livestock.

Cereals in general are not high in protein (usually in the range of 10%-15%) and the amino acid composition of the protein does not completely match the needs of people. Soybeans (and other grain legumes) have protein content higher than that of rice or wheat and the amino acid composition complements that of the cereals. The protein content of a raw soybean is around 35%. Soybean mash, which is bought for feed is around 44% protein after processing. A lot of protein in the world comes from legumes but, unfortunately not all people can afford basic food beyond the cereals and these low protein crops, like rice, wheat, barley, produce about 50% of the protein consumed by people.

In order for humans to use the amino acids in food, we need a full complement of amino acids at the same time from different sources. A prime example of such protein complementarity is the practice of eating rice and beans together. The amino acid composition of such cereals and legumes complement each other and provide more human nutrition that either would when eaten separately. The human body takes a protein from a plant and breaks it down into amino acids and then rebuilds it into our proteins. Our protein and an animal's protein have different ratios of amino acids than that of plants; e. g. , corn is short in lysine. Therefore, we can consume all sorts of protein from corn but its usefulness will be limited by how much lysine there is in the corn in order to make our own protein. There will be many "extra" amino acids that we cannot utilize because the lysine is limiting. One can actually get protein deficiency even though they are taking in a good amount of protein. In a fair and sustainable system, humans should not be relying on cereals for all our protein.

Fig. 15. 1 and Tab. 15. 1 show the world production of principal food crops; figures are in thousands of metric tonnes. It shows that half of the total production is actually cereals. There are three of them, maize (corn), rice and wheat, which make up more than one-third.

A legume in botanical writing is a plant in the family Fabaceae (or Leguminosae), or a fruit of these specific plants. A legume fruit often develops as seed like a cereal's grain, so-called seed legume, is a simple dry fruit that develops from a simple carpel and usually dehisces (opens along a seam) on two sides. Well-known legumes include alfalfa, clover, peas, beans, lentils, lupines, mesquite, carob, soy, and peanuts. Locust trees (*Gleditsia* or *Robinia*), and wisteria.

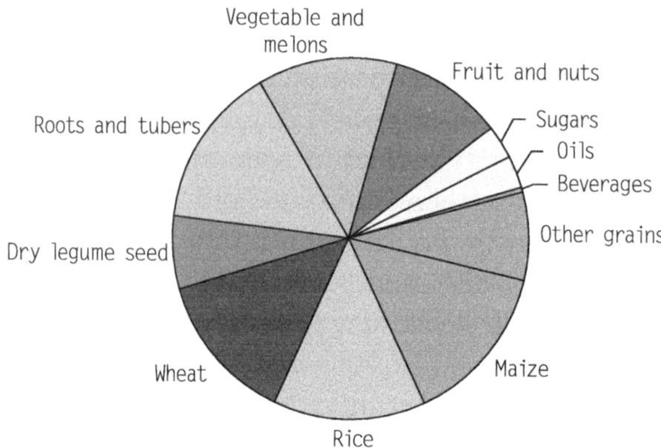

Fig. 15. 1 World production of principal food crops (ranked by tonnage).

Tab. 15. 1 The ranks of world crop in production (FAO, 1982)

Rank no.	Crop	World production ($\times 10^6$ t)	Percentage contribution to world production (%)
1	Wheat	417	15. 7
2	Rice (paddy)	345	13. 0
3	Maize	334	12. 5
4	White potato	228	10. 8
5	Barley	190	7. 1
6	Sweet potato	136	5. 1
7	Cassava	105	3. 9
8	Soya bean	62	3. 1
9	Sorghum	52	2. 0
10	Seed legume	52	1. 9
11	Pearl millet	52	1. 9
12	Oats	49	1. 8
13	Tomatoes	41	1. 5
14	Rye	28	1. 0

15. 2 Cereals for food and feed

15. 2. 1 Domestication and adaptation of crop

Cereals are the most important plants in the world. This section aims to impress upon learners the significance of cereal crops locally and internationally in a broad sense. Among them, rice, more than anything is so integrally linked with culture. For instance, the Chinese greeting word daily is "have you eaten?" translated literally "have you had rice?" If you have not had rice, you have not eaten. In those countries, you have rice three times a day. So rice is part of the history, culture and production.

The temperate cereals evolved around the Tigress and Euphrates rivers in the area of what is now Iran and Iraq; this area is therefore the site of origin where one may find greater species biodiversity. When these cereals were first selected by primitive people they would have been mixed. Under really good conditions, wheat tends to out-compete the barley and the oats but as people moved further north, the barley and oats became more dominant. As they moved with their mixture of harvested seeds, there was natural selection taking place across the world. So the species sorted themselves out across Europe in the places they grew best. The first selections were made by accident as people moved. Things were better adapted to certain places. Since that time, of course, people have done a lot of selection; e. g. , some seeds stored well, and those that didn't store well were planted, the ones that were bigger were planted more, the ones that yielded more, so essentially a lot of the selection for these types of crops occurred thousands of years ago. We have done a huge amount of cereal improvement over the last one hundred years but we started with well-established species through selection by our ancestors. Present day plant breeders now select and breed for a number of desirable characteristics; e. g. , larger seeds for harvest. This is true for quite a number of crops but particularly true for these small grains. We want bigger grains and we want them to harvest easily as well; in other words, we want them to stay on the cob (or head) until we come along with our combine and thresh them. We don't want the seeds to fall off; we don't want the seeds to shatter as they get ripe. Shattering means that as soon as the seeds are ripe they come off. This is a characteristic of wild plants. Most wild plants shatter easily so that they can spread their seed. We don't want our domesticated plants to be successful weeds. We want them to hold onto the seed until we get to them. We breed a lot for ease of harvest, no shatter, and less toxicity. Most wild plants have some sort of chemical protection. Hemp, *Cannabis sativa*, for instance, has tetra-hydrocannabinol (THC) in its tissues to protect against insects foraging on them. If you want to increase the THC in cannabis, you introduce insects into the growing situation because that stimulates the gene to produce more THC. This chemical protection is quite common among wild plants and as they are stimulated by whatever stress there is, they tend to produce more of that protective compound. Wild potatoes have a lot of toxins. We do not eat the leaves of potatoes because they are toxic. That same toxin that is in the leaves was in the roots and in the tubers of the wild precursors of our domestic potato and we have bred it out. In order to domesticate something we have tended to create bigger organs, easier to harvest and less toxic. Lately we have done a huge amount of work on getting whatever substance we want increased. For instance, we have designer oils being bred into canola. Now we are breeding not just for cooking oil; now we are breeding for something of value that can be extracted, put in a little capsule and sell for a premium price.

15. 2. 2 The major cereal crops in the world

The following is a brief introduction of the top three cereals according to Oerke (2006) and Khush (2005).

(1) Wheat

Wheat is grown on all continents and is the most important cereal crop in the Northern hemisphere as well as in Australia and New Zealand. Major wheat producing countries are the PR China, India, the USA, France and Russia. In 2001-2003, almost 564×10^6 t of wheat was grown on 209.4×10^6 hm^2 (annual data from FAO, 2005). With a worldwide average of 2690 kg/hm^2 the yield per unit of area varied from less than 500 kg/hm^2 almost 8500 kg/hm^2 in Ireland.

(2) Rice

Rice is the world's most important food crop and a primary source of food for more than half the world's population. Rice production is largely concentrated in Asia; more than 90% of the world's rice is grown and consumed in Asia where 60% of the earths' people live. Rice accounts for 35%-75% of the calories consumed by more than 3 billion Asians. It is planted on about 154 million hectares annually or on about 11% of the world's cultivated land.

Paddy rice (*Oryza sativa*) is grown under different growth conditions with widely differing yield levels, with irrigated and non-irrigated lowland rice and dryland rice being most important. In West Africa *Oryza glaberrima* is also grown. In 2001-2003, 583×10^6 t rice were produced on 149.6×10^6 hm^2 giving an average yield of 3900 kg/hm^2 (annual data from FAO, 2005). Yield levels varied from less than 800 kg/hm^2 in some Sub-Saharan countries to 9280 kg/hm^2 in Egypt.

(3) Maize

Maize production is highest in the Americas-the USA is by far the greatest producer and exporter -and in East Asia; in Latin America and parts of Africa maize is the staple food for human consumption. In 2001-2003, worldwide maize production reached 612×10^6 ton 139.8×10^6 hm^2 (annual data from FAO, 2005) . The yield per unit of area averaged 4.38 t/hm^2 and varied from less than 500 kg/hm^2 in some African countries to more than 10 000 kg/hm^2 in New Zealand and some countries in the Near East.

15.3 Cereal-based cropping systems

Cereals are not always a cash crop; in many cases they are a rotational crop. They are rotated around some other cash crops that make money. The cost of production for small grains can be almost equivalent to the returns; in some areas of the world, especially under small farm conditions, it is difficult for a grower to make substantial returns on small grains. Most cereals have both spring type and winter type, and a winter type is a winter annual. It is planted in the fall, goes dormant over the winter and is harvested the next summer. It is an annual because it completes its life cycle within one year, but it is a winter annual because it's planted in the fall and harvested the next summer. Spring cereals are planted in the spring and harvested in late summer. In Atlantic Canada, a lot of spring cereals are planted the first week in May and harvested in August or early September. Winter cereals are usually planted in the first part of September and are harvested the end of July to early August of the following year. In Fujian, Southern China, the season is from March to July.

What does a farmer want from a rotational crop? Instead of making money directly, the purpose of the use of cereals in a rotation is to maintain soil integrity, good soil health, good organic matter, efficient use of inputs, and reduce erosion. Keeping the ground covered gives a direct economic return to the growing year toward a really sustainable agriculture. Cereals are rotated with crops like potatoes, carrots, vegetables that can make money and break the disease and weed cycle. The diseases and insects that hit potatoes, don't affect the cereals, thus decreasing the use of fungicides and herbicides. Cereals can also act as a nurse crop for forage crop establishment. For instance, a standard rotation in a potato growing area is grain under-seeded to some forage, such as a red clover/timothy mix. During the year of the cereals, the forage establishes, grows a bit and, when the cereals are harvested, the forage will flourish. The forage can be harvested the next year or ploughed down to improve soil health; the result will be improved soil structure and the disease cycle of the potato will be broken. A three year rotation has been legislated in Prince Edward Island. This is to protect the soil because one of the big problems in PEI is soil erosion. One of the side effects of the 3-year rotation is to improve the grade on potatoes; i. e. , the improved soil makes for better growing conditions for the tubers.

The same sort of thing happens on carrots, on strawberries or other horticultural crops; cereals break disease cycles. They also add value in animal products so the farmer might not make money on the feed but if he/she can grow their own feed that decreases the cost of production of the animal, thus making the money through the sale of the animal.

There are some people who are cash crop cereal producers in the Atlantic Provinces of Canada but not many. If one is cash crop producer, there are a few ways of making money, direct sales, indirect sales of animal products and enhancement of value to other crops and rotation. The highest return a farmer can get for any of these cereals is to grow seed become a certified seed grower. If a farm is producing cereal crops, it is an opportunity. The equipment is available and the farmer just needs to develop enough expertise to grow seed. That seed then gets very high return. The farmer must be very good at growing the grain, with clean product, no contamination of weeds, no disease; if successful, there is a big return here. For direct sales, seed is the highest value; milling is the next for wheat, malt for barley, milling for oats; feed is the lowest value usage. All of these products get graded so that the higher the grade, the better the return. Interestingly enough, there are years when the straw attracts more money than the grain because there is a fair demand for straw some years for spreading on the potato land to keep erosion down, to put on strawberries, and for use by mushroom growers, so there are some other opportunities. There are a few things to remember - aim for the highest market, know the market, and produce quality grain. Any good potato grower does things in a timely fashion, any good strawberry grower; carrot grower does things in a timely fashion. In the same way, a grain grower must do things in a timely fashion or the result is poor quality, low yields and poor economic and environmental impact.

Literatures cited in this chapter

Khush G. S. 2005. What it will take to Feed 5. 0 Billion Rice consumers in 2030. *Plant Molecular Biology* 59: 1-6.

Miflin B. 2000. Crop improvement in the 21st century. *Journal of environment botany* 51 (32): 1-8.

Oerke E. C. 2006. Crop losses to pests. *Journal of Agricultural Science* 144: 31-43.

Wild A. 2003. *Soils, Land and food: managing the land during the 21st century*. New York: Cambridge University Press.

Chapter 16 Vegetable-based production systems

Learning objectives

1. In both global and Canadian context, discuss the importance of vegetables for the economy and for human health.
2. Name the four principal constituents that are deficient in the diet of most of the population in the world.
3. List and briefly explain four ways of classifying vegetables, giving examples for each method of classification.
4. Name two examples of:
   - Tropical vegetables
   - Temperate vegetables
   - Crucifer vegetables (Brassicaceae)
   - Solanaceous vegetables (Solanaceae)
5. Describe the two predominant vegetables in the tropics and one for a temperate country.
6. Explain the profit vs principle concepts of vegetable growing and the impact of solely profit-based systems on the environment.

16.1 The roles of vegetable in human development

Why people grow vegetables? Vegetables are an important component in an agricultural system; they are important for rural diversity, rural sustainability and for human nutrition.

Vegetables are the major source for several essential human nutrients. There is a large diversity of nutrients that exist in vegetables not found in cereals or fruits. They provide iron, Vitamin A, dietary fibers, proteins, essential amino acids and other medicinal properties. Vegetables are consumed not only for nutritional but also health purposes, not as a food but to supplement those nutrients that are essential to our health, they also provide high calories per unit area. When one compares rice to potatoes, about 40 times more calories can be harvested from a piece of land with potatoes.

Vegetables have high productivity; compared to 2-7 tonnes/hectare for rice, carrots can go up to 70-90 tonnes/hectare per year. They can also produce about 2-3 crops per year depending on where they are grown. They also provide a high value in terms of productivity and profit, anywhere from 40 to 300% compared to other crops. They also provide higher employment opportunities; it is estimated that vegetables provide about a 4-5 fold increase in employment opportunities by switching over from a rice-based system to a vegetable-based system.

In order to grow and commercialize vegetables, people need specialized skills such as training, pruning, propagation, nursery and seed production; all these industries can be amalgamated together for a successful vegetable industry. Vegetable production systems provide high diversity; unlike a cereal monoculture, one can have multiple crops, intercrops, in the terrestrial atmosphere and in the rhizosphere. Vegetable systems are also industry oriented; many value-added products and commodities come from vegetables. The seed, nursery, packaging, and processing industries all interlink and add value to a successful industry. At present, there are also efforts to deliver nutraceuticals and biopharmaceuticals through vegetable systems.

Most importantly, there is the concept that "vegetables that can heal" . Vegetables contribute to both prevention and curing of human diseases. There is a list of benefits that are available by consuming vegetables. Vegetables can provide antioxidants, antibacterials and anti-fungal agents; they can help immuno-deficiency disorders. Many have been shown to have anti-cancer properties.

As examples, broccoli contains a high amount of phytosterols; it has curing properties for arthritis and cancer and also contributes to the control of cardiovascular diseases. Onions contain allicin, one of the major components, and there is evidence of anti-viral, anti-fungal and antibacterical properties related to onions. Vegetable effects on cardiovascular disease and anti-cholesterol properties are also being looked at scientifically. Another tropical vegetable is bitter melon. It contains momordicin, an alkaloid which stimulates the pancreas, and diabetes (type A) can be treated with this particular vegetable. Many vegetables have both nutritional and medicinal properties.

The World Health Organization reports on the four principal constituents that are deficient in the diet of most of the population in the world; they are Vitamin A, protein, iron and iodine; all four can be supplied by vegetables. Southeast Asia is one of the chronic areas suffering from anemia due to lack of iron in the diet; about 78% of the population is anemic. The data suggests that what we consume on a global basis is not sufficient and is not meeting the dietary requirements of the World Health Organization. There is a lot of work to be done in that area. Anemia can lead to brain dysfunction; brain dysfunction can lead to paralysis. It is not just anemia but related diseases that could spread due to this deficiency. China, on average exceeds the recommendation and India, Vietnam and Nepal are close to meeting the requirement levels.

In term of the health effect of vegetable and its consumption trends, World Health Organization recommends about 73 kilograms per person per year for the intake of vegetables (WHO, 1990). Several countries are near or just under the line (Fig. 16. 1). Canada is close to that recommendation. This is met from the fresh market and not from frozen or canned vegetables. It is expected that the world population will increase to about 8 billion by 2020 and the major population explosion will happen in parts of Asia. What will happen in that situation when migration is taking place from the country and rural areas to urban cities? It is estimated that 2 million live in the urban cities of Manila and 20 million people live in Calcutta which means there needs to be a regular supply of vegetables to be moved into the urban areas.

Because of their importance to human health and their economic influence, vegetables have a social and economic impact. There is a continuous connection between consuming vegetables, producing vegetables and building a nation. It is not just the

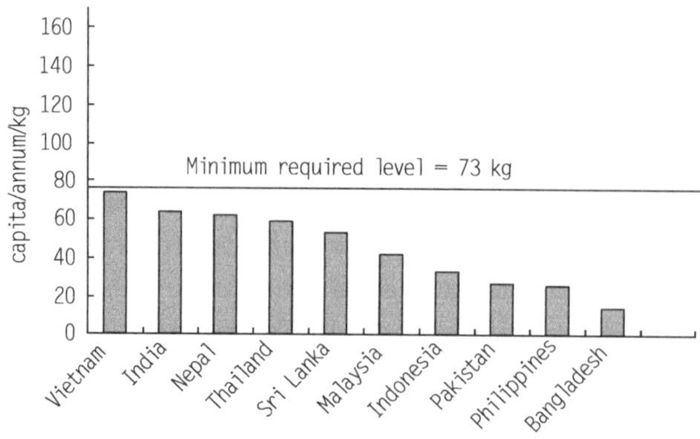

Fig. 16. 1 Per capita vegetable availability of Asian countries in 2000.

vegetable we need to take but it has other socio-political implications in building countries, building continents, building regions, building the whole global situation. For instance, improved nutrition can lead to improved health; it can trigger learning capacity; and improve working capacity; the whole efficiency of a country can be enhanced, thus improving competition among different countries, and enhancing socio-economic development. The improved social economic development could result in improving the infrastructure and institutional development. It will contribute to increased income and ultimately that will serve as grounds for improved nutrition.

16. 2 Vegetable production: Global and regional

In Canada, there are nearly 20 different categories of vegetables; the economic value of vegetables produced is about one billion dollars in farm-gate value. That does not include potatoes which would be a total of 2 billion dollars. There is a tremendous increase in terms of its value by greenhouse production of vegetables, especially in Canada, a fourfold increase in the past five years or so. The top five vegetables that are being produced in Canada are carrots which produce the highest level in terms of fresh market, then onions, lettuce, cabbage and corn. In terms of processing vegetables, tomatoes rank first at 51 million dollars followed by corn, peas, cucumbers, beans and carrots. The value for the carrots is 7 million dollars. In greenhouse production, tomatoes contribute the highest amount, a 255 million dollar industry in Ontario and Quebec. Tomatoes are a major source of income in agricultural commodities in the Ontario region, followed by cucumbers, peppers, and lettuce which all contribute to the greenhouse production of vegetables in Canada.

Ninety percent of Canadian exports in vegetables go to the U. S. The total export is about 411 million dollars which is about 45%-50% of the total production of vegetables. There is an increasing trend toward greenhouse-produced vegetables, especially tomatoes.

16. 3 Scientific aspects of vegetable

16. 3. 1 Classification systems

Vegetables can be classified in 4 ways:

- Botanically
- By the edible parts that are consumed
- By their temperature requirements
- By their life cycles (whether they are annual, perennial or biennials)

There are about 200 species of vegetables consumed worldwide. We consume vegetables from two different botanical classifications, monocots and dicots. Vegetables are not from one particular species or variety; they are a diverse type of food. The classification gives an understanding of how they are assembled in terms of their botanical characteristics; e. g. , the cucurbitaceae family all looks similar in terms of the leaves and some of the reproductive organs and the polygonaceae family looks similar in the morphological and reproductive characteristics.

Vegetables can also be classified based on edible parts. There are a whole spectrum of plant organs we consume; i. e. , roots, tubers, stems, leaves, petioles, inflorescence, immature and mature fruits (Fig. 16. 2). Radish is a root; potatoes have a tuber; onion is a bulb; broccoli is an immature inflorescence; cauliflower is an inflorescence, and tomato and watermelon are fruits. There are also leaf modifications, for example, brussels sprouts and lettuce.

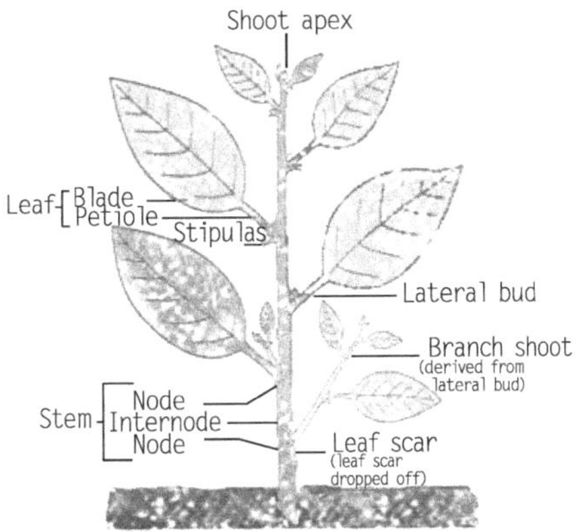

Fig. 16. 2 The edible parts in vegetable plant shoot.

Vegetable varieties can be selected in certain area (e. g. tropics) and growing season (e. g. cool season) according to their temperature requirements. Cool season vegetables include asparagus, broccoli, brussels sprouts, cabbage, and kohlrabi; warm season crops include cucumber, eggplant and tomato that can be planted in tropic area even in summer, whereas, cool season crops can be grown in cool temperatures. This gives an option to growers, especially in warmer climates, as to when those crops can be grown.

Vegetables can also be classified based on the life cycle; i. e. , annual, biennial and perennial. Annual crops like cucumbers, cowpeas and lettuce produce and perish in one season. Biennial crops have two cycles, it has a vegetative cycle and enters the reproductive cycle the second season. Some biennial crops can also be grown as an annual crop; e. g. , carrots. Asparagus is an example of a perennial vegetable which does not have to be re-planted each year and can be harvested year after year.

16. 3. 2 Vegetable-based production system

There are two major categories of production systems, tropical and temperate (Fig. 16. 3). There are sub-categories or classification by cereal based system or year-round production systems, which means the continuous vegetables producing within a year-round on a particular piece of land versus rotation with cereals and other crops within a year-round. There is also a mixed system; e. g. , ten months' cassava in crop duration, with other vegetables planted along with cassava. A year-round production system has two major classes of categories cultivated in a field or in a greenhouse or protected structure system.

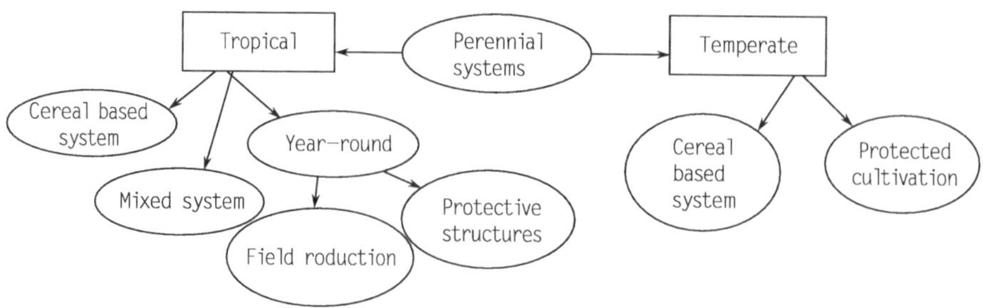

Fig. 16. 3 Global vegetable production systems.

The perennial vegetable system is common for both tropical and temperate areas. An example for the tropical systems is *Moringa*; it has long pods of edible fruits as well as leaves that are fed to livestock. They contain a high amount of iron; it is in many backyards of every country in any tropical region. *Coccinia* is another example of a tropical perennial. It can be grown as a climber and the leaves and fruits can be used. In the temperate region, examples include asparagus and rhubarb. One of the great advantages of perennial crops is they can be planted, managed and then harvested without re-planting. In a cereal-based production system, rice or wheat (also barley or oats) are used in a tropical or temperate climate. The year-round production system produces vegetable after vegetable mostly in a tropical production system.

In a temperate cereal-based production system the wheat or barley is followed by potatoes or carrots or any of the crucifer crops, and corn, cauliflower, cucumbers. Or a forage-based system is followed by onions, watermelons and tomatoes, depending on the market trends.

There are as many as 200 different cropping systems that are available in a temperate vegetable production. Potato, cereals, spinach, and cereals or forages in a particular system followed by a vegetable.

Highland vegetable rotations: In some of the tropical countries the elevation is utilized as an advantage. They also grow vegetables in high elevations where the temperature is generally lower. In principle, it is a potato-based system with potatoes, tomatoes, cauliflower or any other crucifers followed by peas, carrots, onions.

Tropical production systems are cereal-based; some are cash crops. There are nearly 2,500 different production systems related to vegetables in the tropics. It is the experience, the market demand and the industry that determines what kind of cropping system happens within a certain rotation.

Examples of a rice-based system would be rice-cucumber/watermelon/beans-rice; rice cucurbitaceous vegetable-rice; rice-cotton-tomato, a highly cash crop system; rice-tomato-rice; rice-chilies-rice. And also in dry-land area, millets are drought-hardy cereals and you can have millets-chilies-millets.

There are two major categories that are purely vegetable-based systems or cash-crop based system. In a purely vegetable-based system with just vegetables or it may be a cash crop including other things like chilies, cassava or bananas. It depends on whether the farm is supplying vegetables to a contract vegetable supplier, a wholesaler or retailer, or if it is dealing with multiple industries.

There is diversity in the vegetable cropping systems. The year-round production system is very intensive and can happen in an open field condition or in an enclosed system. Both are commonly seen in the tropics and also in temperate climate conditions. The choice of a crop is determined by the market and the choice of the grower. Vegetables can also be grown in an aquaponic system, in which leafy vegetables are grown in this system with about 12 crops per year. The vegetables are produced in a fertilizer floating tub; any type of vegetable can be produced in this way, tomatoes, melons, okras. If there is a problem with a piece of land, very intensive cultivation can be done using this system.

The protective structures are greenhouses, high tunnels or low tunnels or net houses. The most profitable crops identified by the growers are tomatoes, cucumbers, peppers, cherry tomatoes, bitter melon and lettuce. They may be profitable in a protective structure system. Net houses are used to prevent major pests and also to utilize the natural rain for irrigation. In Taiwan, it is very popular to use different size mesh depending upon the insect problem. None of the crops produced under the nets are sprayed with chemicals.

An off-season production system is used to capitalize on the off-season higher prices. This happens mostly in the tropics. When the temperature goes up (April to September) followed by heavy rains, regular production comes down dramatically and prices go up. In order for farmers to utilize a particular time frame and get more profit, it is suggested they go for off-season vegetable production system overcoming the constraints. Profits can be possible in summer and winter if winter crops, such as cabbage and cauliflower, are produced in summer. If a farmer produces tomatoes in summer, he gets a higher price. And has an option to go into production of vegetables during the off-season when it is not available or priced high. The major problem is high rainfall; flooding is commonly seen during April to September, typhoon, heavy rainfall, heavy winds as well as root diseases. To overcome the problems, selecting of the root stocks that could tolerate flooding and high temperature and constructing a shelter to protect against the wind and rain, and grafting with a rootstock can help plants grow better under flooding conditions and withstand high temperatures and withstand bacterial wilt, as well as nematode populations in that particular region.

Intercropping, multiple cropping, cover crops are frequently conducted in vegetable production systems. Intercropping can produce short-term crops under a canopy, while multiple cropping grows several crops together for harvest over a period of time. In relay cropping, one crop succeeds another in a short period of time. Trap crops are utilized to trap certain insects in the trap rows so that the other crops can be protected. An example of that would be a peanut crop which can be used as a cash crop, and castor bean crop can be used as a trap crop. Cover crops are in a tropical used to avoid erosion problems and avoid the impounding effect of the rain on the soil surface.

The vegetable industry is very intensive; people tend to continuously grow one vegetable after another to pursue high economic value so the land will be highly productive and may become exhausted. Therefore, it is extremely important to compromise profits with ecological principles when you grow vegetables to keep your land productive for a long period of time, to avoid the sacrifice of production principles; it is essential to maintain an appropriate methods such as crop rotation, green manure crops in the rotation, inclusion of leguminous crops in the rotation. Obviously, intensive vegetable production system producing potatoes after potatoes or carrots after carrots is not good for the soil or the environment; also using as much of an input possible to harness more yields needs to be avoided. However, excessive fertilizer use and land tillage is commonly seen in many intensive vegetable operations especially in tropical situations. Farmers may till the soil whether it is required or not; they may apply fertilizers whether they are required or not; there is no soil testing commonly practiced. There are a lot of issues that are connected with fertilizer utilization in tropical countries. There is no rest for the soil. The consequences are low fertility, low organic matter, increased compaction and low microbial activity. Some soils have zero microbial activity because of intensive cultivation. In the lower rhizosphere, microbial biodiversity is decreased compared to 2,000 species usually present; there is a less amount of diversity in an intensive system. Short term profit sometimes over-rides the need to have solid production principles.

High pest disease and high amount of pesticide use is commonly seen, which is also a consequence of such economy-based intensive systems. Land erosion is another problem especially in the highland areas. Low water table is another problem in the interior south Asia and in about 2020 that will be a major limiting feature for the production Southeast Asia because they use tonnes of water in intensive vegetable production. Increasing land degradation is commonly seen in Southeast Asia and soil is becoming degraded. Once the soil has become degraded, it is very difficult to bring it back. Any production system must take this into account - take care of the base material; that is the fundamental process for successful production.

Literatures cited in this chapter

Cox D. N., Reynolds J., Mela D. J., Anderson A. S., Mckellar. S., and Lean M. E. J. 1996. Vegetables and fruits: barriers and opportunities for greater consumption. *Nutrition & Food Science*5: 44-47.

World Health Organization. 1990. Diet, Nutrition and the Prevention of Chronic Disease, WHO, Geneva.

Williams C. 1995. Healthy eating: clarifying advice about fruit and vegetables. *British Medical Journal* 310: 1453-1455.

Chapter 17 Sheltered plant production for food and enjoyment

Learning objectives

1. The size, importance and diversity of the ornamental horticulture industry in general.
2. The size, importance and diversity of the greenhouse, nursery and the specialty crops
3. How changes in marketing have changed the technology of bedding plant production.
4. Why greenhouse cut flowers are considered to be an international commodity.
5. How greenhouse vegetable growers get "insects" to work for them.
6. The differences between:

- Wholesale and retail plant nurseries
- Woody and herbaceous perennial landscape plant nurseries
- Field and container production systems used by landscape plant nurseries

17.1 Sheltered plant production: principle and services

There are several other names for sheltered plant production, i. e. "Protected agriculture", "Installment agriculture", "Facilities farming", and "Construction agriculture" and so on, all of them refer to agricultural production by using artificial facilities to alter one or several ecological factors and to gain more appropriate conditions for plant growth in a certain growing season, by which to increase productivity, improve quality and prolong the growth period of crops.

In general, sheltered plant production integrates modern biotechnology, agricultural - ecological engineering, and computer and material technology into a whole to give birth to higher technological content, higher economic attached values, and higher land and labor productivity per capita, and most importantly an environmentally friendly agricultural pattern.

In most countries, sheltered plant production is furnished by plastic green house, while in colder temperature regions for example in The Netherlands of Western Europe, it is mainly equipped by glass greenhouses. Usually sheltered plant production systems are capital intensive, equipped with various environmental controls to regulate factors such as moisture, temperature, light intensity and day length. In the past decade, a new material plastics membrane has been developed in the USA and Japan characterized by being light spectrum selective, temperature reduced, microbial killing and pest resistant. Computer-based greenhouse production systems are now more prevalent in sheltered plant production systems to control the production conditions including CO_2 precisely and automatically.

The species grown in sheltered plant production are most frequently vegetables, ornamental flowers and fruits, among which cucumber and tomato are the most important in Canada and tulips in the Netherlands. The greatest recorded productivity of greenhouse cucumber is 600 tonnes per hectare per year, eight times that of outside cucumber production; the most productive greenhouse flower has been reported in Israel (以色列) that reach 300 million rose per hectare per year.

The trends of the sheltered plant production in developed countries are toward larger green house in size, 2-20 hectare green houses are general in USA and the Netherlands. Another remarkable change of sheltered plant production is to be equipped by mechanization and industrialization, characterized by hydroponic culture (营养液调配技术), carbon dioxide fertilization (二氧化碳施肥技术), bee pollination [蜜蜂授粉 (生物) 技术] and information technology.

17.2 Sheltered plant production in Canada

Canadian greenhouse growers also produce greenhouse-grown culinary herbs and greenhouse-grown vegetables, with an annual value of $1711 Million, and the greenhouse vegetable industry is an important and growing segment of the Canadian agri-food industry, with annual value of $600 Million. Nursery Crops include woody plants (trees and shrubs) and hardy herbaceous perennials used for outdoor landscaping purposes. Three kinds of sheltered plant production industries are introduced as follows.

17.2.1 Bedding plants

Most bedding plant growers are small in size and direct market most or all of their plants to the consumer at their retail greenhouses, and smaller growers usually grow in freestanding (individual) greenhouses. While larger wholesale growers that produce and sell to chain stores and independent garden centers grow in larger gutter-connected facilities, often one acre or larger in size. Fig. 17.1 shows these orange marigolds (万寿菊) are a small part of the production in this large wholesale greenhouse. This gutter-connected house has moveable (or rolling) benches to allow for more plant production since there are fewer walkways in this type of setup. There is usually attached a bedding plant propagation house. The benches have bottom heat for seed germination purposes and mist systems to keep seed from drying out until it germinates and emerges. Some growers propagate their own plants from seeds or cuttings; others buy from other greenhouse operations that specialize in bedding plant propagation. Bedding plant production by wholesale growers is increasingly being mechanized; "transplant lines" are part of this mechanization. Monorail system with shelves is another way of decreasing labor resulting in less walking up and down the aisles carrying flats. Shelved carts are also being widely used to decrease handling.

Fig. 17.1 Green house bedding flower industry in Canada.

17.2.2 Pot plants

Pot (potted) plant production is the second most important commodity group produced by greenhouse ornamental crop growers after bedding plants. These plants are used to decorate the interior of the home. Flowering geraniums are very colourful pot plants grown by a smaller retail grower. Some greenhouse pot plants have been popular for decades; newer products are always being introduced. Miniature roses are a newer pot crop, especially popular at Valentine's Day. Red roses are a symbol of love so that is why this color of the plant is so popular at Valentine's Day (February 14) . Some potted plants are growing on flood (ebb and flow) moveable benches. This type of system waters and fertilizes the plants via sub-irrigation by capillary action when the benches are flooded with a liquid fertilizer solution. The flood bench system is controlled with microprocessor technology. Water and fertilizer levels are monitored and replenished automatically as the plants use them up. The system also floods and drains the benches automatically based on a preset program. The most important potted plant is the poinsettia (猩猩木) which is grown for the Christmas season. Red is the most popular colour even though poinsettias are available in many cultivar colours.

17.2.3 Cut Flowers

Bedding plants and pot plants can be cut flowers in terms of their monetary importance to the greenhouse floriculture industry. Cut *chrysanthemums* (菊花) have always been an important greenhouse grown cut flower. However, Canada imports significant quantities of cut flowers, including chrysanthemums from Colombia, South America. Cut chrysanthemums are a very bright and cheerful flower. Cut roses, however, are the most important greenhouse grown cut flower in Canada. Red is the most popular colour. Roses are the best known flower in the world and have been throughout recorded history. Roses are usually grown in glass houses for maximum light transmission. Rose growers usually have larger operations and produce only wholesale products for the florist trade. Young roses are usually grown in a hydroponic (soilless) system comprised of buckets full of clay pellets. Plants are fertilized with a liquid hydroponic solution. The fixtures hanging from the roof of the greenhouse are high pressure sodium lights to provide supplemental lighting in order to maintain production during the low light levels and short days of Eastern Canadian winters. Greenhouse cut flower crops are usually also fed supplemental CO_2 in order to increase photosynthesis. Ambient levels of 360 mg/kg are usually increased 3 fold to around 1000 mg/kg. This can be achieved by burning high grade propane or natural gas in CO_2 generators

17.2.4 Cut flower outdoor

There exists an outdoor cut flowers industry that grows cut flowers in the field, it is usually a wholesale market but many growers are small in size and they retail the product themselves in order to achieve a better price. Farmers' Markets are a popular place to sell and buy outdoor cut flowers.

17.2.5 Culinary herb production

Culinary herb production is another segment of the greenhouse industry in Canada. It is much smaller than the 3 floriculture components (i.e., bedding plants, potted plants and cut flowers) and the greenhouse vegetable component of this industry. Herb production has become an important part of the greenhouse industry. Herbs are produced as transplants in 7 cm to 15 cm pots for sale to home owners to grow their own culinary (cooking) herbs. Plants produced include: basil, oregano, thyme, rosemary, mints and many others.

Another part of the greenhouse herb industry is the production of fresh cut herbs for sale to restaurants and grocery stores for consumer purchase for in-home food preparation. Some of these fresh cut herbs are grown in soil based production systems; other growers use hydroponic (soilless) systems.

17. 2. 6 Greenhouse-grown vegetables

The greenhouse vegetable industry in Canada has expanded rapidly during the past 10 years. Canada is now the second largest exporter of greenhouse vegetables in North America and Europe after the Netherlands. Most of Canada's greenhouse vegetable export is to the United States. Tomatoes are the most important crop (followed by cucumbers, peppers and lettuce). Most greenhouse grown vegetables are grown hydroponically. Smaller growers usually produce in small, freestanding hoop house structures covered with polyethylene. Larger growers normally grow in large, gutter connected houses, often covered with glass (roof) and polycarbonate side walls (Fig. 17. 2). This house is fully computerized. The crops are grown hydroponically and pests are normally controlled without the use of pesticides. Biological control methods are used as part of the growers integrated pest management (IPM) strategy.

Fig. 17. 2 Larger growers normally grow in large, gutter connected houses.

The device in Fig. 17. 3 hanging in the center of this slide is a "weather station". It is connected to a computer in the office of the greenhouse operation and is used to monitor light intensity, temperature, relative humidity, and CO_2 levels. Note the yellow strips of material running the length of the rows of plants. These yellow sticky tapes are used to trap and monitor pests in the greenhouse. When used in this quantity the sticky tape is actually being used to trap insects as a control strategy.

Fig. 17. 3 The device hanging in the center of this picture is a "weather station".

Fig. 17. 4 Bees are used to pollinate the crop in Green house production.

Greenhouse tomato growers at one time had to pollinate flowers on a daily basis, with a device that vibrated the flower clusters, in order to get good fruit set and yield. Today bees (Fig. 17. 4) are used to pollinate the crop, hence saving a lot of labour. The second most important greenhouse vegetable crop is cucumber. Most of the production is the European or seedless cucumber type.

17.2.7 Landscape Plant Nurseries

Landscape plants include woody plants (trees and shrubs) and hardy herbaceous perennials used for outdoor landscaping purposes. Many smaller retail nurseries direct market to the consumers at the farm (nursery). Larger nurseries are usually more mechanized than smaller nurseries; wholesale container nurseries are usually quite large, producing hundreds of thousands or even millions of container grown plants per year. Woody shrubs for landscaping are often produced in this system.

Another production system is container production. Shrubs grow well in this system. The container-grown plants were part of a research project at the Nova Scotia Agricultural College, Truro, Nova Scotia, Canada to study container-growing media and fertility programmes. Herbaceous perennials like astilbes (落新妇属植物) are also grown in both field production and container production systems. Most container-grown landscape plants are overwintered in hoop houses covered with a white translucent polyethylene. In the summer you will see the container grown plants growing under the hoops since the polyethylene is removed in the spring. When these hoops are covered with plastic in November (to March), the plastic creates a microclimate which will provide sufficient protection for woody plants at temperatures as low as −25℃, ground surfaces in the container nursery are usually covered with materials to suppress weeds. In recent years this system has become more and more popular as a way to grow high quality herbaceous perennials for landscaping.

Chapter 18 Environmental innovations in the "green" industry

Learning objectives

1. Describe the relationship between horticulture, the environment and agriculture.
2. Explain the environmental benefits of plants.
3. Describe the concept of green space and identify the various segments of the green industry.
4. Explain how some basic principles of sustainability can be applied to landscape planning and maintenance.
5. Define the following terms:
   - Horticulture
   - Environmental horticulture
   - Green infrastructure

18.1 The concept of environmental horticulture

The discipline of agriculture is a subsector of Plant Science, and Plant Science consists of three particular groups, agronomy, forestry and horticulture. Horticulture has been defined as the science and art of growing fruits, vegetables, flowers or ornamental plants, the purposes of which are raising plants for food and aesthetics and usually can be broken down into three categories: pomology (fruit crops); olericulture (growth of plants for herbaceous crops); and environmental horticulture (using plants to enhance our environment or our surroundings) . Herein environmental horticulture falls into the latter under horticulture, resulting in the development of the minds and emotions of individuals, the enrichment and health of communities and the integration of the concept of the garden in the breadth of modern civilization. This is part of the overall definition of agriculture which includes the changing of sunlight into healthy, happy people. Environmental horticulture is one of the keys to mental and emotional health of people.

Environmental horticulture, in a broad sense, covers floriculture, nursery production and the concept of landscape horticulture. Landscape horticulture deals with the use and care of plants in the landscape; that may be constructing gardens or creating green spaces, using plants or maintaining those plants, or managing turfgrass, e. g. Golf course management and sod production. In addition, landscape horticulture includes park management and the field of arboriculture (including trees and tree care for communities and municipalities).

Plants enhance our lives, they provide us with oxygen, food, make us happy, and enhance the beauty of our living place and communities. It is difficult to imagine what it would be like without plants, trees, shrubs and turf; plants have become an important part of our culture, like Christmas trees, the multi-million dollar business in the western world. Take the example of a rose flower; in the world, no single plant in history has had as much influence on culture. The Roman civilization had an enormous infatuation with the rose, the concept of meeting "ad roseum" means that anything said inside the meeting would be kept secret and it was always signified by a rose over the top of the door and that comes from Roman civilization.

18.2 The environmental benefits of plants

18.2.1 Capturing carbon dioxide

Plants capture energy from sun and take in carbon dioxide from the atmosphere and provide oxygen through the mechanism of photosynthesis. In particular, the capture of carbon dioxide results in carbon sequestration that reduces carbon dioxide concentration in the atmosphere and mitigates against the global warming trend. A large tree can actually store up to 3100 kg of carbon through the process of photosynthesis as carbohydrates within the plant. Carbon dioxide is a significant part of the whole concept of global warming, so it is significant to sequester carbon from the atmosphere.

18.2.2 Reducing air pollution

Plants are very effective in keeping particulate matter out of the atmosphere. A line of trees along a country road can catch dust which then washes off and goes back into the soil during a subsequent rainfall. The trees are effectively acting as an air filter. Deciduous trees can actually reduce particulate matter by up to 9%. Coniferous trees are even more effective; they are capable of reducing particulate matter up to 13%. Conifers would be more effective than deciduous trees or leafy trees, because they have foliage all year round and more surface area on a conifer than there is on a broadleaf tree. Plants are also effective in reducing air pollution in respect to other chemicals such as sulphur dioxide, carbon monoxide and nitrogen oxide.

18.2.3 Preventing soil erosion

Plants indeed play a very key role in reducing soil erosion; both large trees and shrubs intercept the rain falling from the sky before it hits the soil. Plants intercept and slow down the rain and any leaf litter or organic material that is on the surface help slow down the runoff of the water over the soil. It actually also gives a better opportunity for the water to percolate slowly into the soil. Water is moving over the soil a little bit more slowly so there is more opportunity for it to sink into the soil, thus less opportunity to pick up soil because it is moving quickly and take that to pollute our streams and waterways. When plants die and decay, they break down into organic material which contributes to the soil improving soil structure, making the soil less susceptible to erosion. In addition, the living roots of the plants hold the soil together and take up water.

18.2.4 Conserving energy

It is also important to look at plants in their ability to assist us in conserving energy. Regarding winter heating costs, placing plants around a house can actually reduce the cost of heating a structure by up to 16% to channel air or to protect it from cold winds that remove that heat from the surface. In the summer, a simple tree in the right place provides shade which intercepts the sun's rays and produces a certain degree of relative humidity in the area that can actually reduce the ambient air temperature by up to 9 degrees Celsius.

18.2.5 Limiting ozone production

Plants do not actually absorb ozone but they can help create ozone from forming by keeping the temperature down. Some trees and some tree processes through volatile organic compounds actually contribute to ozone formation but overall, the influence that trees and plants have on our surface temperatures of the earth helps reduce ozone formation.

18.2.6 Benefiting wildlife

Plants create habitat providing diversity, not only in plant life but also in animal life since they offer protection for those inhabitants and provide connectivity between safe habitats. The green spaces are important for wildlife; development is constantly infringing upon their natural habitat and connecting corridors. The roaming animals (such as deer) can use these connecting corridors to move from one area to another.

18.3 Designing an environmental horticulture

In brief, Environmental Horticulture is the use of plants to enhance our environment not only aesthetically, but also ecologically. It is important to understand that when we are working in the environment we are working within an ecosystem. An ecosystem is a community of organisms that are working together with their environment as an integrated unit. Human beings are always working within a landscape with both living and nonliving entities, while developing a relationship, exchanging energy in between. So whenever people make a decision in the landscape, or a decision related to installing or modifying the landscape, or managing the landscape, they are affecting many different living organisms, by changing non-living things (and possibly living things as well), and also modifying their relationships. Therefore, humans need to make design decisions in an environmentally responsible manner. Each design decision should be respectful of and integrated with natural processes that are inherent in the outdoor environment. A number of things need to be considered:

- The universally present forces of nature
- Precipitation
- Sun, how intense is it? how does it affect microclimates?
- Wind
- Seasonal change (how to design things to take advantage of seasonal change; or enhance seasonal change, perhaps)
- Plant development and growth (are the designers aware of how plants develop and grow throughout their lives)
- Ecology of plant and wildlife communities (are the designers aware of how that plant or plants will fit into the ecology of the local community? How will surrounding plants and wildlife respond to the changes of landscape?)

So there are several environmental design fundamentals considered:

18.3.1 Respecting and enhancing site microclimates

Microclimates, for example, are related to energy and some of the universally present forces of nature. They are small scale climatic conditions in localized areas as a result of sun, wind, or maybe protection from structures. It represents climatic conditions that are different; sometimes better, sometimes worse than the surrounding area. They are different and must be kept in mind when planning a landscape. Perhaps a microclimate represents a space to improve. Maybe shade can be introduced to a hot, dry side of a building to conserve energy. Or perhaps a windbreak to reduce the amount of heat-loss from a building can be put up on a windswept hill to make it a more comfortable place to be. Microclimates can easily be created to enhance the landscape and make it more useful.

18.3.2 Encouraging biodiversity

Diversity is another thing that designer needs to think about. Biodiversity is simply the variety of living things. It is not a good idea to have a landscape that is made up of primarily the same living organism. An example of where this went terribly wrong was the planting the elm trees in the northeastern Canada and USA (in fact all over North America). Elm trees were once planted in great numbers throughout the towns and cities. Unfortunately, then finally a great majority of these trees have been lost because of the Dutch Elm disease and insect. The problem actually began when people decided to plant so many of the same species. The insect or the disease occurs naturally. That has had a tremendous impact on the street-scapes of our towns and cities. Diversifying our landscapes makes them more tolerant of environmental stresses and conditions (Fig. 18.1).

Fig. 18.1 Biodiversification in a landscape in Japan.

18.3.3 Reducing inputs

It is also important to minimize inputs like energy, time and water in designing and managing a landscape. The more we can minimize these resources, the more sustainable these landscapes can be. For example, saving water will certainly help conserve water resources; minimizing the amount of fertilizer will save on the cost of the product put on the soil but it would also save us in terms of the cost of the energy required to carry out this procedure.

18.3.4 Maximizing re-usable resources

To reuse or recycle materials in our landscapes, composting is a perfect example. Composting occurs both naturally and under the guidance of people. A tree growing in the forest doesn't receive any extra fertilizer from inputs. But that tree still gets adequate nutrients that it needs to grow. These nutrients are made available through the natural decomposition process -natural composting. It is really a quite elegant scenario that the tree grows, puts on biomass and through the seasonal growth cycle, that biomass -the leaves and debris -falls to the ground, decomposes, creates organic matter, adds to the soil and provides nutrients for the trees. It is a perfect example of reusing and recycling. However, in modern landscapes to clean up any debris and remove it from the site are often encouraged to break a critical chain in this natural decomposition cycle that often produces some disease in the plants. As a result, managers usually end up adding additional fertilizers and other materials to the soil to make up for this material being removed. In this case, it is extremely good to compost this material to recycle those nutrients back into the growth cycle of this tree.

18. 3. 5 Encouraging sustainability

All of these things above add up to help us achieve sustainability. Sustainability means meeting the needs of the present without sacrificing the needs of the future. It can be achieved by perhaps reducing inputs, by taking steps to be more environmentally friendly, perhaps harmonious with nature, and more self-sufficient or self-perpetuating in developing a landscape. Then such a landscape should be functional, environmentally friendly, maintainable, cost effective, visually pleasing and environmentally aesthetic.

Fig. 18. 2 A man-made landscape with plants that never existed naturally.

In achieving above, plants are introduce to be a desirable elements, their textures, lines and colours, to create a sense of place with different forms and mass. Plants also can be used to soften architecture or provide human scale. Fig. 18. 2 demonstrates the totally man-made landscape that never existed naturally. All these trees were planted. It is a man-made ecosystem but it is very successful. It is a good example of aesthetic enhancement to our environment.

This green infrastructure is very important to our communities. Green infrastructure refers to strategically planned and managed networks of wilderness, parks, greenways, conservation easements, and working lands with conservation value that supports native species, maintains natural ecological processes, sustains air and water resources, and contributes to the health and quality of life for communities and people. Often, green infrastructure is underrated when it comes to planning our cities and communities. Green infrastructure it is a critical part of our cities and communities.

18. 4 Green industry

Green industry is the industry that grows, sells, installs, maintains and preserves green infrastructure to enhance living environment, usually such plants are cultivated (sometimes sold) in greenhouses and nurseries with specially designed and structured plants to enhance living surroundings.

Fig. 18. 3 shows a designed landscape between the Highway and Public Park in Fuzhou City in Fujian province of P. R. China, the green industry represents the landscape contractors that are installing these landscapes, creating them, and maintaining them. Some of those specialists are arborists, who deal trees and shrubs within our city street-scapes and urban forests. Golf courses are also part of our green industry. They actually represent a significant part of green infrastructure in many communities. Municipal parks, botanical gardens and arboreta are also very important. It actually represents a huge business with many viable career options. It is difficult to put a value on the green industry but it has been determined that environmental horticulture is the fasting growing segment of agriculture in the United States and elsewhere in the world. It was estimated that the industry was worth over 50 billion dollars in the year

2000 and a recent study in the northeast US determines the value of the industry at 3.8 billion dollars to the local economy. In Canada, it has been determined that in the floriculture/nursery segment of the industry in 2002 the production value was 1.8 billion. That certainly is a very significant figure in terms of agriculture in this country. Indeed, the green industry represents a significant contributor to our economy. It is a significant aspect of agriculture and it is a very viable career option nowadays for graduates particularly of agronomy and horticulture.

Fig. 18.3 A designed landscape between Highway and Public Park in Fuzhou.

Literatures cited in this chapter

Haber W. 2004. Landscape ecology as a bridge from ecosystems to human ecology. *Ecological Research* 19: 99-106.

Fu B. J. and Lu Y. H. 2006. The progress and perspectives of landscape ecology in China. *Progress in Physical Geography* 30 (2): 232-244.

Opdam P., Foppen R., and Vos C. 2002. Bridging the gap between ecology and spatial planning in landscape ecology. *Landscape Ecology* 16: 767-779.

Unit 5 Agroecosystem Management: Issues, Problems and Solutions

Chapter 19 Agroecosystem health and services: Ecology and economics

Learning objectives

1. List at least 5 ecosystem services.
2. Describe the steps in ecosystem management and the theoretical base of agroecosystem management.
3. Explain the difference between ecosystem services and agroecosystem services.
4. Describe the function of agroecosystem services in agricultural production.
5. What do ecosystem goods and services provide for humans?
6. Name three seed dispersal mechanisms.
7. How does people measure an ecosystem service?
8. Can you explain the basic indicator concepts of ecosystem health: vigour, organization and resilience?
9. What are the four categories of agroecosystem services discussed in this chapter?
10. What is the goal of agroecosystem management?
11. Explain the differences between microscopic management and macroscopic management in agroecosystem management.

19.1 Ecosystem services, health and management

19.1.1 Ecology of ecosystem services

Ecosystem services comprise of both ecosystem goods and environmental services. Essentially, ecosystem services sustain all species (including humans) and economies. Ecosystem services, also referred to as natural service or natural capital, provide fundamental life-supporting services such as oxygen production, while also enhancing the quality of human life and functioning of the world's economies. Human economies are merely a subsidy of an ecosystem. A sustainable society lives off the biological income provided by these ecological services without depleting or degrading them. Theoretically, all ecosystems could operate sustainably by using renewable energy and recycling chemical nutrients; Fig. 19.1 shows a conceptual diagram of this process.

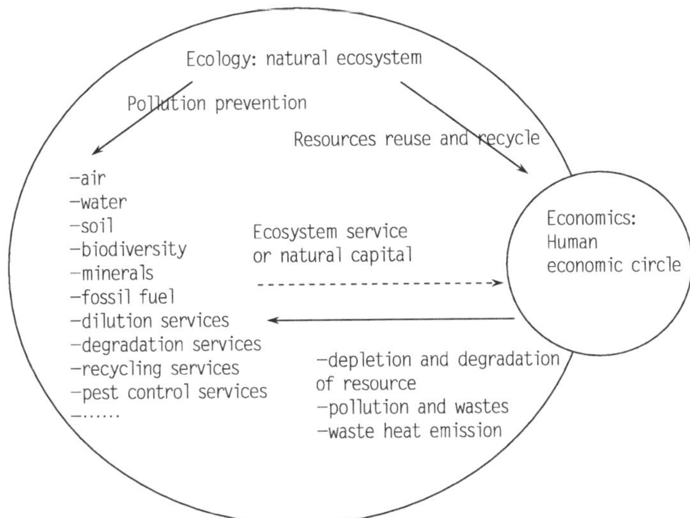

Fig. 19. 1 Ecosystems services (or natural capital) sustain all species and human economies.

Civilizations would cease to exist without the abundance of ecosystem goods and services. Some of the key ecosystems goods and services include:

(1) Production of ecosystem goods

Natural ecosystems provide people with a myriad of goods for human benefit. Goods of this sort include foods, marketable items, labour and materials. Ecosystems offer food in the form of vegetation, fruit, nuts, spices and fish for human consumption. Fish plays a major role in the economy through commercial harvest, sale, sport fishing and other fishing related activities.

Ecosystems also offer marketable goods that stem from animals using grasslands as habitat. These goods include wheat, oats and barley, animal meat such as deer, moose and elk, and animal products such as wool, leather and milk. Animal labour can further be considered as a secondary product of ecosystem services.

Materials derived from natural ecosystems, such as fibre, fuelwood and industrial products also play a major role in society. Most people have become heavily dependent upon these natural materials offered by ecosystems. Fig. 19. 2 below shows the breakdown of some common ecosystem goods.

(2) Generation and maintenance of biodiversity

The generation and maintenance of biodiversity is a crucial component of ecosystem services. Generating and maintaining a multi-scale, interdependent, co-evolutionary array of organisms ensures humans continually benefit from the abundance of biological diversity. Biodiversity supports conventional crops and future food security, genetic and biochemical resources and pharmaceutical enterprises, which exceed $40 billion per year for nearly 80% of the medical systems worldwide (Daily, 1997).

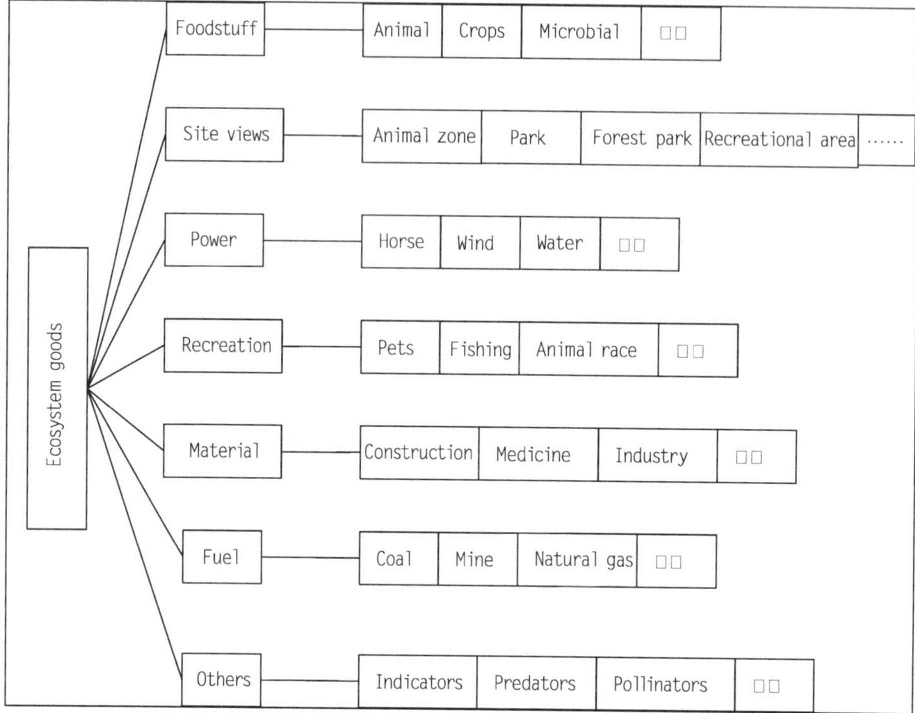

Fig. 19.2 Production of goods that ecosystems provide (Wang, 2007).

(3) Partial stabilization and regulation of climate

Ecosystems help stabilize climate on the global scale and regulate weather and temperature on the regional scale. Natural ecosystems stabilize climate through the prevention of overheating and by the removal of excess greenhouse gases in the atmosphere. The stabilizing mechanisms usually result from natural trends in feedback mechanisms. On a regional scale, ecosystems exert influence over temperature and weather, influencing precipitation, evaporation and transpiration.

(4) Mitigation of droughts and floods

Soil, plants and plant litter soak up the 119, 000 cubic kilometres of rainfall each year, allowing water to permeate through the soil and plant roots into aquifers and streams (Daily, 1997). Protection from soil and vegetation prevents annual rainfall from flooding most of the Earth's surface. On the other extreme, when rainfall is scare soil and plants store water as groundwater and in plant roots to nourish the ecosystems, reducing disruptions in the water cycle and loss of nutrients.

(5) Pollination of crops and natural vegetation

Ecosystems provide habitat for natural pollinators (usually animals) for plants and crops. Pollinators, from bees and hummingbirds to beetles and birds, require many different habitats to complete the different stages of their life cycles. Keeping these ecosystems in tact ensures over 200, 000 species of plants receive pollination. Likewise, many agricultural crops require pollination from wild animals as well. Natural ecosystems provide this service for free, however, if humans were to try and replicate this process it would cost many billions of dollars each year.

(6) Dispersal of seeds

To disperse seeds for germination in areas beyond a plant's rooted zone, plants depend on other mechanisms in an ecosystem such as wind, water and animals. Wind carries seeds such as dandelions, while water moves seeds such as the seafaring coconut. Animals on the other hand, transfer seeds in a variety of ways. Some seeds have evolved to latch onto animals and get carried away; other seeds are disguised as sweet fruits that pass through an animal's digestive track. For instance, the Southern Cassowary in Australia disperses over 200 seeds species many kilometres away from the original plant roots. Other seeds have evolved to have a very specific counterpart, such that only one animal species can disperse the seeds. This ecosystem service provides numerous ecosystem benefits, particularly by protecting plant species from extinction due to natural or human disturbances through multiple seed dispersal mechanisms.

(7) Natural pest control

Pests, competitors of food, fibre and materials, destroy much of the world's harvest and compete for water, light and nutrients. Luckily, natural pest controls in the form of birds, bugs, diseases and other organisms act as biological control agents to limit pest abundance. No chemical pesticide truly competes with a biological control agent, since pests can quickly evolve to resist synthetic poisons acting as artificial prey.

(8) Services Supplied by Soil

Soil provides four interdependent natural ecosystem services:

• Soil shelters plant seeds for germination and provides physical support for plants to anchor their roots and grow

• Soils maintains the cycling and movement of nutrients to plants acting as a buffer to fertilizer and leaching, and giving plants access to a supply of nutrients when needed

• Soil plays an important role in the detoxification and decomposition of dead organic matter and wastes, breaking down chemical bonds through specialized reactions

• Soil regulates carbon, nitrogen and sulfur stored in vegetation

(9) Provision of aesthetic beauty and intellectual stimulation that lift the human spirit

An important but often misunderstood ecosystem service is the aesthetic beauty, intellectual stimulation and renewal of spirituality humans receive from nature. These types of ecosystem services provide people with the opportunity to partake in activities such as hiking, camping and gardening, to observe and internalize nature through art, film and bird watching. A long history of religion, art and cultural traditions highlight the deep appreciation people have for the peace and beauty one may find in nature.

These ecosystem services presented above highlight the many benefits that the natural ecosystem provides to humanity. These ecosystem services support life and maintain the human economy. These free services would otherwise cost humanity billions upon billions of dollars, in addition to the benefits they provide through health and a good quality of life.

19.1.2 Economics of ecosystem services

Valuing ecosystem services proves extremely complex and highly uncertain. Generally measurements rely on marginal values, such as estimating an ecosystem flow or service in terms of how much preservation or destruction would occur due to the loss of a specific area. This qualitative valuation is enough evidence to validate or reject plans on land altering projects. However, replicating or replenishing lost ecosystem services generally far exceeds the estimated worth of those services (Fig. 19.3, Fig. 19.4).

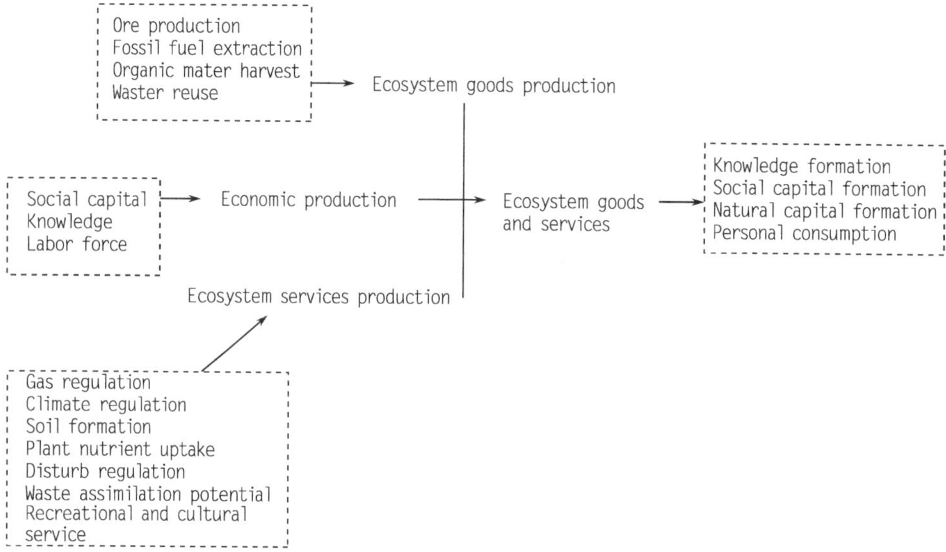

Fig. 19.3 Economic production completely deriving from ecosystem services.

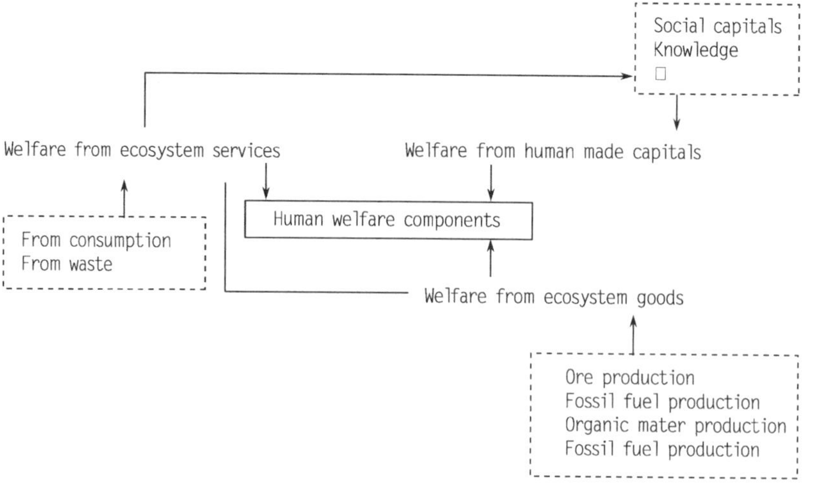

Fig. 19.4 Human welfare deriving from ecosystem services.

The importance of valuating ecosystem services is threefold: ① to aid in macro-allocation decisions between economic production and ecosystem services and between economic infrastructure (including agriculture) and ecological infrastructure; ② to avoid exceeding economic thresholds, where ecological degradation costs will exceed the benefits; and ③ to avoid exceeding ecological thresholds that threaten long term sustainability and intergenerational macro-allocation of services.

The value of ecosystem function, the capacity of natural processes and components to provide goods and service that satisfy human needs, depends greatly on the value of the ecosystem service.

The value of an ecosystem service stems from its ecological, socio-cultural and economic importance. These services can be measured by its use value and non-use value. Fig. 19. 5 depicts a framework for mapping and valuing ecosystem services based on two key concepts: ① valuation—how can we assess the relative value of various ecosystem services? and ② incentives—how can we provide rewards for providing ecosystem services? Fig. 19. 6 explains the valuation process further in terms of use and non-use values.

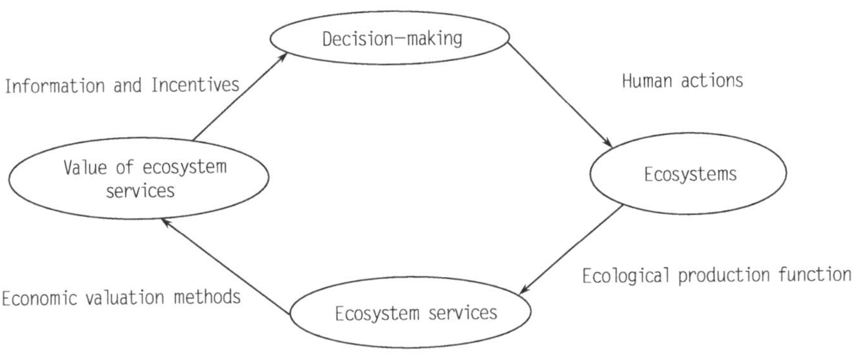

Fig. 19. 5 A framework for mapping and valuing ecosystem services.

Use value in Fig. 19. 6 refers to direct use value and indirect use value. Direct use value includes market and trade values, usually for goods, but can also apply to information and regulation. Indirect use values on the other hand, impart valuation techniques through indirect assessments. Usually indirect use value measures the value of the loss of a service. These measurements include avoided costs, replacement costs, factor incomes, travel costs and hedonic pricing (Groot, 2002). For instance, flood control is considered an avoided cost, or the value people are willing to pay to avoid damages from floods.

19. 1. 3 Ecosystem Health

(1) What is a healthy ecosystem?

In 1990, the Environmental Protection Agency of United States broadened their management goals from protecting human health to protecting ecosystem health (Costanza, 1992). Since then, the science advisory board has improved management to reflect linkages between human health and ecological health in the U. S. national environmental policy. Public awareness about sustainability has broadened the scope of

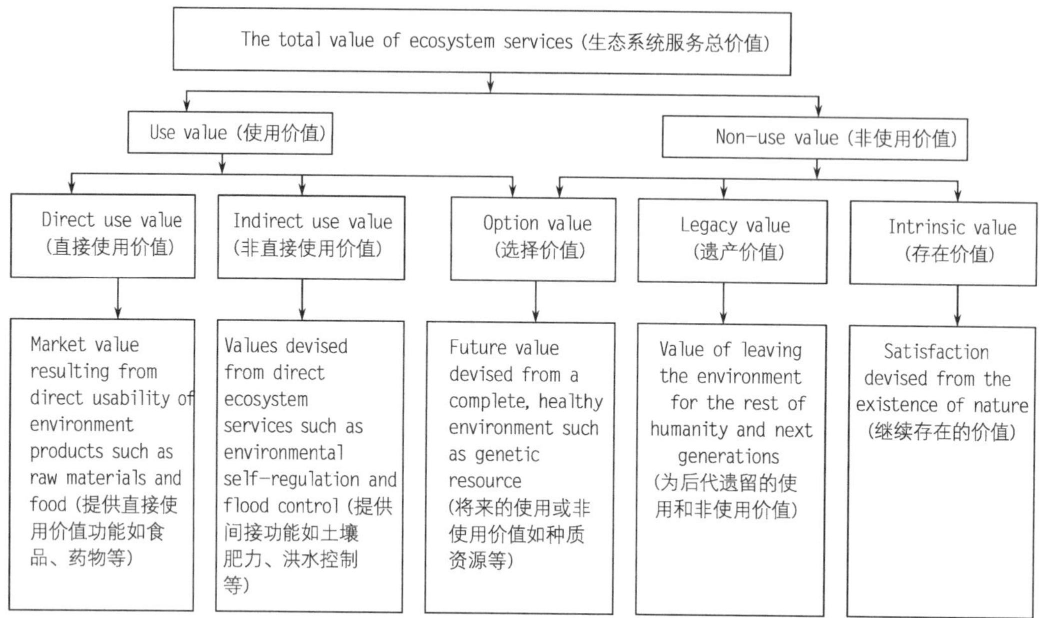

Fig. 19. 6 Value classifications of ecosystem services (Wang, 2007).

ecosystem health into a social objective. Ecosystem health, as analogous to human health, can take on many different definitions, including but not limited to:

- Health as homeostasis
- Health as the absence of disease
- Health as diversity or complexity
- Health as stability or resilience
- Health as vigour or scope for growth
- Health as balance between system components

In 1990 and 1992 Costanza developed the following two definitions of ecosystem health: ① "An ecological system is healthy and free from 'distress syndrome' if it is stable and sustainable" —that is, if it is active and maintains its organization and autonomy over time and is resilient to stress; and ② the concept that "ecosystem health is a comprehensive, multi-scale, dynamic, hierarchical measure of system resilience, organization, and vigour." A healthy ecosystem must maintain structure (organization) and function (vigour) over time, in the face of external stress (resilience). The definition of a healthy ecosystem must also stay within the parameters of the larger system of which it is part (context) and the smaller system it creates (components).

(2) measuring ecosystem health

Fig. 19. 7 demonstrates an approach to measuring ecosystem health. Since measures of health are inherently less precise and difficult to obtain, this model shows the progression from "indicators" directly measured from the status of a component, to composites of these indicators, referred to as "endpoints", to "values" of health.

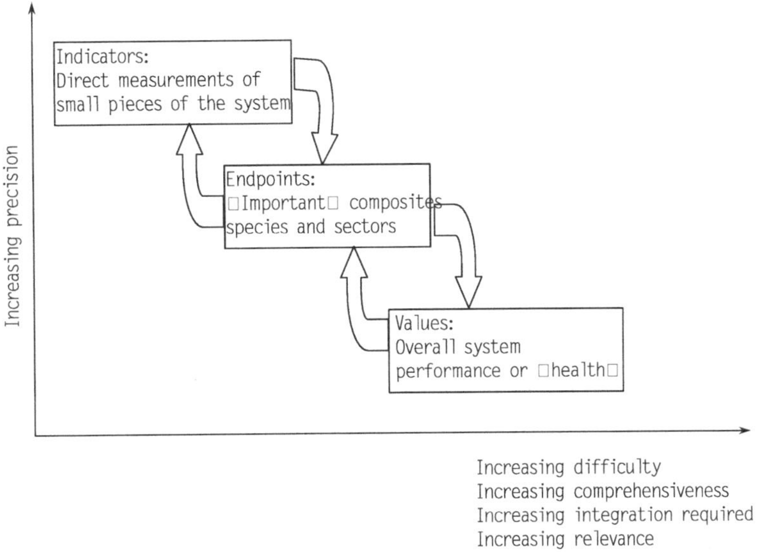

Fig. 19.7 Relationship among indicators, endpoints and values (Costanza, 1992).

Each component of an ecosystem, whether it is a cell, organism, species or biosphere, has a finite lifespan. A healthy and sustainable ecosystem in this context indicates a component attains its full and expected lifespan.

Cutting short the life span of an ecosystem component is an indicator of poor health. The key, however, is differentiating between changes due to normal lifespan limits and succession, and changes that actually cut short the life span of the ecosystem component. Distress syndrome refers to the breakdown of an entire system, in an irreversible process where the normal lifespan is cut short (Costanza, 1995). A fairly comprehensive assessment of overall system performance and health combines three basic concepts: vigour, organization and resilience (Fig. 19.8). Here, Vigour is generally quantified as a measure of activity, metabolism or primary productivity. For instance, methods that already exist in the system such as gross primary productivity and gross domestic product measure the overall activity, metabolism or economic growth in the system. While these measures help valuate vigour easily, vigour alone does not indicate overall health. Organization refers to the interconnections within ecosystems, affected by the diversity of species within the system and the exchange pathways between them (Costanza, 1995). Unlike vigour, organization measurements are not straightforward; they involve complex analyses such as an Input-output (I/O) analysis or an ecological/economic mass-balance model. Resilience pertains to the ability of the system to withstand stress disturbances and perturbations. The concept of resilience consists of two main aspects: ① time for the system takes to recover from stress, and ② thresholds for absorbing stress in which the system can no longer recover (Costanza, 1995). Measuring resilience requires dynamic simulation models for prediction, which makes true results difficult to obtain. The most accepted method of resilience measurement is the Recovery Time (R_t), or the maximum magnitude of stress (MS)

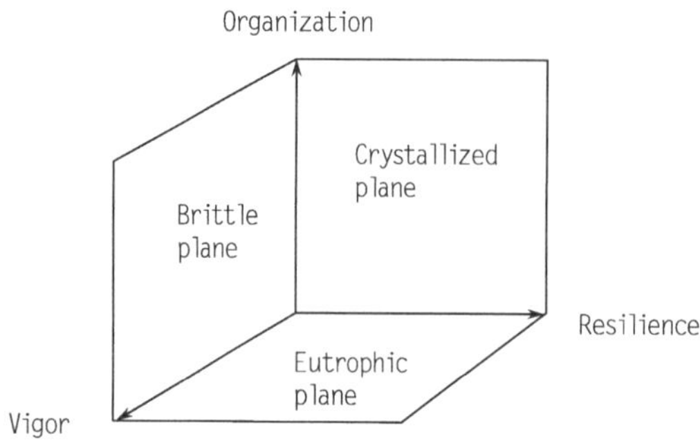

Fig. 19.8 A three-dimensional plot of system vigour, organization, and resilience (Costanza, 1995).

divided by the Recovery Time, as an estimate of the time it takes for the overall system to recover.

Fig. 19.8 also offers a three-dimensional plot for measuring the overall health of an ecosystem with respect to vigour, organization and resilience. A healthy ecosystem exhibits a balance among these three components, whereas a system that exhibits less of one or two of these components shows signs of crystallization, brittle or eutrophic features. For instance, nutrient rich lakes showing early succession have little organization and should be considered "eutrophic". Ultimately imbalanced, unhealthy ecosystems hinder the human economy, as remediation requires trillions of dollars and often still cannot offer the full range of ecosystem services naturally derived.

19.1.4 Ecosystem management

No standard definition exists for ecosystem management (EM), but rather, over 50 EM definitions with respect to values and working fields are referenced in literature. Grumbine (1994) offers a general but very comprehensive definition: "Ecosystem Management integrates scientific knowledge of ecological relationships within a complex socio-political and values framework toward the general goal of protecting native ecosystem integrity over the long-term."

Based on the ten dominant EM themes presented by Grumbine in 1994 (hierarchical context, ecological boundaries, ecological integrity, data collection, monitoring, adaptive management, interagency cooperation, organizational change, humans embedded in nature, and values) in 1999 Pavlikakis and Tsihrintzis developed the following steps to EM methodology (Fig. 19.9):

- Localization of issues: determining most important issues
- Participation of the population: public participation in the decision-making process
- Political, legislative and economic analysis: conducting political, legislative and economic analysis before beginning process
- Definition of goals: stating clear goals and communicating them to the public
- Definition of the boundaries of the ecosystem: understanding local restrictions and opportunities; understanding the needs and expectations of local residents
- Development of a plan: Involving all entities in the planning and communication process; securing funding and human resources
- Monitoring: collecting high quality scientific data and information
- Evaluation: continually evaluating the EM project to reach stated and expected goals

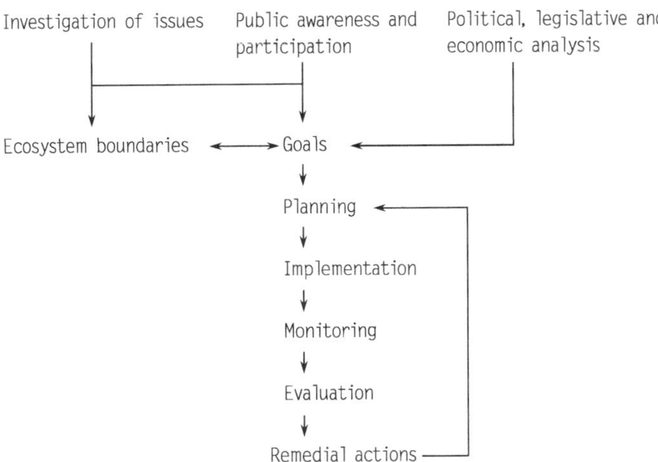

Fig. 19. 9 General steps in ecosystem management methodology (Pavlikakis, 2000).

19. 2 Agroecosystem services, health and management

19. 2. 1 Ecology and economics of agroecosystem services

As we recall from Chapter 3, agroecosystems are critically important managed ecosystems. Ecosystem services from agricultural land provide important non-market goods and services imperative to sustain life at all levels and agriculture. Therefore, maintaining and restoring ecological functions to an agroecosystem is of paramount importance for agricultural sustainability.

Agroecosystem services build upon ecosystem services discussed earlier in this chapter. Agroecosystem services refer to the provisioning, regulating, cultural, and supporting services. Provisioning services include the six "F's" —food, fuel, fibre, fodder, fish and forage; this class also includes other tangible goods produced in agroecosystems and marketed in our social system such as genetic resources, biochemicals, natural medicines and fresh water. Regulating services include pollination, water regulation and purification, erosion regulation, disease regulation, pest regulation and flood control. Cultural services consist of cultural diversity, spiritual and religious values, inspiration, aesthetic values (scenic qualities), recreation and tourism. Supporting services includes soil formation, primary production, nutrient cycling and water cycling.

The management of agriculture and agroecosystems has huge effects on the quality and quantity of agroecosystem services that contribute to human production. Suitable management practices ensure agroecosystem health and overall ecosystem health.

19. 2. 2 Agroecosystem health

Agroecosystems are an important component of the larger ecosystem. Human participation differentiates agroecosystems from all other ecosystems, allowing for a complex integrated nature-economy-society system that naturally changes over time. Therefore, ideal agroecosystem health accounts for variation with time and space without limiting the system's ability to uphold functional and structural characteristics to produce agroecosystem end products and services. Broadening the ecosystem health assessment method based on the dynamic characteristics vigour, organization and resilience (maintenance), in agroecosystem health we also assess structural, functional or organizational characteristics.

Structural components include resource availability, accessibility, diversity, equitability and equity. Functional criteria include productivity, efficiency and effectiveness. Organizational criteria include integrity, self-organization, autonomy and self-reliance. Generally, measurements of agroecosystem health recognize important linkages between agroecosystem health and: soil and water quality; human health; Integrated Soil Management (ISM) and Integrated Pest Management (IPM); ecological impacts of biological indicators, genetically modified crops (transgenic crops); roles and impacts of agricultural inputs, policy and landscape ecology; and green food development.

Agroecosystems sustain Earth's life support systems. Unsurprisingly then, agroecosystem health plays an important role in agricultural stability and sustainable development of human society. Research on agroecosystem health provides a scientific basis and diagnostic tools for monitoring and managing agroecosystems. Rational human intervention can enhance healthy system dynamics and sustainable development, while irrational human intervention may interfere with overall system health, resulting in damage, ecosystem degradation, and ecological disaster. An agroecosystem management model must combine sound ecology, biology, economics, information science and other disciplines. Agroecosystem health and agroecosystem management highly depend upon each other and require a symbiotic relationship to pursue sustainable agricultural development.

19.2.3 Agroecosystem management

(1) The theoretical basis for Agroecosystem management

Agroecosystem management derives from a holistic perspective of agroecosystems, including all environmental and human elements. From this point of view, agroecosystem management aims to attain sustainable use and management of natural resources accomplished by using social, cultural, economic, political and ecological methods. Sustainable use and management refers to sustainable agricultural production, an ecologically based assessment of structure, function and multi-dimensionality, and spatial scale of food systems. Combining these principles, agroecosystem management can provide ecological guidelines to design and manage sustainable agroecosystems.

(2) Modelling agroecosystem management

In theory, agroecosystem management should be highly applicable to different types of agroecosystems and easily implemented. In practice however, the application of agroecological principles proves challenging. Maintaining a resource with minimal outside artificial inputs, good nutrient cycling within the system with few "leaks", control of pests and diseases through internal regulating mechanisms, and resilient to human and harvest disturbances requires a balance among vigour, organization, structure, resilience and equality. One agroecosystem health assessment model established uses a four-stage framework with 36 indicators (Zhu, 2010a):

Level 1. Object: evaluate objectives and composite index of agroecosystem health

Level 2. Item: determine subsystem of agroecosystem

Level 3. Evaluation factors: determine specific elements for each item

Level 4. Index level: detail indicators to express evaluation factors

An agroecosystem management model should also develop in consideration of local conditions, with a design adapted to the local environment making full use of information technology, biotechnology and ecological engineering technology to carry out Integrated Plant Nutrient Management, Soil Management, Water Management, and Pest Management. Conceptually, agroecosystem management must focus on desired objectives, microscopic and macroscopic management.

- Microscopic management

Microscopic management in an agroecosystem refers to the monitoring and regulation of the interactions and energy flows within the ecosystem. Optimal behaviour of agroecosystems depends on the level of interactions between various biotic and abiotic components occurring in the soil, water and air. In addition, energy flows and nutrient cycles within the air, water and soil also form a basic component of agroecosystem services. In essence, microscopic agroecosystem management should effectively regulate these flows to achieve the most efficient use of energy and resources in an agroecosystem, managing both microscopic organisms to field wide species.

- Macroscopic management

Macroscopic agroecosystem management must account for the larger ecosystem in which it exists (context). Macroscopic management practices go beyond the relationships found on the farm, to integrate into the larger economic, systemic, social and cultural driving forces, linked by policies and connecting producers and consumers. Thus, a good agroecosystem management strategy can achieve its goals through implementing decision-making, legal, participatory and ecological mechanisms.

In summary, both ecosystem and agroecosystems provide goods and services without which, society would cease to exist. These goods and services range from essential activities such as keeping the environment suitable for life to offering aesthetic pleasure from the simple existence of nature. There are nine key ecosystem services discussed in this chapter: ① production of ecosystem goods, ② generation and maintenance of biodiversity, ③ partial stabilization and regulation of climate, ④ mitigation of droughts and floods, ⑤ pollination of crops and natural vegetation, ⑥ dispersal of seeds, ⑦ natural pest control, ⑧ services supplied by soil and ⑨ provision of aesthetic beauty and intellectual stimulation that life the human spirit. Somewhat well defined methods of valuing and measuring ecosystem health rely on vigour, organization and resilience. Agroecosystem health branches out from ecosystem services and health, which makes it slightly more difficult to measure. In this chapter a theoretical basis for agroecosystem development is discussed, with a model for overall agroecosystem health, microscopic management and macroscopic measurement. Research continues to monitor and evaluate methods for both agroecosystem management and methods to value and measure agroecosystem health.

Literatures cited in this chapter

Altieri M. A. 1989. Agroecology: a new research and development paradigm for world agriculture. *Agriculture, Ecosystems and Environment* 27: 37-46.

Conway G. R. 1985. Agroecosystem Analysis. *Agricultural Administration* 20: 31-55.

Costanza R., Sklar F. H., and White M. L. 1990. Modeling coastal landscape dynamics. *BioScience*, 40 (2): 91-107.

Costanza R. 1992. *Toward an operational definition of health. In: Costanza R., Norton B. and Haskell B. Ecosystem Health: New Goals for Environmental Management*. Washington, D. C.: Island Press.

Costanza R. and Patten B. C. 1995. Defining and predicting sustainability. *Ecological Economics* 15: 193-196.

Daily G. C., Alexander S., Ehrlich P. R., Goulder L., Lubchenco J., Matson P. A., Mooney H. A., Postel S., Schneider S. H., Tilman D., and Woodwell G. M. 1997. Ecosystem Services: Benefits Supplied to Human Societies by Natural Ecosystems. Ur6: http://www. wms. org/biod/value/Ecosystem Services, html, Search date. Nov. 15. 2011.

Daly H. E. and Townsend K. N. 1993. *Valuing the earth: economics, ecology, ethics, Steady state economics: the economics of biophysical equilibrium and moral growth*. Boston, Massachusetts

Gliessman S. R. 1998. *Agroecology: ecological processes in sustainable agriculture*. Michigan: Ann Arbor Press.

Groot R. S., Wilson M. A., and Boumans R. M. J. 2002. A typology for the classification description and valuation of ecosystem functions, goods and services. *Ecological Economics* 41: 393-408.

Grumbine R. E. 1994. What is ecosystem management? *Conservation Biology Essays* 8 (1): 27-38.

Holling C. S. 1986. The resilience of terrestrial ecosystems: local surprise and global change. In: Clark W. C. and Munn, R. E. *Sustainable Development of the Biosphere*. Cambridge University Press.

Holmes T. P. and Kramer R. A. 1995. *Economic Values, Ethics, and Ecosystem Health, Southereastern Center for Forest Economics Research*. Research Triangle Park, http://www. srs. fs-usda. gov/eion/pubs/scfer/scferso. pdf.

Jackson L. E., Pascual U. and Hodgkin T. 2007. Utilizing and conserving agrobiodiversity in agricultural landscapes. *Agriculture, Ecosystems, and Environment* 121 (3): 196-210.

Mageau M. T., Costanza R. and Ulanowicz R. E. 1995. The development and initial testing of a quantitative assessment of ecosystem health. *Ecosyst Health* 1: 201-213.

Pavlikakis G. E. and Tsihrintzis V. A. 2000. Ecosystem Management: A Review of a New Concept and Methodology. *Water Resources Management* 14: 257-283.

Pimentel D., Harvey. C. Resosudarmo P., Sinclair K., Crist S., Shpritz L., Fitton L. Saffouri R., and Blair R. 1995. Environmental and economic costs of soil erosion and conservation benefits. *Science* 267: 1117-1123.

Rapport D. J. 1989. "What Constitutes Ecosystem Health?." *Perspectives in Biology and Medicine* 33: 120-132.

Rapport D. J. 1992. What is Clinical Ecology? In: Costanza R., Norton B. G., and Haskel B. G. *Ecosystem Health: New Goals for Environmental Management*. Washington, D. C.: Island Press.

Wang S. L. 2005 Information technology: toward the way to the sustainable management of agroecosystem. *Agriculture Network Information* 8: 4-12.

Wang S. L. 2007. Ecosystem Services Assessment and Management. In: Lin W. X. *Ecology*. Beijing: Science Press.

Zhu W. F., Wang S. L., and Caldwell C. D. 2010. Agro-ecosystem service and its managerial essence. *Chinese Journal of Eco-Agriculture* 18 (4): 889-896.

Zhu W. F., Wang S. L., and Caldwell C. D. 2010. Pathways of Assessing Agroecosystem Health and Agroecosystem Management, presented in the 2nd International Workshop on Ecosystem Assessment and Management (EAM), Lanzhou, Gansu, China, July 20-25, 2010.

Chapter 20 A framework for enquiry into agroecosystem management

Learning objectives

1. Define Sustainable Agroecosystem Management and integrated farm management.
2. Explain neoclassifical microeconomics in farm systems analysis.
3. Discuss the differences between the models for neoclassical economics and heterodox economics in farm systems analysis.
4. Draw and explain the conceptual framework for integrated farm management.
5. Explain the overall goal of farm system management.
6. What is an agroecosystem unit?
7. What is the difference between an economic analysis and a financial analysis?
8. Name three assumptions in the neoclassical paradigm.
9. How does Farm Systems Research (FSR) work?
10. How do neoclassical and heterodox economic models differ?
11. Explain the term "agroeconomics".
12. Do you think agricultural policy is based on economic evaluations or true farm values? Explain.
13. What are two methods of integrated farm management?
14. Identify the level each component of integrated farm management falls within.

Sustainable Agroecosystem Management (SAM) uses an ecosystem-based approach for the design and management of natural resources in sustainable agroecosystems. In doing so, SAM addresses the economics and formation of agricultural production (economic, biological and ecological), the agriculturally fragmented landscapes and bio-diversification within its management strategies. Following this school thought, multiple methods of integrated farm management have emerged to achieve the goals of SAM.

20.1 Farm management systems: Goals and units

A farm management system seeks to better agriculture as a business, allowing farmers to determine risks and opportunities associated with farming activities. A holistic design for a farm management system might incorporate concerns of farmers, farm suppliers, environmentalists, local community members, consumers and the general public. To address issues for each of these interest groups, farmers need to understand business management as much as farming. Overall, business management must allow farmers to maintain profitability while balancing on-farm activities such as soil quality and wildlife habitat. The business management activities may include quality insurance of crops, farm productivity and workplace health and safety.

Before deciding on a business management scheme, a farmer must first define the parameters of the farm system. A farm system unit, or "agroecosystem unit," will represent a defined area for a farm management system. The agroecosystem unit proposed here represents a study entity in both the biological and social sense, and is intended to reconcile atomistic and holistic approaches.

Fig. 20. 1 represents a farm unit operating within two superimposed contexts: the farmer and the farm. A farm unit in this sense incorporates social, economic and biophysical characteristics. The farm context deals with natural (ecological) issues such as soil integrity and crop diversity, which imposes some constraints on farmers in operational practices. The farmer, or farm operator, deals with ever-changing social contexts from finance and governance to cultural and spiritual beliefs. A farm system management scheme should aim to achieve the goals of Sustainable Agroecosystem Management on both levels of management and treat the farm as a business.

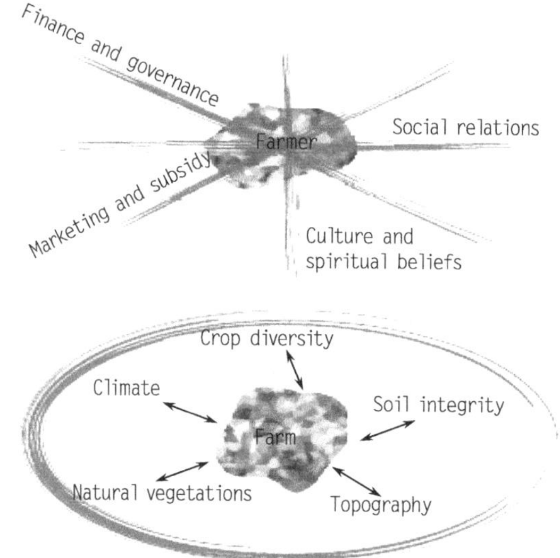

Fig. 20. 1 A farm unit operates within two contexts, the farmer and the farm, and incorporates social, economic, and biophysical characteristics.

A successful farm operation must balance these farm and farmer responsibilities within the agroecosystem unit simultaneously. Balancing livestock on a farm is one such example. Farm animals consume food energy to maintain metabolic processes: the farm persists as a recognizable entity only if the farmer plans and acts to keep appropriate feeds available. Guidelines for feed and animal ethics must be in accordance with governance standards, buying and selling animal necessities fall within marketing and subsidy plans and grazing land must have the right topography, climate and soil integrity for vegetation the animals prefer. In short, both ecological and social (economic) dimensions need to be considered in the overall farm operation (Fig. 20. 2).

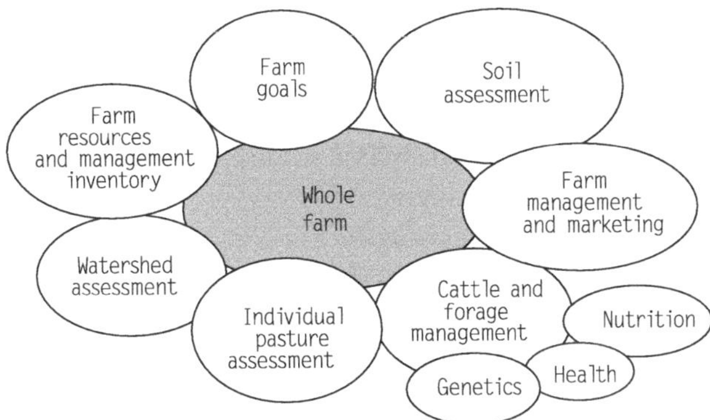

Fig. 20. 2 A farm consists of a complex matrix of entities, which must be considered when managing the agroecosystem unit.

20. 2 Farm systems analysis: Economic and political perspectives

20. 2. 1 Economic perspectives

Using an economics framework for farm system analysis has contributed to agricultural studies since the late 1800's, helping farmers make choices about achieving desired objectives within the limitations of natural resources. An economic analysis addresses a broad scope of farm system concerns, from resource sustainability to agricultural household economics. An economic analysis does not imply profitability as the farm scheme's sole objective, although it often includes a financial analysis: a subset of economic analysis relating to monetary values related to the farm.

Economists generally conduct farm system research with one of two goals: problem solving or knowledge oriented. The underlying concepts behind these research designs can fall within a myriad of disciplines within economics. In this chapter we will discuss neoclassical-based microeconomics and heterodox economics for farm systems analysis.

(1) Neoclassical-based microeconomics

The neoclassical paradigm for farm system analysis has a critical focus on scare resource optimization and allocation, and increased efficiency for determining supply, demand, income, outputs and prices (Collin, 2000). This paradigm is characterized by several assumptions: ① people have rational, stable preferences; ② people focus on equilibrium between farm production and profitable income; and ③ people practice methodological individualism and an atomistic decision-making process. Both modern farm management and agricultural household economics illustrate neoclassical economics to some extent. Most farm system studies of a neoclassical economic analysis relax certain standards or assumptions of the neoclassical paradigm; therefore these study systems are merely extensions of the neoclassical model rather than fundamentally different systems.

Farm Systems Research (FSR) on modern farm management generally uses descriptive statistical analyses, formal surveys of farmer practices and data from farm record keeping programs. Common features of an FSR model include (Colin, 2000):

- Action orientation
- Develop improved technology adapted to local conditions
- Focus on target farmer groups
- Address farmer objectives and constraints
- Teamwork from several researchers and disciplines
- Direct researcher-farmer contact
- Rapid, qualitative data collection
- Technology evaluation from a whole-farm perspective
- On-farm trials with farmer participation
- Commentary with commodity and disciplinary research

While this research takes into account a full range of household and farm related activities, including linear programming, often these analyses overemphasize economics and under represent agronomic variables.

FSR on agricultural household studies addresses a host of activities beyond farm production, such as consumption, domestic household production and off-farm wage employment. The school of thought behind agricultural household studies has four assumptions: ① the household objective is to maximize utility of goods consumed and leisure; ② production factors include time and materials; ③ household goods consumed include purchased market items and non-traded commodities (Z-goods) such as nourishment; and ④ production and consumption decisions are separable and function independently in the market. Problem-solving agricultural household studies differ from knowledge-oriented studies in that the former does not employ a mainstream model whereas the latter generally standardizes studies based on a formal model. Fig. 20. 3 demonstrates an FSR neoclassical agricultural household economics model.

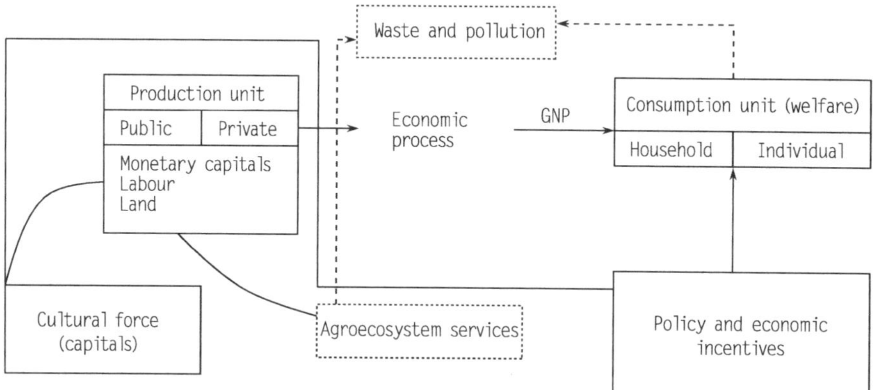

Fig. 20. 3 Neoclassical agricultural household economics model for a farm agroecosystem. Social capitals include monetary capital, cultural force and policy incentives. Natural capital, or agroecosystem services, with the exception of land are discarded with wastes and pollution emissions from production and consumption (Antle and Capalbo, 2002).

(2) Heterodox economics

Heterodox economics combines resource and environmental economics with behavioural and system science orientations, thereby creating "agroeconomics" with socioeconomic ideals. Heterodox refers to the concept of not conforming to the accepted beliefs or standards. Therefore, heterodox economics refers to a paradigm with explicit or implicit distance from the neoclassical paradigm in both research methods and issues. The heterodox economics perspective focuses on the value associated with actual costs and returns of a resource in production, consumption and environmental impact. Fig. 20. 4 illustrates multidisciplinary heterodox economics. Notice the slight differences in this model compared with the neoclassical economics model; heterodox economics counts wastes and pollution emissions differently, in addition to including a simultaneous investigation into economic and ecological processes.

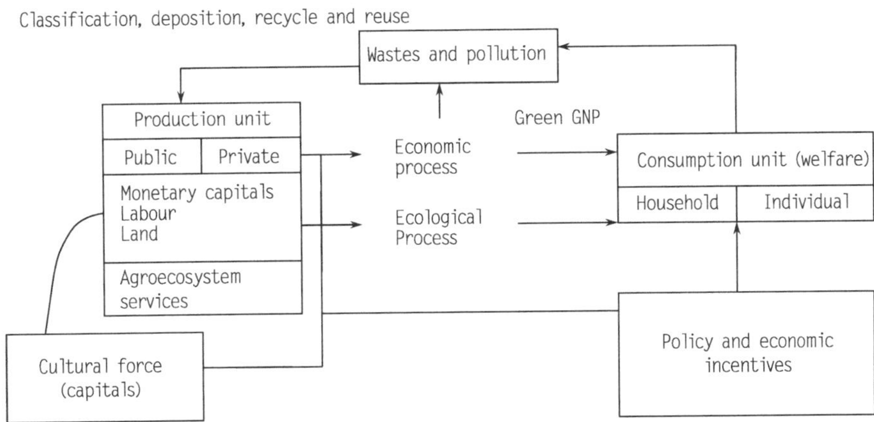

Fig. 20. 4 Heterodox economic model for a farm agroecosystem. Social and natural capitals are recognized in the same way as neoclassical economics; however, economic and ecological processes are simultaneously investigated. In addition, wastes and pollution emissions from production and consumption are counted as costs, which are reused in production by classification, deposition, recycling (Antle and Capalbo, 2002).

Formal mathematical models and quantitative analyses often disregard crucial ecological processes concerning the environment and resource limitations. Future economic models must develop more reliable quantitative tools for understanding economic and social dimensions of natural resource utilization.

20. 2. 2 Political implications

Agricultural policy usually derives from economic analyses that evaluate the production of marketed commodities and utilization of resources. However, what if we consider non-commodity (NC) services relating to health, moral, ethical and sustainability values? If the incentive for agricultural policy lays in raising the value of the agricultural system in the sense that incomes of the rural poor increase and farm production resources and services are met efficiently, then an economic analysis fails to evaluate those necessary components of the farm system. From this standpoint, political implications that do more than correct a market failure require different analysis objectives that address NC services derived from an agricultural resource base.

Several well-known policy options exist to analyze efficient resource utilization for implementing science-based agricultural policy when NC services are public goods (Antle, 2002):

- Command-and control regulatory approach

- Imposition of performance standards
- Creation of marketable assets for emissions or environmental services
- Market for pesticide risk

Both environmental and health economics have tried to value non-market goods and services for decades. While no standard approach has been adopted for valuing NC services, agroeconomics ultimately aiming to influence policy must recognize and distinguish among these multi-attributable decision models for farm system analysis. This paradigm requires adequate information regarding tradeoffs associated with competing resources, valuations required for human health and environmental quality, and the long-term livelihood of the farmer. If agroeconomics could achieve an integrated model combining agricultural sciences and the production of goods and services, it could have a profound implication for policy: moving the current regime of agricultural policy (driven by interest group politics of income redistribution), towards science-based agricultural policy needed to make efficient use of the natural resource base.

20. 2. 3 The future of farm sustainability

One of the greatest challenges facing agriculture in the foreseeable future is to resolve conflicts between allotting natural resources for the growing demands of agricultural goods and services and for non-agricultural services dependent upon those same resources. In addition, we must find a way to provide resources for the present demands without depleting from the future availability of those resources.

In this way, agricultural sustainability refers to the long-term livelihood of agroecosystems. This requires the premise of farm management and FSR to incorporate regional characteristics, enabling trends and potential barriers, future impacts and promotional strategies to determine decision making, problem solving and political implications related to agroecosystem management.

Since governmental policy determines many decisions concerning the agroecosystem, practicing economic research that incorporates NC will ensure political implications based on true farm values. In our current system, FSR general application is based on producing the highest profit for farmers, owners and stockholders. Increasingly so, global recognition of the need to incorporate future values, sustainability and NC prosperity is becoming well recognized. Future economic research will need to incorporate the internal and external costs of goods and services, the cost of removing pollutants from the atmosphere and the opportunity and cost-benefit relationships associated with the allocation of natural resources.

20. 3 An agro-ecological framework for Integrated Farm Management (IFaM)

One of the key concepts of farm system management deals with recognizing the need for a holistic approach to agroecosystem management for farm sustainability. Integrated Farm Management (IFaM) systems act as a collective approach to agricultural management that incorporate numerous factors involved in agroecosystem production and consumption.

One method of an integrated system for farm management, or ISFARM, manages agricultural production at the farm level with algorithmic and non-procedural methods and linear programming models. This strategy allows quantitative measuring of activities and resource values for dynamic decision-making. Linear programming models use a systematic technique to find the most profitable combination of enterprises subject to resource restrictions. Simulated applications of linear programming models have shown ISFARM methodology can improve the decision-making process, especially when operating under severe uncertainty at the farm level (Amir, 1991).

Another method to designing and integrating farm management research relies on systems engineering and reductionist approaches. This approach uses four systematic steps: ①defining the problem; ②identifying factors that possibly affect the solutions; ③developing problem-solving concepts; and ④quantify tradeoffs associated with each solution. Research to support this method has shown that systems engineering and reductionist approaches can help plan complex agricultural projects incorporate the concerns of multiple interest groups (Karlen, 1994).

Fig. 20. 5 gives a conceptual framework of Integrated Farm Management. Different organizational levels exist within IFaM, such as Integrated Field Management, Integrated Crop Management, Integrated Weed Management, Integrated Water Management, Integrated Pest Management, Integrated Soil Management and Integrated Plant Nutrient Management. Each component acts as a complementary tool for IFaM.

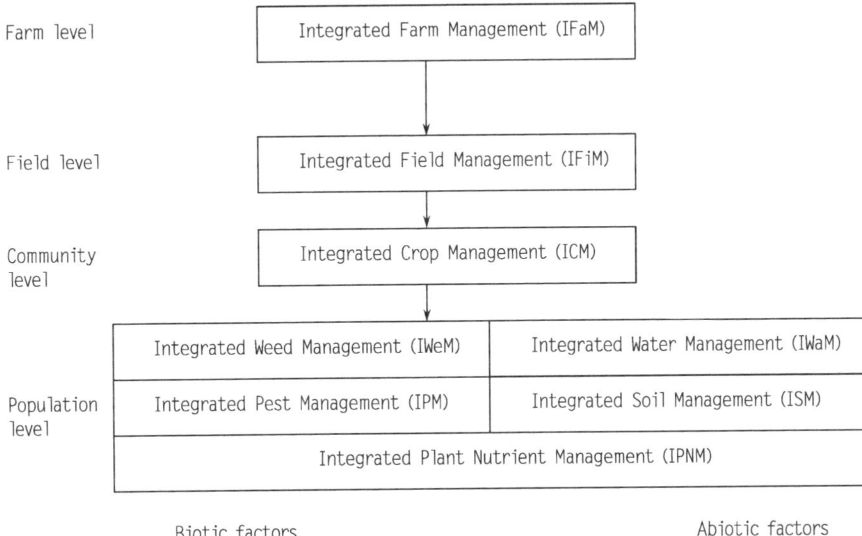

Fig. 20. 5 A conceptual framework of Integrated Farm Management

20. 3. 1 Integrated Field Management (IFiM)

Integrated Field Management incorporates biotic and abiotic field components in the design of cropping systems.

20. 3. 2 Integrated Crop Management (ICM)

ICM optimises efficiency and profitability of crop production while minimising risks to human health, natural and manmade environments. ICM requires farmers to make complex decisions based on a sound understanding of the relationships among economic, social and technical factors. These relationships range from hydrology, climatology, agronomy, entomology, helminthology, arachnology and mycology to post-harvest distribution and nutrition. .

20. 3. 3 Integrated Weed management (IWeM)

IWeM focuses on how crop yields and weed interferences are affected by changes in management (e. g. tillage, herbicide application timing and rates, cover crops, and planting patterns). Acceptance of IWeM will depend on the recommendation of specific strategies that manage weeds and maintain crop productivity. IWeM must shift from a descriptive strategy to a predictive strategy for long-term impact. Linking management changes with crop-weed modelling that includes components such as weed population dynamics and the ecophysiological basis of competition can help predict future weed problems and solutions, along with the economic risks and benefits of intervention. In agroecosystems, IWeM designs must incorporate the interactions among organisms (including humans) and the environment.

20. 3. 4 Integrated Water Management (IWaM)

Agricultural development has negatively influenced the availability of clean water resources. Developing water management technologies to conserve water and use the existing water resources more efficiently will help meet the growing demand for clean water. Existing agricultural water management technologies, such as drip irrigation, mulching, reduced tillage, windbreaks cover management for shade control and water harvesting, have the potential to double or even quadruple rain-fed crop yields (Zhu et al, 2010) (see Chapter 6).

20. 3. 5 Integrated Soil Management (ISM)

Soil Quality is a critical factor in the management of natural resources. It provides many essential ecosystem functions, among them the ability to slowly release water to plants when needed. ISM prevents or reduces the discharge of pollutants into storm water that will eventually be taken up by plants. Pre-construction surveys, inspecting excavations regularly and remediating contaminated soil promptly helps prevent soil pollution. ISM can be put into effect through: ① minimum or reduced tillage; ② mulch the soil year round to minimize the compaction forces of rain and sprinkler irrigation; ③ add organic matter to clayey soils; ④ avoid cultivating or working a clayey soil when wet, and use a raised bed with established walkways and avoid walking on the growing bed; ⑤ increase nitrogen contributions from legumes; and ⑥ use of manure or cover crops.

20. 3. 6 Integrated Pest Management (IPM)

IPM refers to the natural control of agricultural pests (i. e. , weeds, fungi, vertebrates). IPM controls agricultural pests such as insects, pathogens, nematodes, weeds, and vertebrates, through preventative practices, biological, cultural and behavioural control. IPM seeks to use alternative methods to pesticides for reducing the population of pests that destroy crops. We discuss IPM in depth in Chapter 23.

20. 3. 7 Integrated Plant Nutrient Management (IPNM)

IPNM is a system used by farmers to manage the amount, source, placement, form, and timing of nutrient applications. Nutrient applications can come in the form of manure, commercial fertilizer, or soil amendments to plants. Supplying plant nutrients optimises forage abilities and crop yields, while minimizing non-point source pollution. IPNM can either improve the nutrient balance or minimize the negative impact of the nutrient imbalance.

In summary, understanding the goals, units, economic analyses and political implications in farm systems is a key to attaining Sustainable Agroecosystem Management. Furthermore, learning different integrated management plans within integrated farm management is important for the application of Sustainable Agroecosystem Management. In this chapter we discuss farm management as a business, where farmers seek to achieve high profitability while increasing efficiency in farm production. Treating a farm as a business helps the farmer in the decision making process. In addition, economic analysis of an operational farm allows the farmer to increase productivity and helps government make agricultural policy. FSR continues to look for ways to improve both economic analyses and political implications to adapt to changing farmer and interest group goals of sustainability. One way in which farmers have adapted to achieve the goals of Sustainable Agroecosystem Management is incorporating different organizational levels within integrated farm management (IFaM). These levels include Integrated Field Management, Integrated Crop Management, Integrated Weed Management, Integrated Water Management, Integrated Pest Management, Integrated Soil Management and Integrated Plant Nutrient Management.

Literatures cited in this chapter

Altieri M. A., Farrell J. G., Hecht S. B., Liebman M., Magdoff F., Murphy W., Norgaard R. B., and Sikor T. O. 1995. Agroecology: The Science of Sustainable Agriculture. London : Intermediate Technology Publications Ltd (ITP).

Amir I., Puech J., and Granier J. 1991. ISFARM: An integrated system for farm management: Part I—Methodology. *Agricultural Systems* 35 (4): 455-469.

Amir I., Puech J., and Granier J. 1993. ISFARM—An integrated system for farm management: Applicability. *Agricultural Systems* 41 (1): 23-39.

Antle J. M. and Capalbo S. M. 2002. Agriculture as a Managed Ecosystem: Policy Implications. *Journal of Agricultural and Resource Economics* 27 (1): 1-5.

Colin J. P. and Crawford E. W. 2000. Economic Perspectives in Agricultural Systems Analysis. *Review of Agricultural Economics* 22 (1): 192-216.

Denyer R. 2000. Introduction: Integrated Crop Management (ICM). *Pest Management Science*, 56: 945-946.

Karlen D. L., Shannon M. C., Schneider S. M. and Amerman C. R. 1994. Using Systems Engineering and Reductionist Approaches to Design Integrated Farm Management Research Programs. *Journal of Production Agriculture* 7 (1): 144-150.

Pardo G., Riravololona M., and Munier-Jolain N. M. 2010. Using a farming system model to evaluate cropping system prototypes: Are labour constraints and economic performances hampering the adoption of Integrated Weed Management? *European Journal of Agronomy* 33 (1): 24-32.

Zhu W. F., Wang S. L., and Caldwell, C. D. 2010. Pathways of Assessing Agroecosystem Health and Agroecosystem Management, presented in the 2nd International Workshop on Ecosystem Assessment and Management (EAM), Lanzhou, Gansu, China, July 20-25, 2010.

Chapter 21 Animal welfare: A good life for animals

Learning objectives

1. Describe the range of attitudes from "animal welfare" to "animal rights" as those terms are used in the present day debate on the use and care of animals in agriculture.

2. Describe the principal animal welfare issues in modern animal agriculture, and illustrate the issues using examples from poultry, swine, beef cattle, fur and dairy farming.

3. Explain the importance of the physical environment, the social environment and the human-animal relationship to farm animals' quality of life.

21.1 Animal welfare: Concept and principles

21.1.1 Concepts of animal welfare

In the current debate about animal welfare, there is a spectrum of opinions among those who are concerned for animals; some consider themselves animal welfare advocates and others take a more radical animal rights position.

Animal welfare means concern for the quality of life of animals under our control (Beaver, 2010). A more extreme position is that of animal rights, which would hold that animals are separate nations and should be free to live lives unencumbered by our interference. Animal welfare, therefore, would allow the raising of animals for food, to be eaten, as long as their quality of life is high, and slaughter is humane. Animal rights position would not allow raising animals for food and many who hold this view would also be opposed to keeping animals as pets. In discussions of agricultural systems, the concern is usually focused on animal welfare rather than animal right, i. e. the concern for the quality of life of animals under our control while we raise domesticated animals for food. However, the positions taken by animal rights activists have had an effect on agriculture by making us examine more closely all animal care.

21.1.2 Principal animal welfare issues in modern animal agriculture

There are many issues surrounding the welfare of animals in agricultural systems; those issues usually include both housing and production procedures.

Crates for veal calves, cages for laying hens, gestation stalls for sows, long term tethering of dairy cows, and caging of foxes and mink are the concrete examples of housing issues. Fig. 21.1 shows a crate for a veal calf. These are usually cull Holstein bull calves that are housed in small pens and often fed diets that are liquid and that may be somewhat low in iron, so as to produce a more pale meat; the lack of exercise also tends to produce a more tender meat than that of veal calves that are given roughage to eat and opportunity to move freely. Many consider this type of treatment to be cruel and unnecessary.

Cages for laying hens is one of the main sources of criticism from animal welfare groups in North America and Europe. Keeping hens to lay eggs in batteries or cages, small cages that may house anywhere from 3 to 6 birds, where they are kept for a period of one year.

Fig. 21. 2 demonstrates the Gestation stalls for sows. Gestation here refers to the pregnancy period of the sow, and during the sow's pregnancy, she may be kept in a small stall like this, where she is tethered or confined by bars. It does not allow her any exercise, it does not allow her to interact with other animals of her kind and there may be serious chafing around the neck in situations such as the one you're looking at where the sow is kept on a short tether.

Fig. 21. 1 Crates for veal calves.

Fig. 21. 2 The Gestation stalls for sows.

Although the dairy industry is usually not criticized but rather is seen as sort of a model of the classical farm animal outside on pasture it looks like everyone's idea of the agrarian ideal. Nevertheless, dairy cow systems are becoming more intensive, although the barns are of high quality and the feed is of excellent quality. In some dairy systems there is long-term tethering of dairy cows and this can be seen as a welfare problem. In some dairy production systems the cows are not put on pasture, in North America this is called a zero grazing system, and if the barn is of a tie-stall design, then the dairy cow may be tethered and kept on a rather short tether for many weeks without having any chance to exercise.

The last example is caging of foxes and mink. Keeping animals for fur production is often viewed quite differently than keeping animals for food production. Food is a necessity; furs are not. Furs can be replaced by other synthetics; many would argue therefore that this is a luxury that we should ended. In order to keep fixes and mink in a healthy environment, without parasites it is necessary to keep them off the ground separating the foxes and the mink from their feces. This helps to control parasites, but it also gives a very simplified boring environment without much stimulation for the animals. It does not allow much interaction with others of their kind.

So these, then, are some of the main housing concerns when it comes to farm animal welfare: handling of veal calves, laying hens, sows, to some extent, long-term tethering of dairy cows and overall the keeping of foxes and mink on fur farms.

Other animal welfare issues in modern animal agriculture have to do with procedure. Cattle are subjected to castration, branding, dehorning, and ear notching. Pigs are subjected to castration, teeth clipping, mixing with other animals especially at a young age, and early weaning, sometimes as early as about a week to 10 days. Poultry are subjected to beak trimming, disposal of day-old chicks (males) and spent hens (hens that have completed their year of egg laying) and other procedures that may cause pain and discomfort for the animals. They are most often done without anesthetics, and are part of the sometimes widespread criticism for the way animals are reared for food production.

21.2 Animal welfare: Observations and research

21.2.1 Observations

Fig. 21.3 Cattle grazing on broad pasture.

Because people cannot talk directly with animals, it is difficult to determine if animals have a good life. However, using our somewhat subjective judgment and ethics combined with observation using proven scientific methods, some answers are emerging. In many cases, our intuition is a reasonable guide to carefully observing field scenarios. For example, Fig. 21.3 shows Cattle grazing on a broad pasture by the ocean. These cattle are in an environment close to their natural environment, an environment to which they are well adapted. There is complexity to the environment, they are able to interact with others of their kind and express natural behaviors.

Comparatively, cows over-wintering in snowy woods may be judged by some to be a cruel situation because it appears that the cow is in an inhospitable environment with so much snow; however ruminants are well adapted to the cold, the cow has shelter in the forest and is eating snow the way wild ruminants do. While steers in a feedlot may shows the problems of lack of environmental complexity, forced crowding, mixing of cohorts and aggressive interactions. Environments like these begin to pose some problems for animal welfare. From a production standpoint, the feedlot is an efficient system for growing steers at an optimum rate for maximum profit.

Fig. 21.4 Heifer calves in a barn.

A dairy cow in a tie-stall looks content: she has comfortable bedding, enough food and water and is kept healthy through regular care. One does observe that sheis on a short tether and the question is can she adopt comfortable resting positions on this short tether? Is this overall a good situation that allows for the animal to express its natural behaviours?

Fig. 21. 4 shows replacement heifer calves in a barn sometime in the next few months. In your opinion, do they have a good quality of environment? Is their resting area comfortable, are they allowed to interact the way cows normally would? What is good about the environment?

Apart from the observation above, there is also the scientific approach to assess quality of life or animal welfare, the main tools in our arsenal are the study of animal behavior, the study of physiology, and the study of epidemiology, or health status of animals in certain confinement and production systems. These give us some objective, clear data to help us make our decision or help animals to cope with confinement (Broom, 2010).

21. 2. 2 Scientific research

There are three main areas in terms of scientific research; one is the physical environment, both how much space and of what quality the space is; another is about the social environment, and the third is the quality of the animal-human relationship.

(1) Physical environment

How much space do animals need? sows during their pregnancy are being housed and tethered. The gestation period of a sow is somewhere around 115 days and for much of this time the sow would be kept confined with no opportunity to exercise and they exhibit considerable repetitive behavior, such chomping on bars. Normally a sow would try and build a nest during her gestation. These sows will sometimes go through some of the movements of that but cannot do it.

The next consideration for the mother pig is how much space and what structure is needed for a farrowing sow. The answer has to consider the comfort of the sows and the safety for piglets (i. e. , they have to be protected from being crushed by the sow when she lies down). Pigs are an animal where the adults are very big and the newborn are very many and very small. It is very easy for piglets to be crushed accidentally by their mother. She is so big, if she lies down on top of them, they die. Farrowing crates are constructed in order to protect the piglets from their mother. So it is probably a fairly good environment for the piglets, but the sow can only do one thing, stand up and lie down. She cannot interact with them, beyond nursing, she cannot turn around, and she is limited in how comfortable she can make herself for the duration of the nursing period, which is usually about three weeks.

Some modified farrowing crates can allow the sow to get up and lie down, but also allows her to turn around and make herself more comfortable, it's a bit broader, yet it also gives protection to the piglets from accidental crushing. A more improved crate shown in Fig. 21. 5 is a Norwegian farrowing pen. These are commonly used in the pig production industry in Norway and provide more freedom of movement. The sow can explore her surroundings a little bit, she can turn around, lie down, stand up, and there's also a small area in the corner underneath the heat lamp where the piglets can rest and get warm and can be protected from being accidentally crushed by the mother.

(2) Environmental enrichment

Besides the size, the quality of space is also important; the crate in Fig. 21. 6 includes some straw bedding and there is no area where the piglets are totally away from their mother but there is enough complexity there, enough small corners combined with the straw that make this a good system. Given sufficient straw, even if the sow accidentally lies down on top of her piglet, there's usually enough cushioning that she can get up again and the piglet may not be injured.

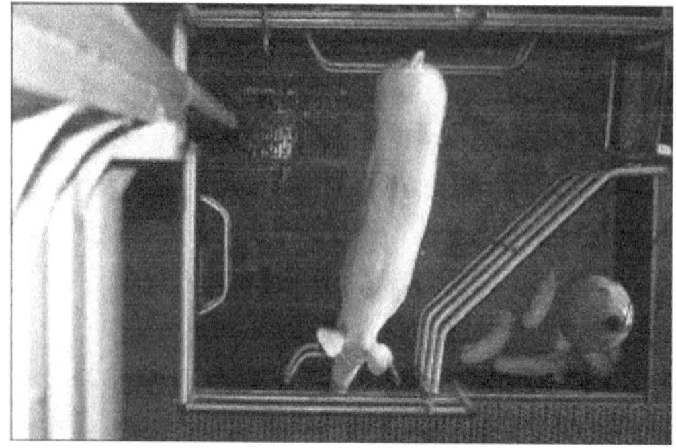

Fig. 21. 5　A farrowing pen giving sows more freedom while still giving piglets a protected place to rest.

Fig. 21. 6　Farrowing pen crate including straw bedding.

In short, the quality of space depends much on environmental enrichment which usually described as "bringing nature into captivity" . Environmental enrichment should also be functional. Fig. 21. 7 demonstrates a sow with her head just poking out from the straw which is a good material for thermo-regulating, so that the pig can dig themselves down into it if the weather is cold, they can also eat some of it, they can root in it, and rooting with their snout is such a common behaviour of pigs in the wild that to entirely prevent pigs from doing that might be unreasonable and it is reasonable to give them something that they can root in. Also with some straw, a sow will make a nest before farrowing. This sow is about to farrow and she is housed in a barn that has a lot of straw, so she can carry that straw around and will actually build a nest or cushioned area where she will give birth.

Fig. 21. 8 shows a farrowing system with both ample physical space and environmental enrichment. The sows are in groups with their piglets, so in this group there may be six sows each with about 10 piglets or so, so you have a group of six adults and about 60 young pigs and this really helps build a high quality of life. They interact with others of their kind and they have a complex environment with which they can also interact.

In nature, sows live in groups. Free ranging and feral pigs in various parts of the world organize themselves into groups of sows, maybe 10 or a dozen or so and all their piglets, and the system you're looking at here, the production system, duplicates that in a sense. The environment shown in Fig. 21. 8 is socially complex and physically complex, in which the sows do not fight and they do not hurt each other's piglets. One can add even more environmental complexity by bringing the animals outdoors and giving them even more space to move around in. Allowing pigs to graze in pasture can also can make an important nutritional contribution; however, sometimes they will eat grass and root soil in earth with their snout. So forest area is better to be a pig farm

Fig. 21.7 Functional environmental enrichment

Fig. 21.8 Ample physical space with environmental enrichment for animal.

than a pasture, herein pigs will root for grubs and roots under the ground and will sometimes root up vegetation and actually help clear forested areas. There are problems with housing pigs outdoors in some very hot or cold climates and ease of handling by the farmer is reduced as freedom of movement for the pigs is increased.

During dry periods, farmers may have to create wet wallowing areas for outdoor pigs. It is also possible to have sows giving birth outdoors in mobile pens that act like farrowing areas and then she and her piglets can move around outdoors in quite a natural way, giving an apparent high quality of life.

(3) The animal-human relationship

How humans interact with animals is important; the nature of our relationship will mean that the animals can be at ease, content, calm in our presence, or be nervous and frightened and stressed.

The nature of the relationship can affect the productivity and the welfare of farm animals. Such relationships are formed by way of the interactions between humans and animals, and these interactions can be positive, neutral, or negative.

A recent experiment illustrates that pigs were given either pleasant handling, in which the handler would walk in, squat in the pen, and allow pigs to approach and interact (Fraser, 2009); either give minimal handling, would have no exposure to humans except during feeding and weighing; or were given unpleasant handling where a handler stood in the pen and delivered a brief shock if a pig approached.

The results of this experiment showed that pigs that were handled in a pleasant way were more likely to become pregnant when bred in the other two treatments. Those sows handled in an unpleasant way were perhaps stressed and perhaps the physiology of stress, which really contradicts the physiology of growth and reproduction, had an effect here.

Furthermore, pigs showing a high level of fear of humans had up to an 11.3% reduction in growth rate, so the physiology of stress and the physiology of growth are at odds, are contradictory to each other in many ways, and if for no other reason than that. This makes us re-think how we handle animals and the kind of relationship we have with our livestock.

In summary, as managers of animals, farmers control many factors that are very important to their welfare, the nature of the physical and social space and the quality of our relationship with them.

Literatures cited in this chapter

Beaver B. V. 2010. Welfare of Animals: Introduction. In: Breed M. D. and Moore J. *Encyclopedia of Animal Behavior*. Pittshurgh: Academic Press: 585-589.

Broom D. M. 2010. Welfare of Animals: Behavior as a Basis for Decisions. In: Breed M. D. and Moore J. *Encyclopedia of Animal Behavior*: 580-584.

Fraser D. 2009. Animal behaviour, animal welfare and the scientific study of affects. *Applied Animal Behavior Science* 118: 108-117.

Chapter 22 Integrated Pest Management (IPM): Case studies

Learning objectives

1. Explain the difference between a key pest, occasional pest and non-pest.
2. Discuss the usefulness of economic injury level (EIL).
3. List five IPM strategies.
4. Outline the main six steps in implementing an integrated pest management program.
5. What is the pest tetrahedron?
6. What are three factors that affect the economic importance of pest control?
7. What is an example of a key pest species? Occasional pest? Non-pest?
8. Explain the three basic components of IPM procedures.
9. What is the difference between altering cultural and genetic practices in host manipulation?
10. How can IPM implementation differ in scale and level?
11. What symptoms develop as a result of LB on potatoes?
12. Describe three different strategies used for effective and economic crop management of rice varieties in China.
13. Why is it important to understand pest behaviour to achieve successful pest control?
14. Why is it important to monitor an integrated pest management program?

22.1 Understanding pests and pest control

22.1.1 What is a pest?

A pest refers to an unwanted living organism that causes damage or illness to people, plants or property. Fig. 22.1 describes multiple pathways of abiotic and biotic factors contributing to crop losses. Pests such as weeds, pathogens and animals can infect crops and plants for human consumption, while other sources such as carpenter ants destroy furniture or wood. Among those factors, pests differ across cultural landscapes; for instance, a cockroach in North America represents a common pest while in Thailand certain species are considered a food delicacy. In this chapter we will look at Integrated Pest Management, with a focus on crop pests.

(1) Pest tetrahedron

The "pest tetrahedron" is a tool for visualizing interactions of pests and their environment (Fig. 22.2). A pest tetrahedron has four components:

- Pest presence
- Environment
- Susceptible host
- Time for the pest-host interaction to occur and cause damage

A successful Integrated Pest Management (IPM) program addresses multiple components in this relationship; for instance using good air circulation within a crop to encourage crop growth and reduce the environment supportive of pest growth. The IPM approach encourages agroecosystem managers to determine when a pest problem arises, methods to address a pest issue and benefits of using a naturally integrated strategy to obtain optimal pest control.

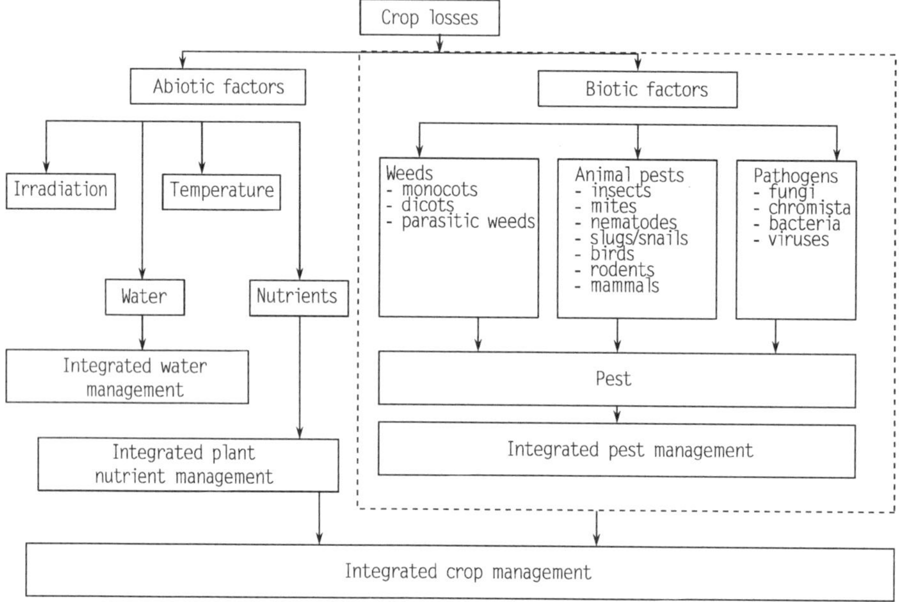

Fig. 22. 1　Abiotic and biotic factors contributing to crop losses (Oerke, 2006).

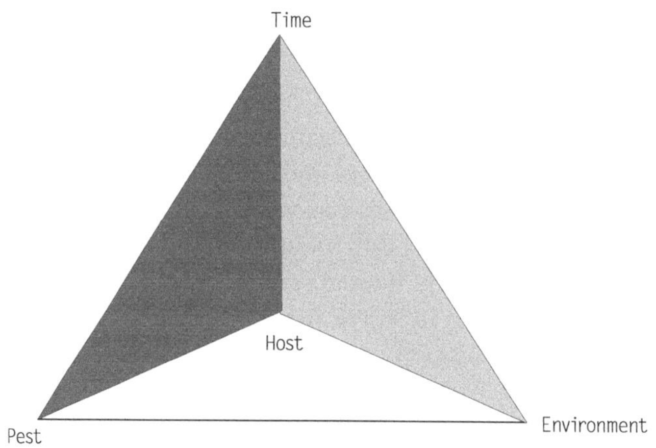

Fig. 22. 2　Conceptual diagram of pest tetrahedron.

(2) Economic injury level

Often determining the level of pest disturbance depends on its relative economic importance. Action threshold, equilibrium position and aesthetic thresholds influence the economic importance of pest control. Economic injury level (EIL) values the population that produces incremental damage equivalent to the cost of preventing that damage. Therefore, it makes sense to control a pest population before it exceeds its EIL. The action threshold refers to this population at which control measures make economic sense.

(3) Equilibrium position

Equilibrium position is the average density of a pest population over a long period of time in the absence of any human control mechanism. The equilibrium position determines the occurrence of pest activity from the organism, such as every year, once in awhile, or never. The equilibrium position of a specific pest helps determine the most appropriate pest management programs for that particular pest.

(4) Aesthetic threshold

Sometimes controlling pests for aesthetic reasons outweighs the desire to preserve yield output or dollar value of pest control. Aesthetic values are commonly taken into consideration in the landscape industry. Similar to the economic threshold, the aesthetic threshold in the landscape industry depends on a measure of visual acceptability. Therefore, aesthetic thresholds evolve as social norms of visual value change. A pest in this sense refers to an organism that causes a visually displeasing landscape. In some cases for instance, dandelions may decrease the visual appearance of a landscape, lowering the aesthetic threshold.

(5) Are all "pests" pests?

An important question to ask when considering IPM management is: are all pests "pests"? Understanding and identifying non-pests species can significantly reduce unnecessary pesticide use in the ecosystem. A key pest refers to a pest population that fluctuates around the action threshold or the economic threshold annually and requires yearly intervention and control. For example, in many areas of the world the Colorado Potato Beetle (CPB) is a key pest of potatoes, peppers, tomatoes and eggplants. Control of a CPB population must take place within the initial 24-48 hours of invasion to avoid total devastation of the crop. In Atlantic Canada, the action threshold of CPB averages two larvae per plant in a 12-metre area, or about 20 CPB per square foot. When the CPB reaches this action threshold, farmers are advised to apply control measures.

An occasional pest refers to an organism that only reaches the economic threshold occasionally, with a large difference between the action threshold and the economic injury level. Normally the population fluctuates below the action threshold but reaches or surpasses the EIL every once in awhile due to natural or human induced perturbations. Generally, natural biological controls regulate an occasional pest population. However, if the biological control diminishes (or if it is biotic in nature and is killed off) then the pest population increases quickly requiring pest control. For instance, under natural biological control (from beneficial insects and disease) the green cloverworm, an occasional pest, nibbles on soybean plant leaves without causing significant damage. However, an overabundance (over 150 green cloverworms per 100 sweeps) can cause defoliation, reduce photosynthate production and inhibit seed development. An IPM program could prevent soybean plant damage during a green cloverworm fluctuation.

A non-pest population fluctuates but always remains below the action threshold and can co-exist with other organisms without causing damage or illness. An example of a non-pest, the larva of the *Pyrrharctia isabella* moth and commonly called a "banded woolly bear", has a long growth period when it eats plants. By September or October when the banded woolly bear reaches a size where it can cause a tremendous amount of damage, the crops have already fully matured.

22.1.2 Population regulation

Understanding reproduction and life cycles in both host and pest organisms is important for regulating pest populations. Two types of reproduction can occur: sexual reproduction and asexual reproduction. In sexual reproduction each parent passes half of its genes to the offspring, resulting in a new genetic makeup. In asexual reproduction an organism passes down its entire set of genes to the next generation. For example, many plants re-grow from their root system in asexual reproduction or vegetative reproduction. A dandelion also reproduces asexually, but it requires pollen for fertilization. Vivipary, a form of sexual reproduction, refers to the process whereby offspring are born alive, such as in humans. Aphids (common pest) typically reproduce through vivipary. Pseudovivipary refers to the asexual reproduction process similar to vivipary.

IPM requires knowledge of host and pest species reproduction, and the amount of time required for reproduction. For instance, some pests can reproduce in very short time. Bacteria reproduce within an hour, producing several generations rapidly. Spider mites, aphids, some nematodes and pathogens can reproduce within days, while many insects, nematodes, pathogenic fungi and small vertebrates take weeks. Yet some insects, pathogens, large vertebrates and weeds require months and large vertebrates, perennial weeds and a few arthropods take years to reproduce. Reproduction time determines the rapidity of population increase per year and therefore has serious implications for the management strategy used. In addition, the timing of the interaction of host and pest may influence if the pest population is in fact considered a "pest" problem.

22.2 Integrated pest management: a strategy of alternatives

Integrated Pest Management (IPM) is an alternative strategy to pesticides for controlling pest populations. Although IPM does not inherently decrease pesticide use, integrated pest management arose in popularity as a means to reduce chemical control. After awareness grew about the negative side effects of chemical pesticides and the need to protect agrobiodiversity, the United Nations conference on Environment and Development (1992) stated explicit goals of making IPM the standard in crop protection.

22.2.1 IPM key concepts

In this textbook we define IPM as a sustainable and systematic approach to managing pests by combining biological, cultural, physical, and chemical tools with careful monitoring in a way that minimizes economic, health and environmental risks. The dynamic nature of IPM allows this strategy to adapt to many different pest problems. IPM has great strength in this adaptability, at the same time however, IPM lacks concrete methodologies for control of all pest populations. Rather, each pest population and host requires different management techniques. The concepts for specific IPM techniques derive from cultural, physical, chemical, horticultural and biological needs of the crop. Management decisions for IPM programs should develop with the aim of controlling the most economically threatening pests.

To encourage successful crop growth, IPM management must also focus on maintaining an actively growing and healthy crop environment. A suitable growing environment program for the crop must fit within the overall crop management system (Oerke, 2006) and integrate features such as fertility management, water management and soil conservation.

Two other important aspects of IPM include safety and financial burden. Carrying out safe and effective pest control remains as the core objective of any pest management program. Ensuring safety, especially with respect to pesticide use, for both the initial user and the end users who may come into contact with a sprayed lawn or consume food products is of the highest importance. Managers must also consider the economic cost of an IPM program. If pest management is not economical, a farmer may end up losing money in an attempt to control a pest. Cost incurred for training, application tools and monitoring programs should be evaluated prior to implementing an IPM program.

22.2.2 IPM strategies

The following strategies, based on Simberloff (2011), underlie the procedures for carrying out an effective IPM program, according to time at which pest identification takes place and economic injury levels.

(1) Prevention

Preventing a pest organism from establishing population levels above the economic injury level threshold is ideal for IPM. Although often unfeasible, this strategy pertains especially to invasive and non-native species.

(2) Temporary alleviation

Temporary alleviation contains, localizes and limits pest outbreaks. This strategy is most useful on an emergency basis, and although unsustainable, can keep pest populations hovering around the economic injury threshold rather than exploding at an exponential rate.

(3) Ongoing management

Maintaining pest populations at tolerable levels allows managers to contain and control pest population within a crop field. This approach requires acknowledging that eradication is likely unfeasible, but overall crop production can continue with tolerable levels of pests.

(4) Area-wide pest management

When the extent of pest population goes beyond one managed crop unit, the IPM approach must reach a broader area for pest management. This strategy extends to a larger geographic region and applies to especially mobile pests that spread beyond a single managed crop unit.

(5) Eradication

Eradication as an IPM strategy applies to limited population sizes and/or geographic regions as an endpoint in pest management. Often eradication proves most appropriate for infestations and of non-native organisms. However, eradication is not always necessary. At low levels, some pest populations may prove beneficial for a crop.

22. 3 Integrated pest management procedures

IMP strategies comprise of three basic components: know ledge of the pest species, decision-making and management tactics (Fig. 22. 3). The very basic level includes gaining knowledge about the pest, the host and the ecosystem biology. This crucial information includes knowledge about the pest's life cycle, behaviour, cycles per season, generations per season, population dynamics, and how the population increases or decreases over the season.

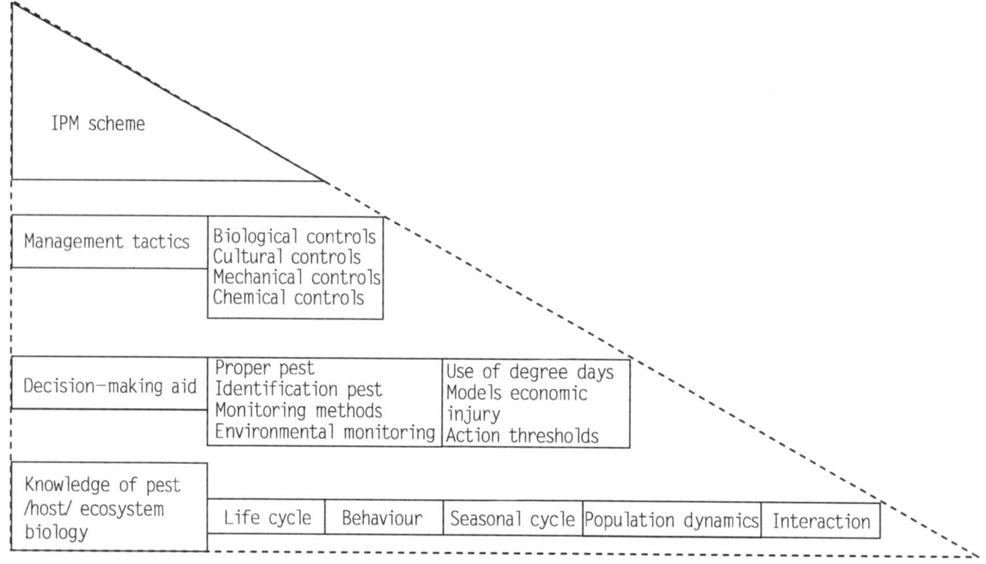

Fig. 22. 3 Schematic of IPM.

The second level, decision-making, includes understanding pest monitoring methods, environmental monitoring and management options available. Comprehensive knowledge of the pest along with educated information about decision-making options will enable managers to make informed decisions about monitoring techniques, choosing a management program and the overall IPM process.

The top level focuses on options and tools available for controlling the pest, including biological, cultural, mechanical and chemical controls. These controls may have the intended purpose of manipulating the host crop, pest organism or the environment.

22. 3. 1 IPM steps

(1) Identifying the pest

As mentioned in the beginning of this section, identifying the pest plays a major role in adapting a specific IPM program to a crop's needs. Detecting the specific pest causing damage or illness to the crop and understanding its basic biology components, population size and limitations drives the IPM process in a certain direction. For instance, knowing that an organism has a large number of degree-days over a season means the manager may have more time to adopt an IPM strategy than a faster reproducing organism. Degree-days are a unit used to measure pest growth through a generation. In the example of the Colorado potato beetle however, a manager must react within 1-2 days with effective management tactics. Without knowledge of the pest's life cycle and reproduction, an IPM program would not help control these pest populations efficiently.

(2) Defining the crop management unit

A farmer must decide the geographic extent of the pest problem. For a farmer who may have 5 or 10 different fields, each field may require different treatments, or alternatively the farmer may treat their entire farm as one unit. A successful IPM program aims to reduce, localize and/or contain a pest population. Determining the boundaries of integration will help an agroecosystem manger define the extent of the IPM design and cost of implementation.

(3) Developing viable monitoring techniques

Developing viable monitoring techniques provides accurate information needed to make pest management decisions. Asking the questions "what pests are present and what is the cause or source of the pests?" allows managers to determine the best monitoring tools to determine pest problems early. Let's look at the blueberry maggot example. Blueberry growers should be aware of blueberry maggots that lay their eggs inside the berry. Controlling this insect before it lays its eggs will ensure a viable crop and income for the blueberry season. Some monitoring techniques for the blueberry maggot include: simple observations, traps, regular pest counts, sweep nets.

(4) Establishing the economic thresholds or aesthetic threshold

Economic thresholds and aesthetic thresholds indicate a pest problem, rather than an incidence of a non-pest or occasional pest. Establishing threshold values enables managers to determine when a pest population fluctuation has reached a level that will result in potential damages and economic losses.

(5) Developing an effective and economical crop management strategy

Developing an effective and economical crop management strategy depends on identifying pests, their damage and natural control agents that reduce negative side effects. The IPM tactics used should intend to practice host manipulation, pest manipulation or environment manipulation; physical, biological, cultural, behavioural, mechanical and/or chemical controls play a major role in pest manipulation.

Host manipulation can occur through alterations in cultural or genetic practices. Altering cultural practices might include changing harvesting schedules, sowing dates, changing irrigation patterns or rotations (Simberloff, 2011). Altering genetic practices changes the host plant resistance through specific, intentional plant breeding techniques.

Pest manipulation refers to using physical, biological, behavioural and chemical controls to naturally reduce pest populations. Biological controls focus on using higher-trophic level organisms to feed on pest species. Biological control offers the advantage of naturally reducing pests through successive generations of plants, however disadvantages include a potentially long lag time where pests can accumulate and a very small likelihood of 100% eradication. Behavioural control, tricking these pests into finding a desired location, although not applicable to plants and pathogens, can effectively reduce pest organisms with a nervous system and reliance on sensory signals (visual, auditory and olfactory). Chemical control usually refers to pesticide use and should be used a last resort. Generally IPM programs intend to minimize pesticide use, but in certain cases a pest will not respond to other tactics.

Selection of an IPM strategy should consider overall benefits to the entire crop management system. Environment manipulation can inhibit pest growth or harbour beneficial organisms that can predator the pests, but the overall changes made to the fields should continue to support crop growth. Environment manipulation often alters patterns of irrigation, flooding and heat and cold applications.

(6) Evaluation

Evaluating an IPM program and its controls can help a manager determine effects and the efficiency of management decisions previously made. If the IPM program falls short in reaching desired goals, strategy modifications can be made.

22. 3. 2 IPM implementation

IPM implementation can occur on three scales and three levels (both increasing in complexity):

- Scale I: Single managed ecosystem such as one crop field
- Scale II: Whole farm requiring complex assessment of ecosystem interactions
- Scale III: Landscape or regional scale with multiple managed units
- Level I: Monitoring of pest populations and scheduling of pesticide application
- Level II: Integrating all pest management practices for a single pest species
- Level III: Integrating all pest management practices and controls for the regional ecosystem

22. 4 Case studies in IPM

22. 4. 1 IPM of the late blight of potatoes in Canada

Potato (*Solanum tuberosum*) production is one of the five most important food crops in the world, with an average production of 16,150 kg/ hm^2 per year (Hijmans, 2000). Therefore, pests of all types are treated with high economic importance. The oomycete (fungus-like organism) pathogen *Phytophthora infestans* causes late blight (LB), the most prominent and threatening pest of potatoes in North America today. LB emerged in Canada in 1840, the same year LB infected potatoes across Europe and caused the Irish potato famine.

Without crop protection in some form, pests would reduce attainable potato production by nearly 75% through pathogens, viruses, animal pests and weeds. Implementing an IPM strategy for potato late blight is an important aspect of Canadian agriculture, specifically in Prince Edward Island and New Brunswick where most of the national potato production occurs. Let's take a look at how to integrate an IPM strategy for potato late blight according to the IPM procedures described in section 22. 3. The first step requires the ability to identify disease symptoms. Fig. 22. 4 shows signs of infected potato leaves and tubers. Common LB signs appear as water-soaked lesions on leaf edges and tips. These lesions enlarge daily becoming brown with a light green border as moisture (rain, dew or irrigation) increases. White growth and spores develop on the underside of leaves, which is most recognizable in the early morning. In addition, symptoms of LB can occur on tubers as irregularly shaped and depressed brown or purple spots.

Symptoms appear four to eight days after LB has infected the potato species. Without a quick response to control the pathogen, LB will destroy the entire crop. *P. infestans* spores will move many kilometres from farm to farm by wind rain. Fig. 22. 5 shows the extent of damage late blight causes when uncontrolled. The picture on top indicates signs of LB in the darker brownish-green plants. The picture below shows a similar farm ravished by LB overnight.

Fig. 22. 4 Symptoms of infected late blight fungi on potato.

Fig. 22. 5 The consequence of late blight on potato field.

Potatoes that do not make grade for sale are thrown into a cull pile that can serve as a source of inocula for LB. Legislation in both Prince Edward Island and New Brunswick requires potato farmers to manage those cull piles in one of the following ways: burying, composting, winter spreading on the field (thereby freezing and killing the fungus), or summer covering in plastic (thereby heating up and killing the fungus). These methods help control the possible spread of late blight.

Tab. 22. 1 explains step-by-step IPM techniques for late blight on potatoes with detailed measures taken for each element.

Tab. 22. 1 Elements of Integrated Management of Late Blight on Potatoes

Elements	Measures
As a holistic part of overall crop management system	• Position and data analyses of IPM in the system of Integrated crop management in the defined field unit
Early detection of "hot spots" essential to successful management	• Practice monitoring, set up field equipment and collect data
Healthy "seed" preparation	• Obtain healthy, disease-free seeds from sources with effective disease management practices, i. e. inspected seed production systems • Examine all seeds prior to use

Continued

Elements	Measures
Crop varieties and cultivars	• Use resistant varieties and cultivar
Sanitation and cull clean-up	• Consists of sanitary storage facilities and equipment • Proper management of cull piles • Bury, compost, feed to livestock, spread on fields in winter and/or bake under black polyethylene sheets during growing season
Cultural practices and rotation	• Crop rotation (minimum 2 year with non-late blight hosts) • Destroy volunteer potatoes • Control weed hosts of fungus • Use well-drained soils with good exposure to drying winds and without excessive shaded areas • Well-spaced plants • Rapid destruction of "hot spots"
Forecasting techniques and scouting techniques	• Predict the likelihood that a disease outbreak will occur • Provide information on when to start fungicide applications and adjust timing • Scout for signs of disease for predicting outbreaks
Scheduled fungicide applications	• Incorporate into disease prevention program • Apply fungicides before late blight occurs • Prevent initial development of disease and delay rapid development • Time first spray by forecasting, coordinated with stage of crop development
Application technology	• Complete coverage of foliage is essential • Use equipment designed and appropriate for fungicide application • Calibrate proper equipment • Use drift reduction technology
Harvesting, grading and storage monitoring	• Harvest only when vines are completely dead • Harvest shaded areas, wet areas or areas suspect of disease after the rest of the harvest is finished • Grade potatoes and remove infected tubers before they are put in storage • Monitor storage for signs of rotting • Manage air flow, humidity and temperature

22.4.2 IPM strategy in tropical paddy rice agroecosystems in China

According to a tetrahedron scheme (refer to Fig. 22.2), host plant resistance plays an important role in crop disease control. Controlling rice pests has played a key role in sustaining rice productivity throughout tropical Asia. Rice variety IR8 (released in the mid-1960s) revolutionized gains in rice productivity helping many countries achieve food security in Asia (Leung, 2003). However, yield increases had a price in the form of huge fertilizer and pesticide inputs, insecticide resistant insects, soil degradation and food safety issues frequently occurring. The deployment of yield advantage varieties dominating the field resulted in the loss of rice diversity as well. A few methods have helped reduce some of the problems associated with monocultures in Chinese paddy rice agroecosystems. For instance, using multiple rice cultivars and mix-planting methods in the field has led to an increase in agroecosystem diversity, maintenance of production stability, and a decrease in pest and pathogen occurrence, ultimately resulting in a significant decrease in pesticide use. This tactic is an effective form of Integrated Pest Management. As a case study, we will look at three IPM strategies in the development phase of effective and economical crop management in both the Yunnan Province and tropical areas in China, where rice culture dominates land use.

(1) Strategy I: Sequential release of resistant varieties in time and space

Releasing successive gene varieties of rice allows farmers to replace one variety with another as they become susceptible to disease. This replacement method offers a way to deal with multiple diseases and the changing needs of farmers and consumers. Since 1973 IRRI rice varieties released have had resistance to blast, bacterial blight, tungro (Leung, 2003). Sequential release of different gene varieties over time and space diversifies the crop and increases resistant genes used in the field. However, this strategy looses usefulness if the rapid loss outweighs the investment in developing a new variety. In addition, sequential release requires ongoing support and large amounts of survey data.

(2) Strategy II: Gene pyramiding

Gene pyramiding, combining multiple resistant genes in breeding lines is based on the theory that a pathogen will not develop multiple virulence mutations at the same time. Using an evolutionary risk assessment model and 2 to 3 years' evaluation in "hot spot" areas in farmers' fields, gene pyramiding showed resistance to bacterial blight under high disease pressure and out-yielded the check (Leung, 2003). Overall, gene pyramiding offers the development of a variety resistance to a single pathogen. Alternative or complementary approaches would render this method much more effective in practice.

(3) Strategy III: Multiline and cultivar mixtures

Heterogeneity offers a natural solution to increase resistance to pathogens. Disease susceptible rice varieties planted with this strategy had an 89% higher yield and 94% less severe damage than monoculture rice varieties (Zhu et al. , 2000). Multilines and cultivar mixes offer the most expansive genetic resistance of these strategies. These interplanting experiments conducted in Yunnan demonstrate that simple methods coupled with strong extension support are critical in disseminating new approaches to disease management.

In summary, Integrating an IPM strategy in agroecosystem management allows farmers to benefit from natural biological controls to encourage healthy crop production while reducing pest growth and environmental damage. The ability to identify a key pest and understand its biology and life cycle is instrumental in controlling the pest through an adaptive IPM approach. Depending on the scale and level of IPM implementation, procedures may eradicate a pest or slowly reduce the population to a level below the economic injury level. The economic injury level assesses the potential damage due to a pest considering economic importance. Equilibrium position and aesthetic thresholds both contribute to the economic importance of a pest, the most important factor in determining when to use an IPM strategy for pest control. There are six steps or procedures in Integrated Pest Management: ① identify the pest, ② define the crop management unit, ③ develop viable monitoring techniques, ④ establish economic and aesthetic thresholds, ⑤ develop an effective and economical crop management strategy and ⑥ evaluation. IPM strategies have successfully helped control late blight in potatoes in Canada and pest and diseases threatening rice paddies in temperate and tropical China. As IPM continues to evolve, strategies to increase pest control while decreasing undesired environmental damage continue to increase as well.

Literatures cited in this chapter

Hijmans R. J. , Forbes G. A, and Walker T. S. 2000. Estimating the global severity of potato late blight with GIS-linked disease forecast models. *Plant Pathology* 49: 697-705.

Leung H. , Zhu Y. , Revilla-Molina I. , Fan J. X. , Chen H. , Pangga I. , Cruz C. V. , and Mew T. W. 2003. Using Genetic Diversity to Achieve Sustainable Rice Disease Management. *Plant Disease* 87 (10): 1156-1169.

Mangan J. and Mangan M. S. 1998. A comparison of two IPM training strategies in China: The importance of concepts of the rice ecosystem for sustainable insect pest management. *Agriculture and Human Values* 15: 209-221.

Muller-Scharer H. and Scheepens P. C. 1997. Biological control of weeds in crops: a coordinated European research programme (COST-816). *Integrated Pest Management Reviews* 2: 45-50.

Oerke E. C. 2006. Crop losses to pests. *Journal of Agricultural Science* 144: 31-43.

Simberloff D. and Rejmanek M. 2011. *Encyclopedia of Biological Invasions*. Los Angeles, CA: University of California Press.

Teng P. S. , Wang Z. , and Mundt C. C. 2000. Genetic diversity and disease control in rice. *Nature* 406: 718-772.

United Nations Sustainable Development, Agenda 21. 1992. Promoting sustainable agriculture and rural development (14. 1-14. 104). *Proceedings of the United Nations Conference on Environment and Development*, Rio de Janeiro, Brazil.

Zhu Y. , Chen H. , Fan J. , Wan Y. , Li Y. , Chen J. , Fan J. X. , Yang S. , Hu L. , Leung H. , Mew T. W. , Teng P. S. , Wang Z. , and Mundt C. C. 2000. Genetic diversity and disease control in rice. *Nature* 406: 718-722.

Zhu Y. , Wang Y. Y. , Chen H. , and Lu B. 2003. Conserving Traditional Rice Varieties through Management for Crop Diversity. *Bio-science* 53 (2): 158-162.

Chapter 23 Trends in organic production

Learning objectives

1. What is organic agriculture?
2. Explain the impacts of consumer demands on agriculture.
3. Discuss the reasons for organic food regulations.
4. What are the challenges in organic production in China?
5. How are organic products marketed?
6. Why do consumers purchase organic products?
7. Who grows organic food and why?
8. What are the types of regulations imposed on organic agriculture?

Massive contradictions have arisen from modern fossil fuel oriented agriculture. In the midst of large-scale agriculture, hunger and malnutrition still widely exist; and there is a loss of biodiversity in agroecosystems due to the prevalence of narrow genetic base varieties grown in monoculture. There also exists environmental destruction and food contamination due to indiscriminate use of biocides and synthetic fertilizers, resulting in reductions of multiple ecological services from agricultural landscapes. Modern "organic" agriculture initially evolved as a reaction to the industrialization of agriculture, stimulated by fear of food produced with various chemical inputs and a will to return to a method of agriculture more in tune with the ecosystem. Although organic agricultural methods cannot resolve all of the above contradictions, it has great potential to stimulate production of enough safe food to feed the entire world in a food system based on agroecological production principles (Badgley, 2007).

23.1 Definition, origins and demands of organic agriculture

23.1.1 What is organic agriculture?

Some consumers define organic agriculture as farming without synthetic pesticides and fertilizers. However, the National Organic Standards Board (NOSB) in the USA provides a more suitable definition of organic agriculture as "an ecological production management system that promotes and enhances biodiversity, biological cycles and soil biological activity. It is based on minimal use of off-farm inputs and on management practices that restore, maintain and enhance ecological harmony." In this sense, organic agriculture pursues an "organizational principle," seeking to manage a complex farm as a nearly closed system using holistic approaches. Although many production methods supportive of the environment and the organizational principle exist, organic production systems differ in that they follow specific and precise standards of production, aiming to achieve economically, socially and ecologically sustainable agroecosystems.

Food produced by means of organic agriculture is marketed as "organic food." The organic food label pertains to organic food products produced in accordance with a certification organization or authority like the International Federation of Organic Agriculture Movements (IFOAM) (Fig. 23.1). Therefore, the "organic" label refers to a process claim rather than a product claim, which includes different standards throughout the food making processes. Since the organic label does not stand for a product claim, organic foods are not necessarily healthier, safer or "all natural." Simply put, organic labels mean the product follows the defined standard of production and handling. "Organic" standards often require strict regulations in addition to the regulatory compliance standards of producers and processors such as food safety regulations, pesticide registrations, general food and nutrition labelling.

Fig. 23.1 The IFOAM label of accreditation for organic product certification bodies.

IFOAM accreditation, marked by the label in Fig. 23.1, ensures fair and orderly trade of organic products. IFOAM accreditation seeks to standardize organic food certification bodies globally. The four fundamental principles of organic agriculture according to IFOAM include:

- The principle of health
- The principle of ecology
- The principle of fairness
- The principle of care

23.1.2 Origins of organic agriculture

Two writings from 1943 contribute to the origins of modern organic agriculture: *An Agricultural Testament*, by Sir Albert Howard and *The Living Soil*, by Lady Eve Balfour. Both publications helped espouse that the health of plants, soil, livestock and people are interrelated (Karen, 1998). As a result, organic farming techniques often include practices such as composting, manure application, and shallow cultivation to minimize the disruption of soil microorganism activities. During that same decade, J. I. Rodale popularized organic farming in the United States through the magazine Organic Farming and Gardening, advocating farming methods in tune with natural ecosystem elements and cycles rather than attempting to manipulate and control them.

Chemical intensive agriculture increased agricultural productivity at low monetary costs in the late 1940s and 1950s, overpowering the attention and attraction of the organic movement. However, in 1962 the publication of Rachel Carson's book, *Silent Spring*, brought worldwide attention to the risks and effects of chemical intensive agriculture, specifically highlighting concerns over DDT pesticide use. This book spurred a large-scale environmental movement into the late 1960s and 1970s. The environmental movement focused on the relationship between agriculture and resource conservation by emphasizing the limited use of non-renewable resources. Innovative cultural practices emerged from this movement as solutions to the problems associated chemical and energy intensive agricultural systems. Some of these cultural practices include Integrated Pest Management, biorational pesticides, and pheromone confusion.

The term "sustainable agriculture" developed at the beginning of 1990s as public concerns with the negative impacts of conventional farming grew. During this time period the organic movement refined some goals to promote environmentally benign, economically sound and socially just agriculture. Ultimately, public support deemed organic agricultural products an economic basis in the marketplace. This growing success led to the standardized labelling of organic commodities by sanctioned certification entities. Certification agencies along with legislation such as the federal Organic Foods Production Act of 1990 (OFPA) directed these regulation efforts at improving the complete processes of food manufacturing from the soil to the table. Regulations unique to organic agriculture force organic farmers to operate under a set of constraints in addition to the regulations enforced upon their conventional counterparts.

Upon the onset of the 21st century, significantly increased public awareness dramatically expanded the organic farming industry. One of the ways in which focuses have shifted is evident in the education system. Beginning in the 1970s, universities and institutes have included courses and degrees geared towards environmentally sound and sustainable food systems. Today, institutes of higher learning continue to adapt and expand these education opportunities. In addition, public agricultural institutions are beginning to dedicate resources to support the needs of the organic sector.

23.1.3 Demands for organic agriculture

As just discussed, consumer preferences and perceptions of the quality and safety of food and its environmental impact during harvesting has driven growing demands for organic foods and organic agricultural practices. According to the U. S. Food and Agriculture Organization (FAO) this growth in demand is expected to continue into the foreseeable future. Consumers expect government agencies, industry and consumer groups to carefully examine organic food related issues and make necessary interventions to ensure an appropriate level of consumer protection.

While the demand for organic food in the United States, Europe, and elsewhere continues to grow rapidly, market shares remain quite small (Erkan, 2002). Organic food sales in the US have grown at an average annual rate of 18-20% between 1990 and 2010, with an estimated market share at retail food value of 5% in 2010. The market share in Denmark has grown to 7% of the retail food market since government subsidies and industry promotions have lowered price premiums for organic products. In contrast, organics account for only 1% of the retail food value in France.

Organic products now appear in both conventional supermarkets and large food chains to compete with natural food specialty shops (Thompson, 1998). The array of organic food products has expanded from traditional varieties of produce to include baby foods, dairy and meat products and cosmetics.

Consumer preferences have broadened beyond the initial focus of sustainable agricultural production for organic products. Today, a growing interest can be seen in the desire for foods with health-promoting benefits in addition to nutritional values. One of the industry responses to this demand is the creation of Genetically Modified Organisms (GMOs), which have raised many controversial debates around the world.

23.2 Approaches to organic agriculture

Soil and pest management presents two notable differences between conventional and organic agriculture. Successful organic farmers use adaptable methods of integrated management to work within the natural biological interaction processes rather than trying to manipulate them for short-term agricultural gains. While certain aspects of farming remain the same in conventional and organic systems (land preparation, planting operations, cultivation and irrigation, soil and pest management), integrated soil and pest management approaches are significantly different.

23.2.1 Soil management

Soil conditions, including physical, chemical, biological and microbial processes, affect the ability of plants to uptake available nutrients. Organic fertilizing methods include using cover crops, livestock manure and compost. Often these methods require time for decomposition and mineralization.

Cover crops, as a method of soil fertility management, aim to increase soil organic matter, nitrogen fixation, and beneficial insect populations, reduce weed growth and control soil erosion. Certain situations require supplemental fertilizers and soil amendments, for instance gypsum, fish, kelp and limestone. Negative influences on the farm from cover crops include increased costs for planting, cover crop management and specialized equipment; in addition, cover crops may attract more pests and interfere with irrigation systems.

Livestock manure and composts may improve soil structure and aggregate stability through the addition of organic matter and nutrients. The additional organic matter and nutrients increase soil physical properties by stimulating soil microbial activity and diversity. Livestock manure and composts also improve soil-water relationships, help control soil erosion and soil-borne pathogens. However, as we learned in Chapter 11, improperly handing compost can lead to a host of environmental and on-farm problems.

23.2.2 Pest management

Pest Management refers to an alternative approach to pesticide and herbicide use to control pest and disease populations. Common practices on organic farms include a combination of management approaches such as water management, sequential planting, diversification, crop rotation and cover crops and controlling diseases and weeds by enhancing beneficial insect populations. All of these strategies can fall under the larger concept of integrated pest management (IPM), discussed in great detail in Chapter 22.

Farmers may take advantage of strategic land use by using certain areas as buffer zones, biodiversity habitats or left fallow (to break disease and pest cycles). Pest control materials that are relatively non-toxic with few ecological side effects are sometimes called "bio-rational" pesticides, although there is no official definition of this term. Some, but not all, biorationals qualify for use on organic farms. The major categories of bio-rational pesticides include botanicals, microbial, minerals, and synthetic materials.

23.3 Organic food regulations

Regulating organic food requires international adoption of a unified set of guidelines pertaining to the farm preparation, storage and transport, labelling and marketing principles of organic production and trade. The first major step towards these goals occurred in 1991, when the Codex Alimentarius Commission (CAC) adopted specific guidelines concerning organic food production, processing, labelling and marketing practices. Inspection and certification bodies enable mechanisms for quality assurance of organically produced foods, affirming strict adherence to these guidelines.

As consumer and producer relationships grow further apart, inspection and certification ensures consumer trust of the "organic" production process. While some consumer demand expresses preference for locally grown organic food, at the same other consumers expect a variety of products year-round rather than seasonally appropriate foods. To meet these expectations, the FAO Committee on Agriculture has sought opportunities for developing world organic farmers to engage in export and trade. In order for a developing world farmer to market and trade their product with developed countries, they must accrue an organic certification organization label. Often small businesses find these costs prohibitive, constraining the growth of organic farm exports from developing countries. Furthermore, this expectation has jeopardized the quality of export produce, with a lack of trustworthy inspection capacity and capability for food control and infrastructure. The FAO currently seeks to better the organic certification infrastructure in developing countries that intend to export with developed countries.

The World Trade Organization (WTO) and the CAC has created important requirements for organic food based on equivalence, transparency and least trade restrictiveness principles. Similarly, export requirements from third world countries into EU countries require that the developing country demonstrate organic food production according to EU legislation and standards. The following topics express several key areas for inspection.

23.3.1 Chemical hazards

A critical point of inspection for organic certification revolves around the avoidance of chemical applications in the forms of synthetic pesticides, fertilizers, herbicides and fungicides.

(1) Pesticide residues

Organic food standards restrict pesticide residues, although complete independence of pesticide use is not required. Organic certification schemes do however require chemical-free land for up to three years prior to beginning organic production, as a means to lower levels of contaminants found in the soil. Natural pesticides (created from natural sources) are subject to a safety evaluation before use in organic fields. International guidelines may differ slightly according to the substances and accepted levels of post chemical pesticides and natural pesticides allowed in organic food production. However, consumers from the organic movement want pure biological control as a method of pest management.

(2) Nitrates

Foods with high nitrate concentrations increase the risk of methemoglobinemia and ingesting carcinogens. Methemoglobinemia results from the impairment of the ability for blood to carry oxygen, while the risk of ingesting carcinogens results from the food content conversion to nitrosamines. The FAO reported that organic foods have significantly lower nitrate content than conventionally grown crops, specifically referring to nitrophilic leaf, root and tuber crops.

(3) Environmental contaminants

Chemical hazards from environmental pollution found in air, water and soil equally affect both organic and conventional agriculture. Environmental contaminants include chlorinated hydrocarbons and heavy metals in the soil, biosolids from wastewater treatment facilities and air pollution from mining and smelting activities. Overall activities that exhibit greater environmental responsibility such increasing organic agriculture and lessening the dependence on fossil fuels will reduce environmental contaminants in the air, water and soil, ultimately lowering contaminant levels in food.

(4) Veterinary drugs and contaminants in animal feeds

Consumer concerns about veterinary drugs and contaminants in animal feed includes microbial resistance to antibiotics such as Bovine Somatotropin (BST) and pesticide residues, industrial and agricultural chemicals, heavy metals and radioactive nuclides in animal feeds. According to the FAO, U. S. consumer demand for organic dairy products is growing at a rate of 35% annually; in the EU, where current organic dairy products available already surpass availability in the U. S. , consumer demand has also risen rapidly. Organic production systems make the best use of animal health management based on appropriate measures of breed and strain selections, high-quality diet and favourable environments. However, as previously discussed, environmental contaminants exist in organically grown products from the atmosphere. Therefore, environmental pollutants may still be present in organic food from animals.

23. 3. 2 Microbiological hazards

Natural fertilisers and manures can lead to microbiological contamination through the mistreatment of manures, biosolids and soil nutrient agents. In organic agriculture, the use of mistreated fertilisers and manures can contaminate water, food and source human pathogens. Typical microbiological hazards include *E. Coli* and mycotoxin contamination. The Codex General Principles of Food Hygiene gives basic guidelines for ensuring food safety for all foods.

23. 3. 3 Mycotoxins

Mycotoxins refer to toxic by-products of mould. Mycotoxins grow on specific types of food products and moulds in suitable conditions. The most toxic mycotoxin compounds, Aflatoxins, can cause liver cancer from prolonged ingestion in small doses. All mycotoxins present a major microbiological health hazard and carefully conducted research continues to examine how best to reduce mycotoxin content in food products through good agricultural, handling and storage practices. To date, no research has shown evidence whether organic agriculture lowers the risk of mycotoxin content when compared with conventional agricultural products.

23. 3. 4 Organic food quality and processing

Organic and conventional food production differs in that CAC and EU organic food guidelines restrict non-agricultural origin food ingredients in the processing of organic foods. Both standards for organic and conventional agriculture prohibit irradiation on food and individual ingredients.

(1) Food irradiation

Food irradiation refers to foods subjected to ionising radiation. Irradiation is used to help control various deteriorative changes that occur in food, insects, parasites and pathogenic bacteria. Although food irradiation has no associated food safety risks and can be carried out in accordance with internationally accepted guidelines, every consumer segment has been reluctant to accept this technology. Therefore, most countries require irradiation labelling to alert consumers to foods subjected to irradiation.

(2) Other aspects of organic food quality

Organic food offers products according to specific guidelines for chemical content, processing and storage characteristics, appearance and taste. However, organic food quality also incorporates considerations associated with ethical and environmental values, such as animal welfare, energy efficiency and social impacts. Organic farming also seeks to enhance genetic biodiversity of soil organisms, wildlife, flora and cultivated crops.

In summary, the history of modern organic agriculture stems from two popularized writings, *An Agricultural Testament* and *The Living Soil*. Since the 1940s popularity and trends in organic agriculture has evolved into the organic culture we see today. Organic agriculture refers to a process claim about food and products produced in a biologically responsible way, minimizing off farm inputs and outputs. To standardize this process certification agencies have arisen to make sure farmers follow specific guidelines. Two notable differences between conventional and organic agricultural practices are soil and pest management strategies. As an extension of these two methods, organic food regulations seek to eliminate chemical and microbiological hazards, such as reducing pesticide residues, nitrates, environmental contaminants, *E. Coli* and mycotoxins. In addition, regulations restrict veterinary drugs and animal feed contaminants. Another aspect of the organic food production system that differs from conventional agriculture includes ethical and moral distinctions, such as the concern over animal welfare and social impact. In this chapter we discuss many international standards for organic foods.

Literatures cited in this chapter

Badgley C. and Perfecto I. 2007. Can organic agriculture feed the world? *Renewable Agriculture and Food Systems* 22 (2): 80-85.

Erkan R. and Turhan S. 2002. Prospects and challenges for developing countries in trade and production of organic food and fibers The case of Turkey. *British Food Journal* 104 (3/4/5): 371-390.

FAO. 2000. Food Safety and Quality as Affected by Organic Farming, Twenty Second FAO Regional Conference for Europe. *Portugal* 7: 24-28.

Goodman D. 2000. Organic and conventional agriculture: Materializing discourse and agro-ecological managerialism. *Agriculture and Human Values* 17 (3): 215-219.

Howard A. 1943. *An Agricultural Testament*. London: Oxford University Press, Inc.

International Federation of Organic Agriculture Movements (IFOAM) . 1998. Basic Standards for Organic Production and Processing. Germany: Tholey-Theley.

Klonsky K. , Tourte L. , Thompson G. D. , Lohr L. , and Krissoff B. 1998. Emergence of U. S. Organic Agriculture: Can we Compete? *Department of Agricultural and Applied Economics*, *University of Gorgia*.

Klonsky K. and Tourte L. 1998. Organic Agricultural Production in the United States: Debates and Directions. *American Journal of Agricultural Economics* 80 (5): 1119-1124.

Li L. 2007. *China's Organic Food Disappoints Consumers*. Washington D. C.: Worldwatch Institute.

Ramesh P., Singh M., and Subba Rao A. 2005. Organic farming: Its relevance to the Indian context. *Current Science* 88 (4): 561-568.

Thompson G. D. 1998. Demand for Organic Foods: What We Know and What We Need to Know. *American Journal of Agricultural Economics* 80 (5): 1113-1118.

Chapter 24 Genetically modified crops and their implications

Learning objectives

1. Define genetically modified organisms (GMOs).
2. Name three technologies used in producing GMOs.
3. Explain three reasons for creating GMOs.
4. Explain five risks of using GMOs.
5. List responsible ways of using GMOs to minimize potentially negative impacts.
6. How is DNA moved from one organism to another to create a GMO?
7. How does a bacteria vector work?
8. What are three advantages to GM crops?
9. How could GMOs further stratify socioeconomic divides in developing countries?
10. Can you explain the relationship between GMOs and the risk of biological warfare?
11. What are some environmental risks associated with GM crop production?
12. How can economics drive GMO production?
13. Do you think we should use genetic engineering in people?
14. Do you think the benefits of GM crops outweigh the risks? Why or why not?

Humans and agriculture share an intertwined history of settlement. When people started selecting specific types of plants to grow, artificial selection began to influence the evolution of crops. However, until recently humans could only favour a specific plant species but were unable to control the actual mix of genetic information. With advances in biotechnology, people have learned how to manipulate genetic information to create genetically modified crops. Biotechnological advancements have led to many changes in the agricultural industry. In this chapter we will discuss genetically modified crops and their implications in commercial scale crop production.

24.1 What is a genetically modified crop?

Molecules, called nucleic acids, store all the genetic information for an organism in the form of DNA (deoxyribonucleic acid) and RNA (ribonucleic acid). Biologists have learned how to manipulate the genetic code in DNA sequences in one organism and build it into another organism's DNA sequence. Similar to a filmstrip, a sequence can be cut, moved and reinserted somewhere else to create a new or different sequence (with different information). Manipulation mechanisms of DNA synthesis include polymerization, ligation and cutting. Fig. 24.1 displays six steps for creating genetically modified corn, based on molecular biology techniques of building new DNA molecules from recombinant DNA, or rDNA (molecular cloning), sequences (Gachet, 1999).

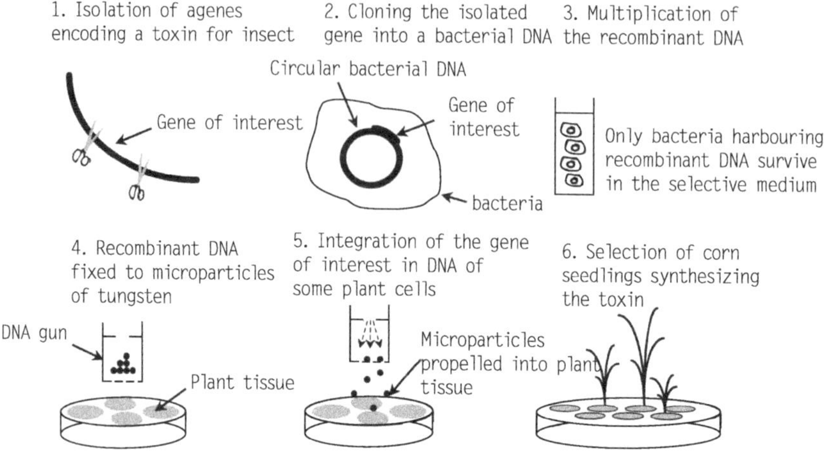

Fig. 24. 1 Steps for the creation of a GM corn variety with an endotoxin gene for insect resistance (Gachet, 1999).

Integrating foreign DNA within an organism yields a new, genetically modified organism, or GMO. Generally, GMOs are created to take on a novel trait from another organism. For instance, a variety of GM corn may have better resistance to pests or a sweeter taste. According to the Canadian Food Inspection Agency, GMOs include "Any organism whose genetic information has been altered by any technique including natural processes, induced mutagenesis, genetic engineering or others" . In Canada, Plants with Novel Traits (PNTs), also refers to genetically modified organisms.

24. 2 GMO technology

Genetic engineering, or genetic modification, refers to the process of inserting an organism with a gene it does not naturally possess. To create a GMO, the desired gene is transcribed onto messenger RNA, or mRNA, and then translated into a protein (a protein corresponds to a specific gene). As long as the organism can synthesize a foreign protein, it can express the genetically modified gene as a trait. Some technology available to carry out this process includes bacterial vectors, microinjection and particle guns. In agricultural crops, genetic engineering has been used to improve crop protection, yield and quality. GMOs present other opportunities for producing high value-added molecules for pharmaceuticals, vitamins or biopolymers for industry, and improved nutritional quality of plants.

24. 2. 1 Bacterial vectors

A common method used to create GMOs is the insertion of genes through bacterial vectors. *Agrobacterium tubefaciens*, a tumour inducing plant pathogen found in the soil is most often used as a bacterial vector, causing the infection known as Crown Gall Disease. The bacterium transfers tumour-inducing (Ti) plasmid that contains regions for the origin of replication located in a section of its DNA, known as T-DNA, into the nucleus of an infected plant cell (Fig. 24. 2). The transfer function of T-DNA encodes for tumour growth. Upon Ti plasmid insertion into a plant, the T-DNA tumour production region causes uncontrolled growth at its base, or crown. During the proliferated tumour growth process, Ti plasmids are randomly inserted into the host plant genome, thereby spreading the new DNA containing the desired trait throughout the plant's genome. Fig. 24.3 displayed this process.

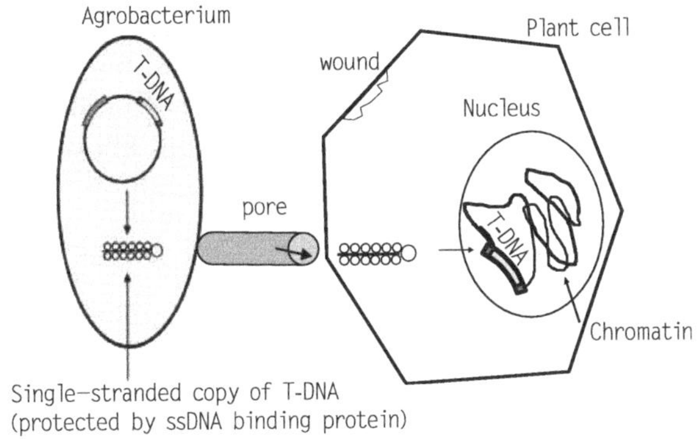

Fig. 24.2 Transfer of T-DNA from *Agrobacterium tumefaciens* to a plant cell.

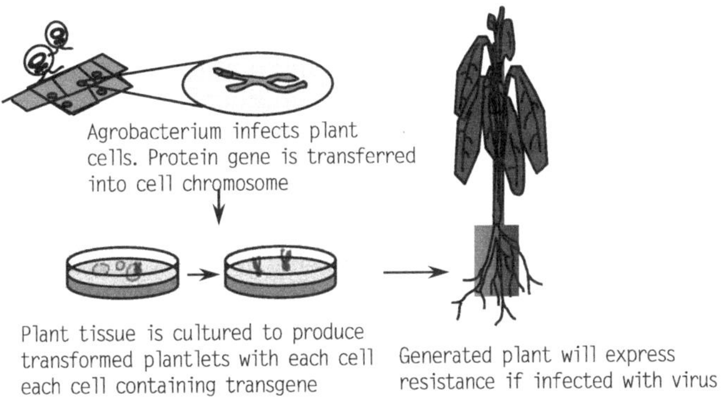

Fig. 24.3 Gene transformation by genetic engineering through the bacterial vector *Agrobacterium tumefaciens*.

24.2.2 Microinjection

Mircroinjection refers to the process of inserting DNA directly into a cell or cell nucleus by way of an inserted cannula for gene expression in a host organism. This whole process occurs under a microscope and does not require a marker gene, as needed in regular injection procedures. Microinjection targets one specific gene to introduce into a cell, which confers a new trait. The transformed cells can be identified with injected dye. Although this process works well in animal cells with stable cell walls, microinjection remains experimental in plant cells. If microinjection could be used for transgenic crops, antibiotic resistant and herbicide resistant markers will become obsolete.

24.2.3 DNA particle guns

A DNA particle gun, or gene gun, transfers genes by placing target tissue in the acceleration path of the microscopic pellets (of gold or tungsten) coated in DNA. This biolistic system requires complex and advanced technology. The gene gun barrel is coated with DNA. When the bullet coated with gold or tungsten pellets is shot through the barrel, DNA adheres to the biologically inert particles of the metal atoms. At the end of the barrel a metal sheet with tiny holes stops the plastic bullet, allowing the pellets with DNA to shoot off of the bullet and through the metal holes at very high speeds to enter the cell wall. Often the DNA contains an antibiotic along with the desired GMO traits. The antibiotic allows researchers to test effective incorporation of the DNA, since cell growth in a petri dish will only occur if the antibiotic produces resistance in the cells. If the cells grow in the petri dish, researchers know that gene insertion of the desired trait has been achieved.

24.3 Advantages of GM crops

24.3.1 Time

Conventional plant breeding is a very slow process, typically taking 12 years for conventional hybrid methods to breed a new crop variety. Biotechnology allows the breeding process to occur quickly, with methods that isolate specific traits in DNA and move them to another organism. In the past, this process might require multiple generations of cross breeding to achieve the same result, if it were possible at all. GMO biotechnology, in an unusual example, could move genes from a fish to a plant and have the DNA encode specific proteins that can be nutritional or medically functional. Genetic engineering offers precise and specific genetic modifications in a short time period.

24.3.2 Benefits to agricultural production

The most widespread benefit in agricultural production from GM crops is the ability to confer resistance to worms, insects and herbicides. One example where genetically engineered crops are able to confer resistance greater than any chemical protection farmers can provide is *Bacillus thuringengis* (BT). Specific BT strains are toxic to Lepidoptera that produce the delta endotoxin crystal. Therefore, GM maize with BT prevents Lepidoptera predation and human body can harmlessly digest it. Scientists have also transferred different strains of BT into cotton, which prevents insect infestation, and allow growth under adverse conditions making it more winter-hardy and more drought resistant. Presently in the USA, BT is used in 30% of cotton, 20% of corn and 5% of potatoes produced.

Other well-known GM crops are Roundup-Ready soybeans and corn, with resistance to Roundup herbicide. Roundup is a non-selective herbicide, which inhibits an enzyme necessary for building aromatic amino acids in plants. Without these amino acids, a plant will die. Genetically engineered Roundup-ready (RR) crops are tolerant to glyphosate, a broad-spectrum herbicide used in Roundup to kill the weeds. Other GM crops resistant to herbicides, fungi and viruses include chicory, papaya, squash, rape seed, wheat, sunflower, beetroot, lettuce, tomato, cucumber and rice.

Another benefit of genetic modification in the agricultural industry includes the ability to make fruits taste better and last longer. For instance, FlavrSavr tomatoes were designed to soften slowly allowing them to stay on the vine longer, which makes them taste better. Similarly, if genetically modifying bananas could make the ripening process slower they would also become tastier. An interesting GM fruit under development is strawberries with the addition of an antifreeze protein from flounder fish to help them grow better in cold climates.

Genetically modifying non-food crops are also important to agricultural production. For instance, GM cotton has been created to grow with coloured fibres. In addition, GM tobacco grows more easily; other research to genetically engineer the poplar tree is underway to improve raw material (cellulose) for making paper.

24.3.3 Health and pharmaceutical benefits

Quite a few GM crops are under development to increase human health. Both tomatoes and strawberries contain natural anti-cancer agents, which GM varieties might enhance for pharmaceuticals. If GM tomatoes and strawberries increase lycopene and ellagic acid respectively, the added health benefits will also help people. GM broccoli with increased levels of both natural anti-cancer agents and antioxidant agents could prevent or slow down the aging of cells. GM corn can be modified to make healthier cooking oils with a reduced saturated fat content. GM potatoes richer in starch will also be used to produce low-fat chips and crisps. Current research is investigating the possibility of creating a GM banana with the hepatitis vaccine. Other GM products underway include a rice variety without an allergen factor and a lettuce variety with lower nitrate levels. Scientists in Sweden have already developed "golden rice" with added Vitamin A, although not enough for significant differences in humans. Other researchers around the work are coming up with new GM rice varieties with added beta-carotene (using genes from daffodil and Erwinia) and iron to combat iron deficiencies. Sometimes, GM crops such as healthier rice ends up acting as a technological fix for a sociological problem, which does not work in practice.

24.3.4 Social benefits

GMO technology has the potential to improve reliability and quality of the world food supply to support population growth, as the food demand of a growing society is expected to double by 2025 and triple by 2050. In addition to offering greater amounts of food, GM crops may offer a cost-effective solution to micronutrient malnutrition, by providing nutrients such as vitamin A and iron-rich crops. At the same time, poverty stricken areas with malnutrition problems face obstacles such as adverse weather and lack the financial capital for input costs to control pests and diseases. GM crops may help achieve the needed productivity in these regions with pest and disease resistant crops, with higher tolerance to drought and soil conditions and with increased durability during harvesting and shipping. For instance, drought-tolerant maize and insect-resistant cassava could benefit both small farmers and poor consumers. Reducing the need for crop protection costs with GM crops can benefit both the environment and overall public health. Furthermore, reducing the need for pesticides, herbicides and cultivating new land for crops helps conserve biodiversity and fragile ecosystems.

24.4 Risks associated with GM crops

While GM crops offer a host of advantages from food security, health and safety standpoints, the rapid development of GMOs has accompanying problems that pose a risk to human health and ecosystems.

24.4.1 Health risks

While GM foods are not intrinsically good or bad for human health, large scale commercial production of GM crops pose a risk of transferring unwanted genes and traits to another species, which may cause allergic reactions. Thus, GM foods require testing for allergy transfers before commercialization. Such testing has avoided an allergen transfer in the past, with the transfer of a Brazil nut gene to soybeans; luckily, testing caught this transfer prior to commercialization. Customers often want better labelling and knowledge of production, although no consumer-producer transparency standard exists for the enforcement of design and safety of GM crops yet.

24.4.2 Ecological risks

Similar to the health risks, GM crops pose an ecological risk through vertical and horizontal gene flows, and GM monocultures. The vertical transfer of genes refers to passing genes to wild flora relatives, while horizontal transfer refers to passing genes to other species and organisms. The risk of passing undesirable traits uncontrollably to both wild relatives and other organisms poses a huge threat for the environment. GM monocultures can critically impair the environment as well, with the creation of super-weeds, rapid development of insect resistance and impacts to soil fauna and non-target organisms. Ecological theory suggests high risks of environmental impacts from GM gene flows and monocultures.

24.4.3 Socioeconomic risks

GM crops pose considerable risk to socioeconomic development and small farmers in developing countries. Without policies and legislation supporting small farmer access to delivery systems, extension services, productive resources, markets, and infrastructure, introducing agricultural biotechnology could actually increase inequalities of income and wealth (Pinstrup-Anders, 2000). In developing countries, large-scale commercial farmers are most likely to benefit from GM crops through early adoption of technology, expanded production, and reduced unit costs.

24.4.4 Biosecurity risks

Biosecurity risks generally include measures needed to protect people and the environment against the malicious use of pathogens or their toxins in direct or indirect actions against crops, livestock or humans (Bork, 2007).

(1) Biosafety

Biosafety risk refers to the (accidental) exposure of crops to infectious agents, which may lead to casualties and disease outbreaks. Although biosafety regulations exist in laboratories settings, for microbial research and in the biotechnology industry itself, one accidental or deliberate release of a microbial pathogen can threaten national and international security.

(2) Biohazards

Two main concerns exist for potential biohazard risks. GMOs become highly infectious and virulent biological agents from the vectors used to introduce genes from on organism to another. As they spread commercially through globalization, the vectors can accidentally introduce alien genes to many different regions around the world. The second biohazard concern addresses GMO impacts on the environment and human health. As novel organisms, the future ecological and heath effects of GMOs remain unknown. Biohazards increase the likelihood of biological terrorism and biological warfare.

(3) Biological warfare

Genetic modification to pathogens and diseases for large-scale release has become a major military concern. The potential for "designer diseases" could quickly and severely harm a large population, ultimately inciting an international biological arms race. "Designer weapons" created from recombinant DNA also pose a threat of biological warfare as they could transcend the limits of old biological weapons.

24.5 GMO debates

Great controversy surrounds the topic of genetically modified organisms, specifically concerning GM crops. While some people fully support the promise of improved world agriculture by using biotechnology for future food security and safety, GM crops causes others to have great concerns about the risks to human health, the environment and biosecurity. These debates go beyond the scope of the advantages and risks associated with GMOs to include economic, political and ethical questions to weigh the risks and benefits of GM crops in our agricultural society.

24.5.1 Economics and politics

Biotechnology for genetic modifications has created an abundance of jobs and investments in the biological sciences. Economic forces can drive biotechnology developments. Positively influencing GMOs in this way gives people greater confidence in biotechnology and brings money to farmers. However, GMO technology has become big business, and the intentions of monopolies and other dominant sellers of GMO products might not be in the best interest of the environment or the people, but rather in their own economic interests. Furthermore, GMOs have the ability to create a greater economic divide that eventually influences the social structure of a society; this is specifically a concern in developing countries. The loss of agricultural diversity in the environment also raises an interesting debate about the future market values of food and non-food crops.

Political debates go hand-in-hand with economical debates. Often economical situations drive political forces. On one hand, bringing biotechnology into attention has given the issue political power for legislation and regulation. However, politics also play a nasty role in GMO globalization and capitalization.

24.5.2 Ethics

A major ethical concern of GMOs is the reduction of plants, animals and microorganisms to mere commercial commodities, bereft of any sacred character. Genetic engineering and "life patents" accelerate this process and exacerbate the issue. The idea of genetic engineering in animals and humans often raises higher concern than the genetic engineering of plants and microorganisms. Genetically modifying traits and characteristics of animals and humans raise some very important and interesting questions. Specifically in humans, we can see many benefits and risks associated with genetic engineering. For instance, having the ability to prevent a baby from being born with autism or preventing Parkinson's from developing later in life would be incredibly beneficial for people. However, genetic engineering could also let people choose their child's eye colour, hair colour and personality traits. This type of genetic engineering refers to "designer babies" and raises the questions, "where do we draw the line?" For this reason among many others, genetic engineering is hotly debated for use in people.

24. 5. 3 Weighing risks and benefits of GM crops

Current debates about GMOs in agriculture reveal major differences in opinions and perceptions about associated risks and benefits. Unfortunately research supports both sides of the debate, and without a long history to examine, it is difficult to deduce the long-term effects of GMOs on agriculture. Economic and political forces drive certain perspectives into the media, which makes it that much more important for trained ecologists to perform reliable research and join the public debate about GMOs with unbiased information (Gray, 2004). Ultimately, every person must make his or her own personal decision about genetically modified organisms. In the future, integrated assessments might bring people from both sides of the debate closer together. An integrated safety assessment of GMOs could create greater consumer confidence in GM biotechnology and focus on hazard identification and exposure assessment (Haslberger, 2006). Integrated views on GMOs might include molecular characterization and international standards for traded foods.

In summary, Genetically modified organisms (GMOs) refer to the integration of foreign DNA from one organism into another organism. This process is done through advanced biotechnology, using techniques such as bacterial vectors, microinjection and DNA gene guns. In this chapter we mostly focus on genetically modified crops and their influence in agriculture. Advantages of GM crops include the ability to quickly develop crops with desired traits, better quality agricultural production, the ability to produce agriculture in adverse environments, pharmaceutical, health, industrial and social benefits. At the same time, serious risks to health, the environment, socioeconomic structure and biosecurity exist. Debates about the topic require weighing the pros and cons of GMOs with economic, political and ethical questions in mind.

Literatures cited in this chapter

Altieri M. A. 2000. The ecological impacts of transgenic crops on agroecosystem health. *Ecosystem Health* 6 (1): 13-23.

Bork K. H., Halkjaer-Knudsen V., Hansen J. E. S., and Heegaard E. D. 2007. Biosecurity in Scandinavia. *Biosecurity and Bioterrorism: Biodefense Strategy, Practice, and Science* 5 (1): 62-71.

Conner A. J., Glare T. R., and Nap J. P. 2003. The release of genetically modified crops into the environment. *The Plant Journal* 33 (1): 19-46.

Gachet E., Martin G. G., Vigneau F., and Meyer G. 1999. Detection of genetically modified organisms (GMOs) by PCR: a brief review of methodologies available. *Trends in Food Science & Technology* 9 (11-12): 380-388.

Gilmore R. 2000. Agbiotech and world food security—threat or boon? *Nature biotechnology* 18: 361.

Gray A. J. 2004. Ecology and government policies: the GM crop debate. *Journal of Applied Ecology* 41 (1): 1-10.

Haslberger A. G. 2006. Need for an "Integrated Safety Assessment" of GMOs, Linking Food Safety and Environmental Considerations. *Journal of Agricultural and Food Chemistry* 54 (9): 3173-3180.

Pinstrup-Andersen P. and Cohen M. J. 2000. *Modern Biotechnology for Food and Agriculture*: Risks and Opportunities for the Poor. In: Persley G. J and Lantin M. M. *Agricultural Biotechnology and the Poor: An International Conference on Biotechnotogy Consultative Group on International Agricultural Research*. Washington, DC: 159-169.

Part Ⅲ Practical Teaching

Practice 1 Supermarket survey

Introduction

Agriculture is a profession worthy of our understanding and respect. However, many first year students who are studying Agroecology are not familiar with the standard procedures of agricultural businesses, the marketing of agricultural products associated with them and the role of the consumer in the food system. This exercise will provide an opportunity for students to observe agribusiness from the view of the consumer you will also become more aware of where your food originates and marketing strategies used by retailers in marketing.

Learning objectives

After completing this survey, discussing the results with your partners and the in-class discussion with instructors, you should be able to:

1. Discuss the strategies that supermarkets use to influence shoppers.
2. Explain the reasons for the floor design of the store.
3. Know the place of origin for several types of food, especially fresh produce.
4. Know the definitions of local, natural, organic, fair trade, functional food and nutraceutical.
5. Compare the relative food value (in terms of sugar, salt and calories) of a variety of foods.
6. Compare the relative prices of several common food products.
7. Discuss the concept of "value-added" using potatoes as an example.
8. Shop in a more informed manner.

Practice procedure and assignment

Select one or two big super marts popular for grocery/food shopping to visit and complete a survey according to the questions below. Your report will be submitted to the instructors.

Work in a group of 4-5 students. Make sure all participants contribute to completing the survey.

1. Sketch the floor plan of the supermarket you have chosen. Label the floor plan with the following sections: dairy products, produce, meat, delicatessen, restaurant, bakery, flowers/plants, frozen foods; non-food items (Note: your store may or may not have all of these sections and it may have other sections that should be included in your floor plan. And with arrows trace the route you would take if you were pushing a shopping cart).

2. List four items of fresh vegetables or fruit which are from Fujian Province . List four items of fresh vegetables or fruit which are from outside Fujian Province and note their place of origin. Where does the majority of the fresh produce come from? Are there fresh products from outside China? What are they and where do they come

from? From which parts of China does the majority of the produce come?

	From Fujian Province	outside Fujian Province (their place of origin)
①		
②		
③		
④		

3. Locate the "organic" or "green" produce section. Where does the majority of the fresh organic or green produce come from?

4. How do the prices compare between "organic" or "green" and "non-organic" fresh products? List 3 products and compare.

	Product	"Organic" or "green" Price	Non-organic or conventional Price
①			
②			
③			

5. There may also be a "processed" organic area. If so, do a similar comparison between prices of "organic" and "non-organic" processed products.

	Product	"Organic" or "green" Price	Non-organic or conventional Price
①			
②			
③			

6. Are there any "organic" or "green" products that surprised you?

7. Find 3 pre-prepared (frozen, boxed or ready made) meals that you would enjoy for your dinner. List the names of the 3 meals and indicate whether they were frozen, dry packaged or fresh. How many people were these prepared foods intended to serve (1, 2, 3, 4 or more?)

8. What is one "snack" item that your family enjoys? How much do they cost? How much did they cost 5 year ago?

9. How many brands of salsa are sold in the store? Name four of them. What is the difference in price?

	Brands	Price
①		
②		
③		
④		
⑤		

10. Looking at the canned fruit section, which USA brand would you judge to be the largest seller? Which cereal has the highest sugar content? Which cereal has the lowest sugar content? Which cereal has the highest calorie content? Which cereal has the lowest calorie content? Find an example of a "natural" granola cereal. List the ingredients and the percentage of sugar and calorie content.

11. Compare the length of shelf space given to the cheapest frozen French fries with that given to the most expensive.

Cheapest (length of shelf space)	
Most expensive (length of shelf space)	

12. What is the most expensive meat available (price per kg)?

13. What is the most expensive seafood available (price per kg)?

14. Find two different brands of tea. Where are the tea leaves grown for the two brands of tea?

15. List as many product names that you can think of that have become the generic name for the product (e. g. CHANGFU, YILI milk).

	Generic 1		Generic 2
①		⑥	
②		⑦	
③		⑧	
④		⑨	
⑤		⑩	

16. Looking at the soft drink aisle, which would you judge to be the most popular soft drink?

17. Find two types of frozen orange juice produced and compare prices. Why do you think the price is different?

	Frozen orange juice	Price
①		
②		

18. Look at the end of aisle displays in the foods section. Which one is most attractive to you and why (3 reasons)?

19. What food items do you often buy that you would want to be able to buy in Canada?

20. Write a summary with 100 words for your survey.

Practice 2 Economic plant tour on campus

Introduction

In Agroecology course, the students have a deep impression of new understanding of agriculture by Dr. Claude Caldwell, i. e. "Agriculture is the science, art, politics and sociology of changing sunlight into healthy, happy people" . That is to say, agriculture initiates by solar energy and plant's photosynthesis. It is plant's primary production support the organisms life rather than others, plant is most important thing for human life. Visiting agricultural businesses for one afternoon is only a small step toward our understanding but it could be the start of a habit of learning from practical people on an ongoing basis. Students with an agricultural background will also benefit by observing other operations and hearing how things can be done differently. Without doubt, this tour will be worth your time in the short and long terms.

Plants, that are important economically, have a wide range of characteristics, diverse structures and a wide variation in their use, because of this, they have many roles in agricultural systems. Students of agriculture should have a good working knowledge of the many terms used to describe plants. This exercise will help students review plant terminology, form and function.

Learning objectives

After completing this practice you should be able to:

Describe general plant characteristics; the wide variation in their use and cultivation and their roles in agricultural systems.

1. Define the following life cycle terms and give an example of a plant for each:
   - Annual
   - Biennial
   - Perennial
2. Give an example of an herbaceous perennial and a woody perennial.
3. Define the following terms with examples:
   - Simple leaf
   - Compound leaf
   - Deciduous tree
   - Evergreen tree
   - Legume
4. Give two examples of diseases, insect pests or nutritional problems seen on campus; name the plant with which they are associated and describe the symptoms. Give the location.
5. Explain the use of row covers and plastic houses to alter environment for plant growth.

In this exercise the class will be divided into 2 groups. Each group will go on a walking tour with an instructor of the campus outdoor fields and gardens. Prior to the tour students should become familiar with the terminology used in the practical exercise questions listed below. This can be done by reviewing the handouts given in class and using the glossary on the Moodle site (the name of courser website) if necessary to identify terms; you may also want to look at the vegetable reading in the resource manual and an Introductory Botany text. The presentations associated with the plants listed in the Plant and Animal ID exercise on Moodle may also prove helpful.

Practice procedure and assignment

During this practical teaching period a tour will be conducted of the outdoor campus plant facilities. Students will meet in a certain place at their scheduled lab time. The class will be divided in 2 groups. Each group will go on a walking tour of the campus grounds with an instructor. Please dress appropriately for the weather and leave heavy knapsacks and extra items in your room if possible.

A follow up exercise will be assigned from the economic plants on campus tour.

Reports from the Economic Plants on Campus tour are due at the beginning of Lecture. Plant characteristics, diversity, the wide variation in their use, habitat and their roles in agricultural systems will be discussed. This assignment may be completed individually or with one partner, directly on the hand-out. Make sure names, student numbers and lab section are listed if you work with a partner. Please write neatly. Submit only one copy if you work with a partner. Answers should be your own; several correct answers are possible for many of the questions; i. e. , do not copy from other groups.

Becoming familiar with the terms used in the questions will make the exercise easier. To do this, you may want to refer to the Vegetable Classification reading and the related textbook or an Introductory Botany text. You may also find the plants listed in the Plant and Animal ID exercise on Moodle helpful or use the glossary on the Moodle site if necessary to identify. Students' report for this practice will be finished according to the following Questions:

1. Define the following life cycle terms and give an example of a plant on campus for each:
   - Annual
   - Winter annual
   - Biennial
   - Perennial
2. Give an example of an herbaceous perennial and a woody perennial growing on campus.
3. Give examples of plants that are commonly used for both ornamental purposes and food production of any kind.
4. Name three fruit trees commonly grown on campus.
5. Find the fruit on the Grapes, how does the grape plant attach itself to a support? How does this differ from the way Kiwis are attached?
6. Name two crops seen on campus grown for their enlarged roots.
7. Give three examples of crops on campus that are harvested at an 'immature' growth stage, or are harvested before complete physiological maturity is reached. (Seeds are not developed or mature).

8. Name two evergreen shrubs growing on campus, one broad leaved and one with needles.

9. How can one distinguish a simple leaf from a compound leaf?

10. ① Name a tree with palmately compound leaves growing in Alumni Gardens; ② Name a vegetable with compound leaves growing in the demonstration garden.

11. What is meant by a deciduous tree? Based on your own experience, name a deciduous tree.

12. What is the tallest member of the grass family you can find on campus?

13. Look at the plants grown with clear plastic covers near the S building where your agroecology class is taught. Why do you think the plastic ground cover is being used? What plants are grown here? Why are they on raised beds?

14. Give three examples of diseases, weeds or pests seen on campus; name the plant or crop with which they are associated, describe the symptoms and the location of the plant.

15. Name three plants on campus belonging to the same botanical family.

16. Name two plants that are primarily used to produce feed for ruminants (cattle and sheep).

17. Name three plants that are primarily consumed by monogastric animals (pigs, people).

18. Look at the cauliflower plants, are their leaves glabrous or pubescent?

19. ① What plant on campus has the largest leaves? ② Were the leaves of that plant glabrous or pubescent?

20. Where will you find peanuts on the peanut plant? Where are they attached to the peanut plant?

21. Name a tree on campus that has flower on it now. Give the Latin name.

22. ① Pea plants are vines. How do they support themselves when climbing on a pole or fence? ② Find another vine type plant and explain how it supports itself.

23. ① Name a crop on campus that is ready for harvest now; ② Name a crop on the campus that has matured and can no longer be harvested; ③ Name a crop on the campus that is not yet ready for harvest.

24. ① Examine wheat planted in the research area. Carefully examine one head without touching or removing it, count the number of spikelets (fan shaped structures containing the developing seeds). How many spikelets are on the wheat head? ② If there are three seeds in each spikelet, how many seeds would you expect to find in the head? ③ If there were 300 heads in one square meter and seeds weighed 35 grams per 1000 seeds, what is the weight of 10 square meters of harvested seed?

25. Many new buildings are being built at FAFU and the grounds have changed a great deal. If you were in charge of designing the re-landscaping or garden type relaxation/recreation areas, what would you include? Use specific plant names or types when possible. Consider how you like to interact with the landscape around you)?

Note: Many ideas were suggested by students, 1-2 points were given according to the effort put into the answer. Students suggested trees, flowers, rock gardens, fountains, sports fields, ponds and pools, fragrant trees, fruit trees etc.

Practice 3 Composting

Introduction

The lecture presentation of "A Compost: Making and Using" has introduced you to the composting process factors and the recommended conditions for active composting. In addition, the lecture briefly outlined some of the activities involved in managing the composting process in order to obtain properly stabilized or mature compost which has value as a soil amendment. This practice teaching is intended to expand your knowledge and understanding of the composting process by teaching you some of the practical skills involved in blending materials and monitoring and evaluating an actively working compost pile.

Learning objectives

After completing this practice, you should be able to:

1. Define the following terms: thermophilic; active composting; feedstock; amendment; bulking agent.

2. Describe three composting process factors which are important in the selection and blending of feedstock materials.

3. Describe three factors which are important in the management of the composting process.

4. Use a compost recipe-formulation computer spreadsheet to determine how much carbon-containing amendment needs to be mixed with manure or other N-containing feedstock.

5. Evaluate an "actively working pile", and troubleshoot to maintain optimum conditions for composting within the pile.

Principles of composting

Composting Process Factors Composting is most rapid when the key composting process factors (e. g. , C : N ratio, porosity, aeration, moisture, etc.), are present within ranges that are optimal for the growth of the composting microorganisms. The recommended ranges of these factors for active composting are summarized below in Tab. P3. 1. Some of the conditions listed in Tab. P3. 1 are established through the selection and blending of the feedstock materials, whereas other conditions are controlled largely through proper management of the composting process. Note that C : N ratio, moisture content, particle size, porosity, and pH are all factors which may be considered in blending materials, whereas aeration, temperature, and moisture are largely addressed during management of the process.

Tab. P3. 1 Recommending conditions for an active composting

Characteristic	Target range
Carbon to nitrogen (C : N) ratio	20 : 1 – 40 : 1
Moisture content (%)	40 – 65
Oxygen concentration (%)	>5
Particle size (cm)	1.25 – 5
Pile porosity (%)	>40
Bulk density (kg/m^3)	475 – 712
pH	6.0 – 9.0
Temperature (℃)	43 – 65

Blending materials

One of the first steps in composting is blending feedstock material (ingredient materials for composting) in a manner and proportions that optimize the composting process factors and balance the mix. Materials added to adjust C : N ratio or moisture content are referred to as amendments, and materials added to open up the compost mix, giving it porosity so air can move through the pile to provide oxygen and cooling, are referred to as bulking agents.

Various approaches are used in blending materials for composting. A quantitative approach involves the use of material testing and calculations to determine mixing proportions based on tested properties of the ingredient materials. Quantitative approaches eliminate much of the "guesswork" in combining materials, and are useful when raw material characteristics are not known or it is important to establish near optimum composting conditions (e.g., for accelerated decomposition, or composting high N ingredients with the least amount of odor or other problems). Part 1 of this field teaching provides you with some practices in using a computer spreadsheet program to formulate compost mixes. In this exercise, you will provide the input values (%C, %N and % moisture) for the feedstock materials, and the spreadsheet calculates the actual weights of materials required to achieve the desired mixture C : N ratio or moisture goal. If the density of materials is known, it is possible to convert weights of materials to more convenient mixing volumes.

Composting mixtures may also be established using qualitative, or more intuitive, approaches. Qualitative approaches include making a best estimate of the correct ratio of ingredients, or combining materials based on composting experience and the look and feel of the mix. When operators are familiar with the feedstock materials and the required conditions for composting, such approaches (while less precise than quantitative methods) are often highly successful. Qualitative approaches are commonly used in on-farm composting and leaf and yard waste composting operations.

Regardless of what method or approach is used to formulate the mix, it is important to bear in mind that composting is a relatively forgiving process that occurs over a wide range of conditions. In other words, provided that you mix materials with an eye to acceptable moisture content and carbon to nitrogen ratio and manage the process properly, you are likely to produce an acceptable compost product. From the lecture presentation, recall that the important requirements in blending materials are:

- Acceptable mixture moisture content (45%-65%)
- Mixture C : N ratio between 20 : 1 and 40 : 1
- Ensuring that the mix includes materials which add porosity and structure (e. g. , straw, wood chips, sawdust)

Process Monitoring and Evaluation

- Once a successful mix is established, and materials are mixed and placed in piles or windrows, the most important composting process management activities are
- Process monitoring and evaluation
- Regular turning (to restore pile porosity, provide aeration, and provide mixing)
- Maintaining moisture within the optimum range
- Troubleshooting composting problems
- Determining when active composting has ceased

Most, if not all, composting problems (e. g. , odours, low pile temperature, excessive temperature, slow or uneven decomposition), indicate process limitations due to an imbalance or deficiency/excess of one of the composting process factors (see Tab. P3. 1). Process monitoring provides important information about the efficiency and rate of decomposition, and is therefore essential for managing the composting process as well as troubleshooting problems which may develop. Process monitoring activities include measurement or assessment of:

- Pile temperature
- Pile moisture level
- Aeration status (as indicated by odours)
- Physical changes in feedstock materials
- Uniformity of temperature, moisture and decomposition within the pile
- The amount of subsidence (shrinkage) in the pile

Practice procedure

Part 2 of this field teaching provides you with an opportunity to visit three active composting piles, established this fall by students in order to practice your skills in process monitoring and evaluation, as well as troubleshooting common composting problems.

Materials and methods

You are encouraged to work in self-selected groups of 2-4 people; this will help in the discussion of what you experience in the practice exercise and in the formation of the data tables; however, the report will be submitted on an individual basis.

Part 1 Using Computer Spreadsheets to Balance C : N and Moisture

Using the downloadable Moisture and C/N Ratio Calculation Spreadsheet provided at the Cornell Composting website, http: //compost. css. cornell. edu/download. html, determine how much carbon-containing amendment needs to be mixed with manure or another N-containing feedstock to achieve a mixture moisture goal of 60% and a C : N ratio of 30 : 1. Develop first a three-ingredient, and then develop a four-ingredient mix. Once you have opened the spreadsheet, in the spreadsheet format appropriate for your computer system, follow the instructions provided below:

Assume you are a commercial farm or agricultural business producing some type of organic waste which you would like to recycle by composting. You will need to find more ingredients to add to your waste to make successful compost according to the desirable characteristics given in Tab. P3. 1. In the first shaded columns of the spreadsheet (rows under ingredient, % moisture, % carbon, etc.), input values are listed for three example feedstock materials. The final column with the amount of each feedstock, allows the program to calculate the % moisture and C/N ratios as shown in the boxes below the table.

Use one of the given feedstocks (e. g. , grass, or leaves or food scraps), but replace the remaining two feedstocks with a suitable alternative. Enter the given values for %N, %C and C/N ratio You will have to calculate the % Carbon using the values given for % N and the C/N ratio (% N dry weight × C/N ratio = % C dry weight). Adjust the amounts of each ingredient (final column) up or down until you have achieved a suitable mix. You may need to select an alternative ingredient if you cannot get a good mix.

If possible, do not include water, but rather use a high moisture feedstock to adjust the moisture content of the mixture.

Once you have determined a three ingredient mix that achieves your moisture and C : N ratio goals, print the table or record the numbers for your report. Next make a four ingredient mix using only 1-2 of the ingredients from the three ingredient mix. Print the table or record the data. Transfer the data for the two mixes to two appropriately titled summary tables, and submit these with your lab report. In the report, please remember to specify the moisture and C : N goals used in the calculations. The format of the tables should be similar to that in the Cornell spreadsheet [i. e. , report % moisture, % C, % N and mass (kg or lbs) for each ingredient]. Reports should include a discussion of the characteristics of your mix based on the components you chose; is it course, fine, smelly, potentially easy to get the ingredients locally, etc. ?

Note that the only acceptable mixtures are those that not only balance C : N and attain moisture goals but also demonstrate adequate porosity. To evaluate porosity, you need to determine the approximate bulk density of the mixture. Mixtures having bulk densities less than 640 kg/m^3 generally demonstrate porosities > 40%, which is considered adequate.

Evaluate the porosities of the mixtures you have proposed and comment on their relative suitability. To evaluate bulk density, use the figures given in the table for each ingredient. Calculate the proportion, by weight, of that ingredient and multiply it times the given bulk density. Add the bulk densities of each portion together to get the total. You may have to use bulk densities of similar materials if none is given for an ingredient. Remember to state your assumed values.

Tips on using the spreadsheet:

Don=t be afraid to play around with the input values (vary levels of N, C, moisture, according to the raw materials used) to achieve the moisture and C : N goals.

Adjust the moisture content first, then adjust the C : N ratio.

The ideal C : N ratio may deviate from the ideal of 30 : 1, according to the availability of C in the amendment. For example, a higher C : N mixture (e. g. , 40 : 1) is acceptable when one of the dry ingredients contains slowly degraded forms of C.

Part 2. Monitoring/Troubleshooting an active composting pile

Take a walk over to the Basic Composting Skills site, you will be asked to monitor, evaluate, and document the composting process in three bins identified by signs as A, B and C (Tab. P3. 2).

Tab. P3. 2 Results of monitoring and evaluation of compost piles

Pile	Temperature (℃)	Moisture status	Observations on decomposition
A			
B			
C			
D			
E			

Working as a group:

Evaluate and take notes on the composting activity in each pile (temperature, signs of microbial activity, extent of decomposition).

Evaluate each pile with respect to moisture status and any additional factors which you feel may be relevant (e. g. , structure/porosity of mix, adequate mixing of materials, pile volume, etc.).

If temperature is not within the target range for active composting, odours are present, or materials are little decomposed, use the Troubleshooting and Management Guide from Rynk (1992) to help you identify possible sources or reasons for the observed condition.

Working independently:

Record the results of your monitoring and evaluation in a table according to the format given below. Note: observations can include any of the following: strong or unpleasant odours, physical appearance of materials, presence of actinomycetes (white, thread-like fungi).

Write a short summary of the results of your inspection of each pile (1-2 paragraphs on each). Comment as to why you think active composting (as indicated by composting temperatures) either has or has not started, or appears to have ceased. If composting is not proceeding well, suggest how you might correct the observed problems.

Marking Scheme

For this report, each student will be given a mark out of 100 possible marks, according to the marking scheme outlined below (Tab. P3. 3).

Tab. P3. 3 Marking scheme for students' reports

Marks	
Part 1	
Recipe tables	25 marks
Discussion re: porosity	20 marks
Part 2	
Pile monitoring table	15 marks
Discussion of results/troubleshooting	30 marks
Spelling and grammar	10 marks
Total	100 marks

Students are encouraged reading the following references before and after the practice:

Dougherty, M. 1999. Field Guide to On-farm Composting. Natural Resource, Agriculture and Engineering Service. NRAES-114. Ithaca, NY.

Richard, T. L. and Trautman N. M. 2000. Moisture and C/N Ratio Calculation Spreadsheet. Cornell Composting website, available at: http: //compost. css. cornell. edu/MIXCALC5. XLS

Rynk, R. (ed) . 1992. On-Farm Composting Handbook. Northeast Regional Agricultural Engineering Service. NRAES-54, Ithaca, NY. (Note: On Reserve in Library)

Lab 1 Vegetables: Classification and anatomy

Introduction

Vegetables are often defined as the edible portion of herbaceous garden plants. They are generally grown as annuals and eaten with the main course of a meal. Although this is a vague definition, it helps us to distinguish vegetables from fruits which are generally perennials (most are woody) and are generally consumed as a dessert.

Vegetables are important for a balanced diet primarily because of their mineral and vitamin content rather than for carbohydrates, proteins and fats. However, some vegetables do supply our diets with high amounts of protein such as beans and peas, and some root crops do contain large amounts of carbohydrates.

Identification of vegetables can be accomplished through their botanical classification; however; other classification systems can also be based on characteristics such as the plant part consumed, plant hardiness, the life cycle or by the cultural requirements such as soil type, nutrition, seeding methods, row spacing and harvesting methods. Vegetables also can be grouped by their preservation method; i. e. freezing, canning (pickling) or drying. This lab will outline the students the above knowledge of vegetables.

Learning objectives

After completing this exercise, you should be able to:

1. Recognize and list vegetables commonly grown in Fuzhou.
2. Place these common vegetables in the correct botanical families and know at least 1 representative vegetable from each of 8 botanical families.
3. Identify the plant parts consumed as vegetables.
4. Describe cultural information about at least 3 vegetables.
5. Utilize what you have learned to design a garden.

Note: You may want to review the following readings accordingly from Biology of Plants and corresponding Chinese textbook if you are not familiar with plant structure.

Lab procedures and assignments

Lab procedures

This lab may be done individually or in pairs. Students will be divided into groups with no more than 40 to complete sections 1, 2 and 3. Students should rotate when finished in each arca.

Sections 1 and 2

Two lab rooms will be set up with displays of vegetables from the demonstration garden and from the supermarket. Vegetables on display will be grouped into their botanical families. Each vegetable will be labelled with the common name and scientific name.

We consume many different parts of plants as vegetables. Students should be able to identify the parts appropriately. Below you will find definitions of these various plant parts (Tab. L1. 1). After reviewing these definitions and observing the vegetables on display, use your knowledge gained from the assigned readings and fill in Tab. L1. 2 on your answer sheet with the common names of the vegetables whose edible portion matches those listed. Please print clearly and only list in these table vegetables that are on display.

Tab. L1. 1 Definitions of edible portions of plants

Bulb	A short, flattened or disc shaped underground stem composed of concentric layers of fleshy scale leaves attached to a stem plate at the base
Fruit	Edible part of the plant (developed from the ripened ovary of the flower) consisting of the seeds and pulpy surrounding tissue
Inflorescence	The flowering structure of a plant or the arrangement of flowers on the stem or axis of a plant
Leaf	The flat, thin parts, usually green growing from the stem of a plant
Petiole	The stalk of a leaf
Root	The part of the plant, usually underground that anchors the plant
Seed	The part of a plant containing the embryo from which a new plant will grow
Stem	Stalk of the plant supporting leaves, flowers or fruit
Tuber	A short, thickened, fleshy part of an underground stem, or a swollen food filled underground stem that bears buds (eyes) along its length

Answer sheets of section 1 needed to be filled in and handed in during the lab are listed below:

Section 1: Edible parts of vegetables. To complete this table, list the common name of the vegetables on display that fit into these categories of the edible portions of the plant. Use the lab handout and knowledge gained from the readings. Please print clearly and only list vegetables in this table that are on display.

Edible portions	Vegetable (s) (Common name)
Bulb	
Fruit	
Tuber	
Leaf	
Seed	
Root	

Continued

Edible portions	Vegetable (s) (Common name)
Inflorescence	
Petiole	
Stem	

Section 2: Botanical families. Tab. L1. 2 is a list of vegetables categorized in their botanical families. Students should become familiar with these families and be able to list at least one vegetable from each of the eight families marked with an asterisk *.

Tab. L1. 2　Botanical family of vegetables

Monocotyledon	
* Alliaceae (Amaryllidaceae)	Onion family
Allium cepa var. *cepa*	Common Onion Spanish, Bunching
A. cepa var. *aggregatum*	Multiplier, Shallot
A. cepa var. *proliferum*	Egyptian topset onions
A. porrum	Leek
A. sativum	Garlic
A. fistulosum	Welsh Onion, Japanese Bunching
A. schoenoprasum	Chive
Liliaceae	Lily family
Asparagus officinalis	Asparagus
Poaceae (Gramineae)	Grass Family
Zea mays var. *saccharata*	Sweet Corn
Dicotyledon	
* Apiaceae (Umbelliferae)	Parsley family
Daucus carota var. *sativa*	Carrot
Petroselinum crispum	Parsley
P. crispum var. *tuberosum*	Rooted Parsley
Apium graveolens var. *dulce*	Celery
A. graveolens var. *rapaceum*	Celeriac
Pastinaca sativa	Parsnip
Foeniculum vulgare var. *dulce*	Florence fennel
* Asteraceae (Compositae)	Composite family
Cichorium intybus var. *folosum*	Belgian endive (Witloof chicory)
C. intybus	Radicchio
C. endivia	Endive
Trag opogon porrifolius	Salsify
Lactuca sativa	Lettuce
Helianthus tuberosus	Jerusalem Artichoke, sunchoke

Continued

Cynara scolymus	Globe Artichoke
Taraxacum officinale	Dandelion greens
* Brassicaceae (Cruciferae)	Mustard family
Brassica oleracea	Cole crops
B. oleracea var. *botrytis*	Cauliflower
B. oleracea var. *gemmifera*	Brussels Sprouts
B. oleracea var. *italica*	Broccoli
B. oleracea var. *gongylodes*	Kohlrabi
B. oleracea var. *acephala*	Kale
B. oleracea var. *capitata*	Cabbage
B. oleracea var. *capitata* f. *alba*	White Cabbage
B. oleracea var. *capitata* f. *rubra*	Red Cabbage
B. oleracea var. *capitata* f. *sabauda*	Savoy Cabbage
B. napus var. *napobrassica*	Rutabaga
B. rapa var. *rapifera*	Turnip
B. rapa var. *Chinensis*	Chinese Mustard, Pak Choi
B. rapa var. *pekinensis*	Chinese cabbage
B. juncea	Mustard Greens
Lepidium sativum	Garden Cress
Raphanus sativus	Radish, Chinese, French
Armoracia rusticana	Horseradish
Eruca sativa	Arugula
* Chenopodiaceae	Goosefoot family
Beta vulgaris var. *crassa*	Table Beet
B. vulgaris var. *cicla*	Swiss Chard
Spinacia oleracea	Spina ch
Chenopodium album	Lambs quarter
Portulaca oleracea	Purslane
Cucurbitaceae	Melon or Gourd Family
Cucurbita maxima	Buttercup, Hubbard
C. pepo	Pumpkins, Acorn, Summer Squash (crook neck), Vegetable marrow, Zucchini, Straight neck
C. pepo	Gourds-yellow flowered
C. moschata	Butternut
C. mixta	Sweet Potato Squash (?)
C. maxima	Gourds-Turban, ornamental squash
Citrullus lanatus	Watermelon
C. lanatus var. *citroides*	Citron
Cucumis sativus	Cucumber
C. melo	Cantaloupe (Muskmelon), Honeydew
Cucurbita maxima	Buttercup, Hubbard
C. pepo	Pumpkins, Acorn, Summer Squash (crook neck), Vegetable marrow, Zucchini, Straight neck
C. pepo	Gourds-yellow flowered
C. moschata	Butternut
C. mixta	Sweet Potato Squash (?)
C. maxima	Gourds-Turban, ornamental squash
Citrullus lanatus	Watermelon
C. lanatus var. *citroides*	Citron
Cucumis sativus	Cucumber
C. melo	Cantaloupe (Muskmelon), Honeydew

Continued

* Fabaceae (Leguminosae)	Pea or pulse family
Arachis hypogaea	Peanut
Pisum sativum	Garden pea
P. sativum var. *macrocarpon*	Edible podded pea
Vicia faba	Broad Bean
Phaseolus vulgaris	Bean (snap, wax, baking, cranberry, pole, bush)
P. coccineus	Scarlet Runner Bean
P. lunatus	Lima Bean
Glycine max	Soybean
Malvaceae	Mallow Family
Abelmoschus esculentus	Okra
Polygonaceae	Buckwheat family
Rheum rhabarbarum (*Rheum rhaponticum*)	Rhubarb
Rumex acetosa	Garden sorrel
Solanaceae	Nightshade Family
Solanum tuberosum	Potato
S. melongena	Eggplant
Lycopersicon lycopersicon (*Lycopersicon esculentum*)	Tomato
Capsicum annum	Sweet pepper
C. frutescens	Hot Pepper
Physalis ixocarpa	Tomatillo
Tetragoniaceae (Aizoaceae)	Carpetweed family
Tetragonia tetragonioides	New Zealand Spinach

Section 3: Botanical classifications. This section will help you place the vegetables on display into their Botanical families. Complete this table, LIST ONLY THE VEGETABLES ON DISPLAY and please print clearly. All vegetables on display will have family and common names beside them.

Answer sheets of section 2 needed to be filled in and handed in during the lab are listed below:

Given vegetable	Botanical family (please write down the scientific name)	List other vegetable (s) that are in this family classification on display
Tomato		
Asparagus		
Lettuce		
Sweet corn		
Broccoli		
Pea pods		
Vegetable		
Celery		
Swiss chard		
Cucumber		

Section 4: Putting your knowledge to work by designing a vegetable garden. Design a garden using the vegetables you selected in section 3, plus the potato example. The garden size is only 5m×5m so efficient use of space is the challenge. Your goals for the garden are:

- Good production in the space provided
- Balanced production; i. e. , a reasonable amount of every product
- Workload should be spread over time

You must decide how many rows of each vegetable you want and where to place them in the garden. Draw a diagram of your garden along with a short paragraph describing your reasons for planting the garden the way you did. You can be as creative as you want as long as you stay within the 5 m×5 m area.

Requirements for Section 4:

1. Use the same vegetables from Section 3 (include the potato example). Or if you would like, you may use 4 other vegetables providing the 4 include:
   - one root vegetable
   - one perennial vegetable
   - one leaf vegetable
   - one "fruit" vegetable
2. 5m×5m area (no limits on height).
3. Labelled diagram of the planting plan.
4. Short paragraph describing your garden and why it is planted this way.
5. Have fun, be creative. Discuss and critically think about this problem as a group using your knowledge from previous classes and this lab (no references are required but you may cite them if they are helpful to your discussion).

This section of the lab may be submitted in the lecture period after the lab.

Lab 2 Soil profile and texture

Introduction

This lab will consist of 2 parts. Part one is a demonstration of soil profile from the natural ecosystem all over china by watching the exhibition in soil laboratory. Part two will be conducted in soil laboratory by mean of soil examination in order to figure out the soil texture for several basic soil components.

Learning objectives

After participating in this lab exercise and preparing the report, you should be able to:

1. Recognize soil profile characteristics and understand the reasons for differences between profiles.

2. Distinguish the major size classes of soil particles.

3. Understand the use of a soil textural triangle to determine the percentages of sand, silt and clay in a soil.

Lab procedures and assignment

Part A: Soil profiles

Soil profiles will be discussed and observed in the soil science laboratory with the assistance of the lab tutors. A soil pit will be demonstrated and available for your observation near the lab. Each student will do the following tasks:

(1) Sketch the designated profile of one of the soils being examined in the lab, including an approximate depth scale, the major horizons (A, B and C), maximum rooting depth and other observable details.

(2) Assess the stone content (material>2 mm diameter) in rough percentages.

(3) Repeat the above for the soil pit profile. Briefly describe the environmental setting of the site and the vegetation growing in the immediate landscape.

(4) In addition for the soil pit, assess the biological activity (if any) of the soil meso/macro fauna (i. e. earthworms; if present, their abundance, depth of activity, size of biopores, plus any other observations on living activity in the soil.)

The sketches and brief answers to questions can be submitted on the answer sheet.

(5) Each working group will take a soil sample from the field designated by the instructor. Divide the soil sampling work evenly among your group so all students have a chance to collect soil samples. The samples should be thoroughly mixed and stored in a bag. Sample to a depth of 15 cm will be shown by the instructor. Assessment of the texture of the combined soil sample will be performed in Part B of this lab.

Part B: Soil texture

In Part B you will examine soil texture. The mineral component of soils consists of inorganic particles in three major size classes. The properties of each of these three particle classes are unique and their content in soils influences how the soil performs. The three classes are sand, silt and clay. Sand has the largest size range of 2. 0-0. 05 mm in diameter, silt is 0. 05-0. 002 and clays are smaller than 0. 0002mm. Further characteristics of each of these classes can be seen in course textbook.

The term soil texture refers to the proportions of sand, silt and clay particles in a particular soil. Soil texture cannot be changed but it is important to be aware of the texture to know how to manage soil. Fine textured clay soils hold nutrients but are easily compacted whereas coarse textured sandy soils are less fertile but are naturally drained and allow more flexibility of timing for tillage and harvesting operations. If fine textured soils are tilled when wet and become compact, water infiltration is restricted and run-off or erosion can result.

Major soil textural classes are defined by the % of sand, silt and clay. The Soil Textural Triangle (Fig. 7. 2) allows one to determine the soil textural class after a particle size analysis has been done.

Think of the Soil Texture Triangle in a simplified form, divided into 3 regions (attached, Fig. L2. 1). It consists of fine textured soils (clays); medium textured soils (silts) and coarse textured soils (sandy). Observe the demonstration on how to use this triangle to determine soil texture class of soils with known sand, silt or clay content.

Answer the following questions by using the Soil Textural Triangle, and record these same answers on the answer sheet provided (see "Students' report format"). Each working group will do the next exercise at a designated station. Four soil samples will be evaluated for texture, three supplied by the instructors plus the one collected from the field plots in Part A.

Determining the textural class by the "feel" method

This is a practical field method for determining textural class and is an important skill acquired by soil scientists. Students will attempt this exercise today but accurate determinations are a skill acquired from practice. Read the attached instructions for performing the ribbon test following the instructor's demonstration:

Do the ribbon test (attached) by performing the following steps to determine the textural class of the soil. The ribbon test is based on the feel of moist soil and how easily it can be moulded. You may also want to use the flow chart supplied as an attachment.

Step 1: Get enough of the soil sample to form a 2 to 3 cm ball. Make sure there is no gravel or plant debris in it.

Step 2: Moisten the soil in the palm of your hand while kneading it firmly, until it is thoroughly and evenly moistened and feels like fresh, warm putty. (Note: sandy soils will never get like putty).

Step 3: Try to extrude the soil between your thumb and forefinger to form a ribbon. Try to form the longest, thinnest ribbon possible for the soil you are testing.

Step 4: Classify the soil into 1 of the 3 major categories fine, medium, or coarse textured, based on the length and strength of the ribbon you make.

(1) If no ribbon less than 1/2 cm thick will form then it is a coarse-textured soil.

(2) If a ribbon of about 1-3 cm will form, then it is a medium-textured soil.

(3) If a long, thin, flexible ribbon forms, then it is a fine-textured soil.

Students' report format

Part A: Draw your profile and answer the questions on the back of this page byusing the Soil Textural Triangle (Fig. 7. 2):

Q1. What is the percentage of sand content of a soil containing 30% clay and 40% silt? What is the textural classification of this soil?

Q2. In what range is the % of clay in a soil classified as a sandy clay loam?

Q3. A soil classified as a clay may also have ________ to ________% silt content.

Q4. A soil containing 35% silt and 45% sand is classified as a ____________ and contains ____________% clay.

Part B: Determine and record the ribbon description and texture of each of the soils in Tab. L2. 1, make brief notes regarding how the ribbons formed and list the predicted soil classification.

Tab. L2. 1 Soil samples of 3 unknowns and one field sample with ribbon descriptions and texture estimation

	Ribbon description	Texture
Unknown A		
Unknown B		
Unknown C		
Field Sample		

Note: Report is due at the end of the lab period.

Lab 3 Seed germination and seedling morphology

Introduction

Germination is the initiation of growth of a seed and begins with water uptake and imbibitions. The seed swells as water is absorbed, food reserves within the seed are metabolized, the expansion of the embryo begins and further development and growth of the seedling continues. The typical stages of germination and seedling development for monocots and dicot seedlings will be examined in this exercise.

Learning objectives

1. At the end of this exercise students will be able to identify and describe the morphological structures of germinating seeds and seedlings of selected monocot and dicot plants.

2. Students will be able to distinguish between monocot and dicot seedlings.

Lab procedure and assignment

Exercise 1: Seed morphology

Each student will observe the samples of crop seeds on display and try to identify the embryo structures as shown in the diagrams (Fig. L3. 1).

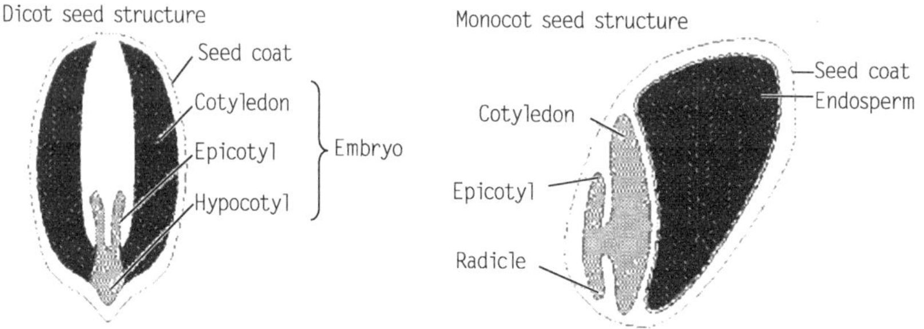

Fig. L3. 1 The structures of a seed.

Note: Instructors will Insert an explanation of the terms "monocot and dicot" and soak some seeds for use in this part.

Exercise 2: Germination

Each student will observe 2 sets of monocot seedlings and 2 sets of dicot seedlings on display at their table. After reading the information on monocot and dicot germination in the handout, students will make detailed drawings of the sets of seedlings on display. All appropriate parts as described in the germination description should be carefully included in the diagram. Label all structures indicated by underlining in the paragraphs.

Use a separate sheet of paper to make your drawings. Please make your drawings neatly and large using the full size of the paper. All structures present should be labelled clearly in each individual drawing. Turn you drawings in at the end of class.

(1) Set 1: Monocot germination

Germination in monocots such as corn, rice wheat, and barley, begins with the emergence of the root closely followed by the developing shoot. A small protective cover called the coleorhiza is the first to emerge from the seed, shortly after, the radical pushes through the coleorhiza and begins to grow downward. Soon, two or more branched seminal roots will emerge. The radical and seminal roots are commonly referred to as the primary root system. The primary root system will support the seedling for several weeks but will eventually be replaced by a secondary and permanent root system.

The shoot growth is beginning shortly after the radical has emerged. Development starts with the emergence of a protective sheath called a coleoptile. The coleoptile protects the young shoot as it emerges through the soil. The coleoptile stops elongating when it comes through the soil surface into the light and the first seedling leaf will emerge, pushing it's way through the tip of the coleoptile. This first leaf will often consist of just a sheath and sometimes has a reduced blade. The second leaf will emerge through the center of the first leaf. The second leaf and subsequent leaves are complete and consist of a leaf sheath and a leaf blade.

The mesocotyl is the portion of the stem below the node where the coleoptile is attached and above the scutellar node at the seed. This internode is where the elongation occurs which pushes the coleoptile tip up through the soil surface. Seed planted deeply will have a longer mesocotyl than shallow planed seeds.

(2) Set 2: Dicot germination

Germination in dicots such as beans and soybeans will first be seen with emergence of the radical from the seed. The radical grows downward forming the primary root system. Unlike the monocot seedling, this root system will continue to grow and support the plant. As the radical grows downward, the hypocotyl, which is the portion of the stem immediately above the root and below the attachment of the cotyledons, elongates upwards forming a hook in the hypocotyl. This hook will emerge up through the soil surface while pulling the cotlyedons, still enclosed in the seed coat, behind through the soil. The seed coat often comes off as the cotyledons are being pulled through the soil. Once the upward facing side of the hypocotyl senses the sunlight, it stops elongating. The opposite side continues to elongate causing the young stem to straighten out and continue to grow upward forming new leaves. The epicotyl is the term used for the portion of the stem above the cotyledon node. The pair of first leaves are attached opposite each other on the stem and are simple leaves the second pair and subsequent leaves are compound leaves having 3 leaflets. The original cotyledons may function as leaves for several days to weeks but will soon become yellow and fall off.

Exercise 3: Calculating germination percent

Students will count the numbers of germinated seeds on display and calculate the percent germination of the seed lot (instructor will Insert an exercise to calculate germination percentages).

Course training on agroecology learning style

Introduction

This course training embraces main the learning style of agroecology that each student has, usually including the instruction of course website use, the paper defined, paraphrasing and citing, library exploitation and so on, which are the basic requirements to learn a course so-called the participatory learning in Canadian universities, most important, the principles of academic integrity that learner involving in the above learning procedures should be taught and observed accordingly.

The instruction of course website use

The instruction begins with Login procedure to the agroecology course website in the computer room (Fig. T. 1), and then explores about 3 learning time to give overall instruction on how to use the tools online and finally an online assignment of PLANT & ANIMAL ID is assigned, the students will finish it step by step along the course period.

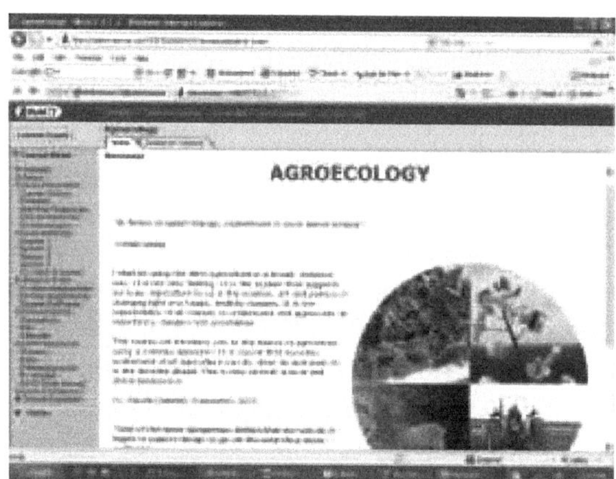

Fig. T. 1 A diagram of agroecology course website.

Paraphrasing and citing

Paraphrasing and citing is the necessary skill when students conduct the assignments of course. Whenever you use information (what is often called "sources") obtained elsewhere—in other words, not something you have come up with yourself—you need to indicate where you have obtained that information. The process of identifying the sources you've used in a paper is called citing or documenting. This instruction and train will give you some examples of document organizing with the various disciplines and the several types of ways to cite the references.

The principles of academic integrity

In every course learning process, the principles of academic integrity must be observed. We will spend 3 course time to exampt the principle of academic integrity and the consequence of violation for students. Particularly, what is plagiarism will be highlighted.

Epilogue

Agroecology: The science of food in the 21st century

1. Food is more than a resource for mankind.

Nothing can be more important than food for mankind on earth, not only because food is the most basic of all resources for human life, food production has effectively diverted more natural landscape to human purposes than any other ecologically significant human economic activity; but also because it endows the gifted right for the human, and it was a light of human civilization—civilization was made possible by agriculture in food production process. Ironically, our human did not recognize those until relatively recently, fear of food shortages and food safety were a concern of most human groups. Such a consciences is not sufficient, as a basic resource, food is limited due to limited agricultural resource and biological growth, the law of Thermodynamic-equilibrium, while as human basic right, population increases exponentially, the Malthusian principle of Population growth. Therefore, fear of famine and treat of toxicity are even lasting issues for mankind.

2. Agriculture is more than an economics.

Mankind is born utilitarian, this can be drawn from the definitions of Agriculture, no matter in Oxford Dictionary defining agriculture as "Science or practice of cultivating the soil and rearing animals", or in the Contemporary Chinese dictionary as "Art, science, and industry of managing the growth of plants and animals for human use. In a broad sense agriculture includes cultivation of the soil, growing and harvesting crops, breeding and raising livestock, dairying, and forestry" and in the Chinese textbook of agronomy as "The infrastructure of national economy, and main source of living, as well as industrial material for human beings" and so on. Those definitions built the ideology of human utilization in modern society, everything inside the economics's account.

Let's back to the food production, the popularity of the Libigian agriculture which led to synthesized fertilizer explosion used and Darwinian agriculture which resting on hybrid varieties of crops both focusing on crop yield as unique goal in food production system resulted from ideology of people center has increased the divide of nature and society, the economic value has been only criteria of food production or agriculture. As a matter of fact, such reductionist food system did not solve the problem of fear of famine, the decline of food productivity stability with depletion of natural resource (and also population increase), there 1. 0 billion hungry people in world this year (2010); but new problem of food contamination occurs with destroyed environment.

Therefore human needs a new ideology or understanding of agriculture, the definition of agriculture can fit into such need by Professor Claude Caldwell, that is, Agriculture, the science, art, politics and sociology of changing sunlight into healthy, happy people. To realize the goal of this agriculture, mankind needs to convert the traditional economics of agriculture to characterize food production in a steady state economy which fit within the capacity of the ecosystems that contain it. Only such conversion can offer answers to questions such as: Can we feed the world? What would people eat and how would it be grown? Would almost everyone be a vegetarian or vegan? Would genetically engineered food play a big role? What about farm subsidies and the role of biofuels? What agricultural practices would be appropriate for so-called sustainable food production system?

A steady state economy would bolster adverse trends by factory-farm dominated agriculture. It would move away from control of food by transnational corporations and toward an increased number and diversity of small and medium-sized farms, and healthy rural communities. Revamped agricultural systems would provide many varieties of food in ways that conserve soil and water and maintain long-term fertility of the land. The best way to achieve sustainable throughput in agricultural systems is to decentralize. Inputs, especially fossil fuel inputs, can be reduced by shifting to local systems of production, distribution and consumption. Large-scale agribusiness contributes a significant percentage of all fossil fuel emissions in the world, stemming from energy-intensive methods of planting, fertilizing, harvesting, packaging, and distributing food supplies. With smaller-scale, more sustainable practices, there is less reliance on fuel to run heavy farm equipment for production and irrigation; less application of pesticide, herbicide, and fertilizers; less reliance on long-distance transportation to ship crops to processing plants and supermarkets; and less use and disposal of plastic for packaging.

3. Agroecology bridging the gap between ecology and economics for sustainable food system.

There are many sciences of agriculture: crop science, food science, chemistry, veterinary science, weeds science, etc. Ecology will be the science of agriculture because ecology is the science at the appropriate level of organization to address most of the scientific problems and issues in agriculture. Because agriculture is a hierarchical system in which each layer is related to the one below and the one above, Most of our agricultural sciences occupy the lower levels of organization, and these lower levels of organization have ability dealing with yield but not quality and other problem attached with the yield center management that are concerned with populations, communities and ecosystems, even more higher that ecosystem level for example landscape and global ecosystem, these are the domains of ecology (Weiner, 2003).

Clearly, those problems must be addressed at the appropriate levels of organization. For example, advances in molecular biology have led many to believe that almost all problems can be addressed at the molecular level, but this is simply not the case. Much agricultural research is at much too low a level for the questions we want to address, and thus represents a type of naive or "crude" reductionism. The future of agricultural research will depend on understanding higher levels of organization, and these are the levels addressed by the science of agroecology, that bridge the gap between ecology and economics for sustainable food system.

One of the other disciplines that look at higher levels of organization in agriculture is economics, the social science of agriculture. Economics and ecology are similar in that they both put agriculture in the context of higher levels of organization. But these higher levels are different. It is not doubt that ecology will, in the future, occupy a position in agricultural thinking similar to that economics has today: ubiquitous. Just as it is not possible to give a lecture on a new technique or idea in agricultural research at an agricultural university or research institute today without being questioned about its cost, so in 10 years it will be equally impossible to avoid questions about the ecological effects of the new idea, both inside and outside the farm ecosystem. agroecology is the science of agriculture, and that will be taken for granted in the future.

Therefore, agroecology , integrating ecology and agronomic science and bridging the ecology and economics science, will be very appropriate to integrate agricultural sector into wholeness and gain the systematic views, with which to predict the problems ahead of time and then to take measures to minimize the adverse impact of the problems.

Regarding what focus of the agroecology will be prior for the future food production, the famous scientific journal of Nature predicted the future researches focuses in agriculture following the paradigm of Agroecology (Marris, 2008). Firstly, The molecular breeding applying molecular biology technologies to increase the resistant ability of crop varieties to pests (disease, insect and adverse environment); secondly, reformation annual crop to perennial crops by means of the combination of traditional hybrid and genetic engineering techniques to decrease the farming practice on soil, agrobiodiversity conservation, decrease of external energy used; thirdly, drought resistance and water saving by ways of phytophysiological and molecular biological technology to safeguard the food security; fourthly, breeding of bioenergy crop such as cassava using biological engineering; fifth but not last, striving for transferring C_3 crop such as rice to C_4 crop to increase the solar energy efficiency.

In conclusion, the Low Carbon Agriculture will be a trend in the coming of low carbon economy era, agroecology will be core science for Low Carbon Agricuolture. This book is the first try to list the framework of future agroecology, we expect the big discussion around the world for the sake of sustainable agriculture that guarantee the world's food security and safety (Francis et al. , 2003).

Literatures cited in the section

Francis C. , Lieblein G. , Gliessman S. , Breland T. A. , Creamer N. , Harwood R. , Salomonsson L. , Helenius J. , Rickerl D. , Salvador R. , Wiedenhoeft M. , Simmons S. , Allen P. , Altieri M. , Flora C. , and Poincelot R. 2003. Agroecology: The ecology of food systems. *Journal of Sustainable Agriculture* 22: 99-118.

Marris E. 2008. Agronomy: Five crop researchers who could change the world. *Nature* 456: 563-568.

Weiner J. 2003. Ecology-the science of agriculture in the 21st century. *The Journal of Agricultural Science* 141: 371-377